CW00540111

THE GLORY OF
GOODWOOD

THE GLORY OF
GOODWOOD

MIKE LAWRENCE, SIMON TAYLOR
& DOUG NYE

Virgin

THE GLORY OF GOODWOOD

"Returning to Goodwood is like going back to an old friend."

STIRLING MOSS

Written by Mike Lawrence, Simon Taylor & Doug Nye
Goodwood motor racing results supplied by Robert Barker

First published in 1999 by Virgin Books,
an imprint of Virgin Publishing Ltd
Thames Wharf Studios, Rainville Road, London W6 9HT

Copyright © 1999 Virgin Publishing Ltd and Goodwood Road Racing Company Ltd

The Goodwood Motor Circuit logo is a trademark of
Goodwood Road Racing Company Ltd. All rights reserved.

This book is sold subject to the condition that it shall not, by way of trade or otherwise, be lent, resold, hired out or otherwise circulated without the publisher's prior written permission in any form of binding or cover other than that in which it is published and without a similar condition including this condition being imposed on the subsequent purchaser.

A catalogue record for this title is available from the British Library

ISBN 1 85227 826 9

Conceived by Derek Slatter and Rob Shreeve
Art direction, design and picture research by Derek Slatter, Diane Meacham,
Emma Murray and Joanne McBride at Slatter-Anderson
Publishing consultant: Philip Dodd

Printed and bound in Italy
Repro by Digital Generations

Above: Freddie, Duke of Richmond, opens the Goodwood Motor Circuit on 18th September 1948 in a brand-new Bristol 400 (painting by Edward I. Halliday, 1953).

Previous pages: the way it was: 7,500 rpm on the clock, star *Scuderia* Ferrari driver Tony Brooks' left hand is reaching for the gearchange of his works 250 *Testa Rossa*/59 as American photographer Jesse Alexander fires the shutter, and the Goodwood infield streams by while Tony shows team-mates Phil Hill and Dan Gurney 'the Goodwood line' - 1959 Tourist Trophy.

CONTENTS

FOREWORD
BY THE EARL OF MARCH

From as far back as I can remember, motor racing at Goodwood has been a major part of my life. As a small boy, I spent every Easter at Goodwood House with my grandfather and those annual visits became the highlight of my year.

For a six or seven year-old, it was heaven. At the Easter meetings, practice was on Saturday, with racing on Monday - there was never any racing on Sunday then, of course - and my grandparents used to host a party for all the drivers on the Saturday evening. The parties were always held in the Long Hall at Goodwood House and I'd be there clutching my little red autograph book, working my way round the room.

There was one time when I went up to a driver whose name I hadn't yet collected. He said, "You don't want my autograph, young man - I'm not famous enough. You want that chap's over there". And he propelled me over to Graham Hill, who was holding forth to a group of guests. I didn't, in fact, want his autograph because I already had it. But Graham looked down at this small boy with his plastic autograph book and said, simply, "Bugger off!" He was always one of my heroes, along with Jim Clark and Jackie Stewart.

When race day came, we used to watch the races from this horrible caravan parked right next to the chicane, so close it's amazing no one ever hit it. We'd sit inside, tucking into a dreadfully English picnic - usually boiled eggs and cold sausages - and, whenever it rained, we were surrounded by a heady smell of wet tweed and wellington boots.

Even then, in the early 1960s, I was much more interested in the older machinery: Bugattis were what I dreamed about and made drawings of all the time. When the Woodcote Cup field - full of mighty racing cars like the 308 Alfa and the '*Thin Wall Special*' - left the grid for the first race of the Circuit Revival, it still blew my mind.

The Revival Meeting was, in part, an attempt to re-capture the special mixture of sights, sounds, machines and fun, but the warmth and strength of people's response took us all by surprise. So we decided to create this book, as a permanent reminder of motor racing at Goodwood, setting out the history of my grandfather, the circuit and the drama of the great races.

It brings together memories of heroic drivers and Goodwood personalities who were so much a part of it all, as well as the Revival meeting itself, of course. Also included are some remarkable photographs, many of which I have never seen before.

This book is a wonderful reminder, as well as an extraordinary insight, into a period when Britain was beginning to establish itself in a sport it now dominates. Goodwood was the beginning - and this is the story.

INTRODUCTION
BY STIRLING MOSS

From the day I arrived at the first ever meeting in September 1948, I knew that the Goodwood circuit had something special - a particular blend of elements that I never found anywhere else in all my racing experience.

Let alone its other qualities, Goodwood had an automatic headstart that September, for the simple reason that it was the first meeting of any real stature that anyone had organised on the British mainland after the War. For all those years since 1939, the fans had been starved of motor racing, and here it was: real, hard, competitive racing. It was like sitting down at a feast.

That day I had driven down from London with all my family - my first visit to those beautiful Downs - and through my youthful eyes this meeting appeared to be seriously sophisticated.

Looking back at the photos now, I can see that, of course, by modern day standards the paddock and pits were pretty rudimentary, but since my only prior experience had been limited to hill-climbs and sprints, with one airfield event at Brough, Goodwood was in a different league.

And then there was Freddie Richmond, a real-live Duke, wandering round the paddock, asking questions, interested in the machinery. Fifty-odd years ago, this was something you didn't see every day, and as a teenager I was impressed that I could rub shoulders with someone so important and yet so friendly.

Goodwood was always extremely sociable. You mixed with everybody, with the other drivers, the mechanics, the spectators. The paying public could get close up to the cars in the paddock in exactly the same way as the Earl of March arranged for the Revival Meeting.

That was one of Goodwood's genuinely unique qualities: the friendliness, the mix of all social classes sharing one over-riding passion, for motor racing. The overall mood had something of the feel of a polo match; in fact, the newspaper race results at the time weren't printed in the sports section, they were part of features run in the news and social pages. You'd see ex-cavalry officers and RAF pilots out with their girlfriends - it was always a good meeting to take a girl to - and so there was this upper-crust veneer, yet never any sense of exclusion. Goodwood had a warmth. You felt it really was your home circuit.

If anywhere came close to the sociability of Goodwood, it was racing in Australia or the West Coast of America, both of which had the same kind of relaxed feel. But Goodwood also had an additional amateur element - not amateur in the sense of driving ability - but in its outlook, and the fun you had there.

Another advantage for Goodwood was that the Easter meeting was the first event of the year, setting the pattern for the season, rather like the Australian Grand Prix does now. A great atmosphere and an excited, knowledgeable home crowd. The other Easter meeting at the time was held at Pau, which was probably fabulous too, but Goodwood was closer to the workshops. You could go down there with a new car, not too far from the factory if everything went horribly wrong...

My first races were in the 500cc Formula 3 cars, which were not too expensive. If you could afford a lot more, you could have a real racer like Reg Parnell's 4CLT/48 Maserati, but if you could only scrape up the necessary for a 500cc car, you could still get stuck into the racing straightaway. So there we all were in the paddock, a mixed bag of drivers ranging from Lord Strathcarron to Reg Parnell, that affable Midlands haulier and pig-farmer! And me, too, full of excitement at being part of it all.

In the '50s I used to stay with John Brierley, who ran the Hare and Hounds at Stoughton. One weekend Ken Carter and some of the other drivers got into my room while my girlfriend and I were having dinner and put cayenne pepper in my pyjamas. I ended up having to sit in a cold bath at two in the morning!

The great thing is that Goodwood never really moved away from the basic approach of providing good racing and a cordial welcome. The events got bigger, and did attract the Tourist Trophy and the best of the Formula 1 drivers, but Goodwood never forgot the welcome. That was down to the Duke of Richmond, and now it's down to Charles March.

But the friendly atmosphere in the paddock didn't mean the racing was any less competitive than anywhere else. Once we were on the track there was absolutely no quarter given. One of my first racing memories at Goodwood is of seeing a terrific tussle between Reg Parnell in that 4CLT Maserati - an impressive piece of machinery - and Bob Gerard in his pre-war ERA. And the presence of the bookies on the circuit added an unusual extra edge of interest...

In many ways Goodwood was not one of the great demanding circuits - not compared, say, to the Nürburgring or Spa. But it did possess one of the most difficult corners: Fordwater. If you had sufficient ability in a 250F or a DB3 you could just take it flat out, coming up over the rise and then letting the car go left, but not too far, before the slight dip. That sorted people out. If the wind - and there was quite often a strong wind at Goodwood - was against you on the straight, then it would be with you at Fordwater, which made the corner even tougher.

The Goodwood circuit taught me a number of things about driving. I remember an American friend, Bob Said, who was easing off at Madgwick in a 500cc F3 car. I told Bob, "You can take it flat out", which he did, but he wasn't as fast as he could have been. Although he had the courage to hold his foot on the floor, the line he was taking meant he was using more steering than necessary, so he was promoting understeer and drag. That was the moment I realised that flat out wasn't necessarily the fastest way round a corner.

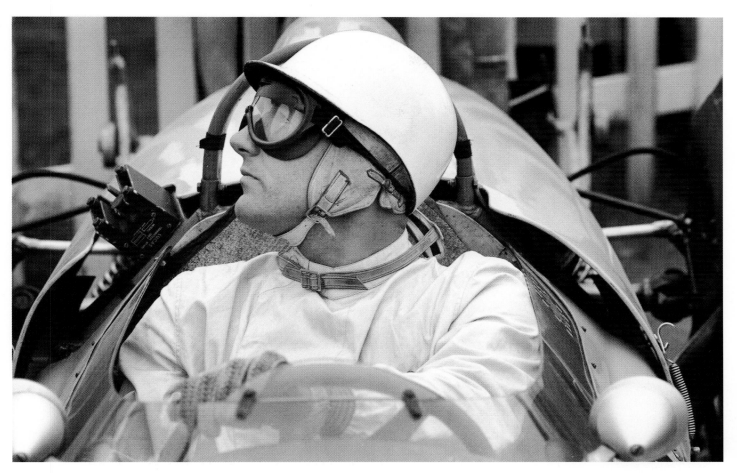

I had some wonderful times racing at Goodwood - the Tourist Trophy in 1959 was probably the best race I took part in - but after my accident in 1962 I wasn't able to get down there much. I'd been unconscious for a month, and paralysed for another six, so I missed the best part of a year - and in any case I've never been a great spectator.

So returning to Goodwood for the Revival was extraordinary. I was amazed at the level of detail Charles March had re-created to take it back in time: the old Shellmex logo, the local postman driving up in his Morris Minor van, and the moment when someone asked for bacon and eggs in the restaurant and was told, "Don't you know there's a war on? Have some Spam."

I had a hectic time during the Revival, driving the Vanwall and the 250GT Ferrari, and my Lola-Climax, and what with all the interviews and the autographs, by the time we got to the Lavant Cup on Sunday afternoon I was feeling a bit tired. There I was in the beautiful green Aston Martin DBR1 - the very car I had used to win the TT 40 years before - and suddenly Willie Green comes by in his Italian-red *Testa Rossa*. Well, it had been Aston versus Ferrari in 1959, so there was no way I was having that!

It was just like it was when I was racing. If I wanted to go faster, I'd simply work harder. Everything started to come back, and I got Willie back by going past him round the outside of Woodcote. Boy, it was a wonderful moment.

Some things - like the Goodwood spirit - should never change.

IN THE BEGINNING

In late 1940 a draughtsman working for the Air Ministry, sitting at his drawing board, designed a superb motor racing circuit, entirely by accident. His brief had been to draw a perimeter track encircling a grass airfield in Sussex. Eight years later, that same loop of tarmac - at RAF Westhampnett - would become the Goodwood Motor Circuit.

During those darkest days of the War, motor racing was far removed from anyone's thoughts. The perimeter track was simply a means of moving 'gas wagons', or fuel tankers, to the fighter planes dispersed around the RAF base.

By a further twist of fate, the airfield site had previously been Westhampnett Farm, whose owner was Frederick Charles Gordon Lennox, ninth Duke of Richmond, fourth Duke of Gordon, Duke of Lennox, Duc d'Aubigny, Earl of March, Earl of Darnley, Baron Methuen, Earl of Kinrara, Baron Settrington, Hereditary Constable of Inverness Castle - and plain 'Freddie' to his many friends.

In 1938 Sir Kingsley Wood, the Secretary of State for Air, had asked Freddie if he would permit part of his estate to be used as an airfield. Freddie was not keen on the idea - understandably, since it seemed to be a further erosion of an already depleted family inheritance. At the turn of the century, the Goodwood Estate had been the fourth largest in Britain, with more than a quarter of a million acres, mostly in Scotland, but death duties imposed in 1935 had seen it shrink to 12,500 acres of Sussex. The site of the county's main fighter base at Tangmere had once been owned by the Goodwood Estate, but had been the subject of a compulsory purchase.

At a subsequent interview, Air Vice-Marshal Sir Charles Portal spelled out what the military saw as Germany's intentions. Freddie, who held a pilot's licence, and the rank of Pilot Officer in the Royal Air Force Volunteer Reserve, agreed to allow part of his

Self suspended upon Charles' auto-wheel-bicycle. 1914

Speed on wheels became the great passion of Freddie Richmond's life.
Above: he tries big brother Charles's auto-wheel bicycle for size, 1914.
Right: looking every inch the part - Freddie with his travel-stained, hard-pressed MG Midget, fresh and ready for the second day's racing, Brooklands Double Twelve, 1931. Victory awaits.

12

13

Through the late 1920s and on into the '30s, Freddie pursued his hobbies of flying and photography. This is 'home', Goodwood House, seen 'from WSW' over the stables with tree lines flanking the famous carriage-circle frontage. The modern Festival of Speed hill-climb runs top right.

estate to be used as a temporary airfield, an Emergency Landing Ground for Tangmere. After the experience of the compulsory purchase of RAF Tangmere, however, he was careful to ensure that the Goodwood Estate retained ownership of the land.

This particular combination of events, people and places led to the farm in Sussex becoming perhaps the best loved motor racing circuit in history.

Freddie, Duke of Richmond, had been born plain Mr Frederick Gordon Lennox, the youngest of four children and the second son of Lord Settrington, the honorary title used by the eldest son of the Earl of March and Kinrara who, in turn, is heir to four dukedoms.

As the youngest by five years, he was a solitary child, but he adored his elder brother, Charles, and shared his enthusiasm for aircraft, cars and motor-cycles.

His mother, Hilda, was a strong-willed woman. She was the grand-daughter of Thomas Brassey, who knew George Stephenson, built railways in Britain, Canada, Australia, India and Argentina, and was renowned for his charitable support. Her father, also called Thomas Brassey was, by turns, Civil Lord to the Admiralty, Governor of Victoria, Lord Warden of the Cinque Ports and an Earl.

Charles Settrington had met Leonard Brassey at Oxford and each had married the other's sister. When Hilda discovered that her new husband was interested only in huntin', shootin' and fishin' - her words - she secured an interview with General

Roberts and returned home to tell her husband that he had been enlisted to the army and was now General Roberts' aide-de-camp.

Freddie was born in 1905, his parents sternly Victorian. He, in contrast, was interested in the twentieth century and all its wonders. When the First World War broke out and the Royal Flying Corps began to train pilots at Tangmere, he would cycle there to watch the flying. When a magazine for boys published plans for a primitive hang glider, he built one. It didn't work, which was just as well because he tried taking off from the edge of the steep Sussex Downs and only 20 or 30 yards out the drop could have been fatal. Neither Freddie nor the magazine had considered that what goes up must come down.

It was not until 1912 that his parents bought their first car, a Ford Model-T Laundelette. Freddie wrote, in an unpublished memoir, "I was spell-bound, unable to concentrate for days on much else, and it is quite incredible the mark this made upon both my brother and myself". The car was entrusted to a coachman, Charlie Tilbury, "who had now assumed deification in my mind". Charlie had been tutored in driving by a local motor trader but, on his first run into Chichester, managed to run into the back of another car.

"One of our brass headlamps folded up like paper. I could have cried; in fact, I did, quite loudly, and, sobbing, pleaded with my father, 'Please, oh please, it wasn't Charlie's fault'. As if this motor car drama was not sufficiently soul-destroying in itself, it became infinitely worse when I heard mother relating it to a neighbour,

Left: the ton-up merchant - Freddie on his AJS 'being tuned for racing', 1923.
Overleaf: Freddie's first fleeting run at Brooklands - the One-Lap Handicap, Junior Car Club's second Member's Day, Brooklands, 1930.

"MY GRANDFATHER WAS A VERY REMARKABLE MAN. IT WASN'T REALLY UNTIL HE DIED THAT I FOUND OUT EVERYTHING ABOUT HIS COACH-BUILDING BUSINESS, HIS AEROPLANE BUSINESS, HIS MODEL-MAKING, AND HIS RACE VICTORIES. HIS OWN RACING CAREER WAS SHORT-LIVED: I THINK MY GRANDMOTHER MUST HAVE ABSOLUTELY HATED IT BECAUSE SHE WAS WORRIED FOR HIM, AND WHEN MY FATHER WAS BORN HE STOPPED. HE WAS A VERY SMOOTH DRIVER WHO TOOK HIS DRIVING VERY SERIOUSLY: HE ALWAYS HAD SOME DOWNTON-TUNED MINI THAT LOOKED BOG STANDARD AND YET WENT LIKE HELL."

THE EARL OF MARCH

"Freddie Richmond was a lovely character. As a young man he just called himself Mr Lennox. He used that name sometimes after he'd become the Duke of Richmond & Gordon, and used to tell the story about arriving at a hotel in New York where he had a reservation. He asked for the room for Mr Lennox, but the hotel disclaimed all knowledge, so he tried his title. 'Ah yes', said the receptionist; 'We have a booking. We've reserved a suite for the Duke of Richmond, with an adjoining room for Gordon'."

JOHN COOPER

the two then lapsing into female laughter over my agony."

As he grew up, Freddie's elder brother, Charles, became his mentor and friend. They even cycled together to visit Sir Henry Royce, in retirement at nearby West Wittering, because Charles wanted to become an engineer and, unlike most members of the aristocracy, was prepared to start on the shop floor.

Charles enlisted in the army in 1918 and saw action in France. He led his platoon into battle and they were slaughtered. He was ordered to retreat and, while heading back to the British lines, picked off a German sniper who was cutting down the remnants of the platoon.

But then the big guns of the British Artllery opened up: he was knocked unconscious by so-called friendly fire and was captured.

Charles was home before Christmas, 1918, but, because of his capture, had to undergo a court-martial - friendly fire or no. He felt humiliated by the experience so, when a friend suggested that the Royal Fusiliers needed a wireless officer for a venture into Russia, to support the White Army in the civil war, Charles volunteered, only to be fatally wounded at Archangel.

Freddie was distraught at the news of his brother's death. Not only had he lost an adored elder brother, but he had inherited his title, as Lord Settrington. Seeing himself referred to by his brother's name on school lists deeply distressed him.

In the time-honoured way of his family, Freddie served his time at Eton before going up to Christ Church, Oxford. Not even Oxford would accept a lord by right and, to win his place, Freddie was sent to a crammer.

It was run by the Rev. Tom Hudson, a man who sat at high table in Oxford colleges. Hudson became a second father to Freddie and also his father-in-law. His daughter, Elizabeth, was six years older than Freddie, but she was the first female of roughly his age who showed a real interest in him. Freddie was smitten - the attraction was mutual, and would last for the rest of their lives.

At Oxford, Freddie was supposed to be studying Agriculture, but he spent most of his time with the university motor club. He won several sprints on his motor-cycle, both in organised events and impromptu drag races, and was a regular spectator at the Brooklands Motor Course, near Weybridge in Surrey.

This was not a recipe for academic success and, before he was due to take his finals in 1923, Freddie jumped before he was pushed. He abandoned university and, through a friend, took a job in the service department of Bentley Motors, at Cricklewood in north London.

It was not an engineering apprenticeship. Freddie was simply a mechanic lying on

Right: Freddie Richmond's personal albums preserve more than mere photography - his captioning reflects much of this remarkably noble man's enthusiasm, friendships and outlook.
Opposite: Mr Settrington's clocking-in cards.

2 Photographs of me taken in 1924 at the Bentley Motors Ltd., Service Department. Myself with the Brooklands racing 3 litre Bentley owned and driven throughout that year by Dr. Dudley Benjefield. Bertie Browning, the fitter with whom I was apprenticed and I looked after this car that year. He took these pictures.

his back on a concrete floor. The underside of a road car was not a pleasant place in the 1920s when there were still millions of horses on the roads. Freddie's outraged parents gave him three months in the job. It was, after all, probably the first time in history that the heir presumptive to a dukedom had taken a 'proper' job.

Freddie entered Bentley as plain Mr Settrington, determined to guard his true identity. Four months into his job, he and another mechanic were removing a back axle from a customer's car when the lad said, "They say as 'ow there's some bloody lord in this place, Fred - d'ye know which one 'e is?" Mr Settrington had no idea.

On one occasion he was rumbled by a reporter from the 'Daily Mail'. Freddie took him to a nearby pub and there buried the story.

Freddie was content in his job, but there was a growing rift with his parents, who not only expected Bentley to be a nine-day wonder but also felt he should find a more suitable match than the clergyman tutor's daughter 'Betty' Hudson. Freddie hated the round of socialite parties. He couldn't bear the vacuous small talk and was always

"Before the war, I always thought of Brooklands as a sort of gentleman's estate where motor racing was allowed to take place - and when Goodwood started up after the war, in many ways it modelled itself on Brooklands."

BILL BODDY
BROOKLANDS HISTORIAN

embarrassed by the grease beneath his fingernails. Besides, he knew where his loyalties lay - with Betty and his pals at Bentley Motors.

When it became clear that Freddie intended to marry Betty, Hilda arranged for Rolls-Royce to offer him a job in America. When he rejected the offer she cornered him in a room and told him that he was going to be aide-de-camp to the Governor of Bombay. She kept him there until he sent a telegram accepting the post.

But once Freddie was released, he sent another telegram, rescinding the first, followed by a letter of explanation to which the Governor replied, agreeing with him. His parents cut off his allowance, forcing him to leave his flat and camp out at friends', but he continued to stick to his guns. Eventually his parents bowed to the inevitable: he married his Betty and restored relations with his family. It may only be coincidence, but standing up to his parents seemed to unleash a period of extraordinary creativity during which he fulfilled all his childhood dreams.

'Mr Settrington' was so good at his job that he was promoted, first to racing mechanic, then to work as a salesman in Bentley's Mayfair showroom. He proved to be a sharp salesman and part of his job was to guide customers to the exact bodywork specification to be built onto their Bentley chassis.

At the end of 1929, Freddie took part in a time trial at Brooklands, driving an Austin Seven. By then he had become Lord March and was writing a regular column for the magazine '*The Light Car*'. It must have occurred to Austin's Sales and Competition Director, Captain Arthur Waite MC, that win or lose, there would be column inches in the exercise. As it happened, Freddie won a Gold award.

Later that afternoon he took part in a one-lap handicap and finished third, beating his far more experienced Austin team-mates.

The following year he shared an Austin Seven two-seater sports car with Arthur Waite in the Brooklands Double Twelve (a 24-hour race run in two daytime legs). They finished seventh overall, first in class and also won a special award based on performance/price.

At one point the rain came down in torrents, conditions which might have fazed many another driver in his first major race, but Freddie kept driving regardless. The handicap field included 6-litre Bentleys and Alfa Romeo Monzas. He had been thrown in at the deep end, but swam immediately.

Freddie then drove in the 1930 BRDC 500, then the world's fastest race - at least for the big car classes. His partner in a works Austin Seven 'Ulster' was S.C.H. 'Sammy' Davis, a past winner at Le Mans and then the Sports Editor of '*The Motor*', while his riding mechanic was the young Charles Goodacre, later a fine works Austin

Above: Freddie March at full flight, bucketing over the Brooklands bumps, in the little MG Midget which he co-drove with racing motor-cyclist and test pilot Chris Staniland - 1931 Double Twelve

Right: armbands from the Brooklands races, and the Gordon Lennox family's Scottish connections mirrored by Freddie's tartan silk scarf from the 1931 Double Twelve victory.

driver in his own right.

The Davis/March won outright. Freddie had driven the whole middle section of 200 miles. Afterwards, '*The Daily Telegraph*' published Freddie's account of the race, including perhaps the earliest reference to the effects of slip-streaming in motor racing.

Freddie was invited to drive a Bentley at Le Mans, but declined on the basis that he was too lightly built to man-handle so big a car over 24 hours. Instead, he attended Le Mans as a spectator and photographed the action. His shots are as good as anything taken at the time, but then Freddie took his photography seriously.

For 1931, Freddie bought three MG C-type '*Montlhéry*' Midgets. He had known MG's founder, Cecil Kimber, while he was up at Oxford and respected his work. Freddie always preferred to race and use small cars, admiring the

BRITISH DOUBLE TWELVE
1930
DRIVER

THE BRITISH
DRIVER
DOUBLE TWELVE
1931 1931

March memorabilia - from
Freddie's scrapbooks, the
minutiae of a very different age
of motor racing.

Clockwise from top left:

500 Miles Race, Brooklands,
1930; 'the practice before',
Brooklands Double Twelve Hour
Race, 1930; the Irish Grand Prix,
1931; pit signals from the 500
Miles Race, Brooklands, 1930;
the Le Mans 24-Hour race, 1929.

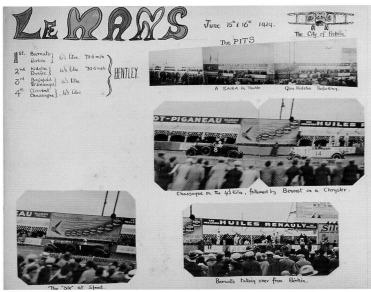

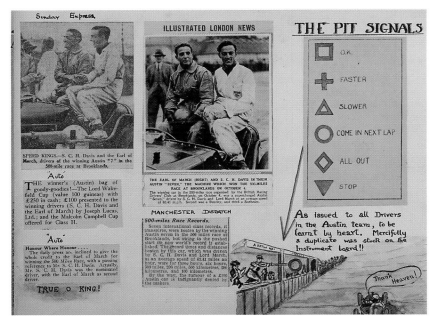

elegance of tuning a small engine to a high standard rather than merely reaching for a bigger one.

In the Double Twelve, with Chris Staniland co-driving, Freddie swept to victory. It seems that the handicapper had been caught out by the speed of the MGs, which filled the first 15 places! Even so, the March/Staniland MG beat 14 others. It was the marque's major win to date, and Freddie would also be instrumental in MG's next two important victories.

Freddie only competed in a handful of events, but he won both major main races held on the British mainland. He would write, "I suppose I had one of the shortest motor racing careers on record, that is if compared to the importance given to it by the press. But I must admit that it was, by luck, unbelievably successful".

After the Double Twelve Freddie turned team manager and guided his cars to victory in the 1931 Irish Grand Prix and the Tourist Trophy - and neither victory was down to luck. A report on the Tourist Trophy said that the March MG driven by Norman Black had won by superior team management. In second place came an Alfa Romeo, entered by one Enzo Ferrari.

Freddie had a rare gift as a team manger in that he could have everyone working together simply to please him. For the Irish races, he had his team up at 5am to run on empty public roads so they could gear the cars correctly. This was so unusual at the time that it was remarked on in the press before the race.

His team of MGs missed out on the one other event it entered, the 1931 BRDC 500, but his cars had taken three of that year's four most important British races. Apart from a time trial at Brooklands in 1933 and a fun day at Goodwood in 1935, that was the sum total of Freddie's motor racing career, as driver and team manager.

In 1929 he had left Bentley to start a car dealership in partnership with Bentley's sales manager, Hugh Kevill-Davies. In its first year of operation, Kevill-Davies & March made a profit of £3,000, a remarkable feat considering the onset of the Great Depression. Following from his interest in sketching,

The adventurous Junior Car Club of the inter-war years was one precursor of the post-WW2 British Automobile Racing Club to whom Goodwood became home. This is the JCC Trophy for their 1930 Double Twelve - Captain A.C.R. Waite and one Freddie Richmond, seventh overall, first in class.

Overleaf: Sweet Victory Mk II - resplendent with 'MG' and 'BRDC' logos stitched onto his overalls, Freddie Richmond savours his 1931 Double Twelve win with Fairey Aviation test pilot and racing motor-cyclist Chris Staniland. Theirs is evidently a popular triumph with Brooklands' 'right crowd'.
Below: the MG Midget during pre-race scrutineering.

and his work helping Bentley customers to choose the right bodywork for their new cars, Freddie started to style coachwork for sale through Kevill-Davies & March. At the time, almost every car had a separate chassis, there were around 250 coach-builders in Britain, and it was not unusual for customers to order special bodies even on cars as humble as the Austin Seven.

With Kevill-Davies & March, Freddie invented the 1930s 'traditional' English sports car look with its cutaway doors, flowing wing line, raised twin scuttles and slab tail tank. You could order a March body for almost any chassis - they appeared on at least a dozen different makes. Cars like the MG TC and SS Jaguar 100, which today

absolutely epitomise the 1930s British sports-car style, were cribs of Freddie March's original line.

Credit has sometimes been given to Eustace Watkins, the London distributor for Wolseley. The real story is that Dick Watkins, son of Eustace, was contacted by Freddie when he was planning a body for the Wolseley Hornet sports car. Dick liked the drawings so much that he introduced Freddie to the coachbuilders used by the family firm used, Whittingham & Mitchel at Putney.

Whittingham & Mitchel then used Freddie's design as the 'Daytona' body on the Wolseley Hornet, sold by Eustace Watkins. It was an obvious copy, but Freddie was too much of gentleman to complain and simply took his business elsewhere.

The Hillman Aero Minx was a March design - as sports car or coupé. Hillman cut corners in the production of the model, to bring it down to a price, but an authentic March body was also available. They were also offered as a factory option on the Riley Lynx in 1933, with more than 60 being made.

From 1934, AC buyers could order a March body - at a premium of about £20 - and almost all AC sports cars, 1934-39, carried March bodies. How many amateur stylists have had their designs put into production by three different manufacturers, and copied by others? Freddie was clearly a world-class car stylist.

He was also a gifted model maker and, in 1934, launched March Models, offering hand-made model racing cars built to order at a typical price of £4 19s 6d - at the time considerably more than the national average wage. A cheaper alternative was to buy two-dimensional car reliefs, hand-carved and painted.

The Shell-BP stand at the 1934 London Motor Show featured a diorama using ten March model cars while others were used by the British government in international exhibitions.

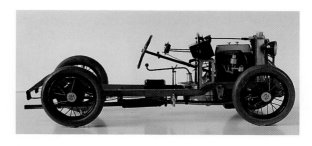

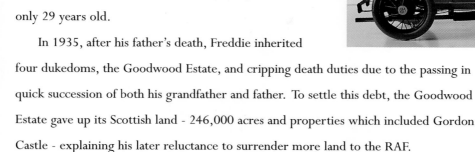

So far Freddie March had been a mechanic, car salesman, racing driver, team manager, journalist, photographer, car stylist and model maker, yet he was still only 29 years old.

In 1935, after his father's death, Freddie inherited four dukedoms, the Goodwood Estate, and cripping death duties due to the passing in quick succession of both his grandfather and father. To settle this debt, the Goodwood Estate gave up its Scottish land - 246,000 acres and properties which included Gordon Castle - explaining his later reluctance to surrender more land to the RAF.

One of the first things that Freddie did when he inherited his dukedoms was to hold a fun day at Goodwood House for members of the Lancia Owners' Club. Kevill-Davies & March was the main Lancia dealer for the Home Counties and Freddie's personal favourite, of all the cars he styled, was his work on the Lancia Aprilia.

Other dukes were wafted around in the back of Daimlers and Rollers. Freddie drove a Lancia because he admired its engineering.

The day at Goodwood included driving tests plus a run up the hill past Goodwood House. Freddie messed up the driving test, but he won the hill-climb and a small trophy. Almost sixty years later, that little social gathering would become the inspiration for the Goodwood Festival of Speed…

At about the same time that he inherited Goodwood, Freddie also met up again with Edmund Hordern, the son of the vicar of Singleton, the parish over the hill from Goodwood where Freddie's family worshipped on occasion. Edmund had gone up to Christ Church, at the same as Freddie, but had left after a term to enrol at Cranwell as an RAF pilot cadet.

Commissioned as a Pilot Officer in 1925, he was assigned to Fighter Command where he became recognised as an outstanding aviator and test pilot. During the 1920s, civil aviation developed rapidly, as did interest in light aircraft for recreational flying. Hordern and some of his friends were fired by enthusiasm and, in 1928, Freddie joined them.

Edmund Hordern had borrowed an Avro Avian, a new civilian biplane. He and Freddie flew it from Hendon down to Goodwood where they landed in the grounds and taxied to the front of the house. Pleased with themselves, they photographed the plane, the house and themselves in every possible combination. Edmund had encouraged Freddie to take the controls during the flight, and he was hooked.

Freddie was frequently air sick, yet he loved flying so much that he was prepared to put up with it. He bought himself an aeroplane and had a hangar built at Goodwood,

Top left: Kevill-Davies & March body style and coach-building brochure pages for (**above**) Hillman, Wolseley, and Riley and (**below**) presenting the 1933 'March Special' Wolseley Hornet. **Middle left:** the hill-climb trophy won by Freddie in his 1935 Lancia Owners' Club day out at Goodwood. **Above:** one of March Models' exquisite scale replicas.

Top: the Hordern-Richmond company enjoyed a busy war, no longer manufacturing aircraft but producing vital laminated-wood propellers for them.

Above: 'The Flying Field' at Goodwood, diagonally opposite the wartime aerodrome, boasted this splendid thatched-roof hangar, home to the Hordern-Richmond Autoplane, 1938-39.

perhaps the only half-timbered, thatched, aircraft hangar ever built. It later burned down, which perhaps explains why Heathrow's terminals remain un-thatched.

Together, Edmund and Freddie designed an ingenious and practical commuter aircraft, the Hordern-Richmond 'Autoplane', intended to be as easy to fly as driving a car. It would carry three people and was stable and docile with a stall speed of just 35 mph. Designed to climb on only one engine, it could glide safely even if both engines failed. A farmer, say, could store his Autoplane in a barn and fly it from a meadow.

The rudder bars were dispensed with, a revolutionary development which not only made the Autoplane easier to fly, but also allowed the pilot to put a rug around his legs - a necessary consideration in an unheated, unpressurised cabin.

The Autoplane was described in the aviation press as 'a design of superb vision… quite unlike anything else ever produced', and a great future predicted for it.

The Hordern-Richmond Aircraft Company was established at Denham airfield where the Autoplane first flew on 16th October 1936, Plans were made to put it into production, but a number of things abruptly changed Freddie's life. A Dutch inventor came knocking on the door promoting a resin-impregnated wood laminate; Hordern-Richmond became the first to see the potential of his concept.

The material - named 'Hydrulignum' - was stronger and lighter than Duralumin, then the favoured material for aircraft propellers. With the encouragement of the government, Hordern-Richmond moved to Haddenham airfield, near Aylesbury, and began making aircraft propeller blades.

In 1936, Freddie decided his closer involvement was required and bought the Old Vicarage in Haddenham, close to the airfield. He moved his family there, with Goodwood becoming their weekend cottage.

He still had such commitments as turning up for the Goodwood horse racing meetings and occasionally entertaining royalty. He was a very close friend of the Duke and Duchess of York and was dining with them in a London restaurant on the night that Edward VIII announced his abdication. The Duke of York promptly became King George VI and the Duchess is better known today as the Queen Mother. Freddie donned the ermine to attend the coronations of George VI and Elizabeth II, at both of which he carried the sceptre. He also served as Deputy Lord Lieutenant of Sussex.

Freddie took all this grandeur in his stride, helped by Betty, whose feet were always firmly on the ground. He walked with kings yet never lost the common touch. One of his closest friends was a mechanic who lived near to Goodwood, another the Estate joiner he persuaded to join him at Horden-Richmond as foreman.

When Freddie died a letter appeared in a local paper from the owner of a garage who had had no idea that the modest man who called regularly to fill up his Vanden Plas 1300 was the Duke of Richmond. He contrasted that to the number of times he'd been berated by people who worked for the Goodwood Estate and thought they should get preferential treatment because of their connection.

As war loomed, the bottom fell out of private aviation. The Autoplane was abandoned. Freddie bought the prototype from the company in 1938, after which Hordern-Richmond concentrated on its propellers while still entertaining some hope of putting the Autoplane into production.

The prototype Autoplane, of which so much was expected, was scrapped during the war. Its two Continental engines had been used by the ARP for pumping water and the rest of the plane was not considered worth preserving.

Above: Freddie Richmond's multiple skills extended to scratch-building these fine miniatures of his own aircraft, the Autoplane (**top**) and the Klemm (**above**).
Middle: Freddie's flying licence.
Below: Magnificent conception - the Hordern-Richmond Autoplane combined car-type utility with the facility of flight but was killed off by the outbreak of World War Two. Here, wings folded, the blood-red prototype shows off one of its Continental A-40 engines.

The first utility car: Freddie Richmond's 'Brakevan' body on a Commer chassis, demonstrating its capacious interior, folding rear blind, collapsible seats and counter-balanced tailgate.

In the meantime, Freddie had designed what may have been the first MPV. His 'Brakevan' was offered on any chassis - at least one Rolls-Royce had a Brakevan body, but more popular choices were Commer and Ford. There was seating for six people in comfort, nine at a squeeze, and the two rows of passenger seats folded flush into the floor when it was being used to carry goods. Freddie patented the system.

The back of the car was vertical, and at the top there was a detachable fabric panel incorporating a window extending about a third of the way down. When detached and folded it was retained by a strap in the roof. Perspex side windows could be slid into the roof and the tailgate folded out to form a platform which was flush with the floor, so it was possible to carry a load which was larger than the cabin space.

The snag was that if you drove your friends to a pheasant shoot, it was a car. If you then drove the shot pheasants to a local game dealer, it became a van which had to observe a speed limit of 30 mph, was liable for higher road tax and also required a special driving licence. Magistrates were divided on the matter.

Still, a photograph of the Rolls-Royce Brakevan conversion appeared in advertisements with a strong recommendation from 'a Sussex owner'. Freddie owned a Brakevan, Goodwood is in Sussex, and Freddie was a successful car salesman...

Kevill-Davies & March was still going strong - it would survive until at least 1959 - but Freddie was playing a less active role. His great period of creativity approached its end as the threat of another war with Germany intensified. Freddie did not move in political circles and, like the majority in Britain, did not fully appreciate the German threat, until his card was marked by Air Vice-Marshal Sir Charles Portal.

The war would change so much. Freddie joined the RAF, initially as a ground controller, sometimes using his experience as a pilot to talk down fliers nursing damaged aircraft - some harrowing exchanges with wounded pilots would stay with him for the rest of his life. Hordern-Richmond was sold to 'Rotol', a joint venture by Rolls-Royce and the Bristol Aircraft Company. Rotol propeller blades would play their part in the Battle of Britain, improving the performance of Spitfires and Hurricanes. Last heard, the laminate was still being made by a company called Permally and marketed under the name 'Jickwood'. March Models folded, never to be revived.

Freddie's career as a car stylist was over. In the post-war market there would be no room for the kind of specialised bodies which he been so brilliant at designing.

By the time war broke out, however, Westhampnett Farm was already under development as part of the war effort and, among other things, Freddie had become the President of the Junior Car Club. The Junior Car Club, an organisation named originally to distinguish it from the RAC (the senior club) was an important race organiser at Brooklands.

In 1946, the JCC would amalgamate with the Brooklands Automobile Racing Club and, in 1949, the joint body would become the British Automobile Racing Club with Freddie Richmond still President. The pieces of the jigsaw were falling into place.

Below: the current Earl of March at Goodwood House with his March-bodied AC.

RAF WESTHAMPNETT

During 1938 and 1939 Westhampnett Farm was flattened, its hedgerows and coppices removed, and the site became RAF Westhampnett - initially an 'ELG', an Emergency Landing Ground for aircraft so badly damaged they were liable to crash on landing and block a permanent runway, as at Tangmere. Until early 1940, Westhampnett was little more than a cleared field, with its handful of personnel camped in tents, but it was speedily upgraded to the status of a satellite station.

Two grass runways were laid out: one running roughly between what would become Madgwick and Lavant Corners, the other bisecting the start-finish straight to finish at Fordwater. The road which runs past the main entrance of the circuit was blocked off a few hundred yards beyond Woodcote Corner. A new access road was driven through from Lavant Village to the A285, alongside what would become the Lavant Straight. For most of its length it came under Air Ministry control as part of RAF Westhampnett.

Former Leading Aircraftman Eric Marsden arrived at RAF Westhampnett with 145 Squadron from Tangmere in the summer of 1940. He recalls, "The official history says that the field was first occupied by 145 Squadron on 31st July, but the official version kept changing. We'd actually come over a few days before and bad weather caused us to return to Tangmere.

" 'A' Flight was based on Madgwick Lane; I was in 'B' Flight on the Lavant Road. Each Flight had two new Nissan huts, so new that the concrete wasn't properly dry. There were no light bulbs inside the huts, but then there was no power either.

"To defend the station we had a 7mm gun lifted from a crashed Heinkel and mounted on a fence post. The rule was that whoever

Images from the 1998 Revival Meeting - in memory of The Few, and of Westhampnett's many.

A War Ministry 'aerial' of RAF Westhampnett taken from 8,000 feet on 29th April 1942, and showing what would become Madgwick Corner, **bottom right**; St Mary's and Lavant, **top left**; and Woodcote, **top right**.

got to the gun first was allowed to use it unless Andy Boyd, one of our fliers, was on the base. He reckoned that since he'd shot down the Heinkel, he had first shout.

"Andy set us a target of getting a kite up within two minutes of the 'scramble' signal because, given the usual amount of advance warning, that would allow the fliers to be up to 15,000 feet when the *Luftwaffe* arrived. In fact, we got it down to 115 seconds and could turn a plane around, from the moment it landed to the time it took off to do battle again, in eight minutes. It was like a Grand Prix pit stop."

On 31st July 1940, ten Hawker Hurricanes of 145 Squadron arrived from Tangmere, with 21 pilots under the command of Sqd. Ldr. John Peel. Next day they were in action, protecting a merchant convoy in the English Channel.

Bombing raids by the *Luftwaffe* had begun on 5th June, mainly directed against airfields, before the Germans began to mount sorties designed to tease out Fighter Command. On 1st August the *Luftwaffe* received their orders. *Adlerangriff* - Eagle Attack - was intended to gain supremacy of the air prior to Operation *Seelöewe* (Sealion), the invasion of Britain planned to commence on 17th September.

Air supremacy was vital because Hitler's ad hoc invasion fleet would be extremely vulnerable to air attack.

On 8th August, 145 Squadron was despatched to defend a convoy under heavy attack from the *Luftwaffe*. It accounted for nine Junkers 87 'Stuka' dive bombers, two Messerschmitt Bf 110 fighter-bombers and four Messerschmitt Bf 109E fighters, but at the cost of five Hurricanes and their pilots. Three days later they lost a further four planes and three pilots. They had inflicted heavy damage on the *Luftwaffe*, but just four serviceable Hurricanes remained, plus a fifth on its nose in the middle of the field. The battered squadron was ordered to stand down on 13th August, 'Eagle Day', withdrawing to Drem, in Scotland, to regroup.

'Eagle Day', *Adlertag*, is the day on which the Germans claim the Battle of Britain began. In fact there is no clear definition of the Battle. The official British view is that it raged from 10th July-31st October, dates chosen so that men decorated in that period could wear a special flash on their medal ribbons. The German view is that the Battle of Britain began on 13th August 1940 and ended in May 1941.

In fact, as good a definition as any is that it was an interlude of roughly four weeks over many months of continuous fighting. It was the period of the *Adlerangriff*, when the *Luftwaffe* concentrated most of its resources on gaining supremacy in the air by attacking military targets, particularly airfields and radar installations.

Within 20 miles of Westhampnett lay four major bases. Apart from RAF Tangmere, there were Fleet Air Arm airfields at Ford and Gosport, and a Coastal Command station on Thorney Island, all placed to defend the enormous Naval base at Portsmouth and Southampton's civilian docks. There was also a major radar

Above: legless fighter ace Douglas Bader flew many missions, including his last, from Westhampnett, and post-war would regularly play golf at Goodwood.
Below: 602 Squadron, RAF Westhampnett, 1940.

"In 1941 my brother Scott and I were both stationed at Westhampnett, flying Spitfires. It was a good place to be, because from the air it didn't look like an airfield, unlike Tangmere, which got bombed to hell. Westhampnett was just four fields on a flat part of the Duke of Richmond & Gordon's land with the hedges taken away to make a grass airfield, and to camouflage it they put big black lines down where the hedges had been. Then it was decided the tankers would have trouble in the winter getting bogged down taking the fuel out to the aircraft, which were just sort of parked around on the grass. So a whole gang of Irish labourers appeared and started constructing a perimeter track." TONY GAZE

"*Flying in the war, I only landed once at Westhampnett, which was a satellite for Tangmere. They needed satellites to accommodate the number of planes coming home at the end of a sweep. Of course, the thing about grass airfields, with no runways, was that twelve aeroplanes could take off at once, in formation.*" RAYMOND BAXTER

installation at Poling, just along the Sussex coast. Satellite station it may have been, but Westhampnett's location put it in the thick of the fighting.

On 13th August the Spitfires of 602 (City of Glasgow) Squadron of the Royal Auxiliary Air Force arrived, under the command of Sqd. Ldr. 'Sandy' Johnstone. As they landed at Westhampnett, they taxied to the outskirts of the airfield to park under the trees which ringed the site. There were as yet no hangars at Westhampnett.

The RAAF was the aviation equivalent of the Territorial Army, training both air and ground crew, who received almost as much flying time as RAF regulars. When war broke out, some RAAF squadrons were already disciplined and integrated fighting units. Indeed, the first German plane shot down over the British mainland was credited to 602's Archie McKellar. The Squadron was ready for action on 16th August, when a total of 1,720 German planes attacked. Tangmere was a prime target and Stukas, supported by Bf 109Es, homed in on the airfield.

The Stukas mounted an impressive display of precision bombing. They destroyed most of the buildings and inflicted heavy casualties. The wounded, some of whom sustained hideous injuries, were rushed to Goodwood House, then under conversion

Top right: aircrew enjoying 'a bronzie' amongst their much-cratered quarters at nearby RAF Tangmere, for which Westhampnett was a safer satellite. A 'Tiffy' sneaks coyly round the hut.
Below: revival for racing entailed the inevitable destruction of some old-time Goodwood structures, but the number was absolutely minimised and each one endlessly debated. The wartime 'parachute building' here, with its 'chute-drying clerestory roof, just had to survive, becoming the circuit shop.

into a medical centre.

Since a Messerschmitt over Tangmere had only a few minutes' fuel to engage in a dogfight, many of the attacking Stukas were picked off by defending fighters on the way home. Tangmere was badly crippled, but remained operational thanks to the far-sighted provision of a back-up Operations Centre and because Westhampnett, un-targeted, was available in support.

On 16th August, the *Luftwaffe* lost 75 aircraft, their highest casualty rate in a single day of the Battle of Britain; the RAF lost 34. 602 Squadron claimed eight kills, six Stukas and two Messerschmitt Bf 109Es, for the cost of two injured pilots and three irreparably damaged Spitfires.

The *Adlerangriff* ended on 17th September when the Luftwaffe ceased concentrating almost exclusively on military targets and shifted its attention instead to the bombing of London. One historian has claimed that 602 Squadron had the second highest number of kills during the Adlerangriff, the lowest casualty rate, and the RAF pilot with the most kills. It is clear that Westhampnett was host to one of the Battle's crack squadrons and played a truly significant role in the fighting.

Over the winter of 1940/41 snow and rain water-logged the field so concrete dispersal points were laid, the perimeter track was built and several pre-fabricated blister hangers erected so that aircraft could be serviced under cover.

Amongst those stationed at Westhampnett were two racing drivers, Tony Gaze and Dickie Stoop. Gaze, born in Australia, and the grandson of Thomas Sadler, a leading Chichester merchant, would later drive as a Grand Prix privateer; Stoop would drive campaign Frazer Nashes both in the UK and at Le Mans.

In 1941 each owned an MG and, when the perimeter track was laid down, they held impromptu races on it. Petrol was rationed, but they filled their cars with low-

The 'Drivers Club' mess and canteen, tailor-made for the Revival Meeting, September 1998.

Above and far right: starring for one night only at the Goodwood revival, the motor course cigarette girls - and clientele - on parade.

grade spirit intended for cleaning engines, which they filtered through old socks while their CO, Wing-Commander Douglas Bader, turned a blind eye.

Bader had moved 616 Squadron to Westhampnett in the Spring of 1941. Part of its attraction for him was the nearby Goodwood golf course. If he was urgently needed while playing a round, a plane would fly over and drop a flare. It would be from Westhampnett that Bader would fly his final mission: forced to bale out after a collision, he spent the rest of the war as a POW.

Apart from Tangmere squadron using their satellite, a further 24 RAF squadrons would be based at Westhampnett (18 of them flying Spitfires) in addition to Polish, New Zealand, American and Canadian units.

From June 1940-April 1941, the RAF fighter planes had been defenders, but afterwards turned to offensive 'Rhubarb' sweeps, or opportunist sorties. Since by 1941 most aircraft were fitted with cannons rather than machine guns, if they found a target they could inflict serious harm.

When America entered the war in December 1941, the 31st Group, United States Army Air Force despatched its pioneering squadrons, in Spitfires, to Westhampnett. They became the first USAAF pilots to see action in the European theatre of war and today a plaque at the circuit commemorates their service.

When they arrived in July 1942, Westhampnett was unrecognisable as the ELG of two years before. It was dotted with Nissen huts, blister hangers, wooden huts, permanent 'Maycrete' buildings, concrete dispersal bays, gun emplacements and searchlight batteries. There were pilots' briefing halls, armouries, a photo-reconnaissance centre, a chapel, a fire station and an extensive Motor Transport section.

The airfield had also spawned no fewer than 11 satellite sites, some up to two miles away. All local roads were under Ministry control so an area of several square miles, including some entire villages, were effectively part of the station.

If you stand on top of the modern circuit pits, anything you can see outside the city of Chichester was part of the station - including the Goodwood racecourse, which had become an accommodation site.

Today, as one drives through the circuit's main entrance, to one's right is the gas clothing and respiratory centre. Beyond are blister hangars, now used as workshops, and at 11 o'clock is the circuit shop with its unusual stepped roof. This was the wartime parachute building, its clerestory roof enabling silk canopies to be hung prior to packing.

A hundred yards or so to one's left is Woodcote Cottage, used in wartime as sleeping quarters, while before it stands the control tower, now used as a restaurant. The landmark Super Shell building was a squadron office and almost immediately behind it, across New Road, is a Type T1 aircraft hangar.

There were no wartime buildings on what is now the circuit infield, but, by 1945, RAF Westhampnett's site inventory included 367 buildings and installations - plus an unknown number of tents - in a two-mile radius. Westhampnett was a substantial station.

Publicans had a busy time during the War, except when they ran out of beer, which was often. In addition to the RAF, large numbers of Navy and Army personnel packed the Chichester area, particularly in the build-up to D-Day in June 1944. Chichester is a small walled city with four main streets. The Navy drank in South Street, the Army in North Street, the RAF in East Street; the Cathedral stands in West Street.

Non-combatant officers and airmen all had their favourite watering holes, but pilots

Overleaf: 'How goes the war?' - the young drama students who reclined at readiness over Goodwood's Revival Meeting weekend lived their roles to perfection.

favoured The Unicorn in Eastgate Square, a large pub run by a jovial Cockney called Arthur King. Most people suspected Arthur of having begun life as a barrow-boy, but, be that as it may, he was a frustrated flier and he 'looked after his pilots'.

The Unicorn was a place where commissioned pilots and NCOs could meet as comrades-in-arms, without the usual divisions demanded by rank, and has been described as an unofficial Operations Planning Centre

Arthur King had contacts on the black market so he could supply special lines of food, drink and luxuries. And nothing was too good for Arthur's fliers.

Just after D-Day, so the story goes, when a landing strip had been established near Dieppe, a Spitfire flew in. Sitting on the pilot's lap was the bulky form of Arthur King. Under the Spitfire's wings, cooling nicely, were two barrels of Henty & Constable's fine ale. On the return flight, the Spitfire carried barrels of brandy.

The story may have become garbled in the re-telling - there's not much spare space in a Spitfire cockpit - or perhaps Arthur flew in a trainer. Whatever the truth, after D-Day he certainly made regular sorties in an old Anson, taking victuals to 'his' pilots in France and bringing back French food and wine, which he handed over to the RAF. Although he was operating in the black market, Arthur made little, if any, profit from his fliers. He was more than a mere publican - Arthur King was an institution.

From the start of the Battle of Britain, Goodwood House had been requisitioned as a medical centre, Freddie Richmond maintaining just a small apartment there. Betty and their two children, Charles and Nicholas, had been evacuated to America and he eventually joined them there, in an official capacity.

His RAF commission saw him first posted to Fighter Command, then to the Ministry of Aircraft Production. In 1943 he was appointed to the staff of a friend, Wing-Commander Geoffrey Lywood.

Lywood was sent to America to persuade the Americans not to scrap, nor cannibalise damaged aircraft, but repair them. Freddie went with him, and the two had a great time since everyone wanted to invite 'the dook' to their parties. They would invite Lywood, as senior officer, casually suggesting that he bring along his ADC.

It wasn't all parties, however, and Freddie did valuable work in persuading the Americans to change their philosophy. He even wrote a ballad on the subject which appeared in the American publication, '*Aviation Maintenance*'.

The magazine noted, "Borrowing useable parts from one airplane to keep a sister aircraft in the fight is not the solution to the spares distribution as is ably pointed out in this ballad submitted to the editors by a Flight-Lieutenant of the Royal Air Force."

From 1943, Hawker Typhoon ground-attack fighters operated from RAF

Westhampnett and proved devastating against ground targets - a Typhoon speciality was 'train busting' - and shipping. These 9-ton, 24-cylinder Napier-engined terrors were formidable fighting machines, but some locals actually complained to the station commander about the din they produced. These people were the spiritual ancestors of those who would complain about the proposed Goodwood Revival in the 1990s.

Shortly before D-Day, the Typhoons were dispersed to surrounding satellite stations, at Merston and Funtington, and Westhampnett was used for last-minute training by Canadians. Once a bridgehead had been established in Normandy, the RAF could move to bases in France and so, before long, Westhampnett became merely a staging post ferrying aircraft across the Channel.

Michael Christie, a friend of Freddie's, and, post-war, a racing driver, recalls, "I used to stay with Freddie in his apartment in Goodwood House if I was in the area. In 1944 Freddie and I were having dinner when an Auster landed just outside the front door. Out climbed an officer together with a sergeant who was carrying a large wicker

Below: upon whose glory the sun shall never set - taxying Spitfire at the 1998 Revival Meeting.
Overleaf: the man who had the big idea - Tony Gaze at speed in his Formula 2 Alta passing the crew hut outside Woodcote Corner which he and his late brother Scott had known in wartime.

"I had an MG J2, my brother had an Alvis, and another Pilot Officer, Dickie Stoop, had an MG PA. When the perimeter track was finished I looked at it one morning and said, 'I think it's time we christened this thing'. By then my brother had been killed - he was just 19. Anyway Dickie and I got into our MGs and went batting round, anti-clockwise as it happened.

After a while we persuaded one or two other chaps to join in, and whenever there was nothing else going on we'd go and have a race round. That's how it went. Later on I bought the old Aston Martin 'LM10', which was a lot faster than the MG.

Just after the war had ended, I happened to be in Charles Follett's showroom in the West End - I'd just bought a car from him, and he was always good for a drink - and there was the Duke of Richmond & Gordon, whom I'd met during the war when he was a Flight-Lieutenant. Someone said 'Freddie's the President of the JCC and they're looking everywhere for a replacement for Brooklands'. I said, 'Don't be bloody silly, he owns one'. And I went over and said, 'You've got an airfield. When are we going to have a sports car race at Westhampnett?' 'Bless my soul', he said, 'What will the neighbours say?'"

TONY GAZE

"Like so many of the exciting things in life the Goodwood Circuit arrived by accident. It was just after the war when I met Tony Gaze, still in RAF uniform. 'When are we going to have a sports car race at Westhampnett?', he asked. I hastened to look at the place and the first impression was hardly prepossessing. Nevertheless within 18 months it was derequisitioned and, with a lot of hard work and improvisation, we were off."

FREDDIE, DUKE OF RICHMOND

basket. They came to the door, the officer saluted and said, 'Your Grace, I thought you'd like some spoils of war', and handed him the basket. Inside were four or five Camembert cheeses, two bottles of old Calvados, and various other bits and pieces. The officer declined an invitation to join us and flew off again."

As the war drew to a close, RAF Westhampnett was mothballed, reactivated briefly to accept aircraft returning home, and on 13th May 1946 finally closed.

It took some time before Freddie was demobbed and returned to manage the Goodwood Estate, but he'd had efficient managers doing that for the whole time he had been Duke, and away at war, so he was little more than a figurehead. Everything which had kept him occupied during his incredibly creative period through the 1930s had gone. March Models had closed, the Hordern-Richmond Aircraft Company had been sold, there was no demand for the special car body styles and, though Kevill-Davies & March still existed, there were precious few new cars to sell. Being President of the Junior Car Club seemed meaningless without a single surviving racing circuit on mainland Britain. Donington Park had become the biggest military transport depot in the land, Crystal Palace had reverted to a public park and Brooklands, which had been turned over to aircraft production during the War, was in the process of being sold to Vickers, hangars cut into its mouldering bankings.

Above: the hauntingly beautiful silver Supermarine Spitfire which is the Scott Gaze Memorial Trophy, awarded by his surviving brother Tony Gaze in the 1950s for each year's fastest racing lap by a British driver. The tacit expectation was that some Continental Johnny would go faster...

Below: Scott Gaze in the garden of a house in Lavant a few days before he was killed.

Right: Tony Gaze in his Spitfire, parked where the Motor Circuit paddock now stands.

It was left to the enthusiastic young Cambridge University Automobile Club and the happy-go-lucky Vintage Sports Car Club between them to organise the first post-war motor race meeting in Britain - on Gransden Lodge aerodrome - in 1947. It was a success; the aerodrome idea could work well. The Junior Car Club, meanwhile, was able to run road races on the island of Jersey in 1947 and 1948, but for most British enthusiasts Jersey was as inaccessible as the far side of the moon.

Then Tony Gaze, who had raced his MG against Dickie Stoop on the

Westhampnett perimeter track, met Freddie at a party and asked him when there would be motor racing at Westhampnett. In the gloomy days of post-war austerity, it was not an obvious idea, and since Freddie was then still in the RAF and stationed away from Goodwood, he had not seen the place.

A day at the races - in this case wheeled rather than four-legged: the Duke and Duchess of Richmond & Gordon, with the Bristol, at their Goodwood Motor Circuit, 1949.

On his next visit to the estate, he drove his Lancia Aurelia to the airfield, and trundled thoughtfully around the perimeter track; it looked promising despite the potholes and the stacks of war surplus and unwanted scrap.

He then called his friend, the journalist and racing driver, Tommy Wisdom, and asked him to look at the perimeter track. Tommy arrived with his wife, 'Bill', also a celebrated pre-war racing driver. They spent almost a whole day at Westhampnett and agreed it really did have potential - provided one could imagine the site without the detritus.

More were invited to inspect the track - officials from the RAC and the JCC - and they were impressed not only by the site itself, but also by Freddie's enthusiasm.

Freddie Richmond decided to run a motor race.

THE CURTAIN RISES

The Duke found so many factors in Goodwood's favour that it seems almost inevitable that the Westhampnett site's perimeter track would become a motor racing circuit. The Air Ministry draughtsman plainly would not have thought 'a fast double-apex right hander at the end of the straight will sort the men out from the boys' but, by pure chance, he had still drawn a great race track. Today, consultants aided by computers still concoct circuits on which overtaking is all but impossible.

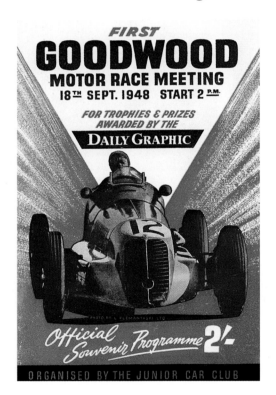

Above: this striking Maserati 4CL image emblazoned the front cover of Goodwood's inaugural meeting race programme, 1948.

The only tarmac on the Westhampnett site formed a perfect road circuit. It was not like other airfields which would be taken up for motor racing circuits using a combination of encircling perimeter track and infield runway. The first three Grands Prix to be held at Silverstone, for example, all used different combinations of the two. What became the Goodwood Motor Circuit was fixed from its inception.

There were dozens of disused airfields dotted over the country, but in 1947-48 only one was owned by a former racing driver. When the RAC wanted to use Silverstone, they had to lease it from the Government, for a one-year experiment, and that involved protracted negotiation with bureaucracy.

Westhampnett, too, had its Air Ministry restrictions, but Freddie had served in the RAF and, when dealing with the Air Ministry, it helped to be on friendly terms with the odd Air Marshal or two.

Not only was Westhampnett owned by a former racing driver, but he was also a Duke. That meant unspoken clout; even though Freddie never stood on his social rank,

First
GOODWOOD
MEETING

"Welcome to our first Goodwood motor race meeting. We're not sure if it will work, but my people have all worked very hard, hopefully to ensure you all enjoy it" - Freddie Richmond's introduction to the 1948 race programme.

WE'LL be quite frank with you at the start. This race meeting is an experiment. We cannot, on this occasion, offer you a seat in a grandstand—or even a seat at all. You'll be able to obtain some refreshments, and the loudspeaker people will do their best to make certain you hear the numbers of the non-starters and of the winners.

We think you'll see some quite good racing, and share our surprise if the programme keeps up to time. But if all the refinements of a fully-developed sporting arena are missing, take our word for it, they will appear eventually—particularly if we have any success with the show to-day.

Meanwhile, months of negotiations have been necessary, just to make to-day's meeting possible. Government Departments have been involved—and you know what that means—but we've stuck manfully to the job, and here we are. To do justice to those with whom we have been called upon to negotiate, we must say that the Government people have been more than helpful. Ministry of Works officials wear collars and ties, drink and eat just like you and I, and smoke cigarettes at 3s. 6d. a packet. Sometimes, though, they do a little better with petrol. And as for local authorities, they seem genuinely keen to see motor sport at Goodwood.

We've been greatly assisted, too, by local farmers, who do not subscribe to the view that dairy cows refuse to come across with the milk if they are within earshot of a racing car.

Naturally, in the J.C.C. we are more than pleased to be staging our first race meeting in England since the war. As someone said the other day, we are a little lucky in having a President with an airfield in his back garden, but it's better to be born lucky than have to pay 19s. 6d. in the £.

12

he was not averse to wielding it if necessary to gain advantage. His proposal to re-deploy the airfield as a motor racing venue found enthusiastic, and practical, support from both District and County Councils - in some contrast to the struggle his grandson would face when attempting to revive it in the 1990s.

As a major landowner, Freddie employed hundreds of labourers and the Estate's horses, carts, tractors and trailers offered all the equipment needed to clear the site. The place was a mess and, at the time, only the owner of an estate could have found the manpower to clear it.

Freddie was also President of the JCC, of course, and, further, his family had nearly 150 years' experience of staging major sporting events at the nearby Goodwood racecourse. The Gordon Lennoxes had been at Goodwood since 1697 and a previous Earl of March had organised the first horse race on Trundle Hill in 1801. All the expertise for running a motor race meeting was thus in place: crowd control, catering, printing programmes and providing public conveniences.

Finally Freddie renamed Westhampnett. It became 'The Goodwood Motor Circuit' - automatically linking this new motor sporting venue with all that heritage: a classic case of 'branding' before its time, but then Freddie had been a successful car salesman.

All the elements were in place for Goodwood to be a success, but it still required an act of faith. When Freddie took the decision to run races, there had been only one motor racing meeting in post-war Britain. The French had run a race for Grand Prix cars on the streets of Paris within four weeks of the surrender of Japan. There would be 26 races for Grand Prix cars in France before Goodwood opened. By then even defeated Italy had found the resources to run the Mille Miglia twice.

Work to convert the airfield into a circuit began in mid-1947, not the happiest of times for Britain. The year had begun with a strike by lorry drivers which caused precious food to rot in warehouses. Then one of the worst winters in history arrived and the whole country was under snow. The weather stopped the railway system altogether and servicemen, even prisoners, were set to work clearing the tracks. Coal failed to reach power stations, leading to wide-spread power cuts. Industry was disrupted and the Royal Family set an example to the nation by using candles in Buckingham Palace.

The economy was thrown into disarray and, in the summer of 1947, the government announced stricter rationing. The meat ration was smaller than it had been during the worst days of war, and even bread was rationed. Imports of items like tobacco and petrol were cut and, from 1st December 1947 to 1st June 1948, the basic petrol ration was withdrawn altogether.

The basic ration had allowed motorists perhaps 30 miles of driving a week but, for six months, unless you had priority (as a doctor or vet perhaps) or could wangle something on the black market, you could not drive your car.

The circumstances were not promising for someone building a motor racing circuit, but build it Freddie did. As well as clearing the detritus of six years' occupation by the RAF, he constructed mesh

Below: the magic moment - the inaugural meeting's Event One, for unsupercharged 3000cc closed sports cars, is flagged away for its three-lap, 7.2-mile duration. Barrington-Brock in his Spa coupé HRG (**left**), the Healeys of Downing, Hall and Haines, and winner Paul Pycroft's 2.6-litre Jaguar. **Overleaf:** September 1998 - the Earl of March re-opens the Motor Circuit in the Bristol 400 (**main picture**) fifty years to the day after his grandfather had completed the first official lap in an identical car (**inset**). The Revival outriders are John Surtees (**left**) and Stirling Moss (**right**).

"THERE'S AN OIL PAINTING HANGING IN GOODWOOD HOUSE OF MY GRANDFATHER OPENING THE CIRCUIT ON SATURDAY, 18TH SEPTEMBER, 1948. HE DID THAT FIRST OFFICIAL LAP IN A BRAND-NEW BRISTOL 400, BORROWED FROM THE MAKERS. SO THE OBVIOUS THING FOR ME TO DO ON FRIDAY, 18TH SEPTEMBER, 1998 WAS TO OPEN THE CIRCUIT IN AN

IDENTICAL BRISTOL 400 - TONY CROOK, A LONGTIME GOODWOOD COMPETITOR, SUPPLIED HIS OWN CAR. AFTER ALL THE PLANNING, ALL THOSE YEARS OF WORK, IT WAS AN EMOTIONAL MOMENT AS I DROVE OUT OF THE PADDOCK. I HAVE TO ADMIT IT WAS MADE RATHER MORE EMOTIONAL BY COMING OUT OF THE CHICANE AND MEETING RAY HANNA FLYING TOWARDS ME UP THE START-FINISH STRAIGHT IN THE SPITFIRE AT AN ALTITUDE OF NOTHING VERY MUCH."

THE EARL OF MARCH

Below: in the then unprotected, pit-less, Goodwood paddock - Harry Lester, MG specialist, with his wife and car.
Right: Patrick Hall (**left**), third in the non-supercharged closed sports car race, stands beside his Healey.

fencing around the entire site - every spectator would be a welcome guest, but they would still have to pay at the gate.

'*The Daily Graphic*' presented a trophy, plus a cheque for £500, for the feature race, and entries flooded in.

Many applicants were to be disappointed because, for each race, only five cars per mile of track were permitted. Since Goodwood was 2.4 miles long, that meant 12 cars per race, which are short rations for a serious meeting. But even short rations can provide a feast when you have been starved of your sport for nine years.

Imagine a young man, his fiancée and an MG setting out from London. The man has a special reason for visiting Goodwood, since he scrambled his Spitfire from the field. He was not an ace, just one of the hundreds of pilots who were based there for a few weeks or months.

The A3 London-Portsmouth road runs through town after town - Esher, Cobham, Send - so, once through Guildford, he takes the back route through Milford, Haslemere and Midhurst. Out of Midhurst he takes the A286 but, instead of going on towards Lavant, he makes a left turn just outside Singleton.

The climb is steep but, at the top of the hill, on one of the highest points of the Sussex Downs, he draws over to the side of the road. Beside him is the Goodwood racecourse, chopped from the top of the Downs by a Lord March who did not have to ask for planning permission.

He tells his girl how he and his friends used to fly in over the Solent or, if they'd been defending London, right over where they're standing. He points out the Isle of Wight and the spire of Chichester Cathedral

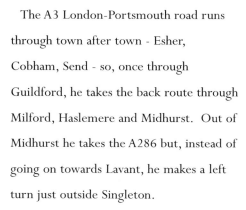

Dudley Folland's supercharged MG Magnette single-seater steals an immediate lead in Event Six, for unblown 2-litre and supercharged 1100cc cars (which became Formula 2). 7.2 miles later Folland will win. His car has been prepared by John Wyer; four years hence Wyer's works Aston Martins will be winning here.

which, for so many pilots, was not only a landmark, but a sign that they were home. It is the heart of the England that he fought for.

And it is England, not Britain. The Downs, the rolling green fields, the Solent, a small walled city with an ancient cathedral: this is England in essence.

It is not the England of smoky chimneys, grimy towns and pitheads. It is not the England of rationing and kids with threadbare clothes and whooping cough. It is not the England of queues for meat, or the England where a banana is an exotic luxury.

It is not the England known by most of its population, where factory chimneys belch out smoke and fumes and where women hang their washing between tenements in the sure knowledge that even the bailiffs will arrive on foot or by bicycle.

But it is the England of landscape artists and the England of which poets write. Goodwood could have been designed by John Constable. It is the England of ideal and the England for which tens of thousands of men and women had so recently laid down their lives.

Our couple drive down the hill between trees, relishing, but not necessarily consciously noticing, the infinite variety of green that only England possesses. At the foot of the Downs lies the new circuit. It does not matter that, apart from a few wartime buildings, it is featureless. The fact that a former military airfield has been turned over to fun and enjoyment is a sign of new and better world.

Our man parks his MG for five shillings (25p), pays ten shillings for two entry tickets, collects a programme for two shillings (10p) and, feeling flush, buys tickets for the paddock at ten shillings each.

Westhampnett is the same, but not quite the same, yet there are still enough familiar buildings to act as landmarks. The field from which he flew is covered by the stubble from freshly harvested wheat - many a meeting would take place with farm workers driving reapers and balers in the infield, stacking stooks or feeding sheaves into a threshing machine. Haystacks on the infield were a feature of Goodwood.

Then he looks in the programme and decides he'll have a flutter, and we'll leave him going to place a bet with a bookie. As at Brooklands, Goodwood had bookmakers.

All round the paddock, people who had known each other from the Brooklands

Left: first meeting, first race. Teetering over the dusty track surface at Woodcote Corner the field pursues eventual winner Paul Pycroft's special-bodied SS Jaguar past the drab remnants of RAF Westhampnett.

days were reunited - sometimes after a separation of nine years.

The paddock consisted of two lines of the competing cars backing on to the start/finish straight with a handful of primitive transporters forming a third line. Spectators stood behind chestnut paling fencing, if they were behind anything - there were not even any straw bales. In order to get a better view, some people scoured the site for planks, bricks and oil cans to create improvised grandstands.

Freddie insisted that the spectators be kept well back for their own safety - ten yards from the track in some cases, with no barriers. Some people, however, argued that the creation of what are now called run-off areas was dangerous because they would instil the drivers with a false sense of security and encourage them to take risks.

A Tannoy system and a couple of beer tents had been set up. The emergency tenders were a breakdown truck and a Jeep.

Freddie had just taken delivery of a new Bristol 400. At two o'clock on 18th September 1948, he drove his Bristol around what was now a circuit and declared The Goodwood Motor Circuit open.

The afternoon's sport opened with a three-lap race for closed sports cars which was won by Paul Pycroft in his very special SS100 Jaguar, fitted with a bespoke enveloping body. It was a closed sports car only in the sense that it ran with its hood up.

A novelty was a race for 500cc cars, a new low-cost category which had grown since 1946 to provide competitive racing, initially for both the special builder but increasingly for serious young drivers using professionally-built cars. The 500 Club set a maximum capacity of 500cc, unsupercharged, a minimum weight of 500 lbs and hoped that no car would cost more than £500. Its rules also noted that 'a body is desirable'.

The knowledgeable noted the name of Stirling Moss in the programme. His was already a name to watch after fine hill-climb performances. At his first race

Below: the Pycroft Jaguar - winner of the Goodwood Motor Circuit's maiden race - was startlingly futuristic by 1940s standards (if never, ever, pretty), not least for its maximum access 'clamshell' bonnet.
Overleaf: Goodwood Motor Circuit, early morning, 18th September 1948, still as yet an obscure corner of rural West Sussex.

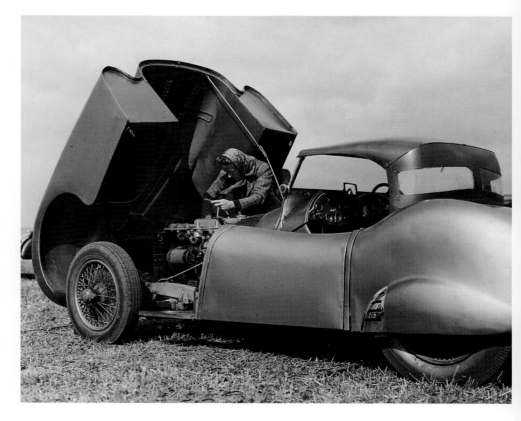

meeting, at Brough in July, he had won his heat, and the final, of a scratch race, and then won a handicap. He won Goodwood's 500cc race at a canter. Even though it lasted only three laps, his mechanic hung out a 'Slow Down' sign, but he still won by 25.8 seconds!

Welsh gentleman driver, Dudley Folland, in a single-seater MG K3, took the Madgwick Cup for Formula 2 cars, but since there were in fact no cars in Britain constructed to the new formula, the race was run to 1100cc supercharged, 2-litres unsupercharged.

The meeting's highlight, however, was the five-lap race for another new category, Formula 1. Reg Parnell's latest model Maserati 4CLT/48, the only pukka F1 car in the race, was pressed hard by Bob Gerard's pre-war ERA. Parnell won by four-tenths of a second, but Gerard set fastest lap, leaving with the outright lap record at 1'42.8", 83.39 mph.

For some time Goodwood's races - even for Formula 1 - were very short, a reflection of both post-war shortages and residual Brooklands tradition. Another tradition began with many races being named after local associations. Madgwick Corner was named after the adjacent Madgwick Lane, which also provided the Madgwick Cup.

Every corner and straight took local names; Woodcote after Woodcote Farm, which had abutted Westhampnett Farm; Lavant after the nearby village and the little river there, shallow enough to be forded, hence Fordwater. St Mary's is both a corner and the church in Lavant village.

The only corner - introduced in 1952 - not to boast a local association would be Paddock Bend, the official name for the chicane, but it never did catch on. Scalextric would sell a length of track which they called 'Goodwood Chicane' - they never sold 'Paddock Bend' - and that is how enthusiasts recall the corner to this day.

The meeting was judged a success. There were thrills and spills, but nobody had been hurt. Joe Lowrey, the technical editor of 'The Motor', had rolled his HRG at Woodcote, but it

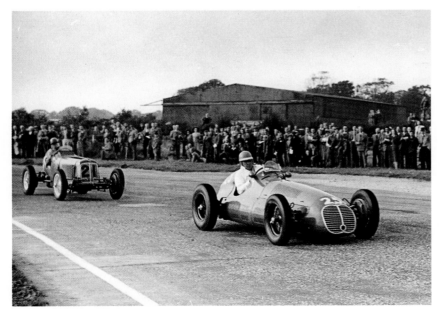

Five laps of pure magic in the inaugural 12-mile Goodwood Trophy race for 1500cc super-charged racing cars as Reg Parnell's raucous new Maserati 4CLT has the legs of Bob Gerard's 'R14B' - the last 'Old English Upright' ERA built at Bourne.

was righted, Lowrey was dusted down, and he drove the car home!

At the gates, 10,478 paid to get in, perhaps 1,000 club members entered by right and an estimated 3,000 more sneaked in. 22 coaches, 1,419 cars, 294 motor-cycles and 36 bicycles were in the car park.

This was a modest turnout by modern standards, but it compared to the best turn-out for any Brooklands meeting. Apart from the austerity measures, there was then no widespread British interest in motor racing. That was to change, and change rapidly. Publicity for the BRM V16 Grand Prix car project had been building momentum since 1946. A fortnight after the meeting at Goodwood, Silverstone hosted the RAC Grand Prix and, the following week, a 500cc race was included in a motor-cycle meeting on an airfield at Dunholme Lodge in Lincolnshire.

Whereas before the War, racing had mainly occurred at Brooklands, in 1948 car races took place in Yorkshire, Sussex, Northants and Lincolnshire - all on disused military airfields. Since such airfields were dotted all over the country, motor racing had the opportunity to go to the people.

Below: first-time victory in a proper circuit race on what would become a permanent racing circuit. The 18-year-old Stirling Moss takes the Goodwood flag in his 500cc cream-liveried Cooper-JAP. **Overleaf inset:** 'Pa' Moss (**right**) helps wheel his son out for the inaugural 500cc race.

"I have good memories of the first Goodwood meeting in 1948 because I hadn't raced properly before - only hillclimbs and sprints, and an airfield event at Brough. The whole family went down to Sussex in my dad's old Rolls-Royce, towing our horse box trailer with my little cream Cooper inside. I practised on the Friday, which was my 19th birthday: after all those hillclimbs I'd never driven my little car that fast, and it was tremendously exhilarating. The first corner, a double right-hander with a hump in the middle of it, I found I could just take flat in top. There was no chicane then, of course, so you were at full chat when you arrived.

Anyway, I was fastest in practice, but the grid positions were decided by ballot. Lining up on a proper starting grid on a proper track for the first time, with other cars around me, was actually fairly daunting: it was my introduction to The Real Thing. But it went all right, and I won the race by 9.4 seconds.

That first time I was very much in awe of the Duke of Richmond & Gordon, because he was a member of the aristocracy, as well as a famous racing name from before the war. Later I found he was tremendously approachable, and he'd come round and ask about the cars. He was always there, like a host. The BARC ran the meetings, but you always regarded it as Freddie Richmond's show, and the rest of the people were just helping him out." STIRLING MOSS

Previous pages: Stirling Moss
poised for his brilliant drive in
'my beautiful Aston Martin' at the
Goodwood Revival Meeting,
September 1998 (**main picture**),
half a century after his first win at
the circuit (**inset**).
Above: ERAs being prepared at
the first meeting. George Nixon is
about to have his first race in
'R2A' (number 56), but he will be
out of luck. Reg Parnell's ERA-
beating Maserati 4CLT (number
25) is on the extreme right.

The crowd at Goodwood was very promising, but the racing had been good and the meeting made a profit of about £1,000. As a result, Freddie decided to forge ahead, to make the Goodwood Motor Circuit permanent, and he formed the Goodwood Road Racing Company to run it. In practice, the company ploughed back most of its profits into improving the circuit.

It was clear the track surface was barely adequate and would soon need improvement. A non-skid 'Resmat' surface was laid down experimentally at Woodcote. Concrete barriers were erected at corners considered dangerous, and would eventually encircle most of the track, soft-faced with straw bales.

The Junior Car Club had absorbed the rump of the BARC (Brooklands Automobile Racing Club). At the JCC's AGM in January, 1949, members voted to change the club's name, since 'Junior' made it sound like a club for schoolboys, and settled on the British

Automobile Racing Club (BARC) instead - a neat piece of continuity.

The club was not to concentrate on Grand Prix cars, but should also cater for the club member with his sports car - a significant decision which not only shaped Goodwood's entire philosophy, but also ensured it would become a breeding ground for new talent.

As BARC President, Freddie arranged for all future meetings at the circuit to be run by the club. That is why people remember Goodwood as an organic whole. Every meeting was run to the same guidelines, by the same people, and to the same style. The BARC was conscious of its roots at Brooklands: most of the leading lights had been involved in organising racing there, and they knowingly carried on the traditions of Brooklands.

Other circuits - Silverstone and Brands Hatch among them - had meetings organised by a great number of clubs, but Goodwood is unique in British motor racing in that every meeting was was run by Freddie and his old friends from the Brooklands days. Chief among them was John Morgan, who would found the Steering Wheel Club in Mayfair, which became a favourite watering-hole of motor racing people.

It was this special arrangement, a circuit run by friends for their friends, which gave Goodwood its individual ethos. And it extended to everybody. Even the casual spectator was made to feel like a guest, not like a punter.

The Goodwood welcome ensured that it would become the best-loved circuit in motor racing history.

Top left: motor sporting aristocracy at Goodwood's opening meeting - the Marquess of Camden, of the RAC, his Marchioness, and son Lord Brecknock. In 1938-39 the Marquess had been one of those who had pointed out the need for fighter airfields to Freddie Richmond.
Middle left: Captain 'Archie' Frazer-Nash, Roland E. Dangerfield (publisher of 'The Motor') and a relieved Freddie Richmond - the meeting is already going well.
Below: film actress Christine Norden and friends.
Overleaf: Reg Parnell collects the trophy for winning the headline Formula 1 race from Denis Berry, a director of the Kemsley Press.

EARLY DAYS

After the success of the first meeting, much was expected of the second, on Easter Monday 1949. Over the years Easter Mondays at Goodwood would become synonymous with everything good about motor racing, but the first one was very nearly abandoned due to the vast crowd spilling over the safety barriers onto the track verges.

Following Freddie's decision to turn Goodwood into the first permanent circuit in post-war Britain, small grandstands were erected at Woodcote and near the start-finish straight. Over the winter the site had been further cleared, but it remained impossible to walk from Woodcote to Lavant because stacks of timber, left by the military, littered the site.

Still, facilities were improving and everything seemed to be in order, but glorious spring weather attracted a crowd of about 40,000, far more than expected. As long queues formed at the gates, many people found other ways of getting in. Indeed, some had come armed with wire-cutters.

When latecomers found themselves at the back of the early arrivals who lined the track, they clambered onto the roofs of huts, tore gaps in the hedges and scrambled over the fences to sit close to the action. Some even parked themselves a yard off the track on the outside of Woodcote Corner.

Marshals restored order only after officials announced that racing would be abandoned if encroaching spectators did not retreat behind the fences. The organisers fumed about the irresponsibility of these 'idiots', but irresponsibility and idiocy are perhaps not the right words. These people were simply ignorant of motor racing. They had no experience of Reg Parnell braking for Woodcote in his supercharged Maserati 4CLT/48 from well over 130 mph, then aiming for a point on the outside of the corner before

Left: perhaps the most-raced individual car in history - Ludovic Lindsay's ex-Prince Bira ERA R5B, *Remus*, at the Goodwood chicane in September 1998 en route to winning the first Goodwood race since 1966.
Below: a regular Goodwood competitor in the early days, Bob Gerard was anything but a fire-breather. 'Mr Bob' was in fact a mild-mannered, bespectacled garage owner from Leicester, whose painstaking preparation and consistent driving brought his three ERAs success through their reliability. It didn't work this time, though: 'R4A' in trouble, Festival of Britain Trophy, 1951.

Easter Monday 1949 - a hat-trick of wins for Reg Parnell's '16-valve Maserati', but no such luck for Walsall industrialist Bertie Bradnack as yet another laborious push-start fails in Goodwood's grassy paddock... and Moss won in his Cooper.

swinging back to the outside verge, where they had been sitting, to line up for the start-finish straight. Nobody would have wanted to have been within a few feet of Reg in full flight.

The errant spectators had come to see motor racing as a Bank Holiday excursion, but they had no clear idea what it was. Goodwood was attracting new people to the sport and was turning a minority interest into a sport with popular appeal.

In the early days at Goodwood, bad weather on a Bank Holiday meant small crowds, good weather attracted large crowds. The area around Goodwood was full of people who had no particular interest in motor racing, but who took their kids and a picnic to the circuit instead of going to the beach at Bognor Regis.

Once order had been restored, the 1949 Easter Monday crowd saw another fine meeting with close racing. There were also some spectacular spins onto the grass, happily without injury to anyone. Even the dimmest spectator who had crowded the track must have been grateful to be behind a fence when they saw a car spin over the spot where they had once been sitting. There would never be a repeat of disorder among the crowd.

The supporting races were extended from three laps to five laps with the feature

Formula 1 race, the Richmond Trophy, held over ten laps, and the number of starters in each race was doubled from 12 to 24.

The day belonged to Reg Parnell, who won three races in his Maserati and set a new lap record at 87.1 mph. Reg, a garage owner and haulier from Derby, who bred pigs for a hobby, had the potential to be a great international star. In 1949, however, he was 37, his best years lost to the War. Still, Parnell was the king of Goodwood in the early days.

Stirling Moss took his second win at Goodwood driving his Cooper fitted with a 998cc JAP engine in one of the handicaps, while Dudley Folland won the Lavant Cup in the first Ferrari to be seen in Britain. It was not just a new car, it was a new sound - a high-pitched shriek just before the up-change.

Folland had commissioned John Wyer, later team manager of Aston Martin, to go to Italy to test the car and arrange the deal. Since there were strict currency restrictions in operation, the cash (about £4000) was handed over in a shoebox in the bar of a London hotel. The car had then been transported from Italy on an Italian carnet, with one of Ferrari's employees in the truck pretending to be the car's owner.

Despite the day's early problems, which had led to a 30-minute delay in the programme, the meeting was again considered a success. '*Motor Sport*' declared,

Above: through 1949 the re-modelled BARC was growing rapidly. Goodwood was established as 'home' and the circuit began to sprout tailor-made structures of its own, but in the sun the observer tower steps would always be the coolest vantage point.

Right: one year on from Goodwood's opening, officials prepare in the Sussex sun for the season's end meeting, September 1949. Every race this day would be a five-lapper (12 miles). Here, from left, Messrs Winstanley and Lord, Mrs Urquhart-Dykes and Captain Archie Frazer-Nash check the handicap timings.

"I always loved Goodwood. Aerodrome circuits were normally miserably bleak places, but Goodwood was different. It was always so merry, like a family party. Even the cosy way the paddock was laid out made it friendly - not like spreading yourself out down some windswept runway.

And I know it did rain there sometimes, but looking back I always think of it as sunny. In my Aston Martin days, when I was at work in my garage business in Tolworth, Reg Parnell used to get on the phone on a weekday morning and say, 'We're at Goodwood to do some testing - you'd better get down here'. I'd look at the rain coursing down my office window and say to myself, 'This is going to be a real waste of time'. But I'd drive down there, windscreen wipers sloshing away, and when I got to the top of the hill by the horse race course the clouds would part, the sun would come out, and I'd know I was in for another happy day at Goodwood.

I know this thing I said years ago is often quoted - 'Give me Goodwood on a summer's day, and you can keep the rest of the world' - but I did say it, and I did mean it."   ROY SALVADORI

"All the old atmosphere of Brooklands prevailed." That was some feat considering that the crowd was nearly three times larger than the best turn-out that Brooklands ever knew and given that everything was still done on an ad hoc basis.

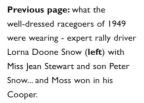

Freddie was worried, however, and he convened an emergency meeting of the BARC Council two days later. There he argued that the International Meeting scheduled for the Whitsun Bank Holiday should be cancelled to allow time for better security measures to be installed.

As well as the spectators, some elements of the BARC also needed to be educated about safety. People who had criticised the generous run-off areas at the first meeting were now silent. The planned International Whitsun Meeting was cancelled while work was put in hand.

More chestnut fencing and concrete barriers were erected. The concrete barriers were pre-cast with internal steel rods and were bolted to the uprights; some survive to the present day. They were the model for the barriers in Scalextric slot-racing sets which were designed and made by Fred Francis, who lived near to Goodwood. On 13th August 1949, the circuit opened for the first Members' Meeting.

Each of the nine races at the first Members' Meeting was a three or five-lap handicap. That was both part of the Brooklands tradition, and also expediency. In 1949, as in 1939, there were not enough evenly-matched cars to run a programme of

Previous page: what the well-dressed racegoers of 1949 were wearing - expert rally driver Lorna Doone Snow (**left**) with Miss Jean Stewart and son Peter Snow... and Moss won in his Cooper.

Right: young star - Stirling Moss in his 'Two-Way' Cooper-JAP. Fitted with a 500cc single-cylinder engine it was eligible for what would soon become Formula 3 racing, with a twin-cylinder 1,000 it proved a winner in Formula 2.

Below: the spirit of Goodwood's *Formule Libre* past at the 1998 Revival Meeting with Julian Majzub booting his glorious 1938-39 straight-eight supercharged Alfa Romeo 308C towards the Autumn sun at Madgwick..

"I had my original audition for the BBC at Goodwood. One of the BBC's producers had heard me doing a public address commentary at a mixed bikes and cars meeting at Shelsley Walsh. As a result I was summoned on Easter Monday 1949 to Goodwood, where I'd never been, to talk about cars, which weren't really my thing at the time. Recording took place in the back of a Humber Super Snipe, kitted out with a thing like an enormous gramophone with a wax disc and a needle. I rattled away for a couple of races about Reg Parnell and the Ashmore brothers, and that was it. But presumably somebody listened to the black disc..."

MURRAY WALKER

scratch races. The handicapper was the redoubtable A.V. 'Ebby' Ebblewhite, the great Brooklands timekeeper; 'Ebby' would be succeeded by his son, Louis, as chief timekeeper and handicapper.

The purpose of the early Goodwood Members' Meetings was to allow club members to race their cars which, as a matter of policy, were all road-going vehicles. The term 'club meeting' has since come to mean a level of racing, but at Goodwood it meant 'club' in the full sense of the word - friends gathering with a common purpose. Nobody could then foresee that Members' Meetings would help to breed a generation of British drivers, including future World Champions.

Two races were won by junior stockbroker Eric Thompson in his HRG, and Eric would soon be driving for Aston Martin. Sydney Allard won in one of his own Allards, a marque which was making a name for itself in America. Dick Jacobs, who would be associated with many of MG's competition activities for the next 20 or so years, was also a winner - in an MG, naturally.

One of the other races was won by Christopher 'Dickie' le Strange Metcalfe. Metcalfe is not one of the sport's great names but, in 1966, he would win the last race to be held at the Goodwood motor circuit. Like his first victory, it was at a Members' Meeting, and it was a five-lap handicap.

Making their debut at the same meeting were two sports cars from a new outfit, Connaught. They finished 1-2 and the success launched the marque which would play an important part in the British motor racing renaissance.

Another entrant was Derek Buckler, in a Buckler. His hero was Henry Ford, the man who brought motoring to millions. Derek's ambition was more modest: to provide the means by which enthusiasts with limited means could enjoy motor sport.

He marketed the world's first kit cars and would be followed by hundreds of other makers such as Lotus, Ginetta and TVR.

The third, and final, meeting of 1949 took place on 17th September. Like the Easter Meeting, it was billed as an International, but that was the licence under which it was run. In the days before sponsorship, there was trade support. To do

Below: modest beginnings - building company magnate Kenneth McAlpine backed Rodney Clarke and Mike Oliver in launching their Connaught marque in 1949-50. This is McAlpine in his Lea-Francis-derived Connaught L2 sweeping through Woodcote Corner towards the chequered flag, 12th August 1950.
Overleaf: Alfred 'Pa' Moss **(left)**, proudly wearing his British Racing Drivers' Club badge on his overalls, helps prepare Stirling's twin-cylinder JAP-equipped 'Two-Way' Cooper - Easter Monday 1949.

well in a race billed as an 'International' meant that a driver qualified for bonuses from spark plug and oil companies. The very word 'International' in the title of a meeting guaranteed larger crowds and better press coverage.

The BARC husbanded its money well, and Goodwood did not often head-hunt international stars, as Silverstone did. For one thing it was attracting large enough crowds without them; for another, it was still in the process of establishing itself, using the profits made at meetings to upgrade the circuit.

The problem that beset Goodwood's fourth meeting in September 1949 was, once again, its sheer popularity. So many people wanted to be there that there were huge traffic jams on the way in, and out. Since most cars had been built pre-war, dozens were stuck by the side of the road with steam rising from their bonnets.

The first race on the card was won by Stirling Moss in his 998cc Cooper-JAP. It was a good way to celebrate his 20th birthday.

The 500cc race was won by Peter Collins, who was then just 17 $^1/_2$ years old. Peter, who would win Grands Prix for Ferrari, had entered the first meeting, but been excluded when it was discovered he was under-age. As in so many races at Goodwood, the finish was close - Peter crossed the line a scant second ahead of the Cooper of the Dutchman Lex Beels.

Like many another driver, including Stirling Moss, Peter stayed at the Hare and Hounds in nearby Stoughton. The pub was run by a former mechanic named John Brierley, who would convert the rooms into a dormitory - John used to pack seven or eight into a room. He recalls, "We did not even have electricity, but the drivers from London loved that. Since there wasn't a bobby for miles around, they could test their cars up the road with nobody minding.

"Then there were all the pranks like the time Stirling Moss and Ken Gregory brought down a couple of chorus girls and the other guys sprinkled cayenne pepper in their pyjamas."

Before the September International meeting Goodwood had liaised with the local police and devised a method, now familiar to every race-goer, of colour-coded routes.

At that meeting, Reg Parnell was once again the star, taking two wins and establishing a new lap record at 89.26 mph. He set the new record in the first race and then, to prove it was

Above: British Hill-Climb Champion Dennis Poore was a Goodwood regular from the first season: here in 1949 driving his ex-*Scuderia Ferrari* Alfa-Romeo 8C-35

Left: 'The Great Farina' - reigning World Champion Dr Giuseppe 'Nino' Farina in full flight with his Maserati 4CLT at St Mary's, Festival of Britain Trophy, Whit Monday 1951. Poor Farina's ageing 1$^1/_2$-litre supercharged Maserati was beaten into 2nd in Heat by Prince Bira's 4$^1/_2$-litre V12 OSCA, and into 2nd in the Final by Parnell's 4$^1/_2$-litre V12 'Thin Wall Special' Ferrari.

Below: Reg Parnell, 'Uncle Reg', the Derby haulier and pig farmer who had become Britain's leading racing driver of the late 1940s and early '50s, won thirteen major races at Goodwood, many in his faithful Maserati 4CLTs.

no fluke, equalled it in the second. In the feature event, the Goodwood Trophy, Reg started from the third row, of four, on the grid, but that was because grid positions were decided by ballot, not by practice times.

The reason for this odd procedure was that if you are running a five-lap race for Grand Prix cars, and the quick guys are on the front row, they are going to disappear into the distance and there will be no competition. With just five laps to make up time, added to the element of chance, Goodwood staged motor racing with overtaking.

Most of the main meetings took place on the Easter and Whitsun Bank Holiday Mondays, with a third meeting in mid-September. At the time no professional sport took place in Britain on a Sunday. Therefore practice for the Holiday Monday meetings would be on the preceding Saturday and, after practice, Freddie would hold a cocktail party in Goodwood House for the drivers and team managers.

Members' Meetings always took place on Saturdays, with practice in the morning and racing in the afternoon followed by a trip to the pub. There was the Richmond Arms which is now part of the Goodwood Marriott hotel, but equally popular were The Crown and The Swan at Chiddingfold on the A285. In the days of light traffic and no breathalyser, it was practically mandatory to gather at a pub and shoot a line.

Before the 1950 season, Goodwood received two blows. First, the government imposed an entertainment tax taking nearly half the revenue both at the gate and at the newly installed grandstands. These were temporary structures because government restrictions on materials and manpower precluded permanent stands. Taking the new tax into account, each seat cost 17s 10d (79p), so charging £1 for a grandstand seat meant a very modest profit. The entertainment tax was a particularly severe blow since the Goodwood Road Racing Company reinvested most of its profits into upgrading the circuit. Consequently, facilities at Goodwood developed at a slower pace than would otherwise have been the case.

Then Goodwood lost two of its three International events. The RAC was keen to tidy up the calendar, and proposed that there should be fewer International meetings so that each would be of a higher quality. Consequently the BARC cut its application from three Internationals to one. The RAC thought that everybody was in agreement but, come the meeting of the FIA (*Fédération Internationale de l'Automobile*) in Paris every other country reneged on the agreement. While Britain reduced its request from fifteen to seven Internationals, France and Italy upped their stakes, to 27 and 23 respectively, and Belgium doubled its quota from four to eight. The result was precisely what the RAC had feared: there were more International meetins on the Continent, but

Left: a practical prize for a period of insouciant political incorrectness - BARC award tankard, 1949.

Right: the BARC of the 1940s to the 1960s was a refined, mannered, capable and very 'British' organisation. From cocktail shaker to cardboard member's pass, BARC memorabilia abounds.

the quality of the entry suffered.

Before the start of the new season, '*Motor Sport*' donated the Brooklands Memorial Trophy for the aggregate best performance at the Members' Meetings. It was virtually the Goodwood Championship - and was the more prestigious because '*Motor Sport*' was then the only British magazine devoted to the sport ('*Autosport*' would arrive in August 1950, however).

More work went on at the circuit over the winter of 1949/50. A pedestrian tunnel was built, linking the outfield to the infield under the start-finish straight. The 'Resmat' experiment at Woodcote had been successful, so the entire circuit was surfaced with it. Resmat was a cold asphalt layer made of crushed furnace clinker coated with bitumen. To the eye it was perfectly smooth, to the tyre it was grippy.

Spectator banks were built at strategic points. The Ministry of Supply cleared the timber from the Lavant Straight. There was a new race control tower on top of an aerodrome building for race officials and commentators. Trees were planted and gardens were planned: Goodwood would become the garden circuit.

As Goodwood progressed, Freddie played a decreasing part in its story, but his influence was everywhere. The flower beds are just one example. They are one reason why spectators felt like guests, not punters.

An ex-War Department telephone system was installed to link the main sites.

In the days when it could take years to be connected to the public phone service, the Post Office was unhelpful, so the BARC laid 20 miles of cable to create its own network; something of an innovation, it remained in place until 1966.

The system was actually conceived and installed by Fred Perry, the mechanic on the Goodwood Estate. Fred was very close to the Duke and not only worked on Freddie's cars, but was involved in most of his schemes. The Boss had no side; he knew the value of a good man regardless of social position. He was, after all, proud to have been a mechanic himself.

The paddock was made four times larger, and three rows of covered stalls constructed so that mechanics could work under cover. The stalls were replicated for the 1998 Revival Meeting.

Other changes came into effect. BARC members who bought tickets for the season received enamel lapel badges, like the Owners and Trainers at the Goodwood racecourse. The catering was formalised with 'lunch wagons' provided locally (step forward Arthur King, landlord of The Unicorn Hotel - Arfur had his finger on the pulse).

The 1950 Easter Monday Meeting took place amid 60 mph gales and rain lashing a bare 15,000 spectators. In the Formula 3 race, John Cooper and Peter Collins retired because the wind was so strong it blew them into a collision. The weather was often bad at Easter, but somehow memory has Goodwood bathed in sunlight - just like the Battle of Britain - even though it snowed more than once at an Easter Monday Meeting.

Once more, Reg Parnell won the feature race, the Richmond Trophy, run over 11 laps. The Maseratis of 'B. Bira' and Count Emmanuel de Graffenried had each led the race, but Bira and de Graffenried were wearing goggles and had to slow when they were blinded by the rain. Parnell always favoured a visor, which he could wipe clear,

Above: pre-war superstar Prince Birabongse Bhanudej Bhanubandh - 'B. Bira' for short - drove his cousin Prince Chula's ERAs and Maseratis to a string of victories from 1936 and ran his own Maseratis and the big V12 4CLT-chassised OSCA at Goodwood 1950-51.
Below: upon its debut, Bira's brand-new OSCA V12 drove Reg Parnell to spin his hitherto almost unbeatable Maserati, then blow it up in his attempted fightback - leaving the Siamese Prince to win the Richmond Trophy, Easter Monday 1951.

and on lap seven he slipped into the lead to win by 14 seconds from de Graffenried.

'B. Bira' was actually Prince Birabongse Bhanudej Bhanubandh of Siam and the grandson of the king of 'The King And I' fame. He had been sent to Eton, stayed on in England, and taken a hat-trick of BRDC Gold Stars between 1936 and 1938. He was an unusually fine driver and very popular with British crowds. De Graffenried, a Swiss, had won the 1949 British Grand Prix, the highlight

of a solid career in international racing.

The 1950 Whit Monday meeting brought another huge crowd. Days before Whitsun, with no warning whatsoever, the government had scrapped petrol rationing. In the morning you needed coupons - by the evening you could have all the fuel you wanted. Come the Bank Holiday, just four days later, the new freedom meant chaos as virtually every car in Britain headed to the coast on a primitive road system. It was the nearest the country has come to total gridlock.

The highlight of the Whit Meeting was the Formula 3 event. The growth of the 500cc movement had been recognised by the FIA who had granted it International status as Formula 3. It was the first time that a new International category had originated in Britain, and so popular had it become that there were 40 entries and only five non-arrivals.

Well into the 1970s, the first thing a commentator told a crowd was the list of non-arrivals - and it was usually a long list. With the arrival of sponsorship that list disappeared. Sponsors were not interested in the fact that the mechanic's wife was having a baby so the car couldn't be ready. In 1950 thirty-five starters from an entry

Top left: Reg Parnell, captured by Sallon of 'The Daily Mirror'.
Below: from the outset, meetings at Goodwood were highlights in the social calendar. The kind of coverage typified by this 'Tatler' spread from May 1949 was unprecedented for this sport of oil, grease and exhaust fumes.
Overleaf: impeccable lines at Woodcote save for one J.G. Sears' MG - BARC Members' Meeting, 17th June 1950.
Overleaf inset: straw bale barricades and chestnut fencing provided the rudimentary safety precautions of the earliest Goodwood meetings.

"AFTER WHAT WE'D ALL HAD TO GET USED TO SINCE THE WAR, GOODWOOD SEEMED TERRIBLY GRAND - FIELDS OF 20 CARS OR MORE RUSHING ROUND TOGETHER - ALTHOUGH LOOKING AT THE REPORTS I SEE THAT MOST OF THE EARLY RACES WERE ONLY THREE LAPS.

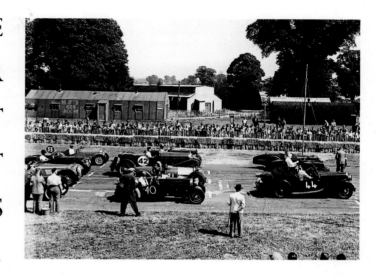

I WATCHED AT MADGWICK, WHICH WAS ALWAYS ONE OF THE BEST CORNERS FOR SPECTATORS. WE'D BE APPALLED NOW: WE WERE STANDING 20 YARDS FROM THE TRACK, BEHIND A SINGLE STRAND OF ROPE, WITH A FEW SIGNS SAYING 'MOTOR RACING IS DANGEROUS'. YET IN ALL THE HISTORY OF GOODWOOD A CAR NEVER WENT INTO THE CROWD. BY THE STANDARDS OF THE DAY GOODWOOD WAS VERY SAFE."

GRAHAM MACBETH

"My first ever race was at Goodwood. I drove my standard MG TC in a BARC Members' Meeting on 17th June 1950, with the windscreen folded flat and wearing goggles and an old flying helmet - crash hats weren't mandatory then. And I spun on my second lap in the middle of the field. " JACK SEARS

Roll up for the magical motor racing tour, but six bob a time was a lot of money then.

of forty showed an unusual level of willingness for the time.

The Formula 3 race was run in two heats and a final over 15 laps, the longest race yet held at Goodwood. It was won by Wing-Cdr 'Curly' Dryden (who, naturally, was bald as a billiard ball) from Peter Collins and John Cooper, all in Coopers. '*The Daily Herald*' recorded that Curly was "richer by £200, and with the title of the world's top small-car racer". Poor Curly was to be killed soon afterwards at Castle Combe.

On 5th May 1950, Silverstone hosted the first race of the new World Championship. Alfa Romeo, then the dominant team, sent four cars. Three were for the regular drivers, Giuseppe Farina, Juan-Manuel Fangio and Luigi Fagioli, while the fourth was ear-marked for 'The King of Goodwood', Reg Parnell, who eventually finished third behind Farina and Fagioli.

The King and Queen attended the Silverstone Grand Prix along with a vast crowd: reports at the time estimated there were perhaps 125,000 spectators, such was the appetite for motor racing.

One reason was geography, both local and national. Goodwood is roughly triangular, bounded by two public roads and the River Lavant. This meant that, in 1950, its absolute maximum capacity was 60,000 spectators.

By contrast, Silverstone had been chosen from a short-list of ex-military airfields, all in the Midlands. The RAC wanted a central location to give access to the greatest number of people. Silverstone was also an ex-bomber station which, by definition, meant that it had been built on a much larger scale.

It is easy to forget how difficult it was to travel around Britain by road before the motorway network was constructed. Since Goodwood is almost as far south as you can go without falling into the sea, it meant that many drivers from the north of England chose not to compete there.

In the late 1950s two drivers dominated the 2-litre Production Sports Car class, both driving AC Aces. They were Peter Bolton from Halifax and Ken Rudd from Worthing. Bolton raced in the north, Rudd raced in the south, and the only time they ever competed in the same race was when they shared a works AC at Le Mans.

Come the September 1950 Goodwood meeting, and the star attraction was the BRM driven by Reg Parnell. This immensely complicated supercharged V16 had made its debut in the '*Daily Express*' International Trophy at Silverstone five weeks earlier. It had taken more than five years to bring this fiendishly complex car to the grid and an efficient publicity machine had raised public expectations to an unreasonable level. It was touted as a world-beater, but had broken its transmission on the startline. Some

members of the public threw pennies at it and the car became the butt of comedians'
jokes. BRM's entry at Goodwood was therefore viewed with a range of emotions, but
most spectators had their fingers crossed for it.

The Goodwood September meeting was run in the wet, which reduced the strain
on the BRM's transmission, and Parnell won both the Goodwood Trophy for Formula 1
cars (completing a hat-trick in the event) and the *Formule Libre* Woodcote Cup.

Parnell put on a show for the crowd, who went crazy at the sight of Britain's great
hope accelerating effortlessly into the distance before Parnell braked gently so that the
others could catch up. The press turned on its head and derision became extravagant
praise. Britain had a 'world-beater' again, except that a few laps of Goodwood against a
thin field was not the same as beating Alfa Romeo and Ferrari over 300 miles.

Over the winter of 1950/51, Goodwood had its quota of International races
increased from one to four and the BARC also introduced a new rule at Members'
Meetings. Any driver who spun twice in a race would be black-flagged. Naturally, this
safety measure had its critics who accused the BARC of putting a damper on the fun.
Later, there would be a one-minute penalty for a spin.

While the BRM project had lurched from disaster to crisis, HWM had become the
first British team in history to undertake a full season's racing on the Continent. HWM
was owned by John Heath and George Abecassis, who ran a garage called Hersham and

Below: Britain expects -
and it was wet enough for a
naval signal fly. Reg Parnell gives
the celebrated V16-cylinder
BRM its first victories,
Goodwood, 1st September 1950.
After abject start-line failure in
its Silverstone debut, the BRM
won the Woodcote Cup, then
the Goodwood Trophy.
Overleaf: fully booked, no room
left in the stalls. Goodwood
Revival 1998, the *Formule Libre*
Woodcote Cup line-up.

Walton Motors (hence HWM) - imagine a small independent garage today running its own grand prix team. John Heath was the heir to an obscure Neapolitan title and, while he could style himself 'Baron', he preferred plain 'John' and getting his hands dirty.

His partner, George Abecassis, had flown Lysanders from Tangmere to drop and pick up SOE agents in Occupied Europe, and had also won the last motor race in Britain (at Brooklands) before the war, and the first (at Gransden Lodge) after it. They shared one car; Stirling Moss, whose talent had first been spotted by Abecassis, drove another; the third was usually driven by Lance Macklin, a fine driver for whom motor racing was merely a part of a raffish lifestyle.

Moss was on hand to drive an HWM in the Lavant Cup, which he won, while the former speedway rider, Alf Bottoms, won the Earl of March Trophy for Formula 3 cars. Bottoms was driving a JBS, a car of his own design, and 'Curly' Dryden, in another JBS, came second. The new JBS marque looked as though it was going to take the initiative from Cooper, but Alf was killed five weeks later in the Luxembourg Grand Prix and the JBS project fell apart. Had Alf Bottoms lived, who knows what JBS might have achieved?

The main race of the day was the Richmond Trophy for Formula 1 cars. Interest, as always, was focused on Parnell who was back behind the wheel of his rapidly ageing Maserati. His main opposition came from 'B.Bira', who had a $4^{1}/_{2}$ -litre V12 OSCA engine, built by the Maserati brothers, in his 4CLT chassis. The race began with a duel between the two which came to an end when Parnell went on the grass and damaged an oil pipe.

If nothing else, Bira's OSCA highlighted the difference that existed at the time between Goodwood and top-flight racing. For the crowds who turned up, however, that didn't matter. They came to see good racing, and they got it. You only need two cars to make a race - the cannon fodder add atmosphere!

1951 was the year of the Festival of Britain, intended to celebrate the fact that the country had turned the corner after the ravages of war. 'The Daily Graphic', which had supported Goodwood from the outset, put up the Festival of Britain Trophy - the event attracted two notable entries. One was the reigning World Champion, Giuseppe Farina, in his private Maserati; the other was Reg Parnell in the 'Thin Wall Special'. Parnell's car was actually an early Ferrari Tipo 125 chassis fitted with a Tipo 375 $4^{1}/_{2}$ -litre V12 engine - not the same 'Thin Wall' that ran from 1952.

The 'Thin Wall Special' was owned by G.A. 'Tony' Vandervell, who had been a supporter of the BRM project, but had left in disgust at all the bickering and endless

John Morgan, Secretary of the BARC, energetically flags home Dr Farina to win the 15-lap '*Daily Graphic*' Trophy for Formula 1 cars, September 1951. Having been beaten in his Maserati here earlier in the year he returned in the World Champion works team '*Alfetta*' to wreak revenge on Reg Parnell in two races, and to beat Moss and Parnell in a third - a 5-lap handicap!

delays. Vandervell had helped Enzo Ferrari overcome a serious reliability problem by supplying him with '*Thin Wall*' engine bearings and the two men thereafter had a love-hate relationship. Vandervell would be the man behind the Vanwalls which, he declared, were designed to "beat those bloody red cars". Calling his car the '*Thin Wall Special*' broke all the rules about sponsorship, but Vandervell got away with it - he was one of perhaps only two dozen millionaires in Britain at the time and when it came to naming his car, he took the view that he owned it so he could bloody well call it what he liked.

The Festival of Britain Trophy in 1951 was run in two heats and a final. Parnell took the first heat and set a new lap record at 93.1 mph. Bira's OSCA took the second heat, five seconds ahead of Farina's Maserati.

Parnell took the final from Farina and, though Farina bettered Parnell's new record, Reg took it back again with a lap at 94.54 mph. For a British driver to beat the reigning World Champion was a sensational result and the popular press made the most of it.

The Formula 3 race was also run in two heats and a final. The *Ecurie Richmond* Coopers of Eric Brandon and Alan Brown each won a heat and a chap called Bernie

Ecclestone was second to Brown in Heat Two. The final, however, was won by Stirling Moss in his new Kieft.

Drivers new to Goodwood had to complete three observed practice laps. The leading Italian driver Piero Taruffi, who had been racing cars since 1923, was entered in a Cooper-Norton in the Formula 3 event, and he duly set off on his three laps. He had covered two and three quarter laps when his engine expired. Taruffi was not allowed to start. The stewards were prevailed upon, but they refused to budge; there could be no exceptions - not even for one of the world's leading drivers. They argued that it was a rule in the interests of safety and there could be no exceptions - not even for one of the world's leading drivers.

The '*Motor Sport*' Brooklands Memorial Trophy awarded at the Members' Meetings was a straight fight between the Fraser Nash of Tony Crook (now owner of Bristol Cars Ltd) and a flamboyant young man driving a rather older $1^{1}/_{2}$-litre 'TT'. The youngster finally pipped Crook by a single point: his name was John Michael 'Mike' Hawthorn.

The final International meeting of 1951 brought Farina and the immortal Alfa Romeo Tipo 158. Alfa Romeo had just announced its retirement from Formula 1, having given Fangio the World Championship, and was making its farewell tour. Alberto Ascari was supposed to drive the '*Thin Wall Special*', but felt that he had a greater obligation to his sick son, Antonio.

Parnell took Ascari's place, but Farina and the *Alfetta* won two scratch races (Parnell was second in both) and a handicap. It was the only time that an *Alfetta* ran in a handicap, and Farina took Moss's HWM a few yards before the finish line. Farina also set a new lap record at 97.36 mph. For comparison, the lap record at Silverstone, also set by Farina in an *Alfetta* was 99.99 mph. The difference was that Silverstone was a much wider track with more room to move spectators back.

The new lap record, combined with some irresponsible driving by some drivers, raised concerns about safety. A favourite trick was to 'straight-line' across the grass at the shallow left-handed kink near the finish line, a ploy which brought cars dangerously close to the crowd. Both problems would be solved over the winter by constructing a chicane officially called Paddock Bend. It reduced lap speeds by about ten per cent and was the only time that the layout of the airfield perimeter track was altered.

The Great Farina accepts the '*Daily Graphic*' Trophy and *Formule Libre* Woodcote Cup from the Duchess of Richmond while former driver John Bolster tells the world the great news, September meeting 1951.

After some initial trepidation from drivers, the chicane became a special, and celebrated, feature of the circuit. It must be the only chicane in the history of motor sport to have been popular, and generations of slot-car enthusiasts did not think their Scalextric set complete without a 'Goodwood Chicane'...

THE
NINE-HOUR RACE

On 16th August 1952, thirty-two drivers lined up on the outside of the track at Goodwood, with their cars in echelon in front of the pits. At 3pm precisely, a flag dropped and the drivers sprinted across the track to their cars, hoping they would still be in the hunt at midnight.

It was the start of the first Goodwood Nine-Hour Race and the first time there had been night-time racing in Britain.

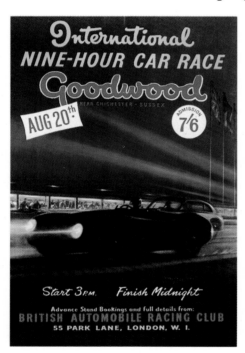

Above: Goodwood's day-into-night Nine-Hour race saw three editions run in 1952, 1953 and 1955. This poster for the last of the three exquisitely sets the scene.

Right: Aston Martin's pit crew in nocturnal action around their 1955 Nine-Hour winning works DB3S, co-driven by Peter Walker and Dennis Poore. Precautions against refuelling fire were, of course, extreme, ahem...

Like so many Goodwood features, the Nine-Hour Race had its roots at Brooklands, which had occasionally run long-distance events. There had been six-hour races, races over 500 kilometres and 500 miles, and the Double Twelve, a 24-hour race run over two days - after completing twelve hours on Day One, the cars were locked up, and brought out again for another twelve-hour stint on Day Two. It allowed Weybridge to sleep at night, but meant that it was the world's only 24-hour race not to include night-time driving.

For Goodwood's Nine-Hour Race, the pits and grandstands were floodlit, the kerbing treated with luminous paint, and strings of lights run between the refreshment marquees. Every effort was made to create an atmosphere similar to Le Mans, although the food was 1953 British and the beer tents had to close before the race ended. The '*News Of The World*' presented a trophy and £2,500 in prize money, with £1,000 going to the winners.

The one overseas entry, from France, was a Lago-Talbot driven by two veteran drivers, Philippe 'Phi Phi' Etancelin and Pierre Levegh. Etancelin, who was then 59 years old, had been a Grand Prix winner pre-war. 'Levegh' was the pseudonym of

Le Mans-type starting line-up for the inaugural Nine-Hour race - C-Type Jaguars for Moss/Walker (1), Rolt/Hamilton (2) and Whitehead/Stewart (3) head the echelon.

Pierre Bouillon, a mere stripling of 48, who had nearly covered himself in glory at Le Mans two months previously when he attempted to drive the entire race single-handedly. His rev counter had broken and he thought that his young co-driver was too inexperienced to trust with a car in that condition. He had driven for 23 hours and had a 25-mile lead when he missed a gear and broke his engine. That let Mercedes-Benz through to score a 1-2. A German win in 1952 meant that Levegh was not the most popular man in France, but his feat made him something of a hero in Britain.

There were three classes in the Nine-Hour Race - the Unlimited Class was headed by three works Jaguar C-types for Stirling Moss/Peter Walker, Tony Rolt/Duncan Hamilton and Peter Whitehead teamed with Ian Stewart.

Heading the list in the 1501-3000cc class was Aston Martin with three DB3 sports racers and a strong driver line-up: Reg Parnell/Eric Thompson, George Abecassis/Dennis Poore, and Peter Collins/Pat Griffith. Their main opposition was provided by two private Ferrari 225s for Bobbie Baird and Roy Salvadori, with Graham Whitehead sharing Tom Cole's car.

Cole deserves a footnote in history because he was the first American driver to race in Europe after the War. In fact, he was British-born, but was raised in America and raced under the American colours of white and blue. A scion of the Vidor battery family, he had fought back to mobility after contracting polio in his youth. Third at Le Mans in 1950, Cole was also fourth in the 1953 Mille Miglia, but he was to lose his life at Le Mans.

The third class, for 1500cc cars, was led by the three Lester-MGs of The Monkey Stable, a group of amateur drivers who employed a professional team manager. Though largely forgotten today, Harry Lester, a regular competitor at early Members' Meetings, was one of the pioneer post-war small-scale constructors. Lester made no more than 20 cars, and had faded from the scene by the end of 1955, after playing a full role in British motor racing's renaissance.

Race day was windy and rain began to fall just before the start. As usual, Stirling Moss won the sprint to the cars, but Tony Rolt had taken the lead by the end of lap one. After the first hour the leaders had completed 30 laps and had lapped some the tiddlers five or six times. Parnell (Aston Martin) led from Rolt (Jaguar), Abecassis (Aston Martin), Moss (Jaguar), and the Ferraris of Baird and Graham Whitehead.

Then the road began to dry, the Jaguars speeded up and both Rolt and Moss passed Parnell, while the Baird/Salvadori Ferrari moved up to fourth. Soon afterwards, the third C-type, with Peter Whitehead at the wheel, crashed - uncharacteristically - at Madgwick and retired. It was joined by the Levegh/Etancelin Talbot.

Unbeknown to its drivers, the Parnell/ Thompson Aston Martin was losing oil from its transmission when Thompson brought the car in on lap 91 to refuel and hand over to Parnell. During refuelling, which was then by churn and funnel, petrol was spilled over the back of the car,

At the 1952 Nine-Hours **(from top)** - the Tom Cole/ Graham Whitehead 2.7 Ferrari will finish second; the Gerry Ruddock/R.F. Peacock Lester-MG was the meat in the 'Monkey Stable' team's 1-2-3 triumph, 1500cc class, 6-7-10 overall; the 'Levegh'/'Phi-Phi' Etancelin Talbot-Lago will fail after running third.

which went up in flames. The two drivers leapt clear but two mechanics were burned and John Wyer, the team manager, who had his head in the cockpit when the car went up, was hurt badly enough to be out of action for six weeks.

The blaze was soon extinguished and Parnell, now out of the race, took over the running of the team - he would later work under Wyer as Aston Martin's team manager. Soon afterwards the Poore/Abecassis DB3 lost its bottom three gears. They kept going, but it meant that, effectively, Aston Martin had just one car left in the race.

At 7.30pm, the half-way point, the Jaguars of Moss/Walker and Rolt/Hamilton led the Collins/Griffith Aston Martin with the Ferraris of Baird/Salvadori and Cole/Whitehead fourth and fifth, and both moving up on the DB3.

Headlights came on at about nine o'clock and, for the first time in Britain, spectators could enjoy the special frisson of night-time racing. Headlights stabbed the darkness to create patterns as the cars went down Lavant Straight before swinging through Woodcote and the chicane. Lights came up on the grandstands, pits and marquees and, as the last remaining daylight faded, the entire circuit was transformed. If you had stood on Trundle Hill, which dominates the skyline, you would have seen the circuit glow in the darkness with the headlights of the cars, constantly changing direction, appearing to be dancing in the night.

The remaining two Jaguars seemed to be cruising to an easy win, with a cushion of five laps between them and the sole healthy Aston Martin. The result seemed inevitable and Freddie took Jaguar's founder, Sir William Lyons, to Goodwood House to celebrate over a few drinks.

Aston Martin's incendiary habits at Goodwood began in this 1952 Nine-Hours pit-stop: the Reg Parnell/Eric Thompson DB2 came in with an overheated final-drive, mechanic Fred Lown spilled fuel as he tipped the churn and smouldering oil in the undertray detonated the flood. Luckless team chief John Wyer and mechanic Jack Sopp were hospitalised for three weeks... but Aston Martin still won the race.

While they were savouring Scotland's product, the race changed dramatically. At about 9.30pm, a half shaft broke on the Rolt/Hamilton car and the Baird/Salvadori Ferrari overtook the DB3 to hold second.

Thirty minutes later there was more drama as Moss brought in the leading car with a broken rear radius arm. It was repaired, but at the cost of nearly an hour in the pits.

"When the Aston Martin pit went up during the 1952 Nine-Hours, our wooden commentary box was just down-wind of the fire. I always had a selection of delightful BBC secretaries to keep my lap charts, and I said to them, "Keep the lap chart going - I'll tell you when we have to get out..."

RAYMOND BAXTER

Salvadori and Baird had a narrow lead over the Aston Martin but, when the Ferrari came in for its final pit stop it hit disaster. First of all, it stopped on a patch of tarmac which had been softened by the fire in the adjoining Aston Martin pit and the jack sank into the ground.

To this day, Roy Salvadori swears that this cost him the race but his memory serves him falsely. It cost him more time than he could spare since the Collins/Griffith Aston Martin was close behind, but his real problem was electrical. The battery was flat.

It took precious minutes to find a new battery and a set of jump leads to get the car going again. Then, in his eagerness to claw back lost time, Salvadori shot out of the pits and promptly spun at Madgwick, stalling his engine. He got going again with a push start, but that cost him a one-lap penalty.

From being a distant third at nine o'clock the remaining Aston Martin went into the final hour with a two-lap lead over the Cole/Whitehead Ferrari, with the Baird/Salvadori car a further three laps adrift.

The position was still the same at midnight as the DB3 claimed its only victory. John Wyer himself was to call it a fluke win - the Peter Collins/Pat Griffith DB3 was not Aston Martin's finest product - but it had run like a train and its young drivers had not put a foot wrong, and that is what endurance racing is all about.

Above: sheep wickets and reflectors show the way - as the 1953 Goodwood Nine-Hours drones on, and on... and again Aston Martin will defeat Jaguar. **Overleaf:** last-gasp drama as the 1953 Nine-Hours is in its final hour and Jaguar's leading Moss/Walker disc-braked C-Type coasts in with engine failure. Moments later the sister Rolt/Hamilton car will fail once again - this is Aston's day, and night.

Though the Moss/Walker Jaguar finished 16 laps down in fifth, it won the unlimited class, while the Lester-MG of Jim Mayers and Mike Keen finished sixth, heading the 1500cc class. The three 'Monkey Stable' Lesters were 1-2-3 in class and won the team prize.

Though the racing itself had been good, and the atmosphere up to usual Goodwood standards, the crowd had been somewhat disappointing. No official attendance figure was released (itself revealing), but it is thought to have been well under 20,000. Some people arrived just as dusk was falling, for the novelty of seeing night-time racing, but many of those were soon bored. Cars were required to illuminate their race numbers at night, but most of the numbers could not be read.

The fact is that most spectators liked to go to Goodwood with their families and a picnic on Bank Holidays when the weather was fine. To them, Goodwood was a 'grand day out'. They were not committed enthusiasts, they wanted to see a programme of short races. Short, closely fought races, and the more the merrier.

Startled winners - Aston Martin DB2 drivers Pat Griffith and Peter Collins on the victory podium after winning the 'News of the World' International Nine-Hours - Mrs Emsley Carr of the newspaper family has just presented the cheque for £1000.

They had a point; not all racing enthusiasts enjoy endurance events. With hindsight, the Nine-Hours Race, which was described in the press as Britain's 'Little Le Mans' was destined to fail as an attraction. For years more British fans have gone to Le Mans to see the same cars and drivers that they could see at Silverstone or Brands Hatch; they don't go for the racing, they go for the *craic*. Le Mans has been described as a 'British Bank Holiday organised by the French', and that about sums it up.

The poor Nine-Hours attendance in 1952 meant that there was no newspaper sponsorship for the second running the following year and, unfortunately, that meant there was scant pre-race publicity which, in turn, produced an even smaller crowd.

It was a pity, because everyone in British motor racing thought that the Nine-Hour Race was a wonderful idea, with the added attraction of a Jaguar vs Aston Martin battle. Two months previously, Jaguar had finished 1-2-4 at Le Mans, while at the British Grand Prix meeting the new works team of Aston Martin DB3S had scored a 1-2-3 in the sports car race.

For the 1953 Nine-Hours, there were just two classes: cars over 2000cc and cars up to 2000cc. Jaguar had three works C-types, fitted with disc brakes, for

Goodwood Revival 1998 - Gary Pearson (**top**) won the Nine-Hour Memorial event in Adrian Hamilton's 1953 Le Mans-winning C-Type Jaguar; Jeremy Agace (**above**) flicks his ex-Cliff Davis Tojeiro-Bristol through the chicane.

Above: Freddie Richmond unveils the new Brooklands Memorial garden, donated by Dunlop and prompted by their veteran Competitions Manager, Norman Freeman. The dark patch at Freddie's feet is a section of Brooklands' concrete ("unbearably nostalgic to some of us", wrote John Bolster).
Right: Shepherds Bush car dealer Cliff Davis hustles his celebrated Tojeiro-Bristol past one of Goodwood's reflective apex markers, 1953 Nine-Hours. He co-drove with Bert Ambrose band drummer Les Leston, finishing 9th despite delays when the spare-wheel tyre in the boot caught fire!

Moss/Walker, Rolt/Hamilton and Peter Whitehead/Ian Stewart. *Ecurie Ecosse*, then a relatively new team, brought along two customer (drum-braked) C-types. One was shared by Jimmy Stewart (Jackie's elder brother) and Bob Dickson, the other by Jock Lawrence and Frank Curtis.

Aston Martin had works cars for Parnell/Thompson, Salvadori/Poore and Collins/Griffith, while HWM had the first of its Jaguar-engined cars for George Abecassis and Graham Whitehead.

Making its first appearance at Goodwood was a new make, Austin-Healey, with a works entry for John Lockett and Ken Rudd. The Healey 100 had been the star at the 1952 London Motor Show - such had been its reception that, after the first day, Leonard Lord, the boss of BMC, had taken Donald Healey to dinner and, next day, it was the Austin-Healey 100. By September 1953, the car was in full production, but, due to the export drive, few remained in Britain.

The 2-litre class was dominated by Bristol-engined cars. It was a rule in the 1950s that any powerful and reliable engine to appear had a class built around it, and in the mid-1950s that engine was the 1971cc six-cylinder Bristol unit. Six of the Bristol-engined cars were Frazer Nashes and there were also others from Tojeiro, Kieft and Cooper. The three Coopers were 1952 Formula 2 cars converted to two-seaters.

The only overseas entry was the fleet little 2-litre Gordini driven by Harry Schell and Jean Lucas. With no outside sponsorship, things were tight in 1953 and the purse for the winners was halved to £500. Jaguar and Aston Martin wanted to be at Goodwood, to put on a show before the home crowd, but many overseas drivers demanded a level of starting money beyond the BARC's resources.

Before the race there was a ceremony in the paddock to open the Brooklands Memorial Garden. The garden had been donated by Dunlop and incorporated a slab of concrete from one of the bankings, courtesy of S.C.H. 'Sammy' Davis with whom Freddie had won the 1930 BRDC 500. Over two dozen former Brooklands drivers

Sartorial style at the Goodwood Nine-Hours.
Above: the 1952 event's Jaguar works drivers - bulky Duncan Hamilton, lanky Tony Rolt, new boy Ian Stewart, pocket dynamo Stirling Moss and veteran gentleman-farmer Pete Whitehead.
Right: time-keeping glamour in the primitive pits.
Bottom right: the contemporary caption reads, "Some of the enthusiastic car racing fans from neighbouring towns made a day's outing of the Nine-Hour Race. But, like Joy and Betty here, they found walking round the course twice in five hours called for a rest..."

were on hand to see Freddie unveil the brass plaque.

Despite the financial constraints, 30 cars lined up before the pits as three o'clock approached, with the drivers standing on the other side of the track, ready to sprint to their cars. For once, Schell beat Moss in the Le Mans start, but the Gordini refused to start and, when it did, it constantly oiled its plugs and was never in contention. Moss therefore led from the start. One diversion was the sight of Cliff Davis's Tojeiro-Bristol, LOY 500, the car which inspired the AC Ace, completing a lap with its rear end ablaze. The fire was dowsed and LOY 500 finished the race.

After the first pit stop, the three Jaguars of Moss/Walker, Rolt/Hamilton and Whitehead/Stewart led from the DB3S of Parnell and Thompson. Then Walker nudged a back-marker at Lavant corner and called in at the pits to have the nose of his car beaten out. Stirling Moss took it over, with a reduced lead, but the Jaguars were eating tyres at an unexpected rate.

Despite that, Jaguar looked as though it was going to cruise to an easy 1-2. After eight hours, the Moss/Walker car led the Rolt/Hamilton C-type. In third was Reg Parnell and Eric Thompson's Aston Martin and, behind, the Whitehead/Stewart works C-type, the Collins/Griffith DB3S and the Ecurie Ecosse C-type of Lawrence and Curtis.

As in 1952, Jaguar should have been triumphant but, in the final hour, the Moss/Walker car threw a con-rod and the Rolt/Hamilton C-type lost its oil pressure. That left the Aston Martin of Parnell and Thompson in the lead and soon afterwards the remaining works Jaguar, in second, slowed with fading brakes and falling oil pressure. The Collins/Griffith DB3S slipped by into second place.

Overleaf: "They're worth *how much?!?*" Frank Sytner enjoys his 'moment' as John Griffith endures his first drive in a strange car, Revival Meeting 1998. Griffith's historic *'Longnose'* D-Type is the Dutch National Motor Museum's *'XKD606'*, the 1957 Le Mans winner. Sytner's is JCB's *'XKD603'*, 1957 Le Mans 2nd place, which one week later led the *Ecurie Ecosse* team's 3-4-5 finish in the *'Monzanapolis'* 500-Miles. There was no steam threshing going on at Monza, and the driving style rather more cultivated...

"I did the three Nine-Hours races - never had much luck, although I led the first two for Jaguar - and my abiding memory is seeing the disc brakes on the Jaguars glowing red coming into the chicane. You never saw that from the pits at Le Mans, because nobody braked on the home straight.

The Nine-Hours wasn't as dangerous as it might have been, because everybody knew the track so well they could do it in their sleep! Plus the drivers

"The first race I saw at Goodwood was the Nine-Hours in 1952. I was 10 years old, and watched the 3pm start, but when night fell I had to be taken home to bed: I wasn't allowed to stay up late."

DEREK BELL

of the slower cars always knew you were there because they saw your lights in their mirrors."

STIRLING MOSS

Right: how traditional can one get? Le Mans-type start drama as the Freddie March Trophy field take off - Gary Pearson's C-type Jaguar (24) leading away - 9.30am, Revival Meeting Sunday, 1998.
Below: a whimsical 1950s view of night-time racing by Russell Brockbank, as published in '*The Motor*'

So Aston Martin took its second win in the Nine-Hours. Reg Parnell and Eric Thompson had two laps in hand over Collins and Griffith while Peter Whitehead nursed his ailing C-type home third. Bob Gerard and David Clarke were sixth overall in their Frazer Nash Le Mans Replica - they also won the two-litre class and Frazer Nash took the Team Award.

Works Jaguars had dominated Le Mans, so why did they fail at Goodwood for the second year in succession? The answer may be found in the fact that Goodwood was then the shortest circuit on which endurance racing took place. It was less than half the length of a lap of Sebring and about a quarter of a lap at Le Mans.

In 1955 John Wyer wrote a letter to '*The Motor*' in which he complained that the drivers had no respite at Goodwood - and that from man who team-managed a hat-trick of wins in the Nine-Hour race. The Goodwood Nine-Hours focused cars and drivers in a way no other endurance did. It was an extremely intense race, with a high rate of wear on the tyres.

Despite the fact the race had been closely fought and dramatic, even fewer spectators turned up in 1953 than in 1952. Behind the jubilation in the Aston Martin and Frazer Nash camps, there were serious problems. The catering was criticised by the BARC Council and the beer tents all shut early. With a diminished crowd and no outside sponsorship, the BARC had made a loss on the event. It was little wonder then that there was no Nine-Hour Race held in 1954, but - perhaps surprisingly - the concept was revived for one final time in 1955.

The 1955 Nine-Hours took place in the aftermath of the terrible accident at Le Mans in June 1955, where over 80 spectators and the Mercedes-Benz driver 'Levegh' were killed. While many countries panicked - races were cancelled, and Switzerland banned racing altogether - Britain and the Netherlands refused to be touched by the same hysteria, but instead undertook detailed examination of circuit safety. Goodwood spent weeks installing new 'defence in depth' concrete crash barriers. Spectators were moved further away from the track and the thickness of the bankings was doubled.

In the two years since the Nine-Hours had last been run, British sports car racing had been transformed, with the arrival of the Coventry Climax FWA engine in 1954 giving a boost to the

Above: it's 3pm, Saturday 20th August 1955. Peter Walker - the eventual winner with Dennis Poore - sprints for his works Aston Martin DB3S as 'Ebby' Ebblewhite has just dropped the flag to start the final Goodwood Nine-Hours classic.
Overleaf: Peter Collins enjoys a cuppa after handing over the 1955 Nine-Hours' leading works Aston DB3S to co-driver Tony Brooks. Team chief John Wyer's wife 'Tottie' guards the pit-board numbers - the loud-hailer did wonders for the pit-crew's energy levels.

1100cc class. Cooper made the mid-engined T39 '*Manx Tail*' sports racer while Lotus's front-engined Mk IX matched it in performance. In 1953 both Cooper and Lotus had been building simple cars for British club racing, yet two months before the 1955 Nine-Hours, both outfits had made their debuts at Le Mans.

HWM had found Formula 1 beyond its means, since it had no suitable engine, and so had switched to making Jaguar-engined sports cars. Lister had begun to make its very successful Bristol-engined cars and Tojeiro was producing bespoke sports racers. In two short years, British sports car racing had changed out of all recognition.

Aston Martin was again present in 1955, with three examples of the ever-improving DB3S. The car now had Girling disc brakes - Jaguar had made sure that no rival could have access to the Dunlop system which it had developed and proved. Pat Griffith had retired from racing at the end of 1954 'to get a proper job' and Peter Collins was paired with young dental student Tony Brooks, who was in only his second race for the team. Peter Walker was driving with Dennis Poore and Roy Salvadori with Reg Parnell. Backing the works team was a private DB3S for Tony Gaze and David

Veteran in the pits - at the 1955
Nine-Hours, the privately-run
Cuff-Miller/Hinde Aston Martin
DB3 (by this time four years old)
was utterly outclassed by the
works DB3Ss and private Jaguars,
but finally finished 15th.

McKay. The works Jaguar team gave the race a miss; perhaps they felt they were
jinxed. There were, however, four private D-types including one from *Ecurie Ecosse* for
Desmond Titterington and Ninian Sanderson, and two ex-works cars from Duncan
Hamilton, one for himself and Tony Rolt, the other for Peter Whitehead and Michael
Head, father of the Williams designer, Patrick.

Count Alfonso de Portago brought his Ferrari 750 Monza, which he drove with
Mike Hawthorn. There were two other Monzas - for Harry Schell and Jean Lucas, and
Jean Jonneret and Ken Wharton - and all three appeared to have some degree of works
support. Stirling Moss persuaded Porsche to send a 550 Spyder which he shared with
Huscke von Hanstein. Their chief opposition was to be an MG-powered works Lotus
IX driven by Colin Chapman and Peter Jopp, while the work's Climax-powered car was
entrusted to Ron Flockhart and Cliff Allison. Ivor Bueb and Jim Russell shared a
Cooper-Climax '*Manx Tail*' entered by the works.

The early stages of the 1955 race were marked by a number of crashes and
retirements. After the first hour, the Aston Martins of Collins and Walker led from
Sanderson's D-type; Hawthorn's Ferrari was in trouble with a gearbox full of neutrals
and Parnell's Aston Martin had retired with a broken wheel hub.

At the one-third distance, the Titterington/Sanderson D-type was first in the field
from the Collins/Brooks Aston Martin and the HWM-Jaguar of Macklin and Hill
Smith. Then Titterington hit a row of markers while avoiding one of the slower cars

and broke a headlight, which took five minutes to replace.

The Collins/Brooks Aston Martin moved into the lead in the fourth hour, but it was to be delayed by ignition problems. The sister-car of Walker and Poore then led, but second gear had gone and the Sanderson/Titterington Jaguar was catching it when midnight - and the end of the race - fell. The Aston Martin had covered 309 laps, the Jaguar was a bare lap adrift, while the Collins/Brooks DB3S was a further three laps down. One newspaper headline ran, 'Grandads Win Little Le Mans'!

So Aston Martin completed its hat-trick of wins at Goodwood at a time when it had still to win a race in the World Sports Car Championship.

1955 was the last time the Nine-Hour Race was run. A spokesman for the BARC said that there was simply no interest in Britain for long races. People who would turn up to a varied programme did not want an endurance event. The spokesman predicted that it would be possibly five or six years before the general public was sufficiently educated in motor racing to accept a long race. It would not be quite that long, since the Tourist Trophy would be run at Goodwood, between 1958-64, and some of those races would feature among the finest ever to be staged at the circuit.

Sweet victory, and a splendid (if sometimes fortunate) hat-trick of Goodwood Nine-Hour Race wins for Aston Martin. **Left to right:** Dennis Poore, company owner David Brown, and Peter Walker on the podium, 1955.

THE BIG BOYS

Over the winter of 1951-52, French race organisers announced that they would run their Grand Prix races to the two-litre Formula 2, instead of Formula 1, which was dying on its feet. Other organisers followed suit and the FIA announced that the whole 1952 World Championship would be run to Formula 2.

The reason was that Alfa Romeo had retired from racing and BRM could no longer be relied on even to turn up. That left Ferrari pitched against old cars from Maserati and Talbot-Lago. To run the World Championship to Formula 1 would have been farcical.

Formula 2 drivers, who had expected to race in relatively minor events, found that they could run in the World Championship. The driver who would make the most of that was Mike Hawthorn. His performances in his first year of racing had so impressed a family friend, Bob Chase, that he bought Mike a Cooper-Bristol, which arrived at the 1952 Easter Monday Meeting, so new it was still unpainted. His father, Leslie, had been spending his time at the Bristol works at Filton, tuning the engine to run on a fuel mix which incorporated nitromethane. Painting the car was not his main priority.

For once there were two great stars present: Juan Manuel Fangio, the reigning World Champion, and his fellow Argentine José Froilán González, winner of the 1951 British Grand Prix for Ferrari. Two stars arrived at the circuit, but three left it.

Hawthorn, in his first single-seater event, put his Cooper-Bristol on pole for the Lavant Cup for Formula 2 cars. Then he realised that he had never practised a racing start in a single-seater. Mike searched in his mind for any descriptions of making a racing start that he might have read.

He need not have worried, leading off the line and setting fastest lap on his way to the flag. Then

Left: spirit of a Grand Prix racing age. Robin Lodge's Ferrari Dino 246 leads Nigel Corner's *'Fire Engine'* Lightweight Maserati 250F and Joaquin Folch's sister Modenese master-piece through the chicane - the Richmond Trophy race, Revival Meeting, September 1998.
Right: through the mid-1950s Roy Salvadori proved himself a formidable opponent on British circuits such as Goodwood. Here he lines up Syd Greene's new Gilby Engineering-entered Maserati 250F for its debut race, the 7-lap Lavant Cup, Easter Monday 1954.

Utterly unconcerned during another day at the office, José Froilán González muscles-on opposite lock as his 'Thin Wall Special' Ferrari slithers at over 100mph onto the Madgwick Corner grass. Although he lost time this way in a preliminary handicap event he would still win the Formula 1 Richmond Trophy – centre-throttle firmly trapped between right foot and firewall – Easter Monday 1952.

he did the same in the *Formule Libre* Chichester Cup - and down in sixth place, driving Alan Brown's new Cooper-Bristol, was Fangio, the reigning World Champion. The great Argentine, shoe-horned in at the last minute, long after preferred not to remember a race in an unfamiliar car which had carburetion problems. As a crowd-pleaser, the stunt was a flop.

The fact that Formula 1 was no longer the Championship category did not mean there were no Formula 1 races, and the Richmond Trophy was run as usual at the Easter Monday Meeting. Actually, only one current Formula 1 car was entered, the fourth in the line of 'Thin Wall Specials' - a Ferrari Tipo 375 with the long wheelbase 'Indianapolis' chassis and the latest twin-spark engine. The rest of the field was a mish-mash which mainly included Formula 2 cars and even Tony Rolt's Delage-ERA, the chassis of which had been built in 1927.

At the start Froilán González took the 'Thin Wall' to a predictable win, but in second place was Hawthorn. Even the most hard-nosed of observers had to admit that two wins and a second place, under the circumstances, was a sensational performance. It is no exaggeration to say that when he woke up next morning Mike was a star as the press went to town on the new sensation. It was no flash in the pan either, and by the end of the year Mike had done enough to be snapped up by Ferrari.

Among Mike's victories in 1952 was the Sussex International Trophy for *Formule Libre* cars at the Goodwood Whitsun Meeting. *Formule Libre*, open to any single-seater, became a popular feature of British racing between 1952 and 1955, since it could

> "The rivalry between Sir Alfred Owen and Tony Vandervell was very intense. Yet the two of them remained good friends. You'd see them at Goodwood, these two millionaires standing side by side watching the racing in their tatty old raincoats, and you wouldn't think either of them was up to much. Yet they both probably could have bought a battleship each."
>
> TONY RUDD

provide large and varied fields. It also provided the fascination of a promotable contest between two fierce rivals.

BRM had been salvaged by the industrialist, Sir Alfred Owen, who found that he had virtually nowhere to run the V16 cars save in *Formule Libre*. It was much the same for Tony Vandervell with his 4 1/2-litre '*Thin Wall Special*'.

The two men made a fascinating contrast. Vandervell was a brash, brusque, flamboyant figure who wore sharp suits and plimsolls - because his feet hurt. He arrived at race meetings with a caravan, orginally built for a Maharaja, which was generously stocked with canapes, caviar and champagne. Sir Alfred was a quiet, ascetic man, a Methodist lay preacher who wore a trilby hat, long mackintosh and a Boy's Brigade pullover. He could be found sitting on the boot lid of his one indulgence, a Bentley Continental, with his packet of sandwiches and a Thermos flask of tea.

You had, therefore, two of the richest men in Britain lined up against each other, and each able to engage the best drivers. So, for the Woodcote Cup at the September 1952 Goodwood meeting, Giuseppe Farina was in the '*Thin Wall*' while BRM fielded Ken Wharton, Reg Parnell and Froilán González. The rest of the field consisted primarily of Formula 2 cars and even some pre-war cars.

Wharton's BRM refused to start, and González led Parnell and Farina, but the former World Champion soon split the BRMs, which was the order they finished in.

Below: 1952, Easter Monday - a sensational single-seat debut for Mike Hawthorn, 'The Farnham Flyer' (depicted by Sallon, **above**), as he negotiates the prototype chicane in Bob Chase's F2 Cooper-Bristol, so new it was unpainted.
Overleaf: Golden Boy - six years of frontline motor racing exacted a price from Hawthorn, Britain's first ever World Champion Driver. Goodwood, Easter Monday 1952 (**inset**), and 1958 (**main picture**).

"Mike Hawthorn really came to fame at an Easter Monday Goodwood. It was 1952, and we'd just brought out our new Formula 2 car, the Cooper-Bristol. I was racing the prototype, and we'd sold cars to Eric Brandon, Alan Brown, and Bob Chase for his protégé Hawthorn to drive. All he'd raced before that was a little pre-war Riley in club events: it was his first big race. He never seemed to be taking things very seriously: he'd like to go to the pub the night before the race and have a pint and a game of darts.

Well, Mike astonished everyone, including himself, by being fastest in practice on the Saturday. In the end I let Fangio drive my car, but none of us could get near Mike; come the Monday he won the F2 race with ease, then he won the *Formule Libre* race, and finally he finished second in the F1 race to González's '*Thin Wall*' Ferrari. He was a household name from then on, and the offer from *Scuderia* Ferrari came five months later.

"There was a story about Mike Hawthorn blowing his car up in practice and going home to Farnham - but then driving all the way back to Goodwood in the evening for drinks with his mates at the Richmond Arms!"

STIRLING MOSS

Soon after that Easter Monday meeting, doing some practice laps, I was going through a corner in my Cooper-Bristol on the limit, as fast as I reckoned I could possibly go. Suddenly Mike in his Cooper-Bristol came round the outside of me, steering with one hand and giving me two fingers with the other. That's when I decided to give up driving racing cars and stick to building them."

JOHN COOPER

Best of the rest was Alan Brown's Cooper-Bristol which actually beat Louis Rosier's 4$^{1}/_{2}$-litre Ferrari 375.

Here is a point to ponder. In today's terms, the BRM had cost many millions to design and build, yet the Woodcote Cup was run over just five laps. Both Vandervell and Owen had hired major stars for a race that lasted eight minutes! Clash of ego hardly begins to describe their rivalry. Both men had supported the BRM project with hard cash, but while Vandervell had left in disgust to do his own thing, Owen had kept the faith and bought BRM.

At first Vandervell wanted only to beat Owen, but then thought that he could build the 'world-beater' that the BRM had promised to be.

Vandervell would have his first Vanwall ready for early 1954, when the new 2-litre Formula 1 came into operation. It would take BRM until September 1955 to bring its own new car to the line, then a further two years before the car was sorted, and another two years before it won its first World Championship race. By the time that BRM triumphed in the 1959 Dutch Grand Prix, Vanwall had won the inaugural Constructors' Cup and had withdrawn from racing.

Just about every competitive British Formula 2 car arrived at Goodwood for the

Ken Wharton competed in anything at any level from mud-plugging trials and speed hill-climbs to Grands Prix and international rallying, but early in his road-racing career he was primarily a 'Nash man - 1952 September International.

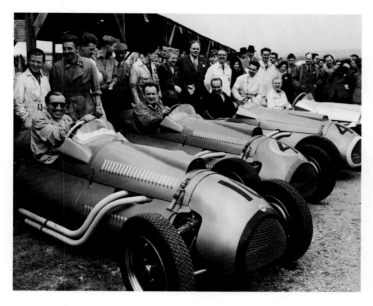

Madgwick Cup in September 1952, from Connaught, Cooper, Alta, Frazer Nash, Aston-Butterworth and ERA - and a couple of Ferraris as well. None of the British cars could match a Ferrari or Maserati, but the sheer diversity of makes underlines how quickly the British motor racing industry was developing.

The surprise winner was Kenneth Downing in a Connaught A-Type, from Dennis Poore in a Connaught with Alan

Below: Time-machine – Alan Miles' Cooper-Bristol running hard to match the pace of Rhoddy MacPherson and Gregor Fisken's sister cars in the Woodcote Cup, September 1998, when even they could not overcome the supercharged 2-litre grunt of Ludovic Lindsay's sexagenarian ERA 'Remus'.
Overleaf: clutches jolt home, juddering wheels spin up, superchargers shriek, 50 cylinders catapult González, Parnell, Alan Brown and The Great Farina off the line - BRM V16s, Cooper-Bristol and 'Thin Wall Special' - September meeting, 1952.

Above: a mob-handed debut for the latest Formula 2 Cooper-Bristols, Easter Monday 1952. The sister *Ecurie Richmond* cars of Alan Brown and Eric Brandon head the line-up, with World Champion Fangio about to have an unhappy day with the works' prototype, and Mike Hawthorn about to enjoy a fabulous day in Bob Chase's still unpainted car.

Brown's Cooper-Bristol third. There had been a multiple crash at the start of the race which, among others, had eliminated Moss's ERA, and a high number of retirements.

That is not to take anything from Downing's achievement. During his brief career he had shown promise and Connaught would be dominant in British Formula Two throughout 1953.

Moss had just completed a wasted season with the ERA G-Type, but while the car was a failure it was, in the best sense, an experimental model. ERA was using it as a learning exercise while preparing for the $2^1/_2$-litre Formula 1 when it would have a bespoke engine. Illness caused the team patron, Jaguar works driver Leslie Johnson, to abandon the project and sell the company. The G-Type remains, however, a statement of intent.

There was another strong field for the Lavant Cup at the 1953 Easter Meeting. Once again it was run over just seven laps and once again, Moss was at the wheel of a lemon - an Alta-engined car based on a Cooper chassis, but with 'improvements' by his team.

Roy Salvadori put his Connaught on pole, 0.2 seconds ahead of de Graffenried's Maserati A6GCM. 'Salvo' led the last lap, but his throttle linkage broke in sight of the line and he coasted to second behind the Maserati of the veteran Swiss.

There were BRMs for Parnell and Wharton for the *Formule Libre* Chichester Cup. Vandervell had entered Piero Taruffi in his car, but the '*Thin Wall*' had been in trouble in a previous handicap. The five-lap race was wet, the BRMs could not find traction on the wet track, and de Graffenried went into the lead to win. Parnell's engine went off and Wharton, in second, could barely keep Ron Flockhart's venerable ERA at bay. It was perhaps this performance that led to Flockhart becoming a works BRM driver.

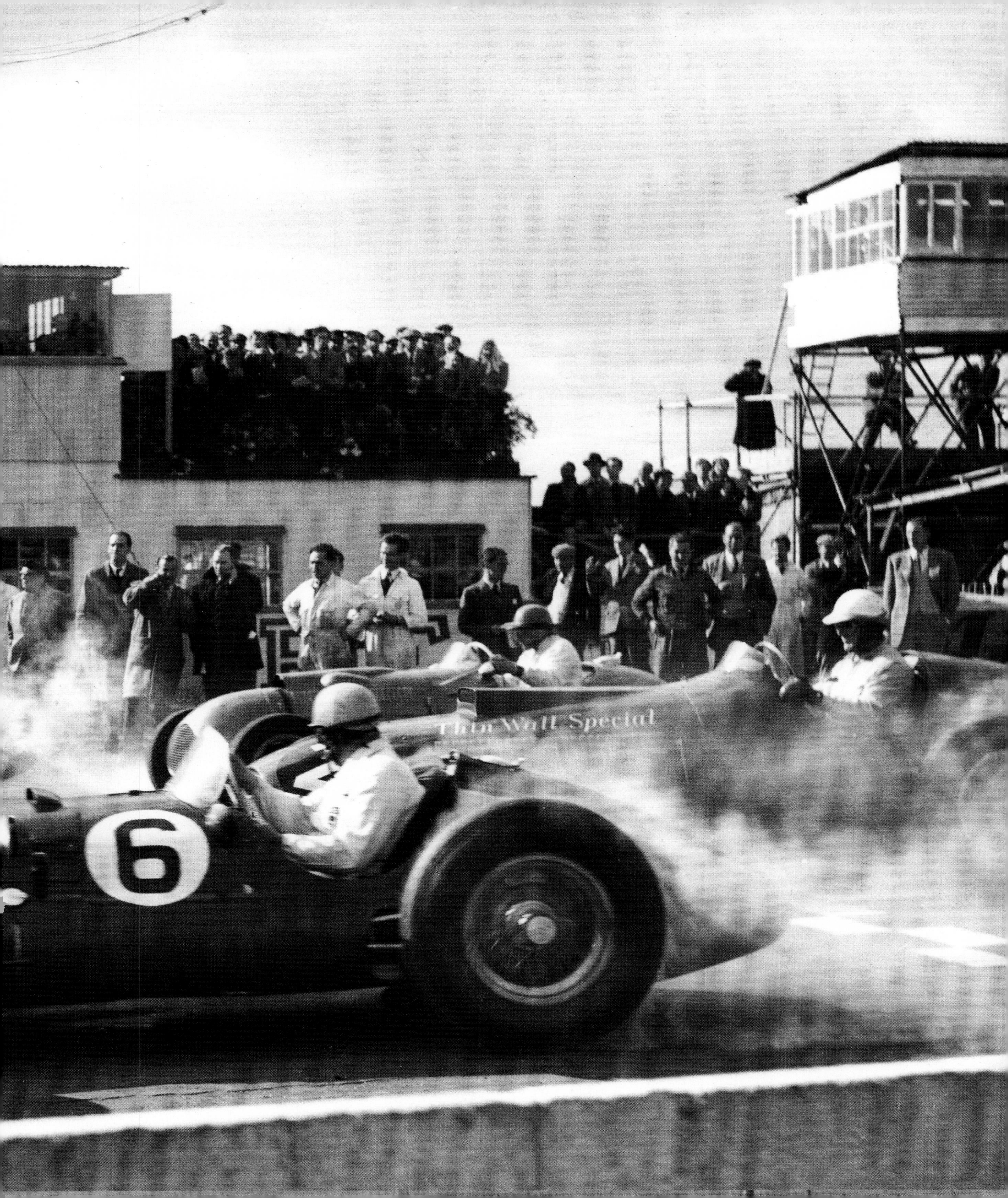

6
Thin Wall Special

Sir Alfred Owen watched the race with BRM engineer Tony Rudd. Owen demanded to know how it was that de Graffenried's Formula 2 car could beat a BRM which had considerably more power. Rudd gave his boss a brief lecture on power/weight ratios and Owen told him to build a lighter car. At once. So the BRM Mk II was born.

A second *Formule Libre* race featured on the same bill, this time over 15 laps, and with Taruffi starting in the '*Thin Wall*'. The track was drier and Wharton won from Taruffi with de Graffenried third. Parnell's BRM retired.

Though there was a Formula 2 race on the bill at the 1953 September Meeting (which was won by Salvadori's Connaught from Moss's Cooper) the main feature was a pair of *Formule Libre* races. BRM hired Fangio to run alongside Wharton while Mike Hawthorn handled the '*Thin Wall*'. Mike returned to Goodwood a hero, a fully-fledged Ferrari driver and winner of the French Grand Prix, where he'd had a race-long duel with Fangio.

This time, there would be no duel, because Mike shot off into the lead to win easily from Fangio with Wharton third. Best of the rest was Moss in his Cooper. By then, the 'Thin Wall' was equipped with Goodyear disc brakes, since the car had ceased to be merely a machine with which to beat BRM and had become a development platform for the Vanwall. The BRM continued to be a cul-de-sac.

In winning the five-lap Chichester Cup, Hawthorn had set a new lap record at 93.91 mph, and he upped that to 94.53 mph on his way to winning the 15-lap Goodwood Trophy, with Ken Wharton 23 seconds in arrears and Bob Gerard's Cooper-Bristol third.

Fangio held second until retiring with gear selection problems while, until he spun, Salvadori's Connaught had been ahead of Wharton's BRM.

Hawthorn had enjoyed a much better season than Moss and the press began to work up a rivalry between them. On the one hand was the tall, blond, extrovert Hawthorn, who was frequently seen with a tankard of beer in his hand and a pipe in his mouth. On the other there was Moss, short but muscular, a dedicated professional. It was just the sort of thing that the burgeoning sport needed to attract public interest.

1954 saw the introduction of the 2-litre Formula 1, but only Vanwall was anywhere near ready. Connaught, HWM, Cooper and Kieft had all hoped to have a V8 engine from Coventry Climax: the FPF 'Godiva' engine was built, and run, but the engineers in Coventry believed the exaggerated power claims which Italian makers issued and though a batch of at least eight engines was built, it was not released.

The Godiva engine is one of the great 'what ifs' of motor racing, because it was as

Fangio wishes Ken Wharton luck before the pair renew battle for BRM, September 1953. Ken revered Fangio and always specified his V16 as the one he wanted to race whenever the great man could not drive for the British team. He identified the car by its horseshoe on the grille - team mechanic Dick Salmon (**left**) would swop it onto whichever car the management decreed Wharton should use...

At Easter Goodwood 1954, Ken Wharton was leading in the V16 BRM - I was chasing in Sid Greene's Maserati 250F. I caught him up, and he was obviously in trouble, because he was going slower and slower in the corners, and the BRM was chucking out oil and petrol which was coating my face and goggles. But he wasn't going to let me by. This went on for lap after lap, and I was getting really fed up, and was waving my arms furiously. Finally, with two laps to go, I got too close at Lavant and hit him hard up the back. Never mind, I thought, perhaps he'll go off.

Instead the BRM went broadside, I hit him in the side, and we both spun. By now my clutch had pretty much had it and my race was over, but Wharton restarted and, because everyone else was miles behind, he won the race.

Sid Greene was so incensed that he put in an official protest against Wharton, although I would have nothing to do with this. Protests never solve anything. In those days, if a driver treated you badly you would never have dreamed of protesting: you just made a mark in your little black book, and sorted it out on the track next time you came up against him. Some time after that battle I unexpectedly received a silver cigarette box from the Duke of Richmond & Gordon, which was inscribed 'In acknowledgment of a splendid show at Goodwood on Easter Monday, April 19th 1954'. I was delighted to get this, because I reckoned it showed whose side the Duke was on - until I found out later that he'd sent Ken Wharton an identical cigarette box…"

ROY SALVADORI

powerful as the Mercedes-Benz W196, with a better power band and more potential for development.

The seven-lap Lavant Cup at the 1954 Easter Meeting was billed as a Formula 1 race, but the only F1 cars were the Gilby Engineering Maserati 250F entered for Roy Salvadori and Reg Parnell's Ferrari 500/625. The prototype Vanwall was entered for Alberto Ascari, but was withdrawn. A sprinkling of Formula 2 cars made up the sparse grid.

But the two Formula 1 cars were enough to make a race, however, and Parnell crossed the line 0.6 seconds ahead of Salvadori. Though often criticised for running such short races, the BARC's policy paid off in terms of close racing. The then record crowd, officially estimated at 55,000, had come to be thrilled, and thrilled it was.

If not even Fangio could win with a BRM something was amiss. While Vandervell had his Vanwall ready, and BRM was nearly two years from racing its first 2¹/₂-litre car, the team from Bourne arrived determined to win the five-lap Chichester Cup. Over the winter they had dissipated their creative energy by building a short-wheelbase Mk II version of the V16.

They had expected to compete against Alberto Ascari in the '*Thin Wall*', but the reigning World Champion had just signed for Lancia, and the company was demanding £700 appearance money, plus expenses. The BARC refused, rather publicly, and Gianni Lancia demanded an apology; the club took the view, 'Why should we apologise to Lancia for them breaking their contract?' It all became very heated for a while.

So it was that the 1954 Easter crowd saw Wharton's BRM win by 0.4 seconds from Salvadori's Maserati, which was 0.8 seconds ahead of Parnell's Ferrari. Flockhart, in his first race for BRM, had been elbowed off at the first bend and he had re-started last. While Flockhart finished 19 seconds in arrears his drive up the field was another feature of what had been an exciting race.

To draw a modern analogy, the few front runners were Formula 3000 cars in a Formula 3 race. The knowledgeable would not be impressed, but the racing was taking place in front of a largely uninformed audience. The public, however, was

Below: Ken Wharton won the Chichester Cup *Libre* race by just 0.4 seconds from Roy Salvadori, Easter Monday 1954. Wharton's brand-new BRM V16 Mark II hustles into the chicane ahead of Roy's gleaming Maserati 250F. The two will collide later the same day, the impact writing off Wharton's alternative V16 Mark I – though he will limp it to the line, and win in a written-off car!

Opposite: Wharton swabs himself down at the finishing line after his battered V16 BRM has treated him to a hot-oil shower bath, and he has been rammed by Salvadori's Maserati. The expression speaks volumes.

growing better informed as motor racing became a more mainstream sport.

The second *Formule Libre* race was run over 21 laps. Flockhart led from the line, but then suffered a misfire. Parnell's Ferrari retired while Salvadori was right on the tail of Wharton's BRM, which led. On lap 19, the BRM went broadside at Lavant and the Maserati hit it. Salvadori retired, but Wharton went on to win with a car which was written off by the works afterwards. The Connaughts of Kenneth McAlpine and Leslie Marr were third and fourth while Flockhart spluttered across the line in fifth.

Salvadori's team did something which was rare at the time, lodging a protest with the Stewards. They, in turn, did something which was usual at the time, and rejected the protest. Apart from discontent in the background, it had been another very successful meeting, even without the presence of Ascari. There was much ill-feeling about the incident, however, and John Morgan was still extremely sensitive on the matter 20 years later.

The 1954 Goodwood Whitsun Meeting saw the first BARC Formula 1 race, run over five laps, with the grid decided by ballot. The field was even thinner than at the Easter Meeting, and most drivers were there because they had also entered the two *Formule Libre* races. Salvadori was slow away, Parnell took the lead, but Roy fought back to within 0.6 seconds at the flag.

The main interest was provided by the two *Formule Libre* races, both won by Peter Collins in the '*Thin Wall*' from a BRM - once from Flockhart, once from Wharton. Each time it was by a clear margin. Collins also won the *Formule Libre* race at the 1955 Easter Meeting, this time in a BRM.

Formule Libre had been fun when it had been a battle between British car against Italian, or Sir Alfred Owen versus Tony Vandervell setting drivers of the quality of Hawthorn, Fangio, Taruffi, Farina and Gonzalez against each other. Hawthorn versus Fangio? Wonderful. Farina versus Gonzalez? Wonderful. Collins versus Wharton and Flockhart? Not so wonderful - Collins was a class or two above either.

There were 21 entries for the Goodwood Trophy, the Formula 1 race at the 1954 September meeting, but only five were F1 cars. Moss in his 250F, entered by the works, won from Collins in the Vanwall by 20 seconds with Salvadori nearly a minute behind Collins.

So far as racing at Goodwood is concerned, this had been the worst feature event ever. Viewed overall, however, it was a very good meeting. Although slightly disappointing that a challenge race for gas turbine cars from Rover, G.M. and Fiat did not come off, the support programme had full grids and close racing. An exception was the Formula 2 event, the penultimate race run to the 2-litre Formula 2.

> "Goodwood was the circuit I started winning races on, as far as Europe was concerned. In fact, I had my first-ever race on British soil there on Easter Monday 1955, in a Cooper-Alta I'd unfortunately bought when I arrived in England. I say unfortunately, because the engine was no good, and we sold it on pretty quick."
>
> SIR JACK BRABHAM

Apart from the performance of individual drivers, notably Hawthorn and Moss, 1954 had been an exceptionally bad year for British racing. Formula 3, which had promised so much, had become a domestic category. So poor had been the year that the SMMT awarded Kieft a stand at the Motor Show on the grounds that its two class wins in the WSCC were the highlight of the year, by a company which did not have a stand.

In the Sebring 12-Hours, a 2-litre Kieft had finished ten laps behind the winning 1-litre OSCCA. A Kieft had also won the 1100cc class in the Tourist Trophy, but there were only three entries and two of those retired. Aston Martin, by contrast, did not win a single point in the WSCC.

Things did not get much better at the 1955 Easter Meeting. Two Vanwalls were entered in the Glover Trophy, but scratched. Moss and Salvadori had their Maseratis and Tony Rolt had the new Connaught Type-B. The rest of the field consisted of obsolete Formula 2 cars. One of the Coopers, however, was driven by Jack Brabham, who was making his debut in Britain. Many of the entries did not turn up, Moss retired and Salvadori won as he pleased.

So far as British involvement in Formula 1 was concerned, at least progress was made during the year. The revised Vanwall made progress, the BRM Type P25 finally appeared in September and, in the Syracuse Grand Prix, Tony Brooks trounced the Maserati works team in his Connaught B-Type, setting a new lap record in the process.

The 1956 Glover Trophy had Moss, Salvadori and and Louis Rosier in private Maseratis. There were also works Gordinis for Robert Manzon and Elie Bayol, but the early promise of Gordini had long gone due to financial constraints, and Manzon's considerable talent disappeared with it. Hawthorn and Brooks were driving in BRMs and there were Connaughts for Archie Scott Brown, Les Leston, Bob Gerard and Reg Parnell. Ken Wharton had a Ferrari entered by Rosier.

It was an interesting grid, which promised much. It certainly attracted 60,000 spectators, Goodwood's largest-ever crowd, and the race was televised. Hawthorn rushed into the lead at the start followed by Scott Brown and Moss - British cars first and second! Hawthorn was demoted to third on lap two, but Moss could do nothing about Scott Brown.

Archie Scott Brown was a severely disabled sportsman who competed at the top

Left: *Wheee!* Jack Brabham's tail-out, power-on, dirt-track driving style quite fazed the BARC *blazerati* when he ran this ex-Peter Whitehead Cooper-Alta at Goodwood on Easter Monday 1955. But the car proved hopeless compared to the Cooper-Brisol '*RedeX Special*' he'd left at home. The nut-brown Australian's skilled development of that car had replaced its standard 56lb clutch with a Harley-Davidson assembly scaling barely 6lbs, which freed the 6-cylinder to rev its heart out. We'd be hearing much, much more from 'Black Jack' - the driver/engineer.

Overleaf: just for once Easter Monday at Goodwood, 1956, was gloriously sunny and a 60,000 crowd was reported. At 32 laps the Richmond Formula 1 race was Goodwood's longest yet. Stirling Moss's faith in his fuel-injected works Maserati 250F was rewarded as Archie Scott Brown's B-Type Connaught (6) would break, Mike Hawthorn's BRM (beyond) would crash, and veteran Bob Gerard's Connaught (8) would finish 4th.

131

level against the able-bodied. His mother had suffered from rubella during pregnancy and Archie was born with a short right arm, which was withered and ended in a thumb and vestigial palm. He had unusually short legs below the knee and club feet - and he'd been born with his feet facing backwards. Though naturally right-handed, he'd had to learn to do everything with his left.

The magazine '*Motor Racing*' once published a diagram of Archie's lines driving his Lister-Jaguar around Goodwood and the car was hardly ever in a straight line.

In the Glover Trophy Archie's brakes began to fade on lap 16 of 32 and Stirling overtook him. A piston in the Connaught's revised Alta engine broke on lap 17. Two laps later, a drive shaft joint seized on Hawthorn's BRM and the car flipped, but without injury to Mike. Brooks's BRM had long gone with no oil pressure.

Moss stroked home from Salvadori and Leston, with the survivors a lap behind. For those looking for hopeful omens of a British renaissance in Formula 1, there was the power of the BRM off the line and the speed of Archie's Connaught. The downside was the fragility of the Alta engine and the failure of the BRM.

A month after the Easter Monday Meeting there was further cause for optimism at the International Trophy at Silverstone where Ferrari had sent cars for Fangio and Collins. Hawthorn led easily until his magneto drive sheared and Moss won in the revised Vanwall (chassis by Colin Chapman, aerodynamic body by Frank Costin) with Scott Brown's Connaught second.

British enthusiasts were still holding their breath at the 1957 Glover Trophy on Easter Monday. There were Connaughts for Scott Brown, Fairman and Lewis-Evans; BRMs for Salvadori and Flockhart; Vanwalls for Moss and Brooks; a Cooper for Brabham; and Lotuses for Keith Hall and Cliff Allison. Jim Russell had a Maserati and Paul Emery ran his Emeryson.

Every driver was British - except for Brabham - and there were five British teams. Even Emery would become a Series 1 constructor in 1961. Surely the first World Championship win could not be far away?

Neither Lotus appeared on the grid - an omen for the season. The brakes of Salvadori's BRM failed on lap one - another omen - and Scott Brown's fuel pressure

Left: 'Old Man Vandervell' saw no merit in running his lovely, toolroom-built Vanwalls in anything less than World Championship-qualifying Grands Prix. Stirling Moss talked him into fielding two cars in Goodwood's 1957 Glover Trophy - he qualified his car on pole at an unofficial record speed of 97.96mph, and led the race. But then both his Vanwall and team-mate Tony Brooks' ignominiously broke their throttle linkages. Only Tony would finish, in 6th. Although he set the lap record at 1 min 29.6, all Tony Vandervell would say was "I told you so" as he stumped out of the paddock.

went on lap seven. Moss led from Brooks in the Vanwalls, but first Stirling, then Tony, retired with broken throttle linkages. Lewis-Evans came through to win from Fairman and Flockhart.

Britain seemed to be doomed to remain in the second division of motor racing, an idea confirmed when Connaught folded a few weeks later when its long-time backer withdrew his support. In the middle four months of the year, however, everything changed. Aston Martin won the Nürburgring 1000 Kms; at Le Mans, five Jaguar D-types started and took 1-2-3-4-6, while Lotus came of age with two class wins and the Index of Performance.

Cooper dominated Formula 2 - Brooks winning the first race at Goodwood. Vanwall won three of the last four World Championship races. Even BRM won a couple of non-Championship races - after Colin Chapman had sorted it.

British enthusiasts looked for auguries in the sky.

By the time that the Easter Monday Meeting came around again, the whole picture had changed. Maserati had withdrawn from racing and Moss had won the Argentine GP in a mid-engined 2-litre Cooper-Climax.

Things had changed at the circuit as well. The car tunnel under the circuit had been built, together with a pedestrian tunnel under the Lavant Straight - and a large grandstand constructed next to the Super Shell building. There were new Members' car parks on the infield with a capacity to take 1,600 cars. The paddock had been

A difference in philosophies – Willie Greene's blaring ex-Reg Parnell/Peter Whitehead 1955-56 Ferrari 555 *SuperSqualo* demonstrates Maranello's agricultural approach to racing car engineering, in stark contrast to Philip Walker's Lotus 16, Colin Chapman's ultra-light last hurrah of a front-engined racing car – which Graham Hill once described as being "all held together by bungee cords and sticky tape"... and both with 2½-litre 4-cylinder engines. Revival Meeting 1998.

'Sacré bleu!' indeed, as French star Jean Behra's luckless BRM season of 1958 gets off to almost the worst possible start. His Type 25 car with new-fangled front end was working brilliantly as he led the first three laps of the 1958 Glover Trophy. But on the fourth he lost the brakes entering the chicane... He was able to walk away, gingerly.

rearranged with new paddock sheds and a competitors' enclosure, separate from the paddock, established. With new viewing from the infield, the capacity of the circuit increased from 60,000 to 70,000. Motor racing was causing excitement.

Vanwall gave the 1958 Glover Trophy a miss, but Ferrari sent a Dino 246 for Hawthorn. Bernie Ecclestone entered Connaughts for Lewis-Evans and Scott Brown, both of who would be dead by the end of the year. There were Coopers for, among others, Maurice Trintignant, Moss, Salvadori and Brabham and Lotuses for Graham Hill and Cliff Allison. BRM sent cars for Jean Behra and Harry Schell.

Behra led off the line but, coming through the chicane for the third time, he managed to both demolish his BRM and most of the wall. That let Hawthorn into the lead with Brabham following. Moss, on pole, had stalled on the line and had just gone past Brabham when a con-rod broke. Hawthorn then won as he pleased with only Brabham on the same lap. Moss and Hawthorn had shared joint fastest lap - one in a mid-engined, one in a front-engined car. The case for putting the engine behind the driver had not yet been proven.

The entry for the Lavant Cup for F2 cars was dominated by Coopers, but then Cooper and Lotus were virtually the only constructors making customer cars for the Formula. It came down to a fine duel between Brabham (Cooper) and Hill (Lotus). Jack led for the first ten laps, Graham for the next four, then the Cooper slipped by on the 15th, and last, lap to win by 0.2 seconds. Hill's was the finest drive ever made in a front-engined Lotus formula car and the first sign of his real talent.

Looking down the entire programme, including the support races, one finds that there are no fewer than 27 British drivers who would end their careers having raced in Formula 1. They range from occasional privateers to future World Champions - and the list naturally includes Stirling Moss.

Easter came early in 1959, so both the Formula 1 and Formula 2 seasons kicked off at Goodwood. The F2 Lavant Cup saw a fierce competition between the Coopers of Brabham and Salvadori, with Jack taking the flag by 0.2 seconds. Coopers would win every F2 race in 1959.

In the Glover Trophy there were BRMs for Harry Schell and Joakim Bonnier, works

Lotus 16s for Graham Hill and the American amateur, Pete Lovely, and David Piper's private car. Cooper was most strongly represented with cars for Moss, Brabham, Salvadori, Masten Gregory and Bruce McLaren. There were also four Maserati 250Fs, which were there just to make up the numbers. Coventry Climax had built a new engine, also designated FPF, which had a new block and a capacity of 2495cc - the earlier FPF could not be stretched beyond 2207cc. This remarkable unit would set the seal on British dominance of Formula 1.

Schell led from Moss, Bonnier and Brabham. Then Brabham moved up to third on lap three. The positions remained static for some laps before Moss made his move on Schell with Brabham following soon after. Moss eased to an easy win ahead of Brabham but, at long last, the BRMs were showing real promise. They were powerful, they handled sweetly and they were reliable. Still, it had taken seven years since the announcement of the Formula for BRM to achieve this.

Vanwall was not present having withdrawn from racing after winning the inaugural Constructors' Cup in 1958. By the end of 1959 many of the teams which had formed British motor racing since the War had gone. Ready to take their place was a new generation (and Cooper) and, as they stamped their authority on single-seater racing, Goodwood assumed an importance even greater than it had enjoyed before.

After qualifying on pole on a wet practice Saturday, Franco-American driver Harry Schell's BRM Type 25 is hotly pursued through St Mary's by Moss's Walker Cooper and Jack Brabham's works car - both by this time packing full 2½ litre Formula 1-sized Coventry Climax engines. This 1959 International '100' ran out Moss-Brabham-Schell, and next day Stirling was sampling the front-engined BRM.

Left: Easter Tuesday, 31st March 1959 - the sensational moment in which Moss acknowledges the signal board brandished by BRM mechanic Arthur Hill as he accelerates Jo Bonnier's Type 25 BRM towards Madgwick Corner. His previous timed lap of 1 min 26.4 has been the first ever 100mph Goodwood lap.
Overleaf: at the start of the Richmond Trophy race, 1998 Revival Meeting - Joaquin Folch gets away first from the grid in the Maserati 250F, from Tony Smith's Aston Martin DBR4 (1), Steve O'Rourke's BRM Type 25 (3) and Willie Greene's Ferrari 555 *SuperSqualo* (17).

GRASS ROOTS

Goodwood developed a unique style of club racing in the 1950s. International meetings were open to all, but Members' Meetings were for the amateur with his or her road car. The shape of Members' Meetings altered, as racing itself did, but the BARC was hesitant to change because it never lost sight of the ordinary member.

Let's go racing! Comparisons are odious - but the Goodwood set-dressers spared few pains to capture the spirit of Meetings gone by - the control tower (**above**) and the paddock (**right**), Revival Meeting, 1998.

As a case in point, there was no single-seater race at a Members' Meeting until 1960. Brands Hatch frequently ran programmes devoted entirely to Formula 3, with ten or more races catering for all levels of competitor, from special builder to rising star. At Goodwood, Formula 3 cars raced only at International meetings.

Other circuits welcomed the 750 Motor Club with their Austin and Ford specials - the specials still raced at Goodwood, but in handicaps as part of the overall scene.

Apart from the Brooklands Memorial Trophy, Goodwood had little truck with championships. There was the odd exception - such as the '*Autosport*' Production Sports Car Championship - but, as with Formula 3, it did not take place at a Members' Meeting.

Goodwood took the view that each race was an individual event. Racing was for racing's sake - it was not to rack up points for a title.

Then again, almost every race at Goodwood was organised by the BARC; the only exceptions were a handful of meetings run by the Vintage Sports Car Club and the Bentley Owners' Club - both of which had a connection with the Brooklands tradition. Other circuits were leased to a variety of clubs, each with its own agenda; Goodwood did not, but remained an essential part of the jigsaw which made up British motor racing. It was the diversity of approaches by different clubs and circuits which allowed motor racing to grow.

Even by 1950 Freddie Richmond had invested in some serious Motor Circuit infrastructure - a wartime RAF building supports the new timekeepers' box and judges' tower overlooking the start of the up to $1^1/_2$-litre sports car race. John Cooper's Cooper-MG (**far side**) will waltz to a handsome win from Jim Mayers' Lester-MG (22) in 2nd - BARC Members' Meeting, 12th August 1950.

Today we know what the term 'club racing' means, but many of the support races in International meetings were essentially club events with an entry virtually identical to that at a Members' Meeting. Things began to change around 1955, but there was still a handicap in the programme of the 1956 Easter Monday Meeting, even if it was only for the big boys like Parnell, Salvadori and Brabham.

The Members' Meetings at Goodwood chart both the rise of British racing and the changing, improving, conditions in the country as a whole.

At the first Members' Meeting in 1949, all seven races were handicaps, but by the second meeting in May 1950 the BARC received so many entries that it was able to run five scratch races together with five handicaps. This 50/50 mix would be typical of a Members' Meeting in the early 1950s. It is noticeable, however, that the scratch races were all run first. It was a fact of life that a fair percentage of the runners in a scratch race would be in no fit state to run twice, even though the races were over only three laps.

Most of the cars had not been run over long distances for more than ten years and when they had been run they had been driven in a way to conserve fuel. Further, the fuel available was low-octane 'pool' petrol and an engine with a high compression ratio was not happy on that.

Virtually every car in the entry lists of early Members' meeting was British. The majority were under 1500cc and some idea of the flavour of the entry for the second Members' Meeting can be gauged by the fact that there two handicaps solely for MGs.

The Jaguar XK120 had been unveiled at the 1948 London Motor Show, but on the home market they went only to selected drivers on the understanding they flew the flag for Jaguar. It was not until 1951 that an XK120 ran at Goodwood.

When the first Members' Meeting took place in August 1949, sports cars like the Austin-Healey 100, Triumph TR2, MGA and AC Ace were still years away. MG was making the TC, a pre-war design, but most were sold to the States. Colin Chapman was building a Ford special for trials driving. John Tojeiro had yet to make his first MG special, Brian Lister was playing his vibraphone in jazz bands and Elva was not even a twinkle in Don Nichols' eye. Cooper had made half a dozen or so sports cars based on the chassis of their 500cc car. Morgan's one four-wheel model had a pre-war Standard 10 engine and HRG was making its 1939 models in small numbers. There were a handful of Allards and Frazer Nashes, and that was about it.

Above: nuts and bolts to the fore as race mechanics labour in untold luxury beneath the Duke's corrugated-iron and timber paddock shelters, welcome sanctuary from the driving rain of Easter Monday 1950.
Below: while new structures went up at Goodwood, the more traditional shape of late summer haystacks remained part of the scenery through the early 1950s.
Overleaf: spirit of an age - Rowan Atkinson wiggle-woggles his illustrious Aston Martin DB2 'XMC 76' through the chicane ahead of Amanda Stretton's Frazer Nash Le Mans Replica at the Revival Meeting, September 1998.

In 1952 the government eased restrictions on the home market and the percentage of total production which was available to the British driver went up from a third to half. This freeing of restrictions created a buyer's market almost overnight. Niche manufacturers such as HRG, Allard, Lea-Francis and Dellow took a dive and all were virtually dead in the water within a couple of years.

But the relaxed restrictions also brought forth marques such as Lotus, Lester, Turner and Tojeiro, which were cars designed for a specific purpose. Up until about the end of 1952 there had been motor racing and a generic activity called 'motor sport'.

For example, when Derek Buckler built his first car, he used it in races, hill climbs, driving tests, trials and rallies. A Maserati was for motor racing, but a Buckler, a Dellow, an MG or an HRG was used for motor sport. And a well-driven general-purpose car could be successful in any category, given that so many races were handicaps. But you couldn't go mud-plugging in an Austin-Healey.

Motor sport began to divide into specialist activities. Dellows had been especially successful in trials but, from about 1952, trials cars were made which could not be used for any other purpose except, perhaps, to undertake a very uncomfortable ride to a muddy hill in winter.

Twins beneath the skin - Tony Crook teeters his post-war Frazer Nash Le Mans Replica through Woodcote Corner ahead of R.F. Peacock's pre-war Frazer Nash-BMW 328 - the Le Mans Rep's 6-cylinder Bristol engine being based on BMW's 1930s design, secured as war reparations for the bombing of Bristol's Filton factory.

At a Members' Meeting, you would drive up in your TR2. The scrutineer would look under the bonnet. If you had a tuning kit fitted, you started after the guy who did

not. After you had passed the cursory scrutineering, conducted along the lines of "Have you got slack in your steering and four wheels and brakes?", you then joined the queue to have your number painted on. A skilled signwriter equipped with a long brush and a padded stick applied on the numbers in a paint that could be washed off after the meeting. The club informed members that they should not leave the circuit with racing numbers on their cars.

Big, brutal, but to many beautiful (no, not the driver, the car). Nobody dozed in the sun when British Hill-Climb Champion and Monte Carlo Rally winner Syd Allard's Anglo-American 'J2' - with its 5.4-litre Cadillac V8 engine - came thundering by.

The chaps got round this stricture by putting white roundels on their cars and wiping off the numbers. The roundels said that you'd been racing - and that was a useful chat-up line.

Looking through the race entries one sees the arrival of the Jaguar XK120, the Austin-Healey 100 and Triumph TR2 which could compete in what we would now call Production Sports Car Racing, but which Goodwood insisted on calling Marque Racing.

Coming to the market were saloons which could be raced - and if something can be raced, it will be. In the earliest days one would see Morris Minors and VW Beetles racing against Aston Martins, in handicaps. It was not until the 1960s that there were scratch races for saloons at Members' Meetings; except the usual description was not 'saloons' but 'four-seat closed cars'.

Grids swelled at Goodwood, as they did at other circuits. It is fascinating to look through the entry lists (and results) of the Members' Meetings and to pick out the new names and makes which suddenly emerge. Suddenly Colin Chapman is driving a Lotus, or Eric Broadley and his Lola Mk1 make their first appearance. You find Archie Scott Brown and Lister, and even Keith Duckworth in 1957. Along the way you come across every British driver who would later become an international star.

Here are names like Don Parker, who would win a record 126 Formula 3 races and three Championships, and Les Leston, who would pip Don to the Championship by half a point in 1954. And Paul Emery whose Emeryson cars would compete in races run to the first four World Championship formulae, a feat equalled only by Ferrari (although it has to be admitted that Ferrari was rather more successful).

These were all semi-professional drivers, but the names of the amateur clubmen also tell a story. They were competitors who began in a modest way, but whose talent shone through. Some went on to become top drivers, but notice also the names of

Overleaf: Members' Meeting memories including Bill Mason (**top right**) in his Bentley, 1952, set against the background of the V.S.C.C's 21st birthday celebrations in September 1955, featuring a 1904 Phoenix basket forecar - hardly a Vintage sports car, but presaging an era in which Goodwood events would present fascinating vehicles of every vintage.

"In my teens I joined the Bognor Regis Motor Club, who supplied marshals for the BARC at club meetings. I did it to get close to the cars, and I certainly did! I used to marshal at Madgwick, and I'd wave my flag from behind a couple of straw bales, with the cars passing within six feet of me: crazy, when you think about it now. But the big moment for me was before the meeting began, driving the few hundred yards down to the post - actually getting, briefly, onto the track itself. I honestly didn't entertain any hopes of being a racing driver then. It was all just a dream...

In my rosy memories, I don't remember it being particularly sunny. It was usually pretty cold out at my marshal's post. But, whatever the weather, the atmosphere was always special: everybody smart, jackets and ties. It was a social event."
DEREK BELL

"I remember sitting having a picnic in the paddock with Ruth Ellis and her boyfriend David Blakely and several of the other drivers. Ruth had brought a hamper and masses of sandwiches - it wasn't long before the night she shot Blakely dead outside a pub in North London. She was a very nice girl, lots of fun: we often used to go to the club she ran in Knightsbridge - but I thought Blakely was an unpleasant man. He didn't treat her very well."
JOHN COOPER

"The Goodwood atmosphere we all remember was partly due to the setting. It was such a beautiful place that even the most thick-headed racing driver couldn't fail to be impressed."
RAYMOND BAXTER

"My father made motor racing films for Shell, and raced his vintage Bentley for fun. There was a famous moment when his 4½-litre Bentley and George Burton's somehow came through the Goodwood chicane side by side. I used to go with him - having three sisters it was a special treat when he and I went off on our own racing - and if he wasn't competing he'd get a photographer's pass. In those days nobody seemed to mind if there was a small boy watching with a photographer. It was an enormous privilege to stand on the mound by the chicane and be able to see everything."
NICK MASON

"John Morgan retired in 1962, and I became Clerk of the Course. One of my jobs was to give any novice drivers a thorough talking-to before their first race, to make sure they didn't do anything too stupid. One young man was having his first race in a new Mini, and managed to turn it over in the chicane, rolling it up into a ball. He was unhurt, but I found him standing by the wreck in the paddock, crying his eyes out. I tried to cheer him up - 'At least you're all right... The car can always be mended'. 'You don't understand', he said. 'It's Mummy's car. She'll be furious.' "
GRAHAM MACBETH

If a BARC member owned it
then he could conceivably race
it - and a very great number of
them did just that at Goodwood
through the 1950s, as this mixed
bag at the chicane amply
demonstrates.

John Coombs and David Murray. Coombs was a useful driver, but would also become a distinguished entrant whose drivers included Graham Hill and Jackie Stewart. David Murray would found *Ecurie Ecosse*, a private team which won Le Mans in 1956 and 1957 and whose future drivers also included Jackie Stewart.

Tony Gaze and Dickie Stoop, the men who had originally discovered the possibilities of the the perimeter track at RAF Westhampnett, were other Goodwood regulars. The competitor lists include Jack Sears, outstanding in saloons and sports cars - and the 1963 British Saloon Car Champion. There is Kenneth McAlpine, who funded the Connaught project from his own income; Ian Raby, who became a Formula 1 privateer; Tony Rolt, who would win Le Mans in 1953; and Jack Fairman, a driver who would drive in Formula 1 and for Aston Martin.

Many drivers who matured into stars of varying brightness included Goodwood as part of their education. To their number must be added those who were fired by the idea of motor racing by first seeing it there - local heroes like David Purley and Derek Bell, and 1970 World Champion, Jochen Rindt, who had been sent to a language school

Above: some prominent names appeared on BARC Goodwood sign-on sheets: Bill Holt drove Connaught Formula cars, Dick Protheroe was the V-bomber nuclear base CO who shone in long-distance Jaguars, and as for Tony Brooks...

in Chichester to brush up his English but, between swimming, sailing and chatting up the local talent, was taken by friends to Goodwood.

Almost any major circuit can cite parallel examples, but there are two talents for which Goodwood can take most of the credit: Mike Hawthorn and Tony Brooks. It was their performances at Goodwood in the early stages of their careers which brought them to the attention of the patrons who advanced their prospects.

Mike Hawthorn's best drive of his rookie year was in the Leinster Trophy, held in Northern Ireland, but that was not much noticed in England. It was winning '*Motor Sport*''s Brooklands Memorial Trophy at Goodwood which brought him to the fore.

In Tony Brooks' case, Goodwood was even more influential. Tony says, "My father was a motor racing enthusiast, but what turned me on was reading Charles Mortimer's book, '*Racing A Sports Car*', where he explained how he had gone racing with a Healey Silverstone. I persuaded my mother that a Healey Silverstone would make an ideal shopping car.

"Ninety per cent of my non-professional races were at Goodwood because I was a member of the BARC. I'd drive down from Cheshire and put up in a B & B in Bognor Regis."

Tony raced his mother's shopping car only a handful of times before a chap called Duncan Hely noticed his smooth style and offered him a drive in a more competitive Frazer Nash. After perhaps 20 races Tony had raced a works Frazer Nash in the 1954 Tourist Trophy and been signed by Aston Martin.

By the time of the Members' Meeting of 26th March 1955, there were handicaps specifically for novices - in these events you find Morris Minors and Ford Anglias mixing it with sports cars. The car which dominated the entry list was the Triumph TR2, but there were also four Jaguar C-types and an Aston Martin DB3S, and the meeting also saw the competition debuts of the AC Ace and the Elva marque.

Two innovations at the 1955 Whitsun International were a Vintage Car Handicap and a three-lap handicap for celebrities. Not so long before, Vintage cars had been competing in mainstream events, now they were getting races of their own.

Below: wartime RAF Westhampnett hero Douglas Bader (**left**) at Goodwood, 1953. Bader was the epitome of gung-ho dynamism in all he did; having lost both legs stunting a Bristol Bulldog in 1931 he fought back to fly again in 1939 and became one of Fighter Command's most charismatic - if controversial - figures.

Beginners, please: six-time Grand Prix winner Tony Brooks and five-time Le Mans winner Derek Bell both began their motor racing careers at Goodwood - and both these fine and extremely popular drivers starred again at the Revival.

The Celebrity Handicap was a bit of a wash-out since so many entries scratched. Enthusiasts were therefore denied the sight of Peter Sellers and Harry Secombe driving their Jaguar Mk VIIs. The race was won by the enthusiastic comedian Richard 'Stinker' Murdoch (Rolls-Royce 20/25), from sports hero Chris Brasher (Jowett Javelin) and the film star John Gregson (Hillman Minx). The experiment was not repeated.

1955 was the year when the Coventry Climax FWA engine became widely available and drivers who had their eyes on Formula 1 switched over from the fast-fading Formula 3 to the 1100cc sports car class. They bought their Coopers and Lotuses and set to.

That suited the BARC down to the ground because of its emphasis on sports cars. From 1956, a typical Goodwood programme would have a scratch race for 1100cc sports cars, one for 1500cc sports cars (which, more or less, meant the same thing) and an unlimited sports car race. The other five events on the programme would be handicaps.

In 1957 there was a scratch race for cars up to 350cc. The BARC was always open to new ideas and so spectators saw a field of Berkeleys plus a Goggomobil entered by Rob Walker. This was another experiment which was not repeated, but at least it was an idea which was tried. And the Berkeleys and the 'Goggo' could always enter a handicap - and did.

The race came about partly because, in 1956, the entrepreneurial John Webb - who would become the supremo at Brands Hatch - ran a 322cc Astra van in a handicap at the September Members' Meeting. Webb came last, but set a new 350cc lap record and gained a lot of publicity.

There was a steady move towards scratch races in the late 1950s. When the Austin-Healey Sprite appeared, so there were scratch races for sports cars up to 1000cc with overhead valve engines, or 1200cc side valve. Sprites and MG Midgets came under '1000cc'; the other option was to allow people who had, say, a Lotus Seven with a Ford 1172cc side valve engine to run as well. The emphasis was on offering the maximum number of people a chance to compete.

Members' Meetings began to change, however, on 19th March 1960 when the

first single-seater race was included in the programme it was for Formula Junior, the direct ancestor of the modern Formula 3, except that no modern Formula 3 race has equalled the historical significance of that Members' Meeting.

For John Surtees, in a Cooper-BMC entered by Ken Tyrrell, it was his first car race. For Jim Clark, it was his first race for Lotus and the start of a legendary association. Three other drivers in the entry would all drive for Lotus in Formula 1: Trevor Taylor, Mike Spence and Peter Arundell.

At the end of lap one Surtees led with Clark inches behind and Taylor a little back. Clark took Surtees at Woodcote on lap two but Surtees passed at Woodcote on lap five; then Clark retook the lead. On lap six Taylor slipped by Surtees and the three circulated so close you could have thrown a blanket over them.

On the tenth, and last, lap Surtees out-fumbled Taylor to reclaim second. Peter Arundell, who had won Britain's first Formula Junior race at the previous year's Boxing Day Brands Hatch meeting, came fourth, but more than half a minute adrift.

Left: BARC Members' memorabilia - the British Automobile Racing Club's Year Book, 1956, and a much coveted windscreen sticker season pass from 1952.

Below: How it all began for the first-ever British World Champion Driver. John Michael 'Mike' Hawthorn in the pre-war 1½-litre 'TT' Riley owned and prepared by his father Leslie. He beat Tony Crook's post-war 'Nash to the '*Motor Sport*' Brooklands Trophy - and £50 prize - by one point, as the most successful driver at BARC Goodwood Members' meetings through 1951.

Arundell was driving a front-engined Elva-DKW, but it would not be long before he was in a works Lotus.

Formula Junior had originated in Italy and, in 1959, replaced the 500cc Formula 3 as the junior international formula. Typically, the Brits were slow to join but, by the end of 1960, if you didn't have a Lotus or a Cooper you might as well stay at home. Between them, they demoralised dozens of rivals all over Europe.

British racing at all levels was entering a Golden Age. Britain dominated Formula 1 and Formula Junior and you could see the stars of both at Goodwood. At a typical Members' Meeting, you would not only get a Formula Junior race, but scratch and handicap races for sports racing cars, production sports car and saloons.

Virtually every car on every grid would be British. All the best production sports cars were made in Britain, and the saloons weren't bad either. If you were in the 1100cc sports racing car class, you would only consider a Climax-powered car. Cars still looked standard - there was tweaking and tuning, but within limits.

Previous pages: in great shape - the immortal Frank Costin-styled Lotus 11 bodyform, Revival Meeting, September 1998.
Below: Miss Elizabeth Jones in her Austin-Healey 3000 before the start of the 10-lap marque scratch race at the Members' Meeting, 11th March 1961.

You could buy an Austin-Healey Sprite and drive direct from the showroom to Goodwood to run it in a handicap with Jaguars, Lotuses and Listers.

Since there was a total of 71 Members' Meetings with between seven and ten races

at each, it is impossible to give more than a brief outline of the overall trend, but one significant, and constant, strand was the contribution of women drivers to the meetings.

Ladies' Handicaps were run in 1955 and 1956 and then the girls were expected to compete with the boys. Most still competed in handicaps and, at Goodwood, the driver as well as the car was given a handicap.

There had been an attempt to run a women-only race in 1951, but only four entries were received.

Just four years on and these races were attracting healthy grids. The first Ladies' Handicap was won by a young woman in her first race. Her name was Pat Moss: she would become one of the greatest rally drivers in history, regardless of gender.

Some of the ladies would become celebrities in the motor racing world: Jean Bloxam, Bluebelle Gibbs, Nancy Mitchell and Hazel Dunham among them. International Rallies always had a Ladies' Cup and if a manufacturer took a win in that, it was splashed in all the advertisements.

There was, however, some contention when Robert Cowell, a former Spitfire pilot and a useful driver, made headlines by becoming Roberta…

Into the 1960s female drivers continued to make their mark. The glamorous Christabel Carlisle could be as quick as most in her Mini, and the equally glamorous Angela Taylor, kid sister of Lotus F1 driver, Trevor Taylor, became a works Ford driver in saloons.

Left top: greatness in the making, Mark 2 - Stirling's younger sister Pat Moss, taking time off from building a great name for herself in equestrian show-jumping, races an MG TF in Goodwood's 1955 Ladies' Cup event. She became the first great woman driver to win world-class International Rallies.
Left below: Mrs Pat Coundley in her Lotus Elite during the opening BARC Members' meeting of March 1961. Her husband John enjoyed considerable club and International racing success in Jaguar D-type and Lister-Jaguar sports-racing cars.

Overleaf top inset: potentially the greatest of them all - the wonderfully talented Christabel Carlisle poised to go to war in her trusty - and very successful - Mini during the 5-lap Handicap, Members' Meeting, 11th March 1961.
Overleaf lower inset: Lady's trophy, won by Mrs Lorna Doone Snow in her Jaguar XK120 Coupe, 18th June 1955 - '*Autosport*' commented " 'Our Lorna' handled her Jag with real verve!"
Overleaf main image: .Revival Meeting, September 1998.

"WHEN I WAS FIRST TAKEN TO WATCH A MOTOR RACE I SAID IT WAS SO BORING THAT I'D NEVER GO AGAIN UNLESS I RACED MYSELF. THE NEXT THING WAS I FOUND MYSELF RACING THE MINI THAT I'D BEEN GIVEN AS A 21ST BIRTHDAY PRESENT. ONE THING LED TO ANOTHER, AND BY MY FIRST VISIT TO GOODWOOD IN 1962, I'D BEEN LENT A 1000cc MINI-COOPER BY ABINGDON. I WAS STILL DOING MY JOB AS A PIANO TEACHER DURING THE WEEK AND RACING AT WEEKENDS. IN PRACTICE ON THE EASTER SATURDAY I THREW A TREAD ON THE VERY GRIPPY NEW DUNLOP SP TYRES WE'D BEEN GIVEN TO TRY. SO I DECIDED NOT TO USE THEM FOR THE RACE. THE WORKS CARS DULY THREW THEIR TREADS AND I WON: THE

"The prettiest car I think I ever 'dressed' must have been an exquisite XK 140, which won the Ladies' Race at Goodwood, notching up a lap record. I'd bought a Maserati racing wheel, very slim, and had it mounted with mother-of-pearl, by craftsmen. All the dashboard knobs, gear lever and brake handle were finished in the pearl. The car was navy and white, piped in navy and initialled, and in the boot were two beautifully fitting suitcases, one with fitted hair brushes, clothes brushes, mirrors and sewing gear. Such elegance, but oh, it was fun."
LORNA DOONE SNOW

NEWSPAPERS WENT A BIT OVERBOARD WITH THEIR HEADLINES ABOUT THE GIRL MUSIC TEACHER BEATING THE WORKS TEAM."   CHRISTABEL CARLISLE

Left: just like old times as
Anthony Williams' 3.8 Jaguar
Mark II saloon heels on port-
tack out of the Goodwood
chicane during the St Mary's
Trophy saloon car race - Revival
Meeting, September 1998.
Above right: BARC member's
pass window sticker. 1961.
Below right: humble set of
wheels, illustrious entrant.
Rob Walker's 293cc Goggomobil
was driven flat-out, nary a
gearchange, by Peter Coleby to
break the 350cc class lap record
set by John Webb with an Astra
van: his time 2 mins 46.4 secs,
51.92mph - May Members'
Meeting, 1957.

Other prominent drivers included Patricia Coundley, whose
husband, John, was a noted exponent of 'big banger' sports racing cars,
and Jean Denton, now Baroness Denton, a title earned for her work
in the motor industry. All had played their part in the history of the
Members' Meetings, which came to a close on 2nd July 1966.

Although Formula Junior/3 had been a usual feature of Members'
Meetings since 1960, the format at the July 1966 Meeting was back to sports
and saloon cars, with one token handicap.

Event One was a ten-lap Special GT race with an entry consisting of cars from
Diva, Austin-Healey, Triumph,
Morgan, Lotus, Ginetta, Marcos
and GSM. Only Triumph and
Morgan had been making cars
when the first Members' Meeting
took place. Next up was a ten-lap
saloon car race for cars up to
1000cc - with Mini Coopers
crowding the entry - followed by
a sports car race which again
included marques in the entry

which had been signposts to the British motor racing renaissance: Brabham, Mallock,
Merlyn and Chevron among them.

Race four was a Marque (Production Sports) event. with a 1001cc-3000cc saloon
car race next on the card; the final ten-lap scratch race was for Clubman's cars, mainly
Mallock U2s and Lotuses.

The very last race to be held at Goodwood, 1948-1966, was a five-lap handicap;
to the very end, Goodwood never lost sight of its roots at Brooklands. That swansong
race was won by the Lola Mk1 of veteran 'Dickie' Metcalfe, who had competed in the
very first Members' Meeting - and many in between.

It was a fitting way to bring to an end nearly eighteen years of a distinct, very
British, style of racing (on the day of the final meeting there were only a handful of
people present who were aware it was the end - not even all the members of the BARC
Council knew).

The Goodwood Members' Meetings left behind their own unique legacy:
Goodwood had not existed to breed champions, but to give Joe Average a chance, and
no other circuit in history has fulfilled its aims with such style and grace.

THE TOURIST TROPHY

When the announcement was made that Goodwood would host the Tourist Trophy on 13th September 1958, it marked the return of the Trophy to the motor racing calendar after an absence of two years. In addition, not only would the event be Britain's round of the World Sports Car Championship, but it would also be the final round, raising the possibility of a 'down to the wire' finish to the season.

The Tourist Trophy was first run on the Isle of Man in 1905 when the main rule was that fuel consumption was not to exceed 22.5 mpg. It was, therefore, a race designed to test touring cars under conditions which bore some resemblance to everyday motoring. The event was dormant between 1914 and 1922, when it became a conventional race.

Following 1922 the Trophy was not run again until 1928, when it took place in Northern Ireland, on the Newtownards road circuit, as a sports car handicap. It was transferred to Donington Park, in 1937-38, then revived once more in 1950, the event returning to Northern Ireland, on the Dundrod road circuit. Following the 1955 running, however, it was clear that Dundrod was inadequate for a top flight sports car race, and so again the Trophy went into abeyance until the news that it would be run at Goodwood.

From 1958 the World Sports Car Championship was limited to 3-litre cars and it was thought by many to be the year when Aston Martin would have a chance of the title. In previous years, competing in an

Left: deerstalker-hatted John Bolster of the BBC interviews Stirling Moss after Aston Martin's sensational Goodwood TT victory, 1959.
Above: the TT statuette presented to Graham Hill after his 1964 victory.
Below: on the grid of the final Tourist Trophy held at Goodwood in 1964 - the two AC Cobra 'Daytona's of Dan Gurney (21) and Phil Hill (22).

Eighteen years after young RAF pilots took their ease on Goodwood's grass, awaiting their call to action, Aston Martin's future Le Mans-winning driver pairing of Carroll Shelby and Roy Salvadori relax by the Duke's hydrangeas before the run-and-jump start of the 1958 Tourist Trophy.

unlimited formula, Aston Martin had always been handicapped by generally running 3-litre engines, but a superb win by Tony Brooks and Noel Cunningham-Reid in the 1957 Nürburgring 1000 Kms had shown the potential of the new DBR1/300, and in 1958 Stirling Moss was back in the team.

It was also confidently expected that even with their engines reduced to 3-litres, Jaguar D-types would remain competitive. In the event, however, the revised Jaguar engines had a habit of breaking con-rods. Aston Martin's best results were a win in the Nürburgring 1000 Kms (Moss/Brabham) and second at Le Mans with the Whitehead brothers' private DB3S. The DBR1/300 was the best car on the grid, until it broke down, outpowered by Ferrari.

Ferrari, therefore, had the Championship sewn up well before the end of the season and decided not to send a team to Goodwood. This was a bitter blow: the race was reduced from six hours to four - and only half points were awarded. Despite that, the home crowd still had a point of interest because Aston Martin was in a position to wrest second place in the Championship from Porsche.

Aston Martin fielded three DBR1/300s for one of the finest teams of drivers ever assembled. Stirling Moss shared with Tony Brooks, Roy Salvadori was paired with Jack Brabham, while Stuart Lewis-Evans drove with Carroll Shelby.

It cannot be said that there was much competition to Aston Martin, just two Jaguar D-types and a pair of Lister-Jaguars in the three-litre class. In fact, the only non-British entries were a couple of works Porsche RSKs. In 1958, the Tourist Trophy was a national event with the sort of field that could be seen at any main meeting in Britain.

The one entry of real interest was the new Lola 1100cc Mk1 which had made its debut at Brands Hatch a fortnight before. There its creator, Eric Broadley, had become the first person to lap the short circuit in under a minute. Unfortunately it had a puncture and since the whole thing was being done on a shoestring there was no spare wheel. The tyre had to be repaired in the pits. But then Eric, a quantity surveyor, had built his special simply because he couldn't afford to buy a Lotus.

While the Nine-Hour Race had not proved popular with the fans, the Tourist Trophy attracted a good crowd despite the poor entry. It would seem that British enthusiasts were prepared to turn up for four hours of Goodwood on a sunny day in late summer whereas night racing had no appeal. Possibly spectators had become more

"I always enjoyed long sports car races, because they'd go on for six hours or so, and you had something to get your teeth into - Grands Prix then only lasted a mere three hours or so."

STIRLING MOSS

sophisticated in the three years since the last Nine-Hour Race. In the interim Britain had leap-frogged from being a second division country in motor racing terms to winning seven of the previous ten World Championship races.

There was also the fact that the Tourist Trophy had become a British institution - and having the same name as the fabulous TT motorcycle races was no handicap. Unlike the Nine-Hour Race, the Tourist Trophy had a long and distinguished history. The two greatest drivers of the 1930s, Rudolf Caracciola and Tazio Nuvolari, had both won it (Nuvolari twice) and Stirling Moss already had three wins to his credit.

Less well remembered, but carrying a certain piquancy in the circumstances, was the fact that Freddie Richmond had been team manager and owner of the MG which Norman Black drove to victory in 1931. More than any other, that race had put MG on the map as far as the rest of Europe was concerned.

The story of the 1958 Tourist Trophy is soon told. The Aston Martins were harried

NEWS OF THE WORLD
SPONSOR THE
23rd R.A.C.
TOURIST TROPHY RACE
GOODWOOD
NEAR CHICHESTER, SUSSEX

SATURDAY, 13TH SEPTEMBER, 1958
Start 2 p.m. — Finish 6 p.m.
PUBLIC ENCLOSURES 7/6 (CHILDREN 4/-)
CAR PARKS 10/- and 5/-
Racing organised by the British Automobile Racing Club
Advance Bookings: 18 SOUTH STREET, LONDON, W.1

Above: everything about Glorious Goodwood was entirely seemly, although many enthusiasts and members could not stifle a ribald comment about the major meetings' sponsoring newspaper - the UK's leading Sunday scandal-sheet...
Left: Jack Brabham vacates the works Aston Martin 'DBR1/1' which he co-drove with Roy Salvadori to finish second in the 1958 Tourist Trophy. The DBR1's grille bars scream '1958' - they were removed before these same team cars disputed the 1959 event.

by Ivor Bueb's Lister-Jaguar for
the first ten laps, before Bueb
('Ivor the Driver') had an off,
damaged his steering and
retired. The three Aston
Martins then cruised home to an
easy 1-2-3, finishing a length
apart and four laps ahead of the
Behra/Barth Porsche. The result
put Aston Martin and Porsche
on 18 points each and they
shared runner-up position.

Left: Aston Martin's works
team pit signal tells the story
of the 1958 TT at Goodwood;
the three works DBR1/300s
are arrayed for the finish -
Moss first, Salvadori second,
Shelby third.

Five weeks later, the
immensely gifted Stuart Lewis-
Evans sustained burns in the
Moroccan Grand Prix to which he succumbed. He had been the third member,
with Moss and Brooks, of the Vanwall team which clinched the inaugural Constructors'
Cup at the Moroccan Grand Prix.

If the 1958 Tourist Trophy had been something of a high-speed demonstration for
the Aston Martin team, the 1959 race was a different matter altogether. Aston Martin
had initially decided to concentrate only on Le Mans, but then sent a single car to
Sebring to please the organisers - it failed to finish.

Then Moss persuaded David Brown, the owner of Aston Martin, to enter one car
at the Nürburgring because he believed he could win. In fact, he offered to pay all the
expenses if Aston Martin would loan him the works spare, which was not required for
Le Mans. It was basically a wager because Moss would keep the start and prize money.

A car was sent and, after his first stint, Stirling had shattered his old lap record on
virtually every lap. He was able to hand over to his co-driver, Jack Fairman, with a six
minute cushion over the works Ferraris and Porsches. After a further six laps Fairman
was forced to swerve to avoid a back marker and landed in a ditch. Alone, Jack man-
handled the car back onto the circuit - he lifted the tail on his shoulders to push it onto
the track - and brought it back for Stirling. It was now more than a minute down, but
Moss came through to win and give Aston Martin its hat-trick in the race. It was
described as one of the greatest drives in history, the stuff of '*Boy's Own Paper*', an epic
performance by a maestro pitted against every top driver in the world.

Three Aston Martins were entered for the 1959 Le Mans: two had slightly detuned engines, in the interests of reliability, while the Moss/Fairman car, which was to act as the 'hare', was tweaked to lure the opposition. Moss led the race at first, according to plan, but shortly after Fairman took over part of an air duct broke and found its way into the engine, which it wrecked. The surviving Aston Martins circulated at a steady pace waiting for the opposition to fall by the wayside, which it did. After 19 hours, the Ferrari of Olivier Gendebien and Phil Hill led easily before developing overheating problems and retiring. This allowed the DBR1s of Roy Salvadori and Carroll Shelby and Paul Frère and Maurice Trintignant to sweep home first and second.

The Moss/Fairman car had done its work and had over-stretched Aston Martin's opposition. With this win at Le Mans, Aston Martin suddenly found it was, with Ferrari and Porsche, capable of winning the 1959 World Sports Car Championship. Only the six-hour Tourist Trophy remained - and Goodwood had been kinder to Aston Martin than any other circuit.

Ferrari and Porsche both sent full-strength teams; Ferrari led with Tony Brooks, Olivier Gendebien, Phil Hill and Dan Gurney. *Ecurie Ecosse* had a D-type and a Tojeiro-Jaguar, and Aston Martin sent three works cars plus Graham Whitehead's private DBR1. Aston Martin had made up an extra car for Whitehead in recognition of the fact that he and his half-brother had finished second at Le Mans in 1958. The 1959

Above: the Italian job - Ferrari works team drivers Phil Hill, Dan Gurney and Tony Brooks discussing prospects, plotting Aston's home-game downfall, prior to the Sports Car World Championship-deciding Goodwood TT, 1959.
Below: an essential part of the scene - Freddie Richmond with Aston Martin works team drivers Jack Fairman, Carroll Shelby, Roy Salvadori and (**second from right**) Ferrari's Californian new boy, Dan Gurney - Tourist Trophy, 1959.

Tourist Trophy was all set.

Stirling Moss may have jumped the Le Mans-style start, but in any case there was no way that anyone was going to get near him. The greatest driver of his day was in the sweetest sports car, even if the gearbox left something to be desired. It is ironical that team *patron*, David Brown, had made his fortune from gears, yet Aston Martin ran the team spare with a Maserati transmission, which all the drivers preferred.

Moss handed over to Roy Salvadori, who duly brought the car into the pits, still in the lead, after two hours. Then came disaster.

The cock on the refuelling hose opened too soon and fuel splashed over the tail of the car before the nozzle could be inserted. The DBR1s were run with high ignition advance and it was common for there to be a blow-back through the exhaust pipe when the engine was switched off. As Salvadori did so, a blow-back occurred and the car went up in flames. Roy was engulfed and rolled out of the car to put out his burning overalls. But the Goodwood marshals dealt with the fire so efficiently that, afterwards, it was discovered that the car, foam-covered, its bodywork melted through in places, was still driveable.

It was the second time that Aston Martin had set fire to the pits at Goodwood. The fact that the company had its name on a fascia over the old pits for many years prior to rebuilding in 1998 often led to some gentle ribbing when Aston Martin used Goodwood for car launches and driving days.

Reg Parnell was team manager, and he and Moss conferred. The upshot was that the second Aston Martin was called in and Stirling took over. Jo Bonnier and Wolfgang Von Trips led in a Porsche RS60. But Moss was on a charge - and Moss on a charge was awesome. He was the greatest all-round driver in history: let's not mince words, we're talking about the best all-rounder there's ever been.

Twenty-five minutes after taking over the second Aston Martin, Stirling took the lead and stayed there, apart from falling

Previous page: best of British - Moss the Maestro in the works sports-racing car he came to regard as "my beautiful green Aston Martin" - the 1959 TT-winning 'DBR1/2', the self-same car which had previously brought Salvadori/Shelby victory at Le Mans. Some 39 years later he drove the same car with the same flair, style and exuberance in the Revival meeting.

Below: "Just to be serious for a moment, Reg, don't let your chaps set fire to my pits again"... Freddie and Aston Martin team manager Reg Parnell with uncharacteristically earnest mien (with Paul Frère beyond), before the start of the Tourist Trophy, 1959, when Aston's fuel supply would, indeed, ignite once more.

back to second when he made a pit stop for fuel and new tyres.

Masten Gregory, driving a Tojeiro-Jaguar for *Ecurie Ecosse*, had a famous accident at Woodcote. He arrived at the corner too fast, realised that he was going to hit the bank and so started to rise from his seat to sit on the back of the car. The Tojeiro thumped the bank and its rear end snapped forward enclosing the cockpit like a steel trap. Half out of his seat, Masten was thrown clear and suffered no more than a broken rib and a dislocated shoulder.

The official story was that Gregory had lost his brakes, but John Tojeiro reckons that he overdid things because he was fired up by the times set by his co-driver. His co-driver was then relatively unknown, but his name was Jim Clark - he was in only his second full season of racing and had gone to Goodwood as a fan of Masten Gregory (who could be mighty in sports cars). The young Scot was astonished to find that he could lap the Tojeiro quicker than Gregory, giving him the confidence that he, too, could be a top driver.

Ferrari had mix and matched its star drivers, entering Tony Brooks and Phil Hill each into two of the three cars. Brooks was sent out to catch the Von Trips Porsche because if he could get the *Testa Rossa* up to second, Ferrari would tie with Aston Martin for the World Sports Car Championship.

Three litres of Ferrari against 1.6 litres of Porsche. One of the greatest drivers ever against an excellent craftsman - Brooks was sublime, but it should never be forgotten how good Porsche was in the 1950s when it was running cars with roughly half the engine capacity of its opposition. Porsche has never been better, winning races outright - and what was a 1.6-litre car doing ahead of Ferrari at Goodwood?

Furthermore, the Porsche was so nimble and reliable that it could be wildly overdriven. It was ideally suited to going sideways round

Above: the advantage of youth, as Phil Hill's latest model factory Ferrari 250TR/59 is waved inside inside Ron Flockhart's three-year old *Ecurie Ecosse* D-Type Jaguar into the second apex at St Mary's - Tourist Trophy, 1959.
Below: "Sorry, Freddie"... Aston Martin do it again - on the fuel hose Brian Clayton has knocked the tap open too soon and an exhaust blow-back has ignited their leading car 'DBR1/3' with Salvadori in the cockpit - Tourist Trophy, 1959.
Bottom: ...and then the blaze spread to the Aston Martin pit's fuel supply!
Overleaf: a patched up 'Salvo' after the conflagration.

"THERE WAS AN ENORMOUS WHOOMPF! AND I SAID TO MYSELF, 'THIS IS FUEL'. I CAME OUT OF THE COCKPIT LIKE A JACK-IN-THE-BOX, KICKING THE HEADS OF THE MECHANICS WHO WERE CHANGING THE FRONT WHEELS. A QUICK-WITTED ST JOHN AMBULANCE MAN SMOTHERED ME IN HIS COAT, BUT MY RIGHT SLEEVE AND GLOVE WERE STILL BURNING, SO HE WHIPPED OFF HIS HAT AND PUT THEM OUT WITH THAT. BY THE TIME I'D GOT BACK FROM THE FIRST AID TENT STIRLING HAD TAKEN OVER

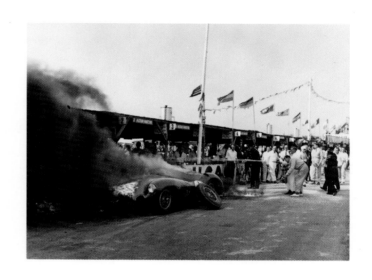

"The whole Aston Martin pit was on fire, and when the fire brigade had put it all out I took one look at the car I'd been driving and realised its race was over." STIRLING MOSS

THE SECOND-PLACED CAR AND WAS DRIVING IT TO VICTORY TO CLINCH THE CHAMPIONSHIP FOR ASTON MARTIN."

ROY SALVADORI

Goodwood's curves, while the Ferrari had to be driven more circumspectly. Brooks ate into the Porsche's lead on the straights, but never quite enough to claw back the time the little silver car gained on the corners.

Von Trips kept the Porsche ahead and crossed the line two seconds ahead of the Ferrari. 'Taffy', as Von Trips was nicknamed, had ignored the optimistic advice from Tavoni, the Ferrari team manager, that he should slow and let Brooks pass him. Jo Bonnier, co-driver to Von Trips, had also held out a 'slow' to Brooks.

So Moss won the 1959 World Sports Car Championship for Aston Martin, just as he had won it for Mercedes-Benz in 1955. Moss is sometimes called the 'greatest driver never to have won a World Championship', but he won two. And when he won them every top driver was competing in sports car racing.

Stirling Moss captured the Championship by two points from Ferrari with Aston Martin taking all the credit. Aston Martin celebrated by withdrawing from racing, just like Vanwall the year before. It seemed that every time that Stirling won a Championship for a constructor, he did himself out of a drive.

The 1959 TT was perhaps the most important race ever held at Goodwood. As well as deciding a World Championship, it was broadcast on television and radio, and the BBC rearranged the scheduling of its Saturday afternoon sports programmes to keep its listeners, not just enthusiasts, abreast of the drama. It was a race that brought the sport alive to people who previously had had no interest.

When Aston Martin withdrew, the World Sports Car Championship became a backwater, lingering on for a couple of years, but it was finished. Top drivers no longer felt that they needed to compete on a regular basis and the names of complete unknowns began to appear in the results.

Goodwood was quick to latch on to the next major trend and in 1960 the Tourist Trophy was for GT cars run over three hours. The World Sports Car Championship was still being run, but soon GT racing would take its place. The BARC and RAC got there first.

The most notable feature of the 1960 TT entry list was that every car in the 1300cc class was a Lotus Elite and

Above: retrieved from the ashes, a fire-damaged sign from the Aston Martin pits.
Below: tragedy averted - Edgar Barth's speeding works Porsche RSK passes the collapsed wreck of the *Ecurie Ecosse* Tojeiro-Jaguar from which Masten Gregory was thrown at the instant of its head-on crash into the Woodcote bank. He escaped with broken ribs and shoulder after scrambling half out of the car an instant before the shattering impact.

every entry arrived, all 11 of them.

Stirling Moss in Rob Walker's Ferrari 250GT SWB went into the lead after the Le Mans start and stayed there. In the view of many people, the 250GT SWB is the best car Ferrari has ever made, since it was equally at home on road and track, had the chassis of the sports racers, and yet was a well-sorted road car. That is not an accusation often made against Ferrari road cars of the 1950s. Roy Salvadori in an Aston Martin DB4GT harried Moss for a while and then had a puncture. Innes Ireland in the second Aston Martin entered by John Ogier took up the pursuit.

After two hours the position was Moss (Ferrari), Ireland (Aston Martin), Salvadori (Aston Martin), Colin Davis (Ferrari), Graham Hill (Porsche) and Jo Schlesser (Ferrari). Davis was the son of S.C.H. 'Sammy' Davis, Freddie Richmond's co-driver in the 1930 BRDC 500 at Brooklands, which they won.

Ireland's race was effectively over when his exhaust pipe came loose, but Moss was anyway uncatchable and it is said that he even turned on the car radio to listen to the BBC commentary on the race. Stirling cruised to his sixth win in the Tourist Trophy ahead of Salvadori and Ireland. Graham Hill brought his Porsche-Abarth Carrera home

Below: Goodwood's finest hour. Despite misfortune, fire, foam and Ferrari, the mission is accomplished for Aston Martin: Moss takes the chequered flag and the marque is World Sports Car Champion - Tourist Trophy, 1959.
Overleaf: blast from the past in his 1961 TT-winning *'Berlinetta'* for Stirling Moss, co-driving chocolate magnate Clive Beacham's ex-Rob Walker/Dick Wilkins team car with Mark Hales in the one-hour Revival TT Celebration - this car being a sister to the Maestro's similarly liveried 1960 TT-winning Ferrari 250GT 'SWB'.

fourth to win the 2-litre class, defeating many bigger cars in the process.

The Lotus Elite class was won by Peter Lumsden and Chris Kerrison from Graham Warner in his car registered 'LUV 1'. They were within sight of each other at the flag having touched at the chicane close to the end. The Elite of Mike Parkes and Sir Gawaine Baillie suffered a puncture while leading the class.

Before the 1961 TT race, the organisers ordered a special cake with seven candles on it. Stirling Moss was on the entry list and few doubted that he would win his seventh Tourist Trophy. Clark, Salvadori and Ireland were in lightweight Aston Martin Zagatos entered by John Ogier, who had also been John Tojeiro's backer.

The senior class was actually fairly thin, and the only other realistic opposition was Mike Parkes who, like Moss, was in a Ferrari 250GT SWB. At the time, one would not have put serious money against Parkes getting a result: he was a very quick driver and actually set fastest practice lap. The 2-litre class featured Graham Hill in a works Porsche, various private Porsches and Morgans, a TVR, an MG, a TR3, an AC Ace and, Heaven forfend, a Sunbeam Alpine, the ultimate hairdresser's car.

Lotus Elites dominated the 1300cc class, but there was one interloper, the Alexander-tuned Turner entered by Michael Christie, a noted hill-climber and one of Freddie Richmond's best friends. This was a one-off built to publicise his Alexander Engineering Company, then a leading supplier of tuning kits.

Mike Parkes was the first away, followed by Clark, Salvadori and Moss. Stirling was second by the end of the first lap and took the lead from Parkes after 17 laps. Mike was quick, but heavy-handed. Stirling was also quick, but he was smooth. The race was won in the pits because Mike rooted his tyres. Everyone did, except the maestro Moss, so he disappeared into the distance. Stirling duly received his cake in the shape of a number seven. He had won the Tourist Trophy for the seventh time, but would not return to the Tourist Trophy since he would crash at Goodwood the following April.

In 1962 the TT race was reduced to 100 laps, roughly two hours on a dry run. The entry was greatly strengthened over the previous two years, with five Ferrari GTOs, for a start, three Aston Martin DB4 Zagatos, and three Jaguar E-types including Dick Protheroe's famous 'CUT 7'.

Jim Clark (Aston Martin) got the best

Left: John Goldsmith in the 1960 Aston Martin DB4 GT Zagato leads Simon Draper's 1963 Aston Martin Project 214 during the RAC TT Celebration race, Revival Meeting, 1998.
Right: Graham Hill in the works Porsche-Abarth Carrera clipping the Woodcote apex - Tourist Trophy, 1960.
Overleaf: the BBC's omnipresent John Bolster, in the pits watching the Ferrari team, (**main picture**) and live and on the hoof (**inset**), 1959.

"ONE OF MY MOST ENJOYABLE RACES AT GOODWOOD, PARADOXICALLY, WAS ONE IN WHICH I FINISHED MILES BEHIND. IT WAS THE 1961 TT, AND I WAS DRIVING A LOTUS ELITE BELONGING TO THE JAZZ MUSICIAN CHRIS BARBER. THE CAR HADN'T HAD ANY PROPER PREPARATION FOR A THREE-HOUR RACE, AND I WAS IN THE PITS SOON AFTER THE START TO CURE OVERHEATING. THEN THE THROTTLE JAMMED OPEN AS I ARRIVED AT THE CHICANE AND I ONLY JUST MANAGED TO SORT THAT OUT. SEVERAL MORE STOPS WERE NEEDED TO GET THE CAR HANDLING PROPERLY, BUT ONCE THE CAR WAS ALL SORTED, IT BEGAN TO GO PERFECTLY. I HAD NOTHING TO LOSE, AND SO I DROVE TOTALLY FLAT OUT, THOROUGHLY ENJOYING MYSELF, FOR TWO HOURS. I FINISHED LAST, 25 LAPS BEHIND THE WINNER IN MY CLASS, AND YET IT WAS ONE OF THE BEST RACES OF MY LIFE."

SIR JOHN WHITMORE

"The first Goodwood broadcast I did was the 1950 Easter Monday meeting, and later on we did TV too. I worked from the commentary box above race control opposite the start line, with Robin Richards describing the scene out at St Mary's, and later on we had John Bolster in the pits."

RAYMOND BAXTER

Piece of cake: having just won the last of his fabulous record seven RAC TT races - and his fourth in succession at Goodwood - Moss, the garlanded Golden Boy, takes delivery while Freddie Richmond presides, August 1961.

start, but was soon passed by the GTOs of Ireland, Surtees and Hill. On the second lap Surtees moved into the lead and shortly afterwards Parkes, who had had a poor start, passed Hill to take third. On lap 62 Surtees came up to lap Clark for the second time. Always the gentleman, Jimmy moved over and lost it on Madgwick's notorious bumps, where cars go light. John couldn't help but ram him and both cars were out, crunched against the safety bank. They walked back together, Jimmy contrite and John philosophical. "That's motor racing", he said.

Innes Ireland inherited the lead and held it from Parkes and Hill, Parkes went in pursuit and made a mistake which let Hill by into second. Ireland slowed to conserve his tyres - Goodwood was notoriously hard on tyres. Hill was catching him at a rate of three seconds a lap and finished a mere 3.4 seconds behind after two hours of racing. It had been a thrilling race with great drivers and with the front-runners in evenly matched cars.

There were two main stories in 1963, one on the track, the other in the pits: during Friday practice, the police arrived in strength to arrest one of the competitors in the main support race (for Formula Junior cars), in connection with the Great Train Robbery, but when they got there, the driver in question - Roy James - was nowhere to be found...

There were also some forced absentees from the Tourist Trophy itself. In 1963 the race had a particularly strong entry, led by six Ferrari GTOs, one of them driven by Roger Penske, for Luigi Chinett's North American Racing Team.

A disappointment to the crowd was the exclusion of two AC (Shelby American) Cobras due to insufficient clearance between the steering arms and the wheels. The decision pleased nobody, but motor racing is a technical sport, it's not show biz.

Aston Martin entered two of its special project DP214 models, but the scrutineer threw out new, wider, wheels which had been fitted. The team had Bruce McLaren and Innes Ireland in the cars, though they were powerless to do much since the cars were skittish on the more narrow tyres which reduced the track by four inches. Ireland had equalled Graham Hill's pole position time on the wide wheels, but was moved back on the grid since only his 'narrow tyre' times were counted.

For the first time at Goodwood the start of the Tourist Trophy was on a normal grid as the RAC had banned Le Mans-style starts on safety grounds (Le Mans itself would

"A young man called Roy James turned up at the first meeting of 1963, rocketed away, set fastest lap, and attacked the leader - literally: both went off. James' car was wrecked, but he turned up at Brabhams on the Monday with a wad of cash asking them to mend it. This kept happening, and rumours started about the source of his money. After the Great Train Robbery, at the TT meeting in August, the police turned up for Roy while the FJ cars were out practising. I took them down to his stall, but when we got there it was empty... After his arrest his FJ was advertised in '*Autosport*' 'as driven to several wins by Roy James, who is currently too busy to race it'."

GRAHAM MACBETH

Tense, poised, clock ticking down: it's Jimmy Clark and the Essex Racing Stable Aston Martin DB4GT Zagato - ten seconds to the start, and the outside bank at Madgwick Corner awaits... Tourist Trophy, 1962.

continue to feature them until 1969 when Jacky Ickx made a point of going slowly to his car so he could strap himself in - safety harnesses had appeared).

First off was Graham Hill, in a Ferrari GTO entered by John Coombs in conjunction with Maranello Concessionaires. Ireland was next up with Parkes (in a sister car to Hill's GTO) third and McLaren, in the other Aston Martin in fourth.

Ireland tried to take Hill at Woodcote, spun and flat-spotted his tyres. Hill took to the grass and Parkes took the lead. Ireland pitted for tyres and rejoined a lap down, but right behind Parkes on the road. Despite the difference in their positions, they went at it hammer and tongs until they both spun at Woodcote, and Hill went into the lead. Parkes, however, was ahead on pit stops.

Hill reeled in his team-mate, who appeared to slow since the deal, allegedly, was that he and Graham would split the prize money. The Coombs/Maranello Ferraris

Pace not haste - the Maranello
Concessionaires team's Ferrari
250GTO receives rapid service
under Colonel Ronnie Hoare's
vociferous direction (in blazer
under pit sign), with Graham Hill
set to resume his seat and hustle
on to victory in the 1963 Tourist
Trophy.

therefore took a 1-2 and Roy Salvadori did well to bring his Jaguar E-type home third
only a lap down. McLaren's Aston Martin retired with a dropped valve and the
exuberant Ireland finally finished seventh.

The final running of the Tourist Trophy at Goodwood was in 1964, when the event
was for sports racers. There was growing interest in 'big-banger' racing which would
lead to the Can-Am Cup in North America and the less-successful *Interserie*
championship in Europe. The entry was divided into two parts: sports racing cars,
with a minimum capacity of 1,600cc and a class for GT cars of at least 2-litres. The
latter had a special point of interest. Shelby American '*Daytona*' Cobra coupés were in
the hunt for the GT Championship and in Dan Gurney and Phil Hill had two of the
finest drivers of the day. They were backed by three open Cobras.

The biggest engines in the race were 5-litre units and this was becoming a
problem. Tyres were getting wider by the month, so cornering speeds were
increasing, and it was clear they would increase even more.

Bruce McLaren was driving the '*Jolly Green Giant*', a Formula 1 Cooper with a
sports car body and a 4-litre Oldsmobile engine, at a time when there was a 1500cc
Formula 1. He led the early laps from Dan Gurney's Cobra and Denny Hulme's
Brabham BT8A-Climax. On lap 8 at St Mary's, Innes Ireland spun his Ferrari
250GTO, Tony Lanfranchi braked to avoid him and John Surtees (Ferrari 250GTO)
rammed into the back of Lanfranchi's Elva, which became a launching ramp. The
Ferrari took off over the top of the Elva and rolled. Surtees was taken off to hospital
with severe concussion.

McLaren suffered a slipping clutch and Clark, driving the difficult Lotus 30, led from Hulme, the Elva of former Lotus F1 driver, Trevor Taylor and Graham Hill's Ferrari 330P. Hill spun at Woodcote, came back on a charge and took the lead while Clark was in the pits being refuelled. The Lotus was suffering fuel pick-up problems, but Clark was flying and nearly caught Hill. Then Clark's front suspension began to fall apart. Hill therefore

won back-to-back Tourist Trophies. David Piper in a Ferrari 250LM was second, a lap down, and Dan Gurney edged Shelby American closer to the GT title by taking third.

That was the end of Goodwood's run of seven Tourist Trophies. Despite featuring stars of the calibre of Hill, Clark, Gurney and Surtees, the 1964 race had attracted only a small crowd. Worse, there was the problem of cornering speeds. Goodwood had suffered its share of serious accidents, and each one had deeply affected Freddie. What if Surtees' Ferrari had bounced off the Elva in a different direction? What if it had gone into the crowd, the enthusiasts who made Goodwood what it was? He began to consider the future of the circuit...

The following year, the Tourist Trophy transferred to Oulton Park, but the interlude when the TT was run at Goodwood is remembered as the Golden Age of the event - a classic race held at the one circuit in Britain which could provide the right sense of occasion.

Above: so much money in the bank - Jimmy Clark has spun the Essex Racing Stable's DB4GT Zagato while trying to give John Surtees' Bowmaker team Ferrari 250GT racing room at Madgwick - 1962 Goodwood TT. Soon Robin Benson's 250GT 'SWB' will spin into them both, inflicting further damage.
Below: Bruce McLaren's Cooper-based McLaren-Oldsmobile V8 struggles for traction off the line in the '64 event, Jim Clark and Graham Hill beyond in Lotus 30 and Ferrari 330P.

Overleaf: grid start of a different nature - the Sussex Trophy race for the great classic sports-racing cars of 1956-60 blasts off during the Revival meeting. Willie Green's JCB 'pontoon-fendered' Ferrari 250TR (9) and Stirling Moss's Aston Martin DBR1/300 (of course bearing his favourite number 7) lead away from Martin Brundle in John Coombs' famous yellow 'Shortnose' D-Type.

TOP OF THE WORLD

1961 was the year that the 'rear-engined revolution' was won. Previously, only Cooper and Porsche had run rear-engined - actually, mid-engined cars - but Jack Brabham's 1959 World Championship changed everything. Lotus and BRM both took the rear-engine route in 1960 and although Ferrari continued to concentrate on front-engined cars, they ran a rear-engined F1 prototype at the Monaco Grand Prix in May.

Only three years previously, Britain had yet to win a World Championship race, but the Glover Trophy at the 1960 Easter Monday Meeting attracted a field worthy of a Grand Prix and every car, and almost every driver, was British. Ferrari was absent, sure, but Ferrari was a make-weight in 1960.

Above: Revival Meeting, September 1998 - American star Danny Sullivan, former Tyrrell Formula 1 works driver, later Indianapolis 500-winner, won the 1½-litre Formula 1 Glover Trophy in Duncan Dayton's 1962 Lola-Climax Mark IV, his first-ever drive in a 'wingless' racing car. "It feels as if it's got a flat tyre, all the way round..."
Right: expatriate Briton, the Hon. John Dawson-Damer flew his much-loved Lotus-Climax 25 all the way from Australia for the revival of the circuit where he had been an avid boyhood spectator. Unafraid of the dirty-hands bit, 'JDD' rebuilds his own Cosworth DFV and Coventry Climax engines.

Cooper entered a car for Bruce McLaren - Brabham was adding lustre to an otherwise thin field at Pau. Tony Brooks was loaned a Vanwall and BRM had entries for Graham Hill, Dan Gurney and Jo Bonnier. There were private Coopers for Stirling Moss, Harry Schell, Roy Salvadori and Chris Bristow. Bristow was a newcomer of extraordinary promise who underlined his potential by putting his car on pole. Team Lotus entered Alan Stacey and Innes Ireland in the new rear-engined Lotus 18.

The main story of the 1960 Glover Trophy is a brief tale: Innes Ireland's Lotus took the lead soon after the start and stayed there, with Moss hounding him all the way and everyone else falling further and further behind. There was nothing Moss could do except hope that Ireland would make a mistake, which he did not.

In pursuit, Moss took four seconds off the old lap record to leave it at 102.13 mph. He and Ireland lapped the entire field up to the fourth-placed man, but Innes took the flag by 2.8 seconds. Almost unnoticed in the excitement, Bristow was third, ahead of Bruce McLaren.

There was a similar scenario in the Lavant Cup where Ireland had a Formula 2

Sudden stardom - Innes
Ireland, Team Lotus works
number one following Graham
Hill's defection to BRM, revelled
in the stunning performance of
his new rear-engined Lotus 18s,
beating Moss's Walker Cooper in
the Formula 1 Glover Trophy
and his Walker Porsche in the
Formula 2 Lavant Cup - Easter
Monday 1960.

version of the Lotus 18 and Moss was in Rob Walker's works-loaned Porsche 718.

Again, Ireland kept his head, this time beating Moss by 6.4 seconds.

The Glover Trophy was Lotus's first win in Formula 1 and Innes Ireland was

unknown to the public at large. Next morning photographs of the Moss/Ireland duels

were on the front page of national newspapers. Just like Mike Hawthorn after the

1952 Easter Meeting, Innes woke up to find himself famous.

At the first round of the World Championship, the Monaco Grand Prix, Stirling

Moss turned up in a Lotus 18 and gave Lotus its first Grand Prix win. Cooper, shaken

by the new Lotus, fielded a new car, the T53 'Lowline', which would take Jack Brabham

and Bruce McLaren to 1-2 in the World Championship.

Sadly, Chris Bristow and Alan Stacey, both drivers with enormous potential, would

lose their lives in the Belgian Grand Prix two months later. Such was the wealth of

Right: smoking permitted - Formula 1's front-liners blast off the line in the 1960 International '100' race for the Glover Trophy. Newboy sensation Chris Bristow on pole in his Yeoman Credit Cooper; Moss in the Walker car; Bristow's veteran team-mate Harry Schell and Innes Ireland in the new works Lotus 18.
Below: wide-angle lens required - bold photographers mark the Madgwick Corner apex as Stirling Moss tries his hardest in the R.R.C. Walker Racing Team's Formula 1 Cooper to catch Innes Ireland's fast fleeing new rear-engined Lotus 18. By the end of the day Stirling will be asking Rob Walker to buy a Lotus.

British talent coming through the ranks, however, that their deaths were not the disastrous blow they would have been to French or Italian racing. Jim Clark and John Surtees would have their first Formula 1 drives within weeks of the tragic race in Belgium.

For the time being, the 1960 Lavant Cup would be the last Formula 2 race at Goodwood. At the end of 1960, the 1500cc Formula 2 became Formula 1. Formula Junior was now the class below Formula 1, but was barred to graded drivers. Just as in 1952, when Formula 2 became the World Championship class, races run to the highest category proliferated.

When the 1500cc Formula 1 was first proposed, the Brits opposed the move, and continued to oppose it until it was clear that they were wasting their time. This led to the two British engine builders, Coventry Climax and BRM, being behind with new engines. It also led to Britain staging a rival series, the Inter-Continental Formula, which was for cars up to 3-litres. In effect, it was a series for surviving 1960 Formula 1 cars.

At the 1961 Goodwood Easter Meeting, the Lavant Cup was run to the Inter-Continental Formula. There was a field of only nine, but it included Moss, Graham Hill, Brooks, Salvadori, Surtees, Gurney and McLaren. To keep the record tidy, there

was also Chuck Daigh in a Scarab and privateer Geoff Richardson in an obsolete Cooper. Moss (Cooper) came from behind to overtake McLaren (Cooper) on the last lap of 15, to win by 0.6 seconds, with Hill (BRM) 20 seconds behind.

The Inter-Continental Formula fizzled out after just five races. All were won by Moss or Brabham in 'Lowline' T53 Coopers. Brabham was contracted to Cooper, but Moss could have chosen to drive a Lotus. In fact, Stirling loved his Cooper, which is a point to ponder when considering the merits of the Lotus 18 and the 'Lowline'.

The feature Formula 1 race, the 1961 Glover Trophy, saw Surtees win in a private Lotus 18. Moss, in a similar car, had easily been quickest in qualifying, but his engine had gone off towards the end of the race. Surtees, however, had led from the start and had resisted all of Moss's efforts to overtake when Stirling still had a healthy engine. It is all too easy to forget how good Surtees was. Actually, 'good' is a weak word; he was sensational.

Although John had begun racing cars in 1960, at a Goodwood Members' Meeting, car racing was fitted in between winning two motor-cycle World Championships for MV Agusta. Surtees had already won the 1961 Lombank Trophy at Snetterton so, at Goodwood, he had taken his second Formula 1 win from fewer than a dozen starts on four wheels.

Behind Surtees came Graham Hill (BRM), Salvadori (Cooper) and Moss (Lotus). Everything looked rosy for the Brits in Formula 1, but Ferrari had taken the new 1500cc Formula 1 seriously, and had two lines of V6 engines ready. Further, these were

Above: the day of the front-engined Grand Prix car is well and truly shading into dusk as Jo Bonnier's best efforts in the powerful BRM Type 25 make no impression upon the rear-engined designs ahead - Easter Monday 1960.

Right: heads up for the first full-blown 1¹/₂-litre Formula 1 race to be held in Britain - Moss (Walker Lotus 18), Surtees and Salvadori (Bowmaker-Yeoman 'Lowline' Coopers) and Graham Hill (works BRM-Climax) poised for the International '100' - Easter Monday 1961. Only 14 starters - but still a good race - which eventual seven-times motor-cycle World Champion John Surtees will win.

fitted amidships in chassis designed on British lines. Ferrari had actually bought a pair of Coopers which were fitted with four-cylinder Ferrari engines and run in a couple of races under a front, *Scuderia Eugenio Castellotti*.

The Ferrari Tipo 156 '*Sharknose*' had a relatively crude chassis, but at least 20% more power than the trusty four-cylinder Coventry Climax FPF unit. The British had a thin time in World Championship events in 1961, except on two occasions when Moss demonstrated his genius and won at Monaco and the Nürburgring, and in a further five non-Championship F1 races.

Things seemed to be better for British teams by the Easter 1962 meeting at Goodwood. V8 engines from BRM and Coventry Climax had begun to appear with selected teams. Goodwood therefore ran two Formula 1 races, the Lavant Cup for four-cylinder cars, and the Glover Trophy for all-comers.

The Lavant Cup attracted mainly privateers and was won with ease by Bruce McLaren in a works Cooper. The Glover Trophy was the race which ended Stirling Moss's glittering career.

Exactly why Stirling crashed remains a mystery. The only footage comes from an amateur 8mm cine film; the photographic evidence is inconclusive. Stirling crashed at St Mary's, on the far side of the circuit from the pits, away from most photographers, who were concentrating on the start and finish of races.

At the time Stirling was trying to unlap himself after paying a visit to the pits to sort out gear selection problems. An eye-witness of the crash declares that Moss had had gearchange problems on previous laps and the car was out of gear when the crash occurred. That would explain why Stirling could not control his car.

He was driving a Lotus designed around a Climax four-cylinder engine which had been converted to take a V8 Climax unit. Colin Chapman himself had looked at the conversion and had basically declared that the rear end of the car had the rigidity of a sponge. Moss had previously had gearchange and throttle problems with the car, both symptoms of a flexing chassis and/or poor engine installation.

That has to remain a theory, one of several, although Stirling himself has admitted it is a distinct possibility. Whatever, the fact is that the career of the greatest driver of his day - some say the greatest driver ever - ended at Goodwood on Easter Monday, 1962.

Since Stirling is the most patriotic of Englishmen, a man who had to search his conscience before driving foreign cars, it is a terrible irony that Easter Monday that year also fell on St. George's Day.

Overleaf: the changing order. Graham Hill will end this season of 1962 as World Champion Driver, while Stirling Moss will end this day gravely injured and comatose in intensive care, his glittering frontline career at an end - Easter Monday, 23rd April 1962. On the right waits Graham's 'stackpipe' BRM P578, poised for victory.

"I've always said I remember nothing about my crash at St Mary's. I do remember a couple of things, though: a party the night before, because I met a bit of crumpet there, a South African girl. Then the next morning, as I was reversing my Lotus Elite out of the Fleece Inn I caught the exhaust on the foot of the gate and pulled it off. I also remember taking a friend of mine, a polio victim called Paul Bates, round to meet the drivers - he was an amazingly brave man: he'd come in his ambulance with his breathing apparatus. But that's all. All the rest of the weekend is just a blank.

The next time I was at Goodwood was some 13 months later to do some laps in a Lotus 19 and decide whether I should start racing again. As I went round Fordwater and into St Mary's I wondered if it would all come back to me and solve the mystery of the crash, but it didn't. It was just a piece of track. Even when I watched the newsreel film of the accident, I still felt nothing.

In fact, believe it or not, I only found out, just before the 1998 Revival, exactly where I'd crashed. I was down there doing a piece for TV, and I said 'I don't really know where I crashed'. There was no 'X marks the spot'! And the chap I was doing the piece with said, 'There. It was just there'. So now I know, roughly."

STIRLING MOSS

"The last time I marshalled was Easter Monday 1962, the day Stirling crashed. I was at Madgwick as usual: he crashed at St Mary's, so I didn't see anything, but it all went terribly quiet. Our only means of communication was one of these 'What happened?' machines left over from the war - you know, you crank, crank, crank with a handle. Nobody would say anything. If there was a bad accident in those days nobody would say anything, so that's how we knew it was bad." DEREK BELL

Previous spread, main picture: the best of care at St Mary's approach, mid-afternoon, Easter Monday 1962. Third from right is an anxious 'Pa' Moss - the days when he eagerly helped prepare his son's Cooper '500' here suddenly seeming long, long, past...
Left: Graham Hill brandishes the Glover Trophy after his first-ever outright race win in Formula 1, Easter Monday 1962, the Duchess and John Morgan to the left.

It is easy to forget how precocious Stirling was. He was signed to lead the Jaguar team on the day before his 21st birthday, and so became the youngest driver in history to lead a works team. At the time of his accident he had won 35 Formula 1 races as well as the Mille Miglia and the Targa Florio, the Nürburgring 1000 Kms (four times) and the Tourist Trophy on seven occasions.

Graham Hill went on to win the Glover Trophy that Easter Monday. It was Hill's first outright Formula 1 win and he was six months older than Moss. Stirling ended his career at the same age that Damon Hill first drove in Formula 1.

Hill subsequently took the 1962 World Championship from Jim Clark and Bruce McLaren. Anglophone drivers filled the top ten places in the final table and British makes filled the top four places in the Constructors' Cup.

As British motor racing grew in stature, so the races at Goodwood grew in quality. British teams ruled the roost and teams and drivers preferred to spend their Easter Bank Holiday at Goodwood. They liked the place, they liked the hospitality, and they liked the easy atmosphere. Organisers of rival races on the Continent had to dangle very large purses to entice them to cross the Channel.

The organisers of the Pau Grand Prix in 1963 did just that, and attracted both Team Lotus and the Rob Walker team. Still, Goodwood had the reigning World Champion Graham Hill, Bruce McLaren in the 1963 Cooper - so new that it was unpainted - and Jack Brabham in his Brabham BT3. The British Racing Partnership entered Innes Ireland and Jim Hall, each in a Lotus 24-BRM. Hall would make his name as an outstanding driver/designer with his Chaparral sports racing cars and more than 30 years later would make a welcome return to Goodwood, at the Festival of Speed.

There may have been only ten starters, but it was a select field which promised excellent racing. Hill led most of the way until part of a fuel tank worked loose and blocked his supply. This let Ireland into the lead and he took the flag with McLaren just five seconds adrift.

The '*News Of The World*' took over sponsorship of the feature Formula 1 race at the 1964 Easter Monday meeting (for years, the Formula 1 race at the Easter Monday Goodwood

Bright new hope. Just like Mike Hawthorn's brand-new Cooper-Bristol, which had raced unpainted on Easter Monday 1952, and Stuart Lewis-Evans's '*Tooth-Paste Tube*' Connaught, which had raced unpainted at Easter 1957, Bruce McLaren's brand-new Cooper T63 was too new for paint here on Easter Monday 1963. One crucial difference - it didn't win.

meeting had, of course, been the Glover Trophy, named for D.M. Glover, head of United Lubricants Ltd). For once there was no clash of dates with the Pau Grand Prix, which was a week later and anyway held for the new 1-litre Formula 2. Ferrari entered two cars, but scratched.

Though John Surtees would win the 1964 World Championship for Ferrari, and Ferrari would win the F1 Constructors' Cup, this was not quite the blow it might have been. A field that was led by BRM, Lotus, Brabham and Cooper and virtually every top Formula 1 driver could not be called disappointing.

Ferrari would come good in 1964, but that was largely due to the influence of John Surtees and Mike Parkes, their two fine British driver/engineers. Britain had a stranglehold on Formula 1. Every car and engine in the 'News Of The World' Trophy was British, as were the top six finishers.

Goodwood was reaping what it had sowed. It had played a significant part in the British motor racing renaissance as both a racing circuit and a test facility. The presence of Ferrari would have been welcome, but it was no longer essential to the running of a top-class event.

"Jackie's time was what!!!!"
An uncharacteristically aghast
Jimmy Clark is told by Team
Lotus senior mechanic Dick
Scammell that BRM's Scottish
newboy, Jackie Stewart, has just
knocked 1.2 seconds off the
World Champion's 1964
Goodwood lap record - practice
for the Formula 1 'Sunday Mirror'
International Trophy race
(Goodwood's last), Easter 1965.

Graham Hill (BRM) led most of the way, with Jim Clark (Lotus) in hot pursuit and Brabham third. Brabham displaced Clark on lap 28 when Jimmy's clutch began to give trouble. Soon afterwards, Jack suffered a broken wheel rim, a tyre came off and he was pitched into a banking, fortunately with little damage to car or driver.

Hill seemed to have the race in the bag, but two laps from home a distributor broke. That let Clark through to win followed at a respectful distance by his team-mate, Peter Arundell, and Trevor Taylor in a customer Lotus.

Winner of the Chichester Cup for Formula 3 cars was Jackie Stewart in a Cooper-BMC run by Ken Tyrrell. It was their second race together, and their second win. One of the most famous relationships in motor racing began when Robin McKay, then the Goodwood circuit manager, told Ken Tyrrell that he should take a look at Stewart. Ken took Robin's opinion seriously and had invited Jackie to a test he was conducting on Cooper's new Formula 3 car, and Bruce McLaren was there to shake it down and set a time.

When it was Stewart's turn, he promptly demolished McLaren's time. Bruce went out again and went faster still, then Jackie beat Bruce's time. Ken was convinced and, in 1964, Jackie raced in 12 major Formula 3 events, winning 11 and finishing second with a slipping clutch in the remaining race.

In the Formula 1 race at the 1965 Easter Monday Meeting, now called the '*Sunday Mirror*' Trophy, Jackie put his BRM on pole, 0.8 seconds ahead of team-mate Graham Hill, and Jim Clark, who had recorded an identical time to Hill. Again, like Surtees, it is easy to forget how blindingly quick a driver Stewart was.

Hill led from Clark during the opening laps while Dan Gurney (Brabham) claimed third ahead of Stewart and Brabham. Clark went ahead on lap six, but Hill hung on until his engine started to lose power, which let Gurney and Stewart into second and third respectively. They both retired on lap 37, and that allowed Hill and Brabham to inherit their places with McLaren's Cooper in fourth place, and lapped.

The race, taken as a whole, was an uncanny predictor of the 1965 World Championship season. Clark dominated, winning seven of the ten rounds. Hill was runner-up, the BRM being less competitive than in previous years. Gurney ran strongly, but had to settle for a string of podium finishes.

Stewart fulfilled his early promise and won the Italian Grand Prix. Brabham had a dreadful season and seriously considered retirement (yet would win the 1966 World Championship) while Cooper slid down the order.

The races held under the 1500cc Formula 1 are arguably the greatest held at Goodwood. Every top team save Ferrari took part and Ferrari was often not a top team. Every major driver took part - not just a case of a Fangio or a Farina being hired

Above: sheer genius times two. Double World Champion Driver Jimmy Clark and Team Lotus chief Colin Chapman enjoy the fruits of yet another Formula 1 race win - Easter Monday, 1965. **Below:** merged as one - the man is the legendary Jim Clark, the machine the marvellous Lotus-Climax Type 33, both victors in Goodwood's last contemporary Formula 1 race - Easter Monday, 1965.

'I was watching the final Member's Meeting of 1963, when I saw this young Scot called J.Y. Stewart driving an elderly *Ecurie Ecosse* Cooper Monaco. And he was clearly very fast. I got in my car and drove across to St Mary's and watched him for several laps. He really stood out. On the Monday after the meeting I gave Ken Tyrrell a call and told him what I thought of young Stewart. Ken phoned Dumbarton the same evening and invited Jackie to come and test the new F3 Cooper. Jackie had never driven a single-seater before, but he seemed very relaxed. Bruce McLaren, who was then Cooper's Number One Formula 1 driver, took the car round to set a benchmark time, and then Jackie went out - and went

"Goodwood was immensely important to me. It was responsible for introducing me to Ken Tyrrell, and the first place I drove a single-seater car. Ken had an immense reputation as a talent spotter, even in those days, and Jim Clark told me he was a good man to go with. All that changed my life."

JACKIE STEWART

"I remember Jimmy Clark bringing the young Jackie Stewart up to the house the first time Jackie raced here, and seeing the two Scots, one already Champion, standing in the Long Hall. My grandfather told me who Jackie was and said, 'Mark my words, he'll be Champion too one day.'" THE EARL OF MARCH

half a second faster. Naturally Bruce wasn't amused, and he went a bit quicker too. And so Jackie replied by going faster still. Ken called a halt then. And John Cooper, who'd been watching down at Madgwick, came back and said to Ken, 'You can put those watches away. This boy's quick...' Jackie would have made it anyway, but I'm glad I made that phone call."

ROBIN McKAY

The start of the 1965 Easter Monday F1 race. Graham Hill (**left**) in the BRM - team-mate Jackie Stewart was on pole - alongside ultimate winner Jim Clark in the Lotus-Climax.

to do the odd five-lap *Formule Libre* race. These were drivers and their teams using the Easter Monday Meeting as a dress rehearsal for the World Championship season.

1965 was the apex of Goodwood's history, but it would all be over by July 1966.

From the beginning of 1966, Formula 1 went from 1500cc to 3-litre cars and when that happened, non-Championship races began to disappear. At least, they did in Europe; nominal F1 races proliferated in Southern Africa. Only three European non-Championship events would be run in 1966.

Most teams were struggling to find a suitable engine for the new formula. Even when they did, costs were escalating at such rate that most circuits could not pay sufficient starting money to make the effort worthwhile for the teams. In a reverse of 1961, when races which had previously been run to Formula 2 were able to be run to Formula 1, so organisers reverted to Formula 2.

"The last time Formula 1 cars raced at Goodwood was Easter Monday 1965. I was driving for BRM then, and it was the first time I'd been on pole position in a European F1 grid. In the race my engine failed, but not before I'd broken the outright lap record. Jimmy Clark did exactly the same time - 1:20.4, 107.4 mph - and so officially we two Scots hold the Goodwood lap record for ever. I'm very proud of that."

JACKIE STEWART

In addition, technology was producing ever wider tyres and cornering speeds increased dramatically. That was not only true of Formula 1, but especially so of a new breed of 'big banger' sports-racer, known as Group 7 in Europe, Can-Am in North America.

At the 1965 Easter Meeting, Jim Clark had set a new Formula 1 lap record at 1 minute 20.4 seconds, but had lapped at 1:20.8 in his Lotus 30 Group 7 car. The difference was the sheer bulk of the sports car over the delicate Lotus 33 F1, and the energy that would have to be dissipated should one leave the circuit. Since the 'big banger' sports racers had no upper limit on engine capacity, one didn't have to be Nostradamus to predict that there would be huge increments in power, representing a potential threat to safety, which was of paramount importance to the Goodwood organisers.

At the beginning of 1966, it was announced that there would be a 3-litre limit for sports cars at Goodwood. Soon afterwards, it was announced that there would be a reduced programme at the circuit.

The reason given at the time was that the Goodwood horse racing course had been granted more dates by the Jockey Club. The core reason was more complex, and involved Freddie Richmond, who had the last say whether Goodwood remained open or not.

One important factor was that Freddie was tired. In 1966 he was 61 years old and was ready to hand over the running of the Goodwood Estate to his son. The men with whom he'd run Goodwood, old pals from the Brooklands days, had either retired, or were about to retire. He did not have the same rapport with the new men in charge of the BARC - they were from a different generation. Running a race circuit involved an

Below: Jackie Stewart in his 1964 BRM P261 participates in the Dream Grid parade at the Goodwood Revival Meeting, September 1998.
Overleaf: Genuine ex-Goodwood veteran (that's the driver) Robs Lamplough in his glorious 1965-type Lotus-Climax 33 on the Goodwood Revival grid, Glover Trophy, 1998.

Time to play with - Jack Brabham demonstrates the understeer effect to the photographer as he hurls his Brabham Racing Organisation 1-litre Formula 2 Brabham-Honda BT18 through Madgwick Corner on the way to crushing victory in the final Goodwood Easter Monday International, 1966.

were from a different generation and there was an increasing amount of bureaucracy which was something he detested. Then there was the way that motor racing as whole was going, with its ever-increasing professionalism.

In short, overseeing the running of the Goodwood circuit was not the fun it once had been. There was a whole parcel of reasons why Goodwood closed in 1966 but, ultimately, it came down to the fact that Freddie did not wish to expend the energy and enthusiasm to solve the problems.

Before the crunch came, Goodwood held its traditional Easter Monday Meeting and, on the surface, everything seemed to be going swimmingly. The feature race, the second Sunday Mirror Trophy, was run to Formula Formula Two and the line-up reads like the sort of menu that some people pocket after a memorable meal.

Savour a selection: Jim Clark, Peter Arundell, Jack Brabham, Denny Hulme,

Richard Attwood, Frank Gardener, Jackie Stewart, Jacky Ickx, Graham Hill, Bob Anderson, Jo Siffert, Trevor Taylor, Jochen Rindt, Alan Rees and David Hobbs. Twelve past or future World Formula One Championships were on the grid - and the supporting cast wasn't bad either.

Since the BARC 200, due to be held at Oulton Park, was cancelled due to snow, Goodwood became the opening meeting of the Formula Two season. Denny Hulme (Brabham-Honda) was quicker than Jack Brabham during qualifying, but he dutifully followed his boss home for a Brabham-Honda 1-2. The works Brabham-Hondas dominated Formula Two in 1966 and won 12 of the 13 rounds. The last round was won, by a short head, by Jochen Rindt in a Brabham-Cosworth from Jack in his Brabham-Honda.

By early summer, Goodwood had closed. The BARC had already secured the use of Thruxton, another airfield circuit and one which was remarkably similar to Goodwood in length and broad style. In 1980, for example, the fastest lap of any class in testing at Goodwood was always two seconds below the lap record at Thruxton. It was uncanny, it was true for every class from Formula Ford 1600 right up to Formula Two.

The BARC was allowed the use of other circuits, notably Silverstone, before it occupied Thruxton in 1968. The club began with a fresh agenda at a new circuit. Motor racing changed dramatically in the 18 months or so that Goodwood closed and Thruxton opened. There was the arrival of Formula Ford 1600, for example, which opened motor racing to a new generation of drivers.

So Freddie left the circuit, and he also left the Estate for whose management he had never had much enthusiasm. He handed over the running of the Goodwood Estate to his son, the present Earl of March's father. Freddie retired to a flat in Mayfair where he and Betty lived a modest life. He confessed to a liking for Marks & Spencer's fine, microwavable meals. That was Freddie to the core - he was surrounded by some of the best eateries in Europe, but he shopped in Marks & Sparks.

Around 1980 he developed cancer of the bone, a condition which people normally die with, not of. He finally slipped his cable in 1989. He was a man of extraordinary gifts: car stylist, salesman, driver, team manager, photographer, model maker, journalist, artist and aviator, but perhaps his greatest talent was his gift for friendship.

If there is a Heaven, Freddie would have looked down on the 1998 Revival Meeting and he would have approved. It was the most relaxed, enjoyable, meeting anyone can remember, but that didn't happen by accident. Underpinning the proceedings was professional precision. That was Freddie's style, to work hard and never let it show.

TESTING TIMES

Almost nobody had gone to the final Members' Meeting on 2nd July 1966 with the knowledge that they would be present at the end of an era. The racing had been up to Goodwood's usual standards and the weather had been perfect. Although everyone knew that the annual programme would be shortened, and there would never again be Formula 1 or 'big banger' sports racers, there was still the September Meeting to look forward to - but it was to remain just a date in the calendar.

There was no closing ceremony at the last meeting, just a brief announcement a few days later. The news took time to sink in and, for many, it was not until they came to plan their Easter Bank Holiday the following year that they realised what they would be missing.

There would be no more easy access to teams and drivers in the paddock. No more picnics on a summer's day. No more being welcomed like a guest to a celebration of a common enthusiasm. There would be no more gatherings at The Richmond Arms or the pubs on the road back to London.

However, although motor racing at Goodwood might have ended, the circuit stayed in operation, as one of the busiest of all British circuits for testing, club sprints and single-stage rallies.

In fact, almost from its inception, Goodwood had been used for a variety of purposes apart from racing. As early as October 1949, for example, it played host to overseas journalists who were in England for the London Motor Show. In the days before international press launches, the Society of Motor Manufacturers and Traders (SMMT) sent cars to the

Left: aristocrat in his element - Lord March in his Lola-Climax Mk I, out amongst the Goodwood corn stooks.
Right: heroes both - former World Champion Driver Denny Hulme captured during pre-Monaco Grand Prix Goodwood testing in May 1974 with his 80-year-old father Clive Hulme VC, fresh in from his New Zealand home that morning to attend a Victoria Cross Association reception at Buckingham Palace. 'Denny the Bear' was absolutely a chip off the old block.

"I WAS 11 WHEN I WAS TOLD THERE WOULD BE NO MORE RACING AT GOODWOOD. I FELT PRETTY ANGRY, BECAUSE I DIDN'T UNDERSTAND WHY MY GRANDFATHER WAS STOPPING IT. I SUPPOSE THE MAIN REASON WAS LOSS OF INTEREST - HE'D DONE IT FOR 18 YEARS, HE WAS 65 YEARS OLD, HE HATED THE BUREAUCRACY AND HATED BEING TOLD WHAT TO DO WITH HIS OWN TRACK. THERE HAD BEEN A TERRIFIC ROW ABOUT THE KERBS AT THE EXIT OF THE CHICANE. HE'D HAD WATTLE FENCING AND THEY MADE HIM PUT SOLID KERBS IN, WHICH HE DIDN'T LIKE AT ALL: HE THOUGHT THEY WERE MUCH MORE DANGEROUS."

THE EARL OF MARCH

"The end was as sad as the start had been euphoric. Nevertheless, comfort was derived from contemplating that Goodwood had played a big part in raising the prestige of British drivers and racing cars from the doldrums of the 1930s to the world supremacy that both had reached 30 years later." FREDDIE RICHMOND

Geoff Duke lapping his 500cc Norton at 89.1 mph in April 1951 - Goodwood's only motorcycle event until the 1998 Revival.

circuit so that visiting journalists could sample them. Like so many aspects of Goodwood's history, there was a personal angle. Freddie Richmond was a Vice-President of the Guild of Motoring Writers in 1949 and would be made President the following year; his close friend, Tommy Wisdom, was a founder member. You can imagine the deal being done with the Guild and the SMMT over a convivial drink.

Journalists all over the world would make a note in their diaries to be at Goodwood. In the days before carefully leaked scoop photographs, and manufacturers offering heavy hints with concept cars, motor shows were full of surprises, even to the press. Furthermore, in 1949, Britain accounted for more than 50% of cars exported world-wide, so the Guild Day was an event with no recent parallel - the Guild Day continued at Goodwood until 1966.

In April 1951, Goodwood hosted its first and only motor-cycle meeting. 20,000 spectators arrived to see Geoff Duke lap his 500cc Norton at 89.1 mph - 'Bira''s outright record at the time was 90.38 mph.

There is some confusion about why the experiment was not repeated. One theory is that the crowd, mainly on motor-cycles, caused trouble on their way home, which embarrassed Freddie personally. At the time, however, Freddie went out of his way to praise the behaviour of the crowd, and the local police concurred. Besides, motor-cycles did not have a poor image, and Freddie himself had been an enthusiastic rider. Another theory is that there was some friction between the ACU (Auto-Cycle Union), who organise British motor-cycle meetings, and the BARC, but they had rubbed along well enough at Brooklands for years, so this seems unlikely.

In the absence of concrete evidence, there remains the possibility that the reason motor-cyclists were not invited back was one of safety. In 1951 Freddie was becoming increasingly anxious about the lap speeds which were being reached, and the top riders had been close to Formula 1 speeds, which themselves had led to the introduction of the chicane.

At the 1998 Revival Meeting, a motor-cycle race (the Lennox Cup) was included as a tribute to the original event, featuring no fewer than 18 Manx Nortons, and guest appearances by Barry Sheene and Damon Hill.

Prince Philip inspects an Aston-Martin shortly before the Nine-Hour Race in 1953, with Aston team manager John Wyer (**left**), and industrialist owner David Brown (**right**). There is a tale that, during one Glorious Goodwood, when Freddie Richmond had arranged for a Jensen 541 to be brought down to Goodwood, Prince Philip took it round the circuit for half a dozen laps. On his return, so the story goes, the Queen requested a go of her own...

In August 1951, the Southsea Motor Club ran its 'Speed Trials' from Lavant Straight to the start/finish line. It was the first event of a tradition which continues to this day. Car clubs have used Goodwood for sprints and single-stage rallies ever since. Although the number of events had to be cut back in 1998 as a trade-off to bring unsilenced racing back to Goodwood, club events are still held, and give grass roots racers the chance to follow in the wheel-tracks of Fangio, Farina, Hawthorn, Moss, Clark, Brabham, Surtees and Stewart. There is no other circuit in the world where that is possible.

A number of record attempts took place at Goodwood, starting in September 1952, when BMC celebrated the fact that the Morris Minor had been fitted with its Series-A (Austin A30) engine. The Minor completed 10,000 miles non-stop - the wheels never stopped turning. To achieve this the car was driven into a special rig towed by a Land Rover, and kept moving while mechanics refuelled it, topped up the oil and even changed wheels.

Other successful record attempts at Goodwood included two Ford Anglias completing 1,000 miles in 24 hours in 1955 - they averaged 40 mph and 40 mpg. Shortly after the 105E Anglia was launched in 1959, Ford staged a demonstration of 'a year's motoring in a week', when an Anglia covered 10,000 miles at Goodwood in under seven days. And in 1964 two enthusiasts surpassed a feat set by a Fiat 508S Balilia at Brooklands pre-war, when the Fiat had averaged 55.11 mph for 1,000 miles; at Goodwood a similar car averaged 55.22 mph - and that despite heavy rain.

On several occasions in the 1950s, Goodwood was used as a high-speed stage for rallies, including the RAC Rally. It also played host to a number of Vintage car gatherings, including one to celebrate the 21st birthday of the Vintage Sports Car Club.

Right: the day we went to Goodwood - any excuse to return to West Sussex in the sun would be eagerly snapped up: the Vintage Sports Car Club ran a well-supported Veteran and Vintage Car Rally there in May 1963.
Below: classic Bugatti beneath the Downs - 'Black Bess' sparkles, while Rolls-Royce loks down its nose...

Another huge gathering of Veteran and Vintage cars took place in 1963 when 300 cars from ten countries used the circuit for driving tests, a *Concours d'Elegance* and a grand parade.

No fewer than 1,100 Rolls-Royce cars gathered at Goodwood in 1964 to celebrate the 60th anniversary of the meeting between Henry Royce and the Hon. C.S. Rolls. Three years later, after the circuit had officially closed, Rolls-Royce and Bentley enthusiasts combined to organise the largest-ever gathering of the two marques.

The Goodwood circuit was also used as a film location: in 1954 Hammer Films chose it as a backdrop to a B-movie called '*Mask of Dust*' (or, in some markets, '*A Race For Life*'). The film, starring Richard Conte, was about a former racing driver who wants to make a comeback against his wife's wishes. Raymond Baxter provided the voice-over race commentaries and, among others, Stirling Moss, Reg Parnell, John Cooper, Alan Brown and Leslie Marr appeared as themselves.

Thirty years later, Goodwood featured in the racing scenes in '*Dance With A Stranger*', the film about Ruth Ellis, the last woman to be hanged for murder in Britain.

She shot her feckless lover, David Blakely, on Easter Sunday, 1955: Blakely had practised his new car, the Emperor-HRG, at Goodwood the day before and was due to race it on Easter Monday. Ruth Ellis ran a night club in London where motor racing people would often go when The Steering Wheel Club closed - she was a popular character with everyone and John Cooper remembers her laying on picnics at Goodwood; she had also helped Blakely finance his car.

One of the more unusual sights at Goodwood came at the 1957 Whitsun Meeting, when Belfast driver, Jim Meikle, demonstrated a Cooper Formula 3 car fitted with a pulse-jet engine: it made a lot of noise, but its performance was way below the claimed top speed of 160 mph. Another slow demonstration was made by Donald Campbell in 1962 when he completed two laps in 'Bluebird'. Since the car was not designed to turn corners, it needed manhandling through the tighter bends. The occasion was a two-day Festival of Motoring to celebrate the Golden Jubilee of the JCC/BARC.

In 1958 the BARC began arranging practice days for members. Their cars had to be scrutineered, but the fee was a modest ten shillings per session. One no longer has to be a BARC member to drive at Goodwood. Apart from driving and racing schools, which have included the celebrated Winfield School (among whose protégés is numbered Alain Prost), there are opportunities to simply drive one's road car, or motor-cycle, on the circuit.

It was also in 1958 that Goodwood became an airfield again. Two landing strips were constructed and 74 aircraft movements recorded at the Easter Monday Meeting that year. Today Goodwood has three runways, five hangars and is home to dozens of aircraft, a flying school, a helicopter charter company and an air ambulance service. With more than 50,000 movements a year it is one of the busiest airfields on the South coast.

In the 1970s, Goodwood staged a number of good quality air shows with RAF jets arriving, but not landing, to fly through their paces. Like the early motor race meetings, they attracted large crowds of both enthusiasts and people who came for a good day out with the family.

From the earliest days, Goodwood was a popular test track. BRM had tested at the circuit before it had raced there at the September 1950 International Meeting, and with so many leading teams based south of London, Goodwood was not only convenient, but the wide variety of corners also made it ideal for testing.

One notable test at occurred when John Surtees was considering trying his hand at car racing. Tony Vandervell arranged for a Vanwall to be taken out of storage in late 1959 and hired Goodwood for three days.

Left: pedal-bin access for the intrepid Donald Campbell as his wheel-driven Proteus gas-turbine powered 'jet car' 'Bluebird' is wheeled out ready for a remarkable and immensely popular 'fish out of water' demonstration at the circuit, 1962.
Above: the mercurial Donald Campbell - committed to building his own self-image after a childhood at the feet of a super-successful yet martinet father - gave his life for his ambition, and for his country. With 'Bluebird' at Goodwood, 1962.

"I first got to know the track itself at Goodwood in the 1970s and 1980s, long after the racing had stopped, because the Aston-Martin and Ferrari clubs used it for sprints. I'd remembered it bustling with people, and now it was deserted. The pedestrian tunnel was damp and echoingly empty - it was an awfully sad place at the time."

NICK MASON

Overleaf: Aston Martin Lagonda and Robin Hamilton launch held at a deserted and rather decrepit Goodwood circuit in 1983 for the lugubriously mis-conceived Aston V8-engined Nimrod Group C endurance racing coupé. James Hunt and Stirling Moss enter the unknown - Roy Salvadori, Jack Fairman and Eric Thompson are happy with the proven World Champion DBR1/300.

"I must have done more miles round Goodwood than anybody else. In 1964 my team was the first to sign up with Goodyear, and for seven years, up to the end of 1970, I did all their tyre testing - thousands of miles. That left-hander out at St Mary's would tell you a lot about how a tyre was behaving. I don't remember any lap times, but by the beginning of the 1970s the F1 Brabham-Repco was going a helluva lot faster than we'd gone when we last raced there in 1965."

SIR JACK BRABHAM

John recalls, "The test was going well, when I phoned Stirling one night to ask him how he took Fordwater. 'Flat out, boy', Stirling said. I tried it the next day and ended up spinning 500 yards down the road, the longest spin in the history of Goodwood. That night, I phoned him again. 'I thought you said Fordwater was flat,' I said. His response was, 'Good grief, you didn't, did you?'..."

John Brierley, who once ran The Hare And Hounds at nearby Stoughton, where drivers tested their cars in the surrounding lanes, and then the Fleece at Chichester, recalls another test session: "There was the time that Aston Martin had built the DBR4 Formula 1 car and booked Goodwood for a secret test. Nobody was allowed into the circuit, but Stirling Moss tipped me off so I disguised myself as a tramp and hung around Lavant Corner. When photographs of the car appeared in '*The Sunday Times*', John Wyer went through the roof."

John Brierley's Fleece pub was a popular venue, and at every race meeting, was filled with drivers. For those drivers returning to London, The Crown Inn and The Swan at Chiddingfold were also favoured.

Aston Martin usually based itself at The Spread Eagle Hotel at Midhurst and the cars were driven to the circuit on the public road. You could see Jaguar D-types on their way to Goodwood, driving round the 15th-century market cross in the centre of Chichester.

The Sussex police used to have a field day with their speed traps. There is a story that Bruce McLaren and John Surtees were both nabbed for speeding, one after the other. They were told that they could go, but they stayed put. When the local constabulary asked why they were hanging around, they chorused, "We're waiting for you to catch Salvadori!"

After 1966, testing continued. In 1974 the noise from a Formula 1 car disturbed lessons in a local school and silencers became mandatory, but this was not too great a problem when most British Formula 1 cars used the Cosworth DFV engine, which took to silencers quite easily.

You could see Hesketh, McLaren, March, Ralt, Toleman, Surtees, Brabham and Tyrrell testing on a regular basis.

One special test session was when local driver David Purley got back into a car having survived one of the worst accidents in racing history, and after spending months in hospital. David lapped his Lec spare car considerably quicker than he'd lapped

Development engineering *al fresco* - Bruce McLaren sorted out the suspension and running gear of his new team's very first prototype McLaren-Oldsmobile M1A here at Goodwood in the winter of 1964-65 before adding the body panels and tuning in its aerodynamics.

Goodwood before. He then ran in a couple of races, to prove that he could, although he was in agony. That accomplished, David was able to walk away from motor racing on his own terms.

Ron Tauranac, whose Ralt-Honda Formula 2 cars continued to test at Goodwood longer than any other top team, says, "When I go testing, I want the most information in the least time. You got that at Goodwood, with its wide variety of corners, whereas Silverstone was just high-speed motoring. We finally had to give up when we failed to meet the noise regulations. We could muffle the exhaust - the problem came with noise from the valve gear and the air rushing into the inlets."

Derek Warwick recalls that when he sent one of his Formula 3 Toyota-Novamotor engines back to Italy for a rebuild in 1979, the factory reported back (although they had not been told) that he'd been testing at Goodwood. Derek was amazed they had guessed this, but the Pedrazzani brothers explained that they knew because the engine showed signs of detonation. Being a Formula 3 unit, it had a restricted air intake, and also had to use a silencer at Goodwood (and only there). The restrictor and silencer, combined with the fact that Goodwood, located at the foot of the Sussex Downs, is prone to wide swings of barometric pressure, had led to the detonation. Elementary...

Formula 1 testing faded in 1980/81 for two reasons. One was the change to turbocharged, cars which were harder to silence, though Toleman did much of its initial testing at Goodwood with a turbocharged Hart engine - Toleman concentrated, however, on systems testing, not on performance testing. The other reason was increased sponsorship, which allowed teams the luxury of testing abroad where the

High-tech R&D at Goodwood as Goodyear tyre designer Bert Baldwin observes his products' behaviour at high speed on the rear of Dan Gurney's 1967 Eagle-Weslake V12. Keeping Bert's enthusiasm warm was not a problem...

weather is more predictable.

McLaren once considered moving its entire operation to Goodwood but its then partner, Honda, did not believe that it could silence the cars to meet the required limits. As Ron Tauranac has pointed out, restricting engine noise is more than a matter of putting silencers on the exhaust pipes. If McLaren did not operate from Goodwood, other makers did. The Respiratory and Super Shell buildings were hosts to a number of small outfits right up to 1998. Martlet and Image Formula Ford cars were made at

"I don't really remember much of Goodwood when my father was racing. I was only five when he did his last event there, the 1966 Easter Monday F2 race. But in 1985, when I was racing in F3, we went there to test. In my mind I'd never been to Goodwood in my life, but as we were driving through the tunnel and up into the paddock I had this weird flashback, and it came back to me that I'd been there as a very small child."

DAMON HILL

Goodwood, as was the JPR Wildcat kit car. And Formula 2 and 3 cars continued to test at the circuit until 1985, when Goodwood agreed to tighter limits on noise.

The official lap record at Goodwood stands at 1 minute 20.4 seconds, set by Jim Clark in the 1965 Glover Trophy, and equalled in the same race by Jackie Stewart. Prior to the 1980 British Grand Prix, however, Nelson Piquet ran a Brabham BT49-Cosworth at Goodwood and lapped in 63.6 seconds. This was beaten in 1989 under unusual circumstances. Onyx Grand Prix, based a few miles from Goodwood, had completed its first car just in time to send it to Brazil, but it hadn't been tested. A car club was running a sprint at Goodwood, so the Onyx transporter arrived at the circuit and parked close to the exit.

Stefan Johansson strapped himself in the Onyx, which had never previously turned a wheel. He did a warm-up lap, one flying lap, and a slow-down lap; with no fine-tuning, Johansson put in a lap time of 62.5 seconds, nearly 142 mph. The car was then hastily packed into the transporter and the team made its escape, since the test had been against all the regulations.

Impressive as the performance of Johansson and his Onyx was, the unofficial record belongs to Denny Hulme who, in 1971, lapped a Can-Am McLaren in 61 seconds, nearly 144 mph. Ted Croucher, the chief marshal at Goodwood, recalls, "A lot of the top drivers were present, including Jackie Stewart. Denny cat-napped on the pit counter until his car was ready. He did his time and then went back to sleep on the counter..."

In affectionate and respectful memory of our friend Bruce - the McLaren-Chevrolet M8D posed for a press photo during pre-series CanAm development testing, mid-summer, 1970.

THE BATTLE FOR GOODWOOD

Every time enthusiasts gathered at the Goodwood motor circuit in the years after 1966, someone would raise the possibility of using it for racing once again. After all, the circuit's continuous use for testing meant that its basic structure had been preserved in good working order. The very idea brought smiles to people's faces as the thought hung pleasantly in the air. Then there would be a rueful shaking of heads - great idea, but...

Freddie Richmond had handed over the running of the Goodwood Estate to his son in the 1968. The Estate, like many at the time, had no money, and so the 10th Duke, who had a background in industry, set about stabilising its financial structure by concentrating on the potential of the horse racing course. The motor racing circuit was not a priority, and he could easily have let it fall into disuse, but - despite his relative lack of interest in motor racing - he nevertheless continued to maintain the motor circuit throughout the 1970s and '80s. Had he not, the revival of the circuit could never have happened.

Above: Ferrari party - Goodwood House is the backdrop as Phil Hill howls by in the magnificent 4-litre Ferrari 330TRI/LM in which he and Olivier Gendebien won Le Mans (yet again) in 1962. The 1997 Festival of Speed celebrated 50 years of Ferrari racing history.
Right: sheer noise - it became the revival movement's experience that for every Goodwood Motor Circuit 'anti-revivalist' there were, fortunately, several dozen albeit less vociferous but undeniably enthusiastic supporters.

In the early 1990s, the time came for the Duke, in turn, to pass the running of the Goodwood Estate to his son, the present Lord March. And Charles March had been deeply influenced by his grandfather, Freddie Richmond, whom he adored. During Easter school holidays, Charles had stayed at Goodwood, absorbing Freddie's love for and knowledge of motor racing, and meeting the great drivers of the late 1950s and early '60s. When the track was closed, Charles was devastated, but never lost his love of speed.

Charles's first job after leaving school was to work alongside Stanley Kubrick on the film '*Barry Lyndon*'. He says, "working with Kubrick taught me about total commitment and the importance of getting every detail right." It was no coincidence

Lord March plans to bring racing back to Goodwood

CHICHESTER
The News
Wednesday, June 8, 1994 — BRITAIN'S BEST-DESIGNED EVENING PAPER

Residents call for public inquiry into Goodwood project

RACING LEGEND BACKS CIRCUIT

By GLYNN WILLIAMS and PETER HOMER
The News

Support grows for race circuit plan

By BEN PROCTOR

ACE SUPPORT: Motor racing veterans (from left) Tony Brooks and John Cooper with Goodwood Supporters' Association committee member Mike Lawrence and Don Parker from Hayling Island, the most successful Formula 3 driver ever.

CHICHESTER
The News
Tuesday, June 7, 1994 — BRITAIN'S BEST-DESIGNED EVENING PAPER

Campaign claims homes would suffer if racing returned

OPPOSITION TO CIRCUIT PLANS

By PETER HOMER
The News

New report ordered after 'flaw' in Goodwood evidence

New noise study

By PETER HOMER

AFFECTED AREA: A Chichester District Council map showing the 'potential disturbance zone' during unsilenced circuit use at Goodwood.

GOODWOOD | Complaints levelled at circuit stars

Residents 'blasted' by race car noise

■ High-powered cars were 'over the top' at festival party.

By PETER HOMER

NOT SO FUNNY ● Rowan Atkinson, one of the drivers

ACCUSED ● Earl of March

TESTS ● Rob Widdows

Noise abaters beware the Earl of March

by Anthea Hall

Laps of honour: Lord March surrounded by mementoes of a motor-racing...

Goodwood noise 'is acceptable'

Council backs racing return

Goodwood plans now go to ministry

By ANDREW ROBERTS

Long way

Goodwood, once one of the country's top circuits, could see no motor racing again after a break of 32 years.

Circuit that attracted the sport's top teams

By PHIL HEWITT

Council votes in favour of nostalgic car races The News 25/9/96

GOODWOOD WIN IN NOISE BATTLE

By PETER HOMER
The News

DJ HAS TO EAT HIS WORDS ● Page 3

THE NEWS 6/11/96
CHICHESTER | Decision shocks objectors to Goodwood plan

Earl wins battle for return of motor racing

■ Plans for event to coincide with circuit's 50th anniversary.

By PETER HOMER
The News

Straight from the horse's mouth - many BARC marshals at the Festival of Speed may retire deaf, but all profess that after being as close to the action as this, they can at least retire happy... That's Eddie Irvine in the works V12 Ferrari.

that the precisely re-created decor of the Revival Meeting in 1998 was frequently compared to a film set.

As an award-winning photographer (a passion for photography was another of Freddie's legacies), and using the name Charles Settrington, Charles worked on many major advertising campaigns. He always knew, however, that photography could not be a career for life, and in the early 1990s, began spending two days a week at Goodwood to prepare himself to take over the Estate.

When his father retired, Charles set about creating the Goodwood Festival of Speed, first run in 1993. It was an 'instant classic'; the first Festival was so stunning that people asked how it could possibly be bettered. The same question has been asked every year since and, with each successive year, the Festival has grown in stature to become the largest event of its kind in the world.

The Festival did not, of course, materialise from thin air. A number of people had proposed some kind of motoring event in the Park. Then Ian Bax of the BARC suggested a hill-climb on the Estate roads adjacent to Goodwood House. Derek Ongaro, the track inspector for the RAC Motor Sports Association, arrived to give the Goodwood circuit its periodic inspection and Charles took him up the hill next to Goodwood House. In the meantime he had discovered that, in 1935, Freddie had staged a light-hearted hill climb there for fellow members of the Lancia Owners' Club.

Derek Ongaro approved, and Aston Martin Lagonda Ltd, a frequent user of the circuit, expressed interest in backing the venture. Charles March drew together a team of experts and enthusiasts - including journalist Rob Widdows, Robert Brooks, the classic car auctioneer, and Doug Nye, the motor racing historian - and an outline began to take shape, based around the concept of great historic and contemporary cars and motor-cycles tackling a hill-climb route running from the Estate's East gates, past the front of Goodwood House and up the hill behind.

The organising team pursued a conscious desire to offer an antidote to the trend in modern motor racing which excludes, rather than includes, the paying public. At the Festival of Speed enthusiasts found themselves with unparalleled access to cars and drivers, and an atmosphere which perfectly complemented the cars.

Once the success of the Festival had been established, it was predictable that Charles would nurture plans for the motor circuit. In fact, he had been in discussion with the RAC over plans to revive the circuit as early as 1991.

Because of its continuous use, the surface of the track was in good condition, and the main safety measures were in place. Derek Ongaro, in his role as the RAC's circuit inspector, suggested modifications, but was persuaded that Goodwood's unique feature was as the only circuit in the world to remain unaltered since 1952. Derek and his colleagues agreed, provided that racing was restricted to cars built no later than 1972.

Below: literally scores of detail drawings had to be created, revised, annotated and perfected before the Goodwood Motor Circuit's revival could progress beyond a glimmer in the eye. **Overleaf:** Stirling Moss, the veteran 'Mr Motor Racing', with Charles March the arch-enthusiast and peerlessly hard-working Earl. Their respect would become entirely mutual - first Festival press day, 1993.

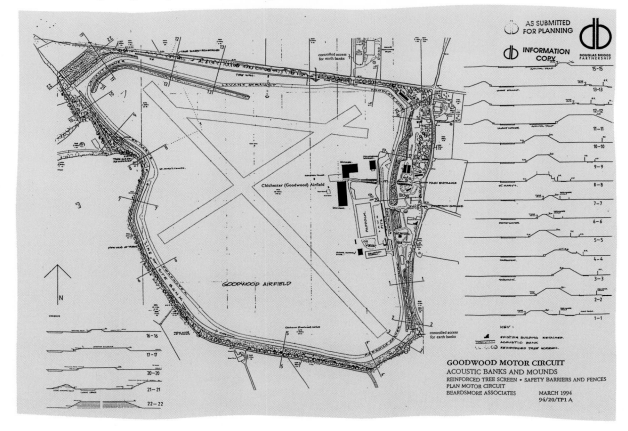

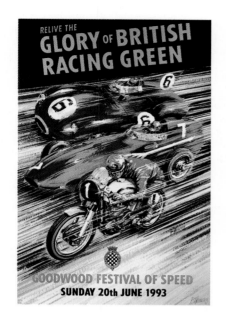

RELIVE THE
GLORY OF BRITISH
RACING GREEN

GOODWOOD FESTIVAL OF SPEED
SUNDAY 20th JUNE 1993

"I think I'd always had the dream in the back of my mind to revive the circuit. Lots of people used to suggest it to me, but naively, with no concept of how much it would take to do it. Actually, my father always saw the potential of re-opening the circuit: it wasn't something that particularly interested him, but it's significant that he didn't just dig it up for gravel, which might have been commercially attractive, or develop it as a valuable site. Because we didn't seem to be getting anywhere with the Motor Circuit, we started the Festival. In 1992 Ian Bax from the BARC asked if I'd ever thought of having a hill-climb on the road past the House. I said I had, sort of, but I wanted something more than a hill-climb... By June 1993 the first Festival was happening. We'd been advised by the RAC that around 2,000 people would turn up - 15,000 came that year. It was a big worry that the success of the Festival would diminish our efforts to get the Motor Circuit up and running. We haven't got endless resources, and we didn't want the two events to compete with each other. But we were all very sure that the Circuit was the goal - we kept having to remind ourselves that was our original plan."

THE EARL OF MARCH

"Charles March is a neighbour of mine. When I heard he wanted to bring racing to Goodwood, and knowing the man, I reckoned he'd bring it off. There's such style to what he and his team do: it's never over the top, nothing's too garish. Everything's done with real aristocratic class."

DEREK BELL

One problem which would dog all negotiations was the decibel limit imposed in 1985 under a Noise Abatement Notice - a limit that had been negotiated with, not imposed on Goodwood. It was understood from the beginning that, in any proposal to restore racing to Goodwood, noise would be an issue. From early in the planning

Gambles' finest - the earth-moving and grading contractors re-profiling the Motor Circuit site and beginning to rebuild the tyre-wall bank frontages, 1997.

stage, Goodwood was advised by Andy Watson, an independent noise consultant, who in turn brought in the Institute of Sound and Vibration Research, an offshoot of Southampton University and a world leader in acoustic science. The upshot was the creation of large, carefully shaped, earth banks which, together with the planting of trees and shrubs, were designed to absorb and deflect noise.

A plan for the circuit was evolved, including the construction of a museum where owners could allow their cars to be housed, and, on 14 days a year, run them on the circuit. An application was made for seven days of unsilenced Historic racing per year and, in return, Goodwood would make concessions in terms of reduced circuit usage. That was the original proposal - then the negotiations began.

As soon as the plans were announced, a public debate erupted in the letters pages of the local press, with writers split into two opposing camps. On one side was a loose alliance of local residents and 'environmentalists', expressing concern about air and noise pollution.

In response, a group of enthusiasts formed the Goodwood Supporters' Association and began by distributing leaflets to all the areas likely to be affected. The GSA grew to a membership of 2,500, running meetings which were addressed by a whole series of stars - drivers, designers, team managers and journalists - all of whom came without payment. Feelings ran high on both sides.

In the meantime, Goodwood was negotiating with the local council, who finally accepted a proposal to allow five days a year of unsilenced Historic racing, but with no 'museum days' and therefore, in the foreseeable future, no museum.

After the Revival Meeting in 1998, the Chichester Observer conducted a readers' poll. It was the first time that the general public had been asked its opinion and 82% of respondents were firmly in favour of the circuit. The opponents to the Revival had perhaps under-estimated the affection and respect in which the local community held Freddie Richmond and Charles March - and some personal, verbal attacks on the family had been ill-judged.

In December 1996, the Council referred its decision to the Department of Transport, for potential review and a possible public inquiry. The planning group had anticipated that there would be a wait of at least six months, but a swift - and favourable - decision, meant that an opening date in September 1998 (fifty years after the first ever meeting) was possible. It was a tall order, but Charles March and his team set about it with a vengeance.

Some of the work had already been done prior to the planning application; now everything had to be put into operation. The team at the heart of the Revival was expanded. Tony Houghton, the manager of Goodwood airfield/circuit, chaired consultative committees and dealt with local councillors and officials; Richard Sutton, a former motoring writer, and the man responsible since 1997 for all the cars at the Festival of Speed including the *Cartier Style et Luxe Concours*, co-ordinated the entries and programme; the architect Brian Beardsmore became the overall designer for the reconstruction of the circuit.

The RAC was deeply involved, and Dennis Carter of the BARC was another stalwart, along with Nigel Draffen, the Goodwood Estate Land Agent and Mark Dugdale, the Estate Manager.

A myriad of planning details remained. One was the installation of noise monitors around the circuit linked to a VDU and, by modem, to a monitoring centre in the local council offices.

Next on the menu - the wartime control tower-cum-postwar cafeteria under siege during the reconstruction process, mid-summer 1998.

Then there was the matter of the 270,000 tonnes of earth required to create the acoustic/spectator banks. Gamble, the civil engineering contractor, built the banks up from soil from other construction sites. The acoustic banks, designed by Funke Associates and Brian Beardsmore in conjunction with the noise consultants, would provide excellent viewing all round the circuit - much better, in fact, than had been the case in 1966.

The Goodwood Estate foresters undertook the massive task of providing mature beech trees - all from the Estate's own forests - which were planted at a rate of six a day for six months, augmented by an additional 20,000 shrubs and saplings. The banks were seeded with grass and wild flowers and tyre walls constructed, each set of tyres planted

with ivy, for camouflage. Then there was new mains drainage to lay, the renovation of every building on the site, pits to build and a paddock to be created. The grandstands had to be temporary structures (as they had always been) and they began to be assembled about a month before the Revival Meeting. Doug Nye had designed the chicane and his woodworker brother, Rod, built it.

Above: gathering pace as the control tower penthouse, hand-rails and members' enclosure fencing have been installed, but still so far to go, so much work still to do - early August 1998. **Right:** "If it moves salute it - if it doesn't, paint it!" Where once ferocious flight-sergeants reigned supreme, the finishing touches are applied: the rebuilt Goodwood pit block awaits set-dressing in the sun, and mid-August 1998 is really racing past.

Sponsors arrived on board; in this the circuit had a certain advantage because of the success of the Festival of Speed. Chrysler and Louis Vuitton had already been involved with Historic motor sport. Aston Martin, Ford, Jaguar, MG, Shell and the RAC had direct historical links with the circuit, and were joined by Omega, Morlands ('Old Speckled Hen' beer) and Veuve Clicquot Champagne.

Then there was the question of the programme and the entry for the first meeting. It was decided that the races should reflect Goodwood's history, with precedence given to drivers and cars with a Goodwood connection. Regardless of the make-up of later meetings, this meant a cut-off point of 1966. Formula Junior and the 500cc Formula 3 were essential, as were handicaps. Both Members' Meetings and Internationals would have to be represented, as well as such landmarks as the Nine-Hour Race and the Tourist Trophy.

Above all, the whole event had to be 'in period'; attention to detail was critical. Charles March's training with Stanley Kubrick was about to come into its own.

As one example, for the Saturday night party, guests would be signed in by WRACs and WAAFs and issued with a orange tin mug filled with Veuve Clicquot Champagne. They were then shown to period MT vehicles, including army tracked personnel carriers, for an open-air drive to the circuit and an aircraft hangar. As the sun set, two Spitfires wheeled low over their heads and, with dusk closing in, searchlights stabbed the sky. The hangar was decked out like a 1940s night club, with cigarette girls, gold nude 'statues', and Goodwood's own chef prepared dinner for over 1,000 guests. The evening was a stunning *coup de théâtre*, but it had not come about by accident.

The Revival was an immense undertaking - and anyone who had visited the circuit regularly witnessed a remarkable transformation from a landscape resembling a Great War battlefield to a modern interpretation of a much-loved circuit. On the day before the Revival Meeting painters and carpenters were still at work, and the last nail was banged in at about 9.30 on the morning of the first day of practice. Within less than two years, the Motor Circuit had been brought back to life - and motor racing was about to return to Goodwood.

REVIVAL

On 18th September 1948, Frederick Charles Gordon Lennox, the ninth Duke of Richmond and Gordon, had driven his new Bristol 400 to open the Goodwood circuit. Fifty years later to the day, his grandson, Charles, Earl of March and Kinrara, drove an identical car around the circuit, and declared it re-opened.

Trumpeters from the Band of the Life Guards played a fanfare and a Spitfire baritoned through between pits and grandstands, barely twenty feet above the start-finish straight. After 32 years, Goodwood was open again. Minutes later, three V16 BRMs were amongst the cars taking to the track for the first official practice session. One driver - passed by Rick Hall in the Donington Collection's V16 - reported that the sound of its open pipes going by "was like having a red hot poker rammed in my ear". Practice all day Friday and on the Saturday morning preceded four races on the Saturday afternoon, eight more on Sunday.

Since the Revival Meeting was intended to reflect Goodwood racing 1948-66, Lord March's team had resolved that no vehicle made after 1966 should be seen. Only period ambulances and tow-trucks were visible - modern high-speed emergency tenders, just as ready, were kept hidden. The only infield car parking accepted pre-1966 competitors' cars.

Unlike any other motor race meeting, Goodwood was kept free of merchandise stalls and the all-pervasive aroma of burgers and chips. Only selected caterers were permitted on-site - including a Champagne tent - while Goodwood's own merchandise was sold from the old 'parachute shed' near the main gate. Spectators were encouraged to dress 'in period'. The

Left: a very English occasion - the Countess of March flying the flag as Ferrari V12s, the fizz of champagne, and the trumpeters of the Life Guards combine at the Revival Meeting, September 1998.
Below: more fly-through than fly-past - the incredible Ray Hanna's circuit-opening run at 9.05 am, Friday, 18th September 1998. At this moment Charles March in the Bristol was just leading the Ferrari trio out of the chicane... towards this Supermarine Spitfire. His first comment on vacating the car was "I saw his eyes!"
Overleaf: an overture from the Band of the Life Guards on the Goodwood grid.

THE GLORY OF GOODWOOD

The Madgwick Messerschmitt: this Merlin-engined '109' starred in the Revival Meeting's spectacular 'tip-and-run' raids, usually drawing the short straw, of course. Amongst the infield corn stooks, pitchforks wielded by tough, tanned men in shirtsleeves, with corduroy trousers gathered beneath the knee, awaited parachuting pilots...

mechanics were white-overalled, while many female visitors adopted hair-styles, make-up and clothes from their mother's or grandmother's era. Jackets and ties were compulsory to achieve access to the paddock and a cap or hat desirable. Baseball caps, anoraks and mobile phones were strictly taboo.

Even the security men eschewed conventional uniform, being dressed instead like John Steed in '*The Avengers*' - with bowler hats, crisp dark suits, collar and tie, a rose in the lapel, and carrying rolled umbrellas. They even smiled... and would be highly praised for their impeccably polite implacability. How could they carry it off? Military Policemen, no less, from Chichester's Roussillon Barracks - the MPs' academy.

All this, pre-event, was fraught with danger. It could so easily have lapsed into vulgarity, but the Goodwood Revival Meeting was not just a race meeting. It was an experience. Comic actor Rowan Atkinson, who raced an Aston Martin, recognised as much, saying "It was like being on a giant film set".

Indeed, during initial planning, Doug Nye had used that same phrase, suggesting the circuit should be dressed in just that way. Charles March had picked up the casual comment and run with it, his fertile imagination roaring ahead unfettered. On the Thursday evening before the meeting he remarked, "We've built the set, provided the props, the actors have arrived - now the script will write itself..."

That became the essence of the entire weekend. To recall Goodwood's considerable wartime heritage as RAF Westhampnett, there were between-race dog-fights and station 'beat-ups' by Spitfires, a Mustang, and a rare flying Messerschmitt Bf109. Local drama students played RAF ground crew and pilots, reading and playing time-killing ball games, before diving desperately for cover as the Messerschmitt screamed in on a strafing run. Grown men had tears in their eyes when the scrambled 'Spits' saw off the attacker. Engine spluttering, it streamed smoke high above the infield, a thunderous cheer welling up from the competitors' enclosure - even hats being thrown in the air.

Chrysler, maker of the modern Jeep, provided a Drivers' Centre which looked externally like a regular marquee but, inside, was decked out like a timber-framed mess hall. Coca-Cola came in curvaceous bottles, not a can in sight. Reprints of period newspapers (for the correct days fifty years earlier) were on hand, and were changed appropriately each day. The catering staff wore RAF uniforms. Spam fritters were served for breakfast.

Right: first-race winner - Ludovic Lindsay's classic ERA '*Remus*' bawled its way to victory in the first Goodwood motor race since closure in 1966 - the 1998 Woodcote Cup.
Below: first-race loser - Julian Majzub's beautiful 3-litre supercharged 1938 Alfa Romeo *Tipo* 308 caught fire briefly just short of Madgwick after a brilliant start.

For years the circuit infield had been farmed, before becoming 'set aside' land. When Charles March saw a Geoff Goddard photograph of the 1955 Nine Hour race, with the cars racing by stooks of wheat, he just had to reproduce that scene. To the rescue came the Downland Museum at Singleton: their staff spent a sun-soaked Revival weekend on the St Mary's infield with a steam-driven threshing machine harvesting the 1950s-style crop. When Rick Hall climbed from Donington's ex-Jackie Stewart BRM P261 at St Mary's after it had popped a drive-shaft joint, he turned to find himself confronted by one of Singleton's finest in braces and neckerchief, brandishing a pitchfork. Rick reported, "I felt like I'd just landed by parachute!"

Before the first race, Canon Lionel Webber, Chaplain to the Queen and also to the British Racing Drivers' Club, blessed the track. The Guards band played while Lord March's actress sister Nimmy led the crowd in singing '*Jerusalem*'. The irrepressibly enthusiastic Canon Webber perhaps shocked, yet also delighted, the crowd as he declared over the PA system, "God is not in Heaven today. He's here at Goodwood. Or, if He's not, He's crackers!"

Overleaf right: his motor racing reverence Canon Lionel Webber - Chaplain to HM The Queen, Chaplain to the British Racing Drivers' Club - is escorted by the Central Band of the Royal Air Force to the circuit blessing dais.
Overleaf inset (left to right): the Earl's sister, Lady Louisa, his mother, the Duchess of Richmond, and the Countess of March.

"THE WHOLE MOTOR CIRCUIT REVIVAL WEEKEND HAD A VERY ODD ATMOSPHERE FOR ME, BECAUSE I DIDN'T FEEL I WAS

HAVING TO RUN IT. THERE WAS SO MUCH GOOD FEELING FROM EVERYBODY THAT I FELT IT WAS BEING DRIVEN ALONG BY ITS OWN ENERGY. I FELL INTO BED ON THE SUNDAY NIGHT WITH A HUGE SENSE OF RELIEF: EVERYBODY HAD HAD SUCH EXPECTATIONS. THE NEXT DAY THE LETTERS STARTED TO COME IN - JUST

"Charles March set out with a dream: he pictured in his mind how it should be, and he never stopped working until he'd realised the dream. He had the knowledge, the enthusiasm, the attention to detail and the energy to get people to co-operate with him." JOHN SURTEES

HUNDREDS OF THEM, MOSTLY FROM PEOPLE I'VE NEVER MET. IT'S QUITE SOMETHING WHEN YOU GET A LETTER FROM A 17-YEAR-OLD SAYING IT WAS THE BEST WEEKEND OF HIS LIFE." THE EARL OF MARCH

Above: flying '500' - Julian Majzub enjoyed better fortune in his beautifully-prepared ex-Peter Collins Cooper-Norton Mark VIII - winning the Earl of March Trophy for 500cc Formula 3 cars.

Below: three more chain-drive solos, this time two-wheeled, with the great British World Champion Barry Sheene, Mick Hemmings and Malcolm Clark astride.

A few minutes later, racing returned to Goodwood, after 32 long years' absence. First race on the card was the Woodcote Cup for Formula 1, 2 and *Libre* cars of the type which raced at Goodwood until 1953. It proved to be not only a fabulous race, but also set the tempo for the entire meeting. Ludovic Lindsay stormed into the lead in what had been his late father Patrick's ex-'Bira' ERA '*Remus*' with the Cooper-Bristols of Roddy MacPherson and Gregor Fisken in hot pursuit.

Into the last lap, Lindsay had leaking lubricant smothering his clutch pedal and, afraid that his oil-soaked left boot might slip on the critical downchange into St Mary's, he reached across to kick it with his oil-dry right boot. He got away with it, and became Goodwood's first motor race winner since 1966. Less than a second covered these first three finishers.

As in the old days, the Earl of March Trophy race was run for 500cc Formula 3 cars. Most of the 32-strong entry were Coopers, interspersed with such rarities as a Swedish Effyh, a Svebe (built by Formula 1 star Ronnie Peterson's father), a Petty and John Fenning's Erskine Staride. As the pack clamoured into Madgwick the Staride locked wheels with a rival, and somersaulted, fortunately without significant injury to its driver, manufacturer of Willans safety belts!

Julian Majzub's Cooper-Norton won from an overjoyed Nick Leston in a Cooper-JAP once raced by his father, Les - the 1954 Formula 3 Champion. On his slowing-down lap Nick admitted to "welling up. It was amazing to experience firsthand some of the racing my father had known."

Seven-times World Motor-Cycle Champion John Surtees helped assemble a superb

field for the Lennox Cup race, admitting 350cc/500cc Group 1 machines, 1948-1966. Two World Champions graced the field: Barry Sheene and Damon Hill, who remarked, "Eddie Jordan has told me that if I hurt myself, he'll operate on me himself - without an anaesthetic".

Barry Sheene (Manx Norton) finished a close second to Mick Hemmings (McIntyre Matchless), ahead of Malcolm Clark's Matchless G50. The

first 350 home was Trevor Barnes' Moto Guzzi. Damon Hill (Manx Norton) set off way down the 30-strong field, but finished tenth after an excellent ride - and loved it.

The Sussex Trophy for customer sports-racing cars 1955-60 saw marques which had been the backbone of the British rise to motor racing dominance rejoin battle at Goodwood . Fastest qualifiers were the 2-litre Lotus 15s of James Shead and auctioneer Robert Brooks - closely involved with both the Festival of Speed and the Revival meeting - while Frank Sytner's powerful 3.8-litre Lister Jaguar lurked in third spot. As they blasted away, Brooks was sandwiched, and James Shead's transmission failed after a single lap, while a spinner on one of the Lister's wheels acted like a can opener on Brooks' car. As it reached maximum speed down the Lavant Straight, air pressure burst half the aluminium tail panel wide open, bending it up in the air, like an enormous tail-fin.

Brooks was flagged in for inspection, but next time round no flag was shown - so he ripped on, the damaged panel remaining firmly attached.

Sytner and Stuart Graham (Lister-Chevrolet) led from Brooks with John Harper's Cooper Monaco fourth. Harper brushed a backmarker and Graham retired. Brooks

Top left: David May (Manx-Norton 350, number 25) and Gerry Jenkins (Manx-Norton 500, number 26) on the Lennox Cup grid.
Below: the Motor Circuit was revived in effect as a movie set, upon which the meeting could unfold as an unscripted drama. But none could have hoped for a more dramatic race than the Saturday's final 15-lap Sussex Trophy, won by auctioneer Robert Brooks's battered Dutch National Motor Museum Lotus 15 after a sensational come-back drive, which had the crowd on tiptoe, roaring him on.

THE EARL AND COUNTESS OF MARCH

REQUEST THE PLEASURE OF YOUR COMPANY AT

GOODWOOD AERODROME TO CELEBRATE THE 50TH

ANNIVERSARY OF GOODWOOD MOTOR CIRCUIT

ON SATURDAY THE 19TH SEPTEMBER 1998

CHAMPAGNE 7.00 PM · DINNER 8.00 P.M

DRESS · MESS KIT & MEDALS OR BLACK TIE

CHAMPAGNE BY VEUVE CLICQUOT

PLEASE BRING THIS INVITATION WITH YOU

REVIVAL MEETING

GUEST OF
THE EARL AND COUNTESS OF MARCH

PLEASE JOIN US DURING THE DAY
AT THE OLD CONTROL TOWER WITHIN
THE MARCH ENCLOSURE

18-20 SEPT '98

50th ANNIVERSARY REVIVAL MEETING
DRIVER
GOODWOOD 18th, 19th & 20th SEPTEMBER, 1998

19 98 PADDOCK

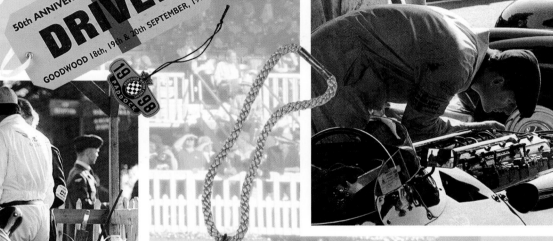

GOODWOOD MOTOR CIRCUIT
50th ANNIVERSARY
1998 REVIVAL

Ford

Right: Gary Pearson in Adrian Hamilton's 1953 Le Mans-winning 'Lightweight' C-type Jaguar appropriately won the Sunday-opening Freddie March Memorial Trophy from this Le Mans-type run-and-jump start. **Below:** Mini-magic leads the way in the St Mary's Trophy as Richard Dodkins' impeccably-driven Austin-Cooper 'S' flickers through the chicane after the rev-limiter of the early leader, Goodwood driving instructor Les Goble's Lotus-Cortina, had progressively re-set itself.

was chasing Sytner like an avenging angel, Harper catching them both. The 'ketch-rigged' Lotus caught the Lister: a first attempt to duck by at Lavant saw the cars bounce apart and press on. A second lunge the next time through Lavant set the crowd roaring as Brooks stole the lead. He held it through the last lap and - at the line - a mere 1.12s covered these three cars.

Many of the casual spectators leaving that evening sought tickets to come back next day. If this was what Revival racing at Goodwood was all about, they wanted more.

That evening saw the competitors' party erupt - the only adequate word - in one of the airfield hangars. The theme was 1940s, a wartime or immediately post-war night club. Military History Enactment enthusiasts provided guest transport to create an unforgettable evening scene as the sun set and dusk rolled in, with black-tie guests ferrying in on Jeep, truck and half-track as two Spitfires buzzed them low on that balmy evening.

Sunday dawned equally glorious. The race programme opened, for the first time since 1963, with a traditional, old-fashioned (and long banned) Le Mans-type run-and-jump start, thanks to special dispensation from the RAC. The entry for the Freddie March Memorial Trophy, evoking Goodwood's Nine-Hour Races, was actually richer than any of the originals. The only deviation from strict historical accuracy was the exclusion of Jaguar D-types on the grounds they might spoil the fun - a typical Goodwood decision, in the best possible taste.

At flagfall the drivers sprinted to their cars with varying athleticism. But an Aston Martin DB2 broke its rear axle, juddering to an immoveable halt just by the timing line.

With the field red-flagged the crowd was treated to not just one Le Mans-type start, but two. This time around, pole position man Andrew Garner's Cooper-Jaguar refused to fire, leaving him second-last away. He drove magnificently, setting fastest lap and recovering to second behind Gary Pearson in Adrian Hamilton's 1953 Le Mans-winning '*Lightweight*' C-type Jaguar. Third, less than two seconds adrift, came Willie Green in another C-type - Simon Draper's Aston Martin DB3S fourth.

While Goodwood had been slow to embrace saloon cars (or 'closed cars' as the BARC labelled them), when it did so, they became a very popular class. The St Mary's Trophy for Group 2 'Goodwood Formula' cars was demanding - specifying period trim: no wide tyres, no alloy wheels and with even such details as period mirrors mandatory. Les Goble's Lotus-Cortina led until its rev-limiter began cutting-in at ever lower revs, allowing Richard Dodkins' rapid Mini Cooper 'S' through to win, with Terry Nicholls' Lotus-Cortina third.

Sir John Whitmore came out of retirement (again) to drive a Lotus-Cortina in positively his last race. The 1965 European Touring Car Champion explained, "I told Lord March I'd drive if he would find me a car I couldn't expect to win in. I didn't think I could keep my competitive instincts under control." Terry Hall's road-tune Lotus-Cortina was exactly as ordered - but loosening manifold bolts caused retirement.

The Lennox Cup was re-run on the Sunday, Damon Hill absent preparing for the following TT. Lennox Cup MkII saw a superb battle, won by Mick Hemmings less than a second ahead of Malcolm Clark with Barry Sheene third.

The one-hour Tourist Trophy Celebration remarkably included veterans of the original series, such as Stirling Moss, Sir Jack Brabham, David Piper, Sir John Whitmore, Bob Bondurant, Phil Hill, Chris Lawrence and John Surtees.

Martin Brundle shared Lord Cowdray's unique Jaguar E-type '*Low-Drag*' Coupé 'CUT 7' with Sir Jack, while Damon Hill drove the Ferrari 250GTO with which father Graham had won the 1963 TT, rebodied in '64 style. Stirling Moss was in the Ferrari 250GT SWB with which he'd won in 1961.

Above: Jaguar wins the 'TT'! The classic Coventry marque's advertising people missed a unique promotional opportunity after the Nigel Corner/'Whizzo' Williams 'Lightweight' E-Type Jaguar led home the Frank Sytner/Gregor Fisken sister car to finish 1-2 in the one-hour Goodwood TT Celebration race.
Below: blind speed - bespectacled coachbuilder Rod Jolley drove like the wind in his 2½-litre Cooper T51 to win the Richmond Trophy, threatened only towards the finish by Derek Bell's less powerful but beautifully-driven Maserati-powered sister car.
Overleaf: the heavy metal pouring through the chicane in a blaze of colour and sound.

Above: finding things somewhat different from Indianapolis - former '500' winner Danny Sullivan's so-elegant ex-Bowmaker Lola-Climax V8 leads Paul Alexander's Lotus-BRM 24 to victory in the feature Glover Trophy.
Below: the Lavant Cup was christened the 'White Choccies' race, its entry of peerless quality like the ultra-special white chocolates from a box, all set aside to be savoured at leisure. Peter Hardman staged a magnificent display of exuberant car control to dominate in this ex-Rodriguez Brothers Ferrari Dino 246S. Pity about the helmet...

Early in the race Frank Gardner's Cobra laid an oil slick around the track, presenting a real advantage to cars quick on the straights by handicapping those nimble through the corners. David Piper - the only man who competed in all seven genuine Goodwood TTs - slithered off at Madgwick in his pole-sitting Ferrari 275 LM, and former World Champion Phil Hill spun his Shelby Cobra Daytona Coupé at St Mary's after some storming early laps. His daughter, Vanessa, was emotional for another reason, explaining, "He retired before I was born and I'm seeing him race for the first time. It's a warrior side of my father I've never seen before".

Lightweight Jaguar E-types finished first and second, Nigel Corner/Barrie Williams heading Frank Sytner/Gregor Fisken while former F1 star Stefan Johansson, sharing Nicolaus Springer's Ferrari 250GTO, grabbed third place from the David Clark/Simon Draper Aston Martin Project 214.

Derek Bell was first away in the Richmond Trophy for Formula 1 cars 1954-60 only for his Cooper Maserati to jump out of gear. Rod Jolley's Cooper-Climax then ran away and hid, until Bell - despite giving away half a litre and never having raced an Historic GP car before - reeled him in to finish a pulsating three-tenths of a second behind.

The crowd delighted in the sight of Sir Jack Brabham, at 73, chin in, elbows out, dirt-tracking his Cooper around just like old times. In the paddock, as he settled into what he thought was his Cooper, its owner/driver tapped him on the shoulder and said "No, Sir Jack, that one over there is yours". The great triple-World Champion just grinned, "I don't mind which one I put me bum in, as long as it's quick".

The Glover Trophy followed for 1½-litre Formula 1 and Tasman Formula cars - those most elegant and intricate single-seaters from the early 1960s. An opening-lap multiple spin at St Mary's thinned the field, without injury or damage, and American Duncan Dayton (Brabham-Climax BT11) led from Paul Alexander's Lotus BRM 24 and former Indycar Champion Danny Sullivan in Dayton's Lola-Climax Mk4. When Duncan retired on lap eight the Alexander/Sullivan tussle became the battle for the lead.

Danny lanced ahead at St Mary's, but ran wide over the wheat stubble, recovering to close again on Paul whose engine had lost its edge at high rpm. Another move at St Mary's this time succeeded, and the Lola howled home to a popular victory. Like Derek Bell, Danny Sullivan had never previously raced an Historic car. Alan Baillie (Lotus

Above: Swiss winner - Jean-Michel Farine took the Chichester Cup Formula Junior event in his beautifully presented and very fast Lotus 20, from 1961.

Below: well-merited second victory of the weekend in the 'Ebby' Ebblewhite Handicap is celebrated by Peter Hardman, in the Ferrari Dino 246S - a real pity about the helmet...

BRM 24) snatched third place from Robs Lamplough's Lotus-Climax 33 on the final lap.

The Lavant Cup race for cars built in the spirit of the 1959 Sports Car World Championship-clinching Goodwood TT was then dominated by Peter Hardman, who staged a tremendous demonstration of natural car control in the Ferrari Dino 246S, powering around the historic course in glorious broadside drifts and slides. Singer Phil Collins' manager Tony Smith finished second in his Maserati T61 '*Birdcage*', ahead of the great Brian Redman, embarrassed by an ungainly roll-over cage on the Aston Martin DBR2.

Behind these leaders not only the Goodwood crowd but also the live TV audience had been enthralled by an incredible early-stages battle for sixth between Stirling Moss's 1959 TT-winning Aston Martin DBR1/300, Martin Brundle in John Coombs' yellow '*Shortnose*' Jaguar D-type and Willie Green's JCB team Ferrari 250 *Testa Rossa*. Brundle spent much of his time broadside in the D-type, yet the man he freely confessed was his 'absolute hero', Moss - three days after his 69th birthday - simply swept by, drifting the Aston through Goodwood's fast curves while waving courteously to the drivers just displaced.

Martin could scarcely believe it. For the backmarker being lapped, Moss's calm salute came as an acknowledgement; for the real competitor who had been battling for a corner with his tyres and brakes almost alight, and his hair definitely on fire, it became a devastating psychological blow...

Brundle's engine went off-song soon after Moss passed, while Willie Green then tried to slink his red Ferrari past Stirling's Aston Martin, so another epic near collision

at Woodcote had the crowd there fit to bust, Willie locked-up and sideways, with Moss flashing that courteous salute again even as he one-handed his drifting steed through the curve. For younger fans here was proof that the old Moss magic really was as fathers and grandfathers might tell.

There was still more. The schoolroom class of Formula Junior had seen many hectic Goodwood battles from 1960-63. What made the 1998 Chichester Cup race so fascinating was inclusion of such pioneering Italian marques as Volpini, Bandini and De Sanctis within the most diverse FJ field ever assembled in Britain. Swiss owner/driver Jean-Michel Farine (Lotus Ford 20), won from Fred Boothby's sister car, Tony Steele (Lola Ford Mk2) and Marcus Mussa (Lotus Ford 18).

To complete the Revival programme two handicap races were run. Virtually every race at Brooklands pre-war was a handicap supervised by the doyen of motor racing timekeepers, A.V. 'Ebby' Ebblewhite. After the War, Goodwood inherited not only Brooklands customs but also 'Ebby' himself. From the first BARC Members' Meeting having consisted entirely of handicaps - the last meeting featured just one, actually Goodwood's last ever before closure in 1966.

The first Revival handicap was named for 'Ebby', admitting sports, GTs and a handful of saloons, with cars being flagged off at intervals. If the handicapper's calculations are correct then the entire field should theoretically reach the finish in line abreast (perhaps thankfully this has never been achieved). Peter Hardman notched his second win of the day in the Ferrari Dino 246S, from Robert Brooks's Lotus 15 - its tail sail safely 'furled' - with Barrie Williams third in the Tojeiro-Jaguar.

The second handicap was named for Scott Gaze, the late brother of Tony Gaze (who was an honoured guest and spectator). In this single-seater handicap Rod Jolley was first across the line, but when his handicap was added, he emerged second, Doug Mockett (Cooper-Ford and seventh past the flag) being declared the final winner of the Revival weekend.

The race was a 'sealed' handicap, a legacy from Brooklands, in which the handicapper decides the handicap for each driver, but does not tell them until after the race. In fact, the race was not intended to be a sealed handicap, but the handicapper's lap-top crashed before the race! So the cars were flagged off as in a scratch race and the handicaps worked out with pen and paper as the race went on. The race passed off with few people the wiser.

The racing had been punctuated by other features, one a cavalcade to honour Stirling Moss, featuring a wide range of the great cars he had raced. The other was the 'Dream Grid' of 58 great Goodwood drivers and motor racing personalities, each in a

Right: The Revival Meeting's 'Dream Grid' line-up reunited great Goodwood cars and characters in an albeit fleeting real-life Hall of Fame. Here Roy Salvadori settles himself into one of the revered Aston Martin DBR1/300s with 1959-60-66 World Champion Jack Brabham beyond in the bottle-green and white colours of Cooper. **Overleaf:** salute the past, relish the present, cherish the future - as the Ferrari escort to Lord March's course-opening Bristol blared back to the finish line, this was a moment for all generations to cherish.

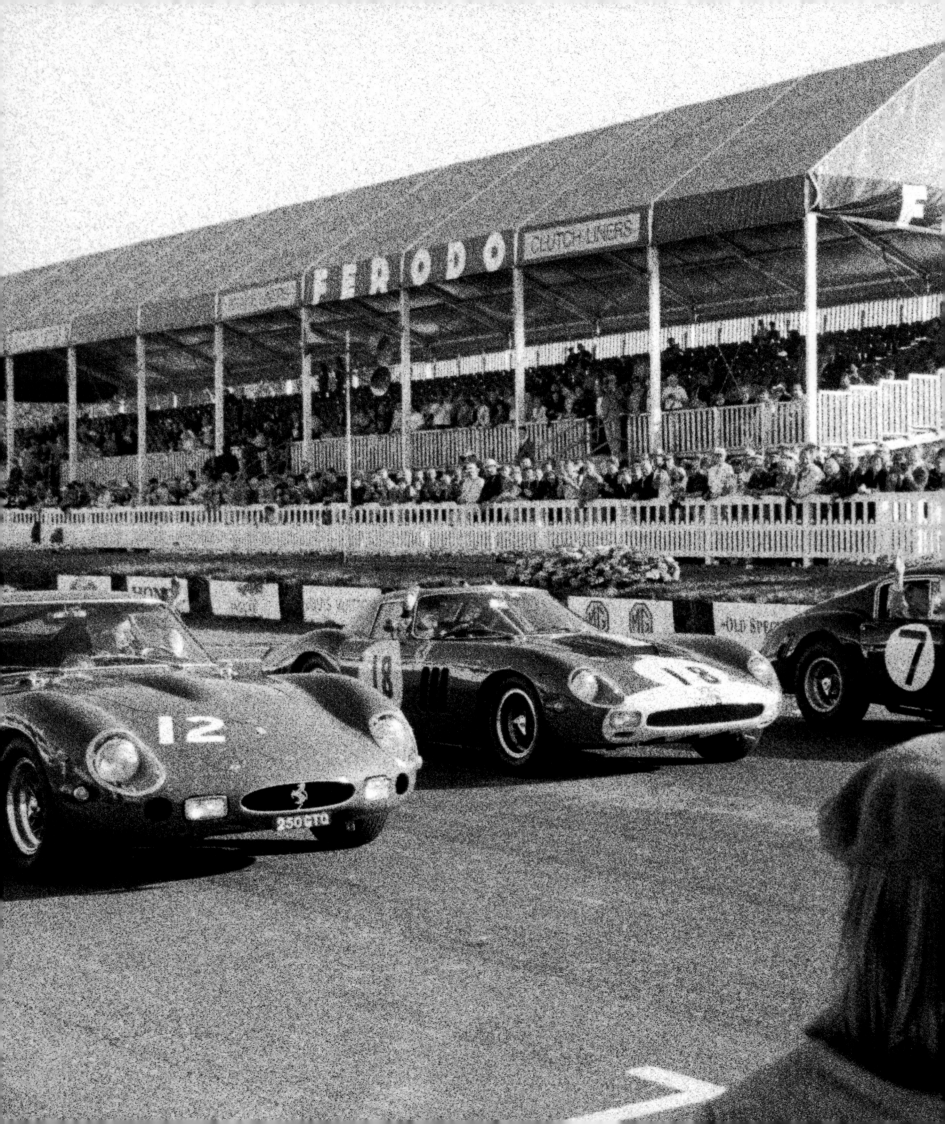

"I've always had a special affection for Goodwood, because it was the first place I ever saw Grand Prix cars in action. By the time I was racing big cars there in the 1960s, like the Daytona Cobra, other tracks had got bigger, but Goodwood never lost its appeal. It always had a certain charm. I thought the Revival was absolutely fabulous, probably the most wonderful event I've been to - and my wife and kids felt the same." PHIL HILL

"When I arrived at the Revival, I walked out onto the track and I saw the flowers all the way down the main straight. That really got to me: I understood then the quality of the detail. It took me back 30 years, and nothing has ever done that to me in my life before. You couldn't do it anywhere else, on any other circuit in the world, because they've all changed. Goodwood didn't change. It just shut, and stayed the same, sleeping." DEREK BELL

"Sitting on the Dream Grid, at the wheel of a Daytona Cobra like the one I ran in the 1964 Tourist Trophy, I was so overloaded with memories it was difficult to put them into words. I was thinking of Goodwood as the place where John Surtees started his four-wheel career, and where Jimmy Clark had some of his first singe-seater races; the place where my hero Stirling Moss ended his career, and where my friend Bruce McLaren ended his life. I found it all very moving."   DAN GURNEY

"It was fantastic to be able to go back and race at Goodwood again. The circuit felt the same - all the corners were the same, all the bumps were in the same places. At the Revival I drove an E-Type, and a 1960 Cooper like the one I won my second World Championship title in, and that hadn't changed much either. I had a good go - that's what I normally tend to do."

SIR JACK BRABHAM

"The whole atmosphere, with everybody in period costume, I've never experienced anything like it. It was just great. I had licence to behave like a lunatic on a motorbike, the first time in a long time for me, and came away in one piece."   DAMON HILL

car associated with his or her career. The participants all returned astonished by their rapturous reception. While the Italian *tifosi* may be the world's most emotional motor race spectators, the British are the most knowledgeable, with the most keenly honed sense of heritage. At Goodwood it always shows.

Former '*Autosport*' photographer Jeff Bloxham, who has covered virtually every major race for the past 30 years, declared the Revival the best meeting he'd ever attended. It was not just the unique atmosphere which enthralled, but also the sheer quality of the racing. Murray Walker, whose audition as a BBC commentator had been at one of the earliest Goodwood meetings, declared, "I have just experienced the best four days of my life, and I don't mind admitting I was close to tears most of the time."

The day after the Revival Derek Bell, twice World Sports Car Champion and five times Le Mans 24-Hour race winner, reflected, "I stayed on late because I dreaded returning to reality. I sat under the wing of a Spitfire, drinking Pimms with friends and watching the sun go down.

"My wife said we should be thinking about getting home to feed the dog, and I said, 'Just this once, the dog can wait. You will never again in your life know another day like this'."

At the Sunday prize-giving on the pit roof gallery, Derek had waxed lyrical after receiving the GRRC 'Spirit of Goodwood' Award, telling the crowd, "Don't go out through those gates over there - because outside those gates is the real world."

While Charles March invited remaining spectators up onto the gallery to share the last of the prize-giving champagne and cake, two of the weekend's younger warriors - both sports-jacketed, one bow-tied - ambled off across the track in a happy daze, clutching their fresh trophies.

Just before Derek Bell's gate into the real world they both stopped, turned and looked back to see the pits silhouetted against the sunset, with the last Spitfire climbing away to the west, and the seated Guards band on top. And the band was playing the Hokey-Cokey. One young warrior turned to the other and murmured, "It doesn't get better than this". The other just gulped, and could not answer. They turned on their heels, found an Army mess tent behind the Chicane grandstand, and ordered pie and chips for supper.

It had been a truly amazing weekend - one which had tugged and teased at every emotion - and above all, so much more than just an Historic race meeting. For Charles March, and his dog-tired but happy team, it was a case of roll the credits. End of movie. Until the next year. After all that time, and so much painstaking trouble, Goodwood had come to life again.

Party time, Goodwood Revival Saturday - after a terrific afternoon's racing on both two wheels and four, competitors and guests repaired to one of the aerodrome hangars, transformed for the night into an extra-ordinarily authentic 1940s nightclub with a circular central bar around a sculptured centrepiece fountain whose gilded nymphs stunned many by abruptly coming to life and climbing down from their perches. More comprehensively attired were the Earl of March's sisters Lady Louisa (with their parents, the Duke and Duchess of Richmond, **centre top**) and Nimmy (**top right**), while guests combined furs and mess-kit, DJs and a General's uniform, and included World Champions and wives, television stars, and stars with cars, but everyone - including Mr Bean - just adored those cigarette girls.

GOODWOOD'S GOLDEN BOOK

Here we list the results of all the motor race meetings held at Goodwood, from the opening meeting of September 1948 to the final Members' Meeting of July 1966, and including the results of the first Revival Meeting in September 1998. The first six are recorded for major Formula 1,2 and other major events (for example the Tourist Trophy and Nine-Hour Races), while the top three are listed for all other Internationals and Nationals. For Members' Meeting races only the winner is given. Where available, additional information is provided for: completed laps; car (or motor-cycle); race times; average speed; and fastest lap. A complete listing of Goodwood results, including every single entry and a narrative on each race, is available in Robert Barker's '*A Record Of Motor Racing At Goodwood*', published as a 2-volume limited edition by St Leonards Press, 4 Station Road, Esholt, Shipley BD17 7QR.

1948

18 SEPTEMBER 1948 - OPENING MEETING

Event 1 - Closed Sports Car Race up to 3000cc non s/c - 3 laps
1	Paul Pycroft (Pycroft Jaguar SS100)	6:30.2, 66.42 mph
2	Ken Downing (Healey Elliott Saloon)	6:36.6
3	Patrick Hall (Healey Elliott Coupé)	6:37.2

Fastest lap: Nick Haines (Healey Elliott Saloon)/Paul Pycroft - 2:06.5, 68.30 mph

Paul Pycroft's special-bodied Jaguar dominating the Goodwood inugural meeting's opening event - 18th September 1948. Who said, "Beauty lies in the eye of the beholder"?

Event 2 - Open Sports Car Race up to 1100cc non s/c - 3 laps
1	Harry Lester (MG L Type Magna)	6:39.4, 64.88 mph
2	Peter Morgan (Morgan 4/4)	6:55.6
3	Len Gibbs (Riley 9 Brooklands)	6:56.2

Fastest lap: Harry Lester - 2:08.6, 67.20 mph

Event 3 - Sports Car Race 1100cc-1500cc non s/c & up to 1100cc s/c - 3 laps
1	George Phillips (MG TC)	6:52.6, 62.82 mph
2	Gerry Ruddock (HRG Le Mans)	6:53.0
3	Charles Meisl (HRG 1500)	6:56.2

Fastest lap: A. B. Hunter (HRG Aero) - 2:11.1, 65.90 mph

Event 4 - Sports Car Race 1500cc-3000cc non s/c & up to 1500cc s/c - 3 laps
1	Ken Watkins (BMW 328)	6:52.8, 62.79 mph
2	Tony Crook (BMW 328)	6:53.0
3	Archie Lusty (MG TC)	7:03.8

Fastest lap: Ken Watkins - 2:12.5, 65.20 mph

Event 5 - 500cc Race - 3 laps
1	Stirling Moss (Cooper-JAP II)	6:00.4, 71.92 mph
2	Eric Brandon (Cooper-JAP I)	6:26.2
3	Curly Dryden (Cooper-Norton II)	6:30.6

Fastest lap: Stirling Moss - 1:58.0, 73.20 mph

Event 6 - Racing Car Race up to 2000cc or 1100cc s/c - 3 laps
1	Dudley Folland (MG K3)	5:49.8, 74.29 mph
2	Frank Kennington (MG K3)	5:57.6
3	Basil de Mattos (Spikins Special)	6:15.8

Fastest lap: Dudley Folland - 1:51.3, 77.60 mph

Event 7 - Racing Car Race over 1450cc s/c - 3 laps
1	Dennis Poore (Alfa Romeo 8C/35)	5:33.4, 77.74 mph
2	Peter Walker (ERA B Type)	5:34.4
3	John Bolster (ERA B Type)	5:35.2

Fastest lap: John Bolster - 1:46.1, 81.40 mph

Event 8 - '*Daily Graphic*' Goodwood Trophy for Formula 1 Cars - 5 laps
1	Reg Parnell (Maserati 4CLT/48)	8:56.2, 80.56 mph
2	Bob Gerard (ERA B Type)	8:56.6
3	David Hampshire (ERA A Type)	9:02.0
4	Cuth Harrison (ERA C Type)	
5	Duncan Hamilton (Maserati 6CM)	
6	Geoffrey Ansell (ERA B Type)	

Fastest lap (RECORD): Bob Gerard - 1:43.6, 83.39 mph

1949

18 APRIL 1949 - EASTER MEETING

Event 1 - Lavant Cup for Racing Cars up to 2000cc or 1000cc s/c - 5 laps
1	Dudley Folland (Ferrari 166)	9:13.6, 78.03 mph
2	Frank Kennington (Cisitalia D46)	9:22.4
3	Jack Fairman (Riley)	9:38.0

Fastest lap: Peter Wilks (Rover) - 1:46.0, 81.51 mph

Event 2 - 500cc Race - 5 laps
1	Stan Coldham (Cooper-JAP II)	10:10.2, 70.80 mph
2	Curly Dryden (Cooper-Norton II)	10:11.0
3	Don Parker (Parker CFS JAP)	11:02.0

Fastest lap: Curly Dryden - 1:55.8, 74.61 mph

Event 3 - Chichester Cup for Cars over 1450cc s/c - 5 laps
1	Reg Parnell (Maserati 4CLT/48)	8:40.6, 82.98 mph
2	Dennis Poore (Alfa Romeo 8C/35)	8:53.4
3	Leslie Johnson (ERA E Type)	8:55.4

Fastest lap: Reg Parnell - 1:40.0, 86.40 mph

Event 4 - First Easter Handicap - 5 laps
1	Frank Kennington (Cisitalia D45)	9:37.6, 74.79 mph
2	George Mackie (Rover)	10:08.6
3	Gordon Shillito (Riley)	10:10.2

Fastest lap: Oscar Moore (OBM) - 1:51.0, 77.84 mph

Event 5 - Richmond Trophy Race for Formula 1 Cars - 10 laps
1	Reg Parnell (Maserati 4CLT/48)	17:22.4, 82.87 mph
2	Peter Whitehead (ERA B Type)	17:26.2
3	Cuth Harrison (ERA C Type)	17:29.2
4	Fred Ashmore (Maserati 4CLT/48)	17:40.8
5	Leslie Johnson (ERA E Type)	17:48.2
6	George Abecassis (Alta)	18:35.4

Fastest lap (RECORD): Reg Parnell - 1:40.2, 86.22 mph

Event 6 - Second Easter Handicap - 5 laps
1	Stirling Moss (Cooper-JAP T9)	9:41.6, 79.76 mph
2	Dick Jacobs (MG TA Special)	10:06.0
3	George Abecassis (Cooper-Vincent T9)	10:06.4

Fastest lap: Stirling Moss - 1:44.8, 82.44 mph

Event 7 - Third Easter Handicap - 5 laps
1	Reg Parnell (Maserati 4CLT/48)	9:38.2, 84.18 mph
2	Tony Rolt (Alfa Romeo Aitken)	9:39.0
3	Fred Ashmore (Maserati 4CLT/48)	9:51.8

Fastest lap (RECORD): Reg Parnell - 1:39.2, 87.10 mph

13 AUGUST 1949 - 1st MEMBERS' MEETING

Event 1 - 3-lap Handicap (A)
1	Len Gibbs (Riley Nine)	7:04.4, 64.49 mph

Event 2 - 3-lap Handicap (B)
1	Eric Thompson (HRG Lightweight)	7:11.2, 66.77 mph

Event 3 - 3-lap Handicap (C)
1	John Craig (Jaguar SS100)	6:47.8, 67.36 mph

Event 4 - 5-lap Handicap (A)
1   Rodney Clarke (Connaught L2)   10:25.8, 73.63 mph

Event 5 - 5-lap Handicap (B)
1   Dickie Metcalfe (Fiat Balilla 508S)   11:39.4, 62.47 mph

Event 6 - 5-lap Handicap (C)
1   Dick Jacobs (MG TA Special)   11:29.8, 68.16 mph

Event 7 - 5-lap Handicap (D)
1   Eric Thompson (HRG Lightweight)   11:11.6, 69.40 mph

Event 8 - 5-lap Handicap (E)
1   Guy Jason-Henry (Delahaye 135M)   10:00.0, 73.80 mph

Event 9 - 5-lap Handicap (F)
1   Sydney Allard (Allard)   10:40.4, 73.68 mph

Progenitor of the post-war explosion in production of quantity-produced racing cars for customer use - the Dante Giascoso-designed Cisitalia D46 popularised the multi-tubular 'spaceframe'-type chassis and contributed greatly to re-establishing Continental motor racing post-war. Frank Kennington's was a rare example to appear in England, Easter Monday 1949.

17 SEPTEMBER 1949 – SEPTEMBER MEETING

Event 1 - Madgwick Cup for Cars up to 2000cc or 1100cc s/c - 5 laps
1   Stirling Moss (Cooper-JAP T9)   8:46.2, 82.10 mph
2   Eric Brandon (Cooper-JAP T9)   8:49.4
3   Bill Whitehouse (Cooper-JAP T9)   9:02.0
Fastest lap: Stirling Moss - 1:42.0, 84.71 mph

Event 2 - Woodcote Cup for Cars over 1450cc s/c - 5 laps
1   Reg Parnell (Maserati 4CLT/48)   8:27.6, 85.11 mph
2   Peter Whitehead (ERA E Type)   8:29.0
3   Cuth Harrison (ERA B/C Type)   8:35.8
Fastest lap (RECORD): Reg Parnell - 1:38.6, 87.63 mph

Event 3 - 500cc Race - 5 laps
1   Peter Collins (Cooper-Norton III)   9:36.4, 74.95 mph
2   Lex Beels (Cooper-JAP III)   9:37.4
3   Stan Coldham (Cooper-JAP II)   9:49.0
Fastest lap: Lex Beels - 1:52.2, 77.00 mph

Event 4 - September Handicap (A) - 5 laps
1   Ken McAlpine (Maserati 8CM)   8:55.6, 83.14 mph
2   Reg Parnell (Maserati 4CLT/48)   9:09.0
3   David Hampshire (Maserati 4CLT/48)   9:10.6
Fastest lap (RECORD): Reg Parnell - 1:36.8, 89.26 mph

Event 5 - September Handicap (B) - 5 laps
1   Tony Rolt (Alfa Romeo Aitken)   9:07.4, 83.49 mph
2   Duncan Hamilton (Maserati 6CM)   9:09.0
3   Peter Walker (ERA E Type)   9:22.6
Fastest lap: Peter Walker - 1:38.4, 87.80 mph

Event 6 - September Handicap (C) - 5 laps
1   Gordon Shillito (Riley)   9:23.4, 80.99 mph
2   Dennis Poore (Veritas)   9:28.4
3   Spencer King (Rover)   9:35.0
Fastest lap: Gordon Shillito - 1:43.8, 83.24 mph

Event 7 - 'Daily Graphic' Goodwood Trophy - 10 laps
1   Reg Parnell (Maserati 4CLT/48)   16:39.6, 86.43 mph
2   Peter Walker (ERA E Type)   16:45.6
3   Bob Gerard (ERA B Type)   16:48.6
Fastest lap: Reg Parnell - 1:36.8, 89.26 mph

Event 8 - September Handicap (D) - 5 laps
1   Gerry Dunham (Alvis 12-70 Special)   10:07.2, 71.15 mph
2   Ron Willis (BMW T40 Special)   10:15.8
3   Ken Downing (Riley Brooke Special)   10:27.6
Fastest lap: Ken Downing 1:52.4, 76.87 mph

1950

10 APRIL 1950 – EASTER MEETING

Event 1 - Lavant Cup for Cars up to 2000cc or 1100cc s/c - 5 laps
1   Bill Aston (Cooper-JAP T9)   9:07.4, 78.92 mph
2   Eric Brandon (Cooper-JAP T12)   9:08.2
3   John Green (Cooper-Vincent HRD T12) 9:32.8
Fastest lap: Eric Brandon - 1:45.0, 82.29 mph

Event 2 - 500cc Race - 5 laps
1   Curly Dryden (Cooper-Norton II)   10:31.6, 68.40 mph
2   Stan Coldham (Cooper-JAP II)   10:31.8
3   Alf Bottoms (JBS-Norton)   10:38.6
Fastest lap: Ken Carter (Cooper-JAP) - 1:51.2, 70.70 mph

Event 3 - Chichester Cup - 5 laps
1   'B. Bira' (Maserati 4CLT/48)   8:55.8, 80.63 mph
2   Baron E. de Graffenried (Maserati 4CLT/48) 9:00.4
3   Dennis Poore (Alfa Romeo 8C/35)   9:01.6
Fastest lap: Peter Walker (ERA E Type) - 1:43.8, 83.24 mph

Event 4 - First Easter Handicap - 5 laps
1   Bill Aston (Cooper-JAP T9)   10:58.6, 73.77 mph
2   Basil de Lissa (MG-K3)   10:59.0
3   Gerry Dunham (Alvis 12-70 Special)   11:18.4
Fastest lap: Bill Aston/John Green (Cooper-Vincent HRD T12) - 1:55.6, 74.74 mph

Event 5 - Richmond Trophy for Formula 1 Cars - 11 laps
1   Reg Parnell (Maserati 4CLT/48)   20:14.4, 78.26 mph
2   Baron E. de Graffenried (Maserati 4CLT/48) 21:00.4
3   Brian Shawe-Taylor (ERA B Type)   21:00.5
Fastest lap: Reg Parnell - 1:46.0, 81.51 mph

Event 6 - Second Easter Handicap - 5 laps
1   Gerry Dunham (Alvis 12-70 Special)   10:38.4, 69.30 mph
2   Jim Byrom (Bugatti T35B)   10:46.4
3   Guy Gale (Darracq T150C)   10:47.6
Fastest lap: Peter Mould (Delage) - 1:57.6, 73.47 mph

Event 7 - Third Easter Handicap - 5 laps
1   Duncan Hamilton (Maserati 6CM)   9:45.8, 76.35 mph
2   Stirling Moss (HWM Alta)   9:48.0
3   'B. Bira' (Maserati 4CLT/48)   10:00.0
Fastest lap: 'B. Bira'/Reg Parnell (Maserati 4CLT/48) - 1:46.2, 81.36 mph

6 MAY 1950 – 2nd MEMBERS' MEETING

Event 1 - 3-lap Scratch Race (B) up to 1500cc non s/c
1   George Phillips (MG TC Special)   6:24.2, 67.80 mph
Fastest lap: Mike Keen (HRG Lightweight) - 2:03.0, 70.21 mph

Event 2 - 3-lap Scratch Race (B) up to 1500cc non s/c
1   Jim Mayers (Lester-MG)   6:14.0, 69.80 mph
Fastest lap: Jim Mayers - 1:57.2, 73.65 mph

Event 3 - 3-lap Scratch Race (A) 1500-3000cc non s/c
1   Ken McAlpine (Connaught L2)   6:00.0, 72.00 mph
Fastest lap: Ken McAlpine - 1:57.0, 73.80 mph

Event 4 - 3-lap Scratch Race (B) 1500-3000cc un s/c
1   Tony Crook (Frazer Nash HS)   6:10.0, 70.01 mph
Fastest lap: Tony Crook - 1:58.2, 73.08 mph

Event 5 - 3-lap Scratch Race over 3000cc non s/c
1   Sydney Allard (Allard-Cadillac J2)   5:56.6, 72.75 mph
Fastest lap: Sydney Allard - 1:54.8, 75.20 mph

Event 6 - 3-lap Handicap for MG Cars
1   Jim Mayers (Lester-MG)   6:31.4, 71.50 mph
Fastest lap: Jim Mayers - 1:55.4, 74.98 mph

Event 7 - 3-lap Handicap for MG Cars
1   John Haesendonck (MG PB)   6:56.0, 66.40 mph
Fastest lap: John Haesendonck - 2:07.6, 67.81 mph

Event 8 - 3-lap Handicap (A)
1   Dick Jacobs (MG T Type Special)   6:50.0, 70.08 mph
Fastest lap: Ken McAlpine (Connaught L2) - 1:55.0, 75.10 mph

The unmistakable 'rasp of ripping calico' between Freddie Richmond's concrete barriers as a Grand Prix car of a very different era powers its supercharged straight-eight way past the old control tower. Back in 1931-32 the Molsheim-made Type 51s such as this contested full-blown ten-hour Grands Prix... By 1950 the ways of racing had changed.

Event 9 - 3-lap Handicap (B)
1   Nancy Binns (Riley Sprite)   6:56.0, 67.50 mph
Fastest lap: Nancy Binns - 2:02.0, 70.80 mph

Event 10 - 3-lap Handicap (C)
1   Guy Gale (Darracq T150C)   6:35.2, 69.11 mph
Fastest lap: Guy Gale - 2:00.6, 71.00 mph

27 MAY 1950 – WHIT-SATURDAY MEETING

Event 1 - 500 International Trophy Heat 1 - 7 laps
1   Eric Brandon (Cooper-JAP)   13:16.6, 75.92 mph
2   Peter Collins (Cooper-Norton III)   13:18.0
3   Dennis Poore (Parsenn-JAP)   13:24.0
Fastest lap: Eric Brandon - 1:52.6, 76.73 mph

Event 2 - 500 International Trophy Heat 2 - 7 laps
1	Curly Dryden (Cooper-Norton II)	13:23.8, 75.24 mph
2	Bill Whitehouse (Cooper-Norton III)	13:26.6
3	Don Parker (Parker Special-JAP)	13:41.6
Fastest Lap: W/Cdr Frank Aikens (Iota-Triumph) - 1:53.2, 76.32 mph

Event 3 - First Whitsun Handicap - 5 laps
1	Basil de Lissa (MG K3)	10:16.8, 73.00 mph
2	John Haesendonck (MG PB)	10:19.6
3	Tony Rolt (Delage 15S8)	10:44.0
Fastest lap: Brian Shawe-Taylor (ERA B Type) - 1:40.2, 86.22 mph

Event 4 - Second Whitsun Handicap - 5 laps
1	Gerry Ruddock (HRG)	10:28.4, 71.95 mph
2	Jim Byrom (Bugatti T35B)	10:43.4
3	John Haesendonck (MG PB)	10:46.0
Fastest lap: Guy Jason-Henry (Delahaye 135M) - 1:50.6, 78.12 mph

Event 5 - 500 International Trophy Final - 15 laps
1	Curly Dryden (Cooper-Norton II)	27:58.0, 77.23 mph
2	Peter Collins (Cooper-Norton III)	27:58.6
3	John Cooper (Cooper-JAP IV)	28:39.2
Fastest lap: Curly Dryden - 1:49.4, 78.98 mph

Event 6 - Third Whitsun Handicap - 5 laps
1	Basil de Lissa (MG K3)	10:13.0, 76.06 mph
2	Gerry Dunham (Alvis 12-70 Special)	10:13.4
3	Tony Rolt (Delage 15S8)	10:14.0
Fastest lap: Tony Rolt - 1:42.0, 84.71 mph

17 JUNE 1950 – 3rd MEMBERS' MEETING

Event 1 - 5-lap Scratch Race (A) under 1500cc non s/c
1	Gerry Ruddock (HRG Le Mans)	10:03.6, 71.58 mph
Fastest lap: John Cooper (Cooper-MG T14) - 1:56.0, 74.50 mph

Event 2 - 5-lap Scratch Race under 1500cc non s/c
1	R E Molyneaux (MG TC)	10:55.4, 65.91 mph
Fastest lap: Leslie Woods (MG) - 2:08.2, 66.83 mph

Event 3 - 5-lap Scratch Race 1500-3000cc non s/c
1	Rodney Peacock (BMW 328)	9:46.4, 73.67 mph
Fastest lap: Rodney Peacock - 1:55.0, 75.10 mph

Event 4 - 5-lap Scratch Race over 3000cc non s/c
1	Guy Jason-Henry (Delahaye 135M)	9:28.8, 75.94 mph
Fastest lap: Guy Gale (Darracq T150C) - 1:50.4, 77.61 mph

Event 5 - 5-lap Handicap (A)
1	John Craig (Jaguar SS100)	11:05.2, 73.84 mph
Fastest lap: John Craig - 1:49.0, 79.30 mph

Event 6 - 5-lap Handicap (B)
1	J. Goodhew (Lagonda LG45)	10:57.6, 70.98 mph
Fastest lap: Jean Mortimer (Healey Silverstone) - 1:55.0, 75.10 mph

Event 7 - 5-lap Handicap (C)
1	Dickie Metcalfe (Fiat Balilla 508S)	11:49.0, 62.25 mph
Fastest lap: Mike Keen (HRG Lightweight) - 2:03.0, 70.20 mph

Event 8 - 5-lap Handicap (D)
1	J.T. Sutherland (MG TC)	11:18.8, 69.93 mph
Fastest lap: J. Goodhew (Lagonda LG45) - 1:54.0, 75.80 mph

Event 9 - 5-lap Handicap (E)
1	R.E. Molyneaux (MG TC)	11:19.2, 65.74 mph
Fastest lap: John Cooper (Cooper-MG T14) - 1:57.4, 72.98 mph

12 AUGUST 1950 – 4th MEMBERS' MEETING

Event 1 - 5-lap Scratch Race up to 1100cc non s/c
1	Dick Jacobs (MG TA Special)	10:41.0, 67.40 mph
Fastest lap: Dick Jacobs - 2:04.8, 69.44 mph

Event 2 - 5-lap Scratch Race 1100-1500cc non s/c
1	John Cooper (Cooper-MG T14)	10:02.2, 71.74 mph
Fastest lap: Gerry Ruddock (HRG Le Mans) - 1:58.0, 73.20 mph

Event 3 - 5-lap Scratch Race 1500-3000cc non s/c
1	Ken McAlpine (Connaught L2)	9:48.0, 73.47 mph
Fastest lap: Rodney Peacock (BMW 328) - 1:53.4, 76.18 mph

Event 4 - 5-lap Scratch Race over 3000cc non s/c
1	Guy Gale (Darracq T150C)	9:23.0, 76.70 mph
Fastest lap: Guy Gale - 1:50.8, 77.98 mph

Event 5 - 5-lap Handicap for non s/c Bentleys
1	J H Bailey (Bentley 3-Litre)	13:11.0, 60.76 mph
Fastest lap: Harry Kemp Place (Bentley 4½ litre) - 2:01.0, 71.40 mph

Event 6 - 5-lap Handicap (A)
1	Guy Templer (Fiat 500 Coupé)	13:44.0, 51.71 mph
Fastest lap: J. Goodhew (Lagonda LG45) - 1:54.2, 75.67 mph

Event 7 - 5-lap Handicap (B)
1	Harry Lester (Lester MG)	11:09.2, 67.79 mph
Fastest lap: Guy Gale (Darracq T150C) - 1:49.8, 78.69 mph

Event 8 - 5-lap Handicap (C)
1	Philip Fotheringham-Parker (Alfa Romeo 8C)	11:03.4, 70.54 mph
Fastest lap: Tony Crook (Frazer Nash HS) - 1:52.8, 76.58 mph

Event 9 - 5 lap Handicap (D)
1	Claude Hamilton (Invicta)	11:12.0, 64.29 mph
Fastest lap: Jean Mortimer (Healey Silverstone) - 1:53.4, 76.19 mph

30TH SEPTEMBER 1950 – SEPTEMBER MEETING

Event 1 - Madgwick Cup up to 2000cc or 1100cc s/c - 5 laps
1	Bill Aston (Cooper-JAP T12)	9:49.0, 73.70 mph
2	Gordon Shillito (Riley)	9:55.0
3	Harry Schell (Cooper-JAP T9)	9:55.4
Fastest lap: Gordon Shillito - 1:55.0, 75.13 mph

Event 2 - 500cc Race - 5 laps
1	Curly Dryden (Cooper-Norton II)	10.10.6, 70.75 mph
2	Stirling Moss (Cooper-Norton IV)	10:16.4
3	Eric Brandon (Cooper-Norton)	10:20.0
Fastest lap: Stirling Moss - 1:59.6, 72.24 mph

Event 3 - Woodcote Cup for *Formule Libre* Cars - 5 laps
1	Reg Parnell (BRM Type 15)	9:10.0, 78.50 mph
2	'B. Bira' (Maserati 4CLT/48)	9:11.6
3	Baron E. de Graffenried (Maserati 4CLT/48)	9:27.4
Fastest lap: Reg Parnell - 1:45.6, 81.82 mph

Event 4 - First September Handicap - 5 laps
1	Horace Richards (Riley Nine)	11:10.0, 64.50 mph
2	John Willment (Bugatti T55)	11:20.4
3	Basil de Mattos (Cromard Special)	11:43.8
Fastest lap: Ray Merrick (Cooper JAP T12) - 1:55.4, 74.87 mph

Event 5 - Second September Handicap - 5 laps
1	Duncan Hamilton (Maserati 6CM)	10:15.0, 75.80 mph
2	Gerry Ruddock (HRG Le Mans)	10:16.0
3	Peter Whitehead (ERA B Type)	10:34.4
Fastest lap: Peter Whitehead - 1:51.0, 77.84 mph

Event 6 - Third September Handicap - 5 laps
1	Harry Schell (Cooper JAP T9)	11:02.0, 72.51 mph
2	J. Goodhew (Alfa Romeo *Tipo B*)	11:03.8
3	Bob Gerard (ERA B Type)	11:05.0
Fastest lap: Bob Gerard - 1:48.0, 80.00 mph

Event 7 - Fourth September Handicap - 5 laps
1	Gordon Shillito (Riley)	10:45.0, 72.90 mph
2	Leslie Johnson (Bentley)	11:03.0
3	George Abecassis (Healey Silverstone)	11:26.4
Fastest lap: Gordon Shillito - 1:54.0, 75.70 mph

Event 8 - '*Daily Graphic*' Goodwood Trophy for Formula 1 Cars - 12 laps
1	Reg Parnell (BRM Type 15)	20:58.4, 82.48 mph
2	'B. Bira' (Maserati 4CLT/48)	21:10.8
3	Bob Gerard (ERA B Type)	21:39.4
4	Baron E. de Graffenried (Maserati 4CLT/48)	21:39.8
5	Brian Shawe-Taylor (ERA B Type)	21:41.0
6	Graham Whitehead (ERA B Type)	21:52.0
Fastest lap: Reg Parnell - 1:41.8, 84.87 mph

1951

26 MARCH 1951 – EASTER MEETING

Event 1 - Lavant Cup for Racing Cars up to 2000cc or 1100cc s/c - 5 laps
1	Stirling Moss (HWM-Alta)	8:54.0, 80.91 mph
2	Eric Brandon (Cooper-JAP T12)	8:54.8
3	Bill Aston (Cooper-JAP T12)	9:24.0
Fastest lap: Eric Brandon - 1:44.2, 82.92 mph

Event 2 - Earl of March Trophy for 500cc Racing Cars - 5 laps
1	Alf Bottoms (JBS-Norton)	9:29.2, 75.92 mph
2	Curly Dryden (JBS-Norton)	9:30.6
3	Ken Carter (Cooper-Norton V)	9:36.2
Fastest lap: Peter Collins (Cooper-Norton) - 1:48.2, 79.85 mph

Event 3 - Chichester Cup for *Formule Libre* Racing Cars - 5 laps
1	Reg Parnell (Maserati 4CLT/48)	8:41.0, 82.92 mph
2	Brian Shawe-Taylor (ERA B Type)	8:43.6
3	'B. Bira' (OSCA G-4500)	8:53.2
Fastest lap: Brian Shawe-Taylor - 1:41.2, 85.37 mph

'The Old English Upright' ERAs formed the high-tensile backbone of British hopes in motor racing immediately after the War. None of the regular road-racing ERAs was more meticulously prepared than Bob Gerard's 'R14B', nine times a winner 1946-51 - here at Goodwood, Easter Monday 1951.

Event 4 - First Easter Handicap - 5 laps
1	Peter Collins (Cooper-JAP T12)	10:06.8, 81.24 mph
2	Mike Keen (HRG Lightweight)	10:16.4
3	Gerry Ruddock (HRG Le Mans)	10:17.4
Fastest lap: Peter Collins - 1:44.2, 82.92 mph

Event 5 - Second Easter Handicap - 5 laps
1	John Cooper (Cooper-JAP T12)	9:02.4, 83.99 mph
2	Brian Shawe-Taylor (Connaught A)	9:03.0
3	E. M. Martin (ERA A Type)	9:51.2
Fastest lap: John Cooper - 1:40.6, 85.88 mph

Event 6 - Richmond Trophy Race for Formula 1 Cars - 12 laps
1	'B. Bira' (OSCA G-4500)	19:44.0, 87.57 mph
2	Brian Shawe-Taylor (ERA B Type)	20:01.2
3	Duncan Hamilton (ERA B Type)	20:09.4
4	Johnny Claes (Talbot-Lago T26C)	20:13.4
5	Stirling Moss (HWM-Alta)	20:34.0
6	Graham Whitehead (ERA B Type)	21:02.6

Fastest lap (RECORD): 'B. Bira' - 1:35.6, 90.38 mph

Event 7 - Third Easter Handicap - 5 laps
1	Len Gibbs (HRG Lightweight)	10:14.0, 72.85 mph
2	George Wicken (Jaguar XK120)	10:21.0
3	John Craig (Jaguar XK120)	10:23.0

Fastest lap: George Wicken - 1:49.4, 78.98 mph

Event 8 - Fourth Easter Handicap - 5 laps
1	Johnny Claes (Talbot-Lago T26C)	8:39.4, 86.50 mph
2	J. Goodhew (Alfa Romeo *Tipo B*)	8:51.0
3	'B. Bira' (OSCA G-4500)	8:58.8

Fastest lap: 'B. Bira' - 1:35.6, 90.38 mph

14 APRIL 1951 - '*MOTOR-CYCLING*'S GOODWOOD SATURDAY

Event 1 - Racing 225-250cc - 10 laps
1	Maurice Cann (Moto Guzzi)	19:27.0, 74.04 mph

Event 2 - Racing 300-350cc - 10 laps
1	Les Dear (AJS)	18:10.4, 79.24 mph

Event 3 - Clubman Production 300-350cc - 10 laps
1	K.R.V. James (BSA)	20:25.4, 70.51 mph

Event 4 - Racing 400-1000cc - 10 laps
1	George Brown (Vincent)	17:23.0, 82.84 mph

Event 5 - Vintage - 7 laps
1	M.C. Tomkinson (Velocette)	15:08.0, 66.61 mph

Event 6 - Racing 400-500cc - 20 laps
1	Geoff Duke (Norton)	33.04.4, 87.08 mph

Event 7 - Sidecars 400-1200cc - 10-lap Handicap
1	Bill Boddice (Norton)	20:10.4, 73.20 mph

Event 8 - Racing 300-350cc - 20 laps
1	Geoff Duke (Norton)	34:28.0, 83.56 mph

Event 9 - Clubman Production 400-1000cc - 10 laps
1	C. Lawrence (HRD)	19:30.4, 73.82 mph

21 APRIL 1951 - 5th MEMBERS' MEETING

Event 1 - 5-lap Scratch Race up to 1100cc non s/c
1	Harry Lester (Lester-MG)	10:14.6, 70.30 mph

Fastest lap: Len Gibbs (Riley Nine) - 1:59.0, 72.60 mph

Event 2 - 4-lap Scratch Race 1100-1500cc non s/c
1	Gerry Ruddock (HRG Le Mans)	9:52.2, 72.90 mph

Fastest lap: Gerry Ruddock - 1:53.2, 76.40 mph

Event 3 - 5-lap Scratch Race 1500-3000cc non s/c
1	Eric Winterbottom (Frazer Nash LMR)	9:14.0, 77.90 mph

Fastest lap: Dickie Stoop (Frazer Nash MM)/Eric Winterbottom - 1:46.6, 81.10 mph

Event 4 - 5-lap Scratch Race over 3000cc non s/c
1	Guy Gale (Darracq T150C)	9:16.4, 77.20 mph

Fastest lap - Bill Holt (Jaguar XK120) - 1:45.6, 81.90 mph

Event 5 - 5-lap Handicap (A)
1	H.J. Wilmshurst (Bentley)	11.09.6, 72.70 mph

Fastest lap: H.J. Wilmshurst - 1:52.4, 76.60 mph

Event 6 - 5-lap Handicap (B)
1	Harry Kemp-Place (Healey Silverstone)	10:53.6, 73.10 mph

Fastest lap: R.F. Walsh (Healey Silverstone) - 1:53.6, 76.10 mph

Event 7 - 5-lap Handicap (C)
1	Cliff Davis (MG N Special)	11:12.2, 71.10 mph

Fastest lap: Dick Jacobs (MG Special) - 1:54.2, 75.00 mph

Event 8 - 5-lap Handicap (D)
1	John Lyons (Connaught L2)	9:45.0, 75.30 mph

Fastest lap: Tony Crook (Frazer Nash LMR) - 1:42.4, 84.30 mph

Event 9 - 5-lap Handicap (E)
1	Dickie Stoop (Frazer Nash MM)	9:55.8, 78.10 mph

Fastest lap: Sydney Allard (Allard J2) - 1:45.8, 81.70 mph

14 MAY 1951 - WHITSUN MEETNG

Event 1 - 500 International Trophy Heat 1 - 7 laps
1	Eric Brandon (Cooper-Norton V)	12:34.6, 80.16 mph
2	David Clarke (Cooper-Norton V)	12:56.2
3	Jack Westcott (JBS-JAP)	13:04.4

Fastest lap: David Clarke - 1:46.0, 81.51 mph

Event 2 - 500 International Trophy Heat 2 - 7 laps
1	Alan Brown (Cooper-Norton V)	12:49.2, 78.63 mph
2	Bernie Ecclestone (Cooper-JAP V)	13:31.6
3	Ken McAlpine (JBS-Norton)	13:34.8

Fastest lap: Alan Brown - 1:47.6, 80.30 mph

Event 3 - '*Daily Graphic*' Race for the Festival of Britain Trophy - Heat 1 - 7 laps
1	Reg Parnell (Ferrari '*Thin Wall Special*')	11:11.6, 90.07 mph
2	Baron E. de Graffenried (Maserati 4CLT/48)	11:24.0
3	Brian Shawe-Taylor (ERA C Type)	11:26.8

Fastest lap (RECORD): Reg Parnell - 1:32.8, 93.10 mph

Event 4 - '*Daily Graphic*' Race for the Festival of Britain Trophy - Heat 2 - 7 laps
1	'B. Bira' (OSCA G-4500)	11:25.2, 88.28 mph
2	Giuseppe Farina (Maserati 4CLT/48)	11:30.0
3	David Hampshire (Maserati 4CLT/48)	11:42.0

Fastest lap: 'B. Bira' - 1:33.8, 92.11 mph

Event 5 - 500 International Trophy Final - 15 laps
1	Stirling Moss (Kieft-Norton)	26:15.4, 82.82 mph
2	Alan Brown (Cooper-Norton V)	26:37.2
3	David Clarke (Cooper-Norton V)	27:05.2

Fastest lap: Stirling Moss - 1:42.2, 84.54 mph

Event 6 - '*Daily Graphic*' Race for the Festival of Britain Trophy - Final - 15 laps
1	Reg Parnell (Ferrari '*Thin Wall Special*')	23:34.2, 91.64 mph
2	Giuseppe Farina (Maserati 4CLT/48)	23:45.0
3	Baron E. de Graffenried (Maserati 4CLT/48)	24:17.8
4	Brian Shawe-Taylor (ERA C Type)	24:18.4
5	Duncan Hamilton (Talbot-Lago T26C)	24:40.6
6	Tony Rolt (ERA-Delage)	24:40.8

Fastest lap (RECORD): Reg Parnell - 1:31.4, 94.53 mph

16 JUNE 1951 - 6th MEMBERS' MEETING

Event 1 - 5-lap Scratch Race up to 1500cc non s/c
1	Mike Hawthorn (Riley TT Sprite)	9:33.0, 75.39 mph

Fastest lap: Mike Hawthorn - 1:52.6, 76.90 mph

Event 2 - 5-lap Scratch Race 1500-3000cc non s/c
1	Tony Crook (Frazer Nash LMR)	9:02.0, 79.70 mph

Fastest lap: Tony Crook - 1:45.0, 82.29 mph

Event 3 - 5-lap Scratch Race over 3000cc non s/c
1	John Craig (Jaguar XK120)	9:08.4, 78.77 mph

Fastest lap: John Craig - 1:46.0, 81.50 mph

Event 4 - MG 5-lap Handicap
1	W.P. Jones (MG J2)	12:20.4, 58.35 mph

Fastest lap: Cliff Davis (MG NA Special) - 1:53.6, 76.20 mph

Event 5 - 5-lap Handicap (A)
1	John de Edwards (Healey Silverstone)	9:49.0, 73.34 mph

Fastest lap: John Craig (Jaguar XK120) - 1:46.0, 81.59 mph

Event 6 - 5-lap Handicap (B)
1	C. Treen (Treen Riley Nine)	10:52.0, 68.35 mph

Fastest lap: Basil Chevell (Alvis Speed 20 Special) - 1:51.8, 77.28 mph

Event 7 - 5-lap Handicap (C)
1	Dickie Metcalfe (Fiat Balilla 508S)	11:01.4, 67.31 mph

Fastest lap: Cliff Davis (MG N Special) - 1:53.2, 76.32 mph

Event 8 - 5-lap Handicap (D)
1	'Twink' Whincop (Bugatti T57S Special)	10:12.8, 73.87 mph

Fastest lap: Tony Crook (Frazer Nash LMR) - 1:44.6, 82.60 mph

Event 9 - 5-lap Handicap (E)
1	Mike Hawthorn (Riley TT Sprite)	10:4.0, 77.47 mph

Fastest lap: Mike Hawthorn - 1:48.6, 79.56 mph

18 AUGUST 1951 - 7th MEMBERS' MEETING

Event 1 - 5-lap Scratch Race up to 1500cc non s/c Grid
1	Mike Hawthorn (Riley TT Sprite)	9:24.0, 76.59 mph

Fastest lap: Mike Hawthorn - 1:49.0, 79.27 mph

Event 2 - 5-lap Scratch Race 1500-3000cc non s/c
1	Tony Crook (Frazer Nash LMR)	9:11.4, 78.34 mph

Fastest lap: Rodney Peacock (Frazer Nash LMR) - 1:46.2, 81.36 mph

Event 3 - 5-lap Scratch Race over 3000cc non s/c
1	Sydney Allard (Allard J2)	8:50.8, 81.38 mph

Fastest lap: Sydney Allard - 1:43.4, 83.56 mph

Event 4 - Bentley Handicap
1	J.H. Bailey (Bentley)	11:00.0, 65.45 mph

Fastest lap: H.J. Wilmshurst (Bentley) - 1:53.8, 75.92 mph

Event 5 - 5-lap Handicap (A)
1	P.B. Merritt (MG NE)	10:15.0, 71.40 mph

Fastest lap: Philip Fotheringham-Parker (Jaguar XK120) - 1:42.2, 84.54 mph

Event 6 - 5-lap Handicap (B)
1	Nigel Mann (Alfa Romeo 8C)	10:11.0, 77.61 mph

Fastest lap: Sydney Allard (Allard J2) - 1:42.2, 84.45 mph

Event 7 - 5-lap Handicap (C)
1	J. Nicholson (MG PA)	10:50.6, 69.27 mph

Fastest lap: J. Nicholson - 2:02.2, 70.70 mph

Event 8 - 5-lap Handicap (D)
1	David Lewis (Alfa Romeo 8C)	10:07.4, 77.50 mph

Fastest lap: Duncan Hamilton (Jaguar XK120) - 1:46.2, 81.36 mph

Event 9 - 5-lap Handicap (E)
1	Ken Downing (Connaught L2)	9:59.0, 75.26 mph

Fastest lap: Tony Crook (Frazer Nash LMR) - 1:44.0, 83.08 mph

29 SEPTEMBER 1951 - SEPTEMBER MEETING

Event 1 - Madgwick Cup for Cars up to 2000cc or 1100cc s/c - 5 laps
1	Stirling Moss (HWM)	8:25.0, 84.83 mph
2	Lance Macklin (HWM)	8:26.6
3	George Abecassis (HWM)	8:27.2

Fastest lap: Stirling Moss - 1:39.0, 86.54 mph

Event 2 - Woodcote Cup *Formule Libre* Race - 5 laps
1	Giuseppe Farina (Alfa Romeo 158)	7:31.8, 94.83 mph
2	Reg Parnell (Ferrari '*Thin Wall Special*')	7:38.4
3	Tony Rolt (ERA-Delage 15S8)	8:09.4

Fastest lap (RECORD): Giuseppe Farina - 1:28.4, 96.92 mph

Event 3 - Sports Car Race - 5 laps
1	Stirling Moss (Jaguar C-type)	8:32.0, 83.67 mph
2	David Clarke (Frazer Nash LMR)	8:45.0
3	Hugh Howorth (Jaguar XK120)	8:58.0

Fastest lap: Stirling Moss - 1:41.0, 84.83 mph

Event 4 - First September Handicap - 5 laps
1	Ken Wharton (Cromard Special)	9:17.0, 81.97 mph
2	Gerry Dunham (Alvis 12-70 Special)	9:22.0
3	Ray Merrick (Cooper-Nor-JAP T16)	9:25.8

Fastest lap: Ray Merrick - 1:38.4, 87.07 mph **Event 5** - Second September Handicap - 5 laps

Event 5 - Second September Handicap - 5 laps
1   Stirling Moss (Jaguar C-type)   9:20.2, 84.16 mph
2   Hugh Howorth (Jaguar XK120)   9:38.8
3   Philip Fotheringham-Parker (Jaguar XK120)   9:41.8
Fastest lap: Stirling Moss - 1:39.6, 86.02 mph

Event 6 - Third September Handicap - 5 laps
1   Giuseppe Farina (Alfa Romeo 158)   8:33.4, 94.50 mph
2   Stirling Moss (HWM)   8:35.4
3   Reg Parnell (Ferrari 'Thin Wall Special')   8:37.8
Fastest lap: Giuseppe Farina - 1:28.4, 96.92 mph

Event 7 - Fourth September Handicap - 5 laps
1   Mike Keen (HRG F2)   9:43.8, 80.91 mph
2   Horace Richards (Riley Brooklands Special)   9:46.8
3   Cliff Davis (Cooper-MG T14)   10:05.2
Fastest lap: Mike Keen - 1:43.4, 82.86 mph

Event 8 - 'Daily Graphic' Goodwood Trophy for Formula 1 Cars - 15 laps
1   Giuseppe Farina (Alfa Romeo 159)   22:31.2, 95.11 mph
2   Reg Parnell (Ferrari 'Thin Wall Special')   22:36.8
3   Tony Rolt (ERA-Delage 15S8)   22:43.0
4   Bob Gerard (ERA B Type)   22:44.4
5   Stirling Moss (HWM)   N/A
7   Ken Wharton (ERA B Type)   N/A
Fastest lap (RECORD): Giuseppe Farina - 1:28.0, 97.36 mph

1952

22 MARCH 1952 - 8th MEMBERS' MEETING

Event 1 - 5-lap Scratch Race (A)
1   Mike Hawthorn (Riley Ulster Imp)   11:06.4, 64.86 mph
Fastest lap: Mike Hawthorn - 2:09.2, 66.87 mph

Event 2 - 5-lap Scratch Race (B)
1   Cliff Davis (Cooper-MG T14)   9:58.0, 72.24 mph
Fastest lap: Cliff Davis - 1:57.2, 73.72 mph

Event 3 - 5-lap Scratch Race (C)
1   Lawrence Mitchell (Frazer Nash HS)   9:51.8, 72.97 mph
Fastest lap: Tony Crook (Frazer Nash LMR)/Dickie Stoop (Frazer Nash MM)/
Lawrence Mitchell - 1:55.2, 75.00 mph

Event 4 - 5-lap Scratch Race (D) over 3000cc non s/c
1   Oscar Moore (HWM-Jaguar)   9:57.2 , 72.36 mph
Fastest lap: Oscar Moore - 1:54.6, 75.39 mph

Event 5 - 5-lap Handicap (A)
1   Ernest Harewood (MG PB)   11:34.8, 67.29 mph
Fastest lap: Ernest Harewood - 2:05.0, 69.12 mph

Event 6 - 5-lap Handicap (B)
1   Jack Fairman (Aston Martin SM)   10:54.0, 70.02 mph
Fastest lap: Nigel Mann (Alfa Romeo 8C)/Cliff Davis (Cooper MG T14) - 1:54.0,
75.79 mph

Event 7 - 5-lap Handicap (C)
1   A.D. Tasker (Healey Silverstone)   10:35.6, 68.68 mph
Fastest lap: Lawrence Mitchell - 1:53.2, 76.32 mph

Event 8 - 5 lap-Handicap (D)
1   Les Leston (Lester-MG)   10:27.0, 73.22 mph
Fastest lap: Oscar Moore (HWM-Jaguar) - 1:52.6, 76.73 mph

Event 9 - 5-lap Handicap (E)
1   Tony Stokes (Jaguar SS100)   11:16.8, 70.59 mph
Fastest lap: Ken Downing (Connaught L2) - 1:57.4, 73.59 mph

14 APRIL 1952 - EASTER MEETING

Event 1 - Lavant Cup for Formula 2 Racing Cars
1   Mike Hawthorn (Cooper-Bristol T20)   10:22.2, 83.18 mph
2   Alan Brown (Cooper-Bristol T20)   10:44.0
3   Eric Brandon (Cooper-Bristol T20)   10:45.0
Fastest lap: Mike Hawthorn - 1:42.0, 84.71 mph

Event 2 - Earl of March Trophy for 500cc Racing Cars - 6 laps
1   Stirling Moss (Kieft-Norton)   11:04.0, 78.07 mph
2   Alan Brown (Cooper-Norton MkVI)   11:09.2
3   John Coombs (Cooper-Norton MkVI)   11:33.4
Fastest lap: Stirling Moss - 1:48.6, 79.56 mph

Event 3 - Chichester Cup for Formule Libre Cars - 6 laps
1   Mike Hawthorn (Cooper-Bristol T20)   10:06.8, 85.43 mph
2   Tony Rolt (ERA-Delage 15S8)   10:16.8
3   Philip Fotheringham-Parker (Talbot-Lago T26C)   10:38.0
Fastest lap: Mike Hawthorn - 1:39.0, 87.27 mph

Event 4 - First Easter Handicap for non s/c Sports Cars - 6 laps
1   Bill Holt (Jaguar XK120)   11:38.0, 75.56 mph
2   Jim Swift (Jaguar XK120)   11:38.2
3   Geoff Duke (Aston Martin DB3)   11:50.8
Fastest lap: Stirling Moss (Jaguar C-type) - 1:44.6, 82.60 mph

Event 5 - Second Easter Handicap for Racing Cars
1   Alan Brown (Cooper-Bristol T20)   11:15.0, 82.15 mph
2   Sydney Allard (Allard J2X Cadillac)   11:24.4
3   Guy Gale (Darracq T150C)   11:26.8
Fastest lap: Alan Brown - 1:41.2, 85.37 mph

Event 6 - Third Easter Handicap for Racing Cars - 6 laps
1   Duncan Hamilton (Talbot-Lago T26C)   10:38.2, 84.67 mph
2   George Abecassis (HWM)   10:56.0
3   Guy Gale (Darracq T150 C)   11:16.6
Fastest lap: José Froilán González (Ferrari 'Thin Wall Special') - 1:37.0, 89.07 mph

Event 7 - Fourth Easter Handicap - 6 laps
1   Eric Thompson (Aston Martin DB2)   12:06.0, 76.34 mph
2   Len Gibbs (HRG Le Mans)   12:07.2
3   Dennis Poore (Aston Martin DB2)   12:09.4
Fastest lap: Eric Thompson - 1:50.2, 78.40 mph

Event 8 - Richmond Trophy Race for Formula 1 Cars - 12 laps
1   José Froilán González (Ferrari 'Thin Wall Special')   19:35.0, 88.23 mph
2   Mike Hawthorn (Cooper-Bristol T20)   20.01.0
3   Duncan Hamilton (Lago-Talbot T26C)   20:08.1
4   George Abecassis (HWM)   20:15.2
5   Graham Whitehead (ERA B Type)   20:32.1
6   Eric Brandon (Cooper-Bristol T20)   21:01.1
Fastest lap: José Froilán González - 1:36.0, 90.00 mph

Altogether of more modest mien than the beautiful if obsolescent Bugattis, Harry Lester's lightweight-bodied, neat and nimble Lester-MGs made the most of the Abingdon marque's T-series production sports car power units. Run most notably by The Monkey Stable team, the cars shone in the hands of such promising drivers as Jim Mayers, Mike Keen and Gerry Ruddock - the former pair sadly fated to die in racing accidents.

17 MAY 1952 - 9th MEMBERS' MEETING

Event 1 - 5-lap Scratch Race (A) up to 1100cc non s/c
1   Len Gibbs (Riley Nine)   10:49.6, 66.55 mph
Fastest lap: Len Gibbs - 2:06.2, 68.46 mph

Event 2 - 5-lap Scratch Race (B) 1100-1500cc non s/c
1   Cliff Davis (Cooper-MG T14)   9:53.0, 72.85 mph
Fastest lap: Gerry Ruddock (Lester-MG) - 1:55.6, 74.74 mph

Event 3 - 5-lap Scratch Race (C) 1500-3000cc non s/c
1   Roy Salvadori (Frazer Nash LMR)   9:42.2, 76.59 mph
Fastest lap: Roy Salvadori - 1:49.4, 78.98 mph

Event 4 - 5-lap Scratch Race (D) over 3000cc nons/c
1   Oscar Moore (HWM-Jaguar)   9:39.0, 74.61 mph
Fastest lap: Phillip Scragg (Alta-Jaguar) - 1:53.2, 76.32 mph

Event 5 - 5-lap Handicap (A)
1   Bert Rogers (Riley)   11:27.2, 62.88 mph
Fastest lap: R.F. Collinson (Aston Martin SM) - 2:07.0, 68.03 mph

Event 6 - 5-lap Handicap (B)
1   Archie Lusty (MG TD)   11:10.8, 64.40 mph
Fastest lap: J. Goodhew (Lagonda LG45) - 1:58.4, 72.97 mph

Event 7 - 5-lap Handicap (C)
1   Tony Brooks (Healey Silverstone)   10:18.4, 69.85 mph
Fastest lap: Oscar Moore (HWM-Jaguar) - 1:48.2, 79.85 mph

Event 8 - 5-lap Handicap (D)
1   Rodney Peacock (Frazer Nash LMR)   10:51.4, 76.66 mph
Fastest lap: Roy Salvadori (Frazer Nash LMR) - 1:49.6, 78.83 mph

Event 9 - 5-lap Handicap (E)
1   Peter Merritt (Aston Martin LM)   11:30.2, 67.47 mph
Fastest lap: Ronnie Symondson (Bugatti T57S) - 1:58.4, 72.97 mph

4 JUNE 1952 - WHITSUN MEETING

Event 1 - 500 International Trophy Heat 1 - 7 laps
1   Bob Gerard (Cooper-Norton)   13:06.0, 76.94 mph
2   George Wicken (Cooper-Norton)   13:06.8
3   David Shale (Kieft-Norton)   13:11.6
Fastest lap: Bob Gerard - 1:50.0, 78.54 mph

Event 2 - 500 International Trophy Heat 2 - 7 laps
1   Don Parker (Kieft-Norton)   13:23.4, 75.29 mph
2   Reg Bicknell (Revis-JAP)   13:24.0
3   Derek Annable (Kieft-JAP)   13:24.6
Fastest lap: Don Parker - 1:51.8, 77.28 mph

Event 3 - First Whitsun Handicap for Sports Cars - 7 laps
1   John de Edwards (Healey Silverstone)   14:17.8, 70.67 mph
2   P G A Bucknall (MG Magnette)   14:18.4
3   A D Tasker (Healey)   14:44.0
Fastest lap: Lawrence Mitchell (Frazer Nash HS) - 1:50.2, 78.40 mph

Event 4 - Second Whitsun Handicap for Sports Cars - 7 laps
1   Bill Lamb (Healey Silverstone)   15:10.8, 73.50 mph
2   Jim Mayers (Lester-MG)   15:44.8
3   Tony Brooks (Healey Silverstone)   15:49.2
Fastest lap: Jim Mayers - 1:52.8, 76.60 mph

Event 5 - 500 International Trophy Final - 15 laps
1   Bob Gerard (Cooper-Norton)   27:42.4, 77.98 mph
2   George Wicken (Cooper-Norton)   27:58.0
3   Don Parker (Kieft-Norton)   28:07.0
Fastest lap: Don Parker - 1:48.4, 79.70 mph

Event 6 - Sussex International Trophy for *Formule Libre* Racing Cars - 15 laps
1. Mike Hawthorn (Cooper-Bristol T20) — 25:22.2, 85.13 mph
2. Bob Gerard (ERA B Type) — 25:24.8
3. Dennis Poore (Alfa Romeo 8C/35) — 26:16.8
Fastest lap: Mike Hawthorn - 1:39.0, 87.27 mph

26 JULY 1952 – 10th MEMBERS' MEETING

Event 1 - 5-lap Scratch Race (A) up to 1500cc non s/c
1. Jim Mayers (Lester-MG) — 9:36.0, 74.87 mph
Fastest lap: Jim Mayers - 1:53.8, 75.92 mph

Event 2 - 5-lap Scratch Race (B) 1500-3000cc non s/c
1. Tony Crook (Frazer Nash LMR) — 9:24.4, 76.53 mph
Fastest lap: Lawrence Mitchell (Frazer Nash HS) - 1:49.0, 79.27

Event 3 - 5-lap Scratch Race (C) over 3000cc non s/c
1. J.K. Hemsworth (Jaguar XK120) — 9:33.8, 75.26 mph
Fastest Lap: Oscar Moore (HWM-Jaguar) - 1:49.6, 78.83 mph

Event 4 - 5-lap Handicap (A)
1. Dickie Metcalfe (Fiat Balilla 508S) — 11:03.0, 66.46 mph
Fastest lap: Jim Mayers (Lester-MG) - 1:50.0, 78.54 mph

Event 5 - 5-lap Handicap (B)
1. Tony Brooks (Healey Silverstone) — 10:07.8, 72.85 mph
Fastest lap: Lawrence Mitchell (Frazer Nash HS) - 1:50.0, 78.54 mph

Event 6 - 5-lap Handicap (C)
1. Bert Rogers (Riley) — 11:48.2, 64.38 mph
Fastest lap: Dickie Metcalfe (Fiat Balilla 508S) - 2:06.0, 68.57 mph

Event 7 - 5-lap Handicap (D)
1. Ronnie Symondson (Bugatti T57S) — 9:55.0, 72.60 mph
Fastest lap: Tony Crook (Frazer Nash LMR) - 1:50.6, 78.12 mph

Event 8 - 5-lap Handicap (E)
1. Peter Gammon (MG TC) — 11:52.4, 72.30 mph
Fastest lap: Peter Gammon - 1:57.4, 73.59 mph

Event 9 - 5 lap Invitation Handicap
1. Roy Salvadori (Jaguar XK120) — 9:41.6, 75.86 mph
Fastest lap: Tony Crook (Frazer Nash LMR) - 1:48.2, 79.85 mph

16 AUGUST 1952 –
'*NEWS OF THE WORLD*' INTERNATIONAL NINE-HOUR SPORTS CAR RACE
1. Peter Collins/Pat Griffith (Aston Martin DB3) — 283 laps, 75.42 mph
2. Tom Cole/Graham Whitehead (Ferrari 225) — 281 laps
3. Bobbie Baird/Roy Salvadori (Ferrari 225) — 278 laps
4. Bob Gerard/David Clarke (Frazer Nash LMR) — 276 laps
5. Stirling Moss/Peter Walker (Jaguar C-type) — 267 laps
6. Jim Mayers/Mike Keen (Lester MG) — 250 laps

27 SEPTEMBER 1952 – SEPTEMBER MEETING

Event 1 - Madgwick Cup for Formula 2 Racing Cars - 7 laps
1. Ken Downing (Connaught A) — 11:53.0, 84.80 mph
2. Dennis Poore (Connaught A) — 12:06.4
3. Alan Brown (Cooper Bristol T20) — 12:10.4
Fastest lap: Dennis Poore - 1:39.6, 86.75 mph

Event 2 - 500cc Race - 5 laps
1. Stirling Moss (Cooper-Norton) — 9:05.2, 79.24 mph
2. Les Leston (Leston Special-Norton) — 9:06.4
3. Reg Bicknell (Revis-JAP) — 9:07.4
Fastest lap: Les Leston/Reg Bicknell - 1:46.8, 80.90 mph

Event 3 - Woodcote Cup for *Formule Libre* Racing Cars - 5 laps
1. José Froilán González (BRM Type 15) — 8:13.0, 87.64 mph
2. Giuseppe Farina (Ferrari '*ThinWall Special*') — 8:19.2
3. Reg Parnell (BRM Type 15) — 8:23.0
Fastest lap: José Froilán González - 1:36.2, 89.81 mph

Event 4 - Sports Car Race 1500-3500cc - 5 laps
1. Tony Rolt (Jaguar C-type) — 8:36.6, 83.62 mph
2. Stirling Moss (Jaguar C-type) — 8:37.2
3. Ken Wharton (Frazer Nash LMR) — 9:03.4
Fastest lap: Stirling Moss - 1:41.2, 85.37 mph

Event 5 - First September Handicap for Racing Cars - 5 laps
1. Tony Gaze (Maserati 8CM) — 9:04.6, 82.82 mph
2. Gerry Dunham (Rover) — 9:17.6
3. Graham Whitehead (ERA C Type) — 9:20.8
Fastest lap: Graham Whitehead - 1:41.0, 85.54 mph

Event 6 - Second September Handicap for Sports Cars - 5 laps
1. Bill Dobson (Jaguar XK120) — 9:30.6, 77.76 mph
2. Michael Head (Jaguar XK120) — 9:47.0
3. Ken Wharton (Frazer Nash LMR) — 9:47.2
Fastest lap: Ken Wharton - 1:45.6, 81.82 mph

Event 7 - '*Daily Graphic*' Trophy for *Formule Libre* Racing Cars - 15 laps
1. José Froilán González (BRM Type 15) — 24:30.6, 88.13 mph
2. Reg Parnell (BRM Type 15) — 24:38.2
3. Ken Wharton (BRM Type 15) — 24:48.8
Fastest lap: Reg Parnell - 1:35.6, 90.38 mph

1953

21 MARCH 1953 – 11th MEMBERS' MEETING

Event 1 - 5 lap-Handicap (A) for closed cars
1. R.L. Woods (Aston Martin DB2) — 12:30.4, 70.88 mph
Fastest lap: R.L. Woods - 1:56.0, 74.48 mph

Event 2 - 5-lap Scratch Race (A) up to 1500cc non s/c
1. Don Beauman (Riley TT Sprite) — 9:40.06, 74.48 mph
Fastest lap: Don Beauman - 1:53.6, 76.06 mph

Event 3 - 5-lap Scratch Race (B) 1500-3000cc non s/c
1. Lawrence Mitchell (Frazer Nash HS) — 8:53.2, 80.97 mph
Fastest lap: Lawrence Mitchell - 1:44.4, 82.76 mph

Event 4 - 5-lap Scratch Race (C) over 3000cc non s/c
1. Oscar Moore (HWM-Jaguar) — 9:30.2, 75.79 mph
Fastest lap: Oscar Moore - 1:49.0, 79.27 mph

Event 5 - 5-lap Handicap (B)
1. John Riseley-Prichard (Riley TT Sprite) — 10:20.0, 74.48 mph
Fastest lap: John Riseley-Prichard - 1:53.2, 76.32 mph

Event 6 - 5 lap Handicap (C)
1. Lawrence Mitchell (Frazer Nash HS) — 10:40.6, 79.93 mph
Fastest lap Lawrence Mitchell/Alan Brown (Bristol T20) - 1:45.5, 81.97 mph

Event 7 - 5-lap Handicap (D)
1. N. Powell (Mercedes-Benz 38/250) — 10:53.0, 68.25 mph
Fastest lap: R.F. Collinson (Aston Martin LM) - 2:02.2, 70.70 mph

Event 8 - 5-lap Handicap (E)
1. Tony Page (Allard J2) — 9:33.2, 78.06 mph
Fastest lap: Oscar Moore (HWM-Jaguar)/Tony Page - 1:49.4, 78.98 mph

Event 9 - 5 lap-Handicap (F)
1. P.H. Scarf (Ford Buckler) — 11:37.4, 63.76 mph
Fastest lap: Peter Gammon (MG TC) - 1:55.0, 75.13 mph

7 APRIL 1953 – EASTER MEETING

Event 1 - First Easter Handicap - 5 laps
1. J. Goodhew (Darracq T150C) — 10:42.8, 74.10 mph
2. Dick Protheroe (Jaguar XK120) — 10:49.2
3. Bert Rogers (Riley Saloon) — 10:54.4
Fastest lap: Bill Holt (Jaguar XK120C) - 1:50.4, 78.26 mph

Event 2 - Lavant Cup for Formula 2 Cars - 7 laps
1. Baron E. de Graffenried (Maserati A6GCM) — 11:30.6, 87.63 mph
2. Roy Salvadori (Connaught A) — 11:43.2
3. Tony Rolt (Connaught A) — 11:50.0
Fastest lap: Roy Salvadori - 1:36.6, 89.44 mph

Event 3 - Earl of March Trophy for 500cc Racing Cars - 5 laps
1. Alan Brown (Cooper-Norton VIIa) — 8:53.8, 80.97 mph
2. Reg Bicknell (Erskine Staride-Norton) — 8:57.8
3. Stirling Moss (Cooper-Norton) — 8:58.0
Fastest lap: Alan Brown - 1:44.8, 82.44 mph

Event 4 - Second Easter Handicap for Racing Cars - 5 laps
1. Ron Flockhart (ERA D Type) — 8:40.4, 85.46 mph
2. Peter Whitehead (Cooper-Alta T24) — 8:45.0
3. Ken Wharton (Cooper-Bristol T23) — 8:51.8
Fastest lap: Baron E. de Graffenried (Maserati A6GCM) - 1:36.4, 89.63 mph

Event 5 - Chichester Cup for *Formule Libre* Cars - 5 laps
1. Baron E. de Graffenried (Maserati A6GCM) — 9:03.4, 79.48 mph
2. Ken Wharton (BRM Type 15) — 9:04.2
3. Ron Flockhart (ERA D Type) — 9:07.4
Fastest lap: Ken Wharton - 1:46.2, 81.36 mph

Event 6 - Third Easter Handicap for Racing Cars - 5 laps
1. Jimmy Stewart (Cooper-Bristol T20) — 9:38.4, 80.22 mph
2. Leslie Marr (Connaught A) — 9:48.4
3. Gerry Dunham (Alvis 12/70 Special) — 9:53.6
Fastest lap: Jimmy Stewart - 1:44.8, 82.44 mph

Despite all Fangio's genius and the enormous respect and affection in which the five-times World Champion was held in Great Britain, he would only ever win one race outright on British soil: the 1956 British GP at Silverstone. Here his V16 BRM is already pivoting around that outside front wheel - Woodcote Corner, Goodwood Trophy, 26th September 1953.

Event 7 - Fourth Easter Handicap for Sports Cars - 5 laps
1. Cliff Davis (Tojeiro-Bristol) — 9:43.8, 76.19 mph
2. Michael Head (Jaguar XK120) — 9:45.6
3. J. Goodhew (Darracq T150C) — 9:48.4
Fastest lap: Duncan Hamilton (Jaguar C-type) - 1:43.4, 83.56 mph

Event 8 - Richmond *Formule Libre* Race for the Glover Trophy - 15 laps
1. Ken Wharton (BRM Type 15) — 23:53.0, 90.47 mph
2. Piero Taruffi (Ferrari '*ThinWall Special*') — 23:59.0
3. Baron E. de Graffenried (Maserati A6GCM) — 24:15.8
4. Roy Salvadori (Connaught A) — 24:47.4
5. Tony Rolt (Connaught A) — 24:57.0
6. Bob Gerard (Cooper-Bristol T23) — 25:08.6
Fastest lap: Ken Wharton - 1:33.8, 92.11 mph

2 MAY 1953 – 12th MEMBERS' MEETING

Event 1 - 5-lap Handicap (A) for Closed Cars
1. Alan Foster (Morris Minor) — 12:50.0, 56.20 mph
Fastest lap: Tony Everard (Aston Martin DB2) - 1:56.8, 73.97 mph

Event 2 - 5-lap Scratch race (A) up to 1500cc non s/c
1   Cliff Davis (Cooper-MG T14)   9:26.0, 76.32 mph
Fastest lap: Cliff Davis - 1:51.0, 77.84 mph

Event 3 - 5-lap Scratch Race (B) 1500-3000cc non s/c
1   Cliff Davis (Tojeiro-Bristol)   9:09.0, 78.69 mph
Fastest lap: Lawrence Mitchell (Frazer Nash HS) - 1:47.4, 80.45 mph

Event 4 - 5-lap Scratch Race (C) over 3000cc non s/c
1   Graham Whitehead (Jaguar C-type)   9:19.8, 77.21 mph
Fastest lap: Graham Whitehead - 1:44.2, 82.92 mph

Event 5 - 5-lap Handicap (B)
1   Ernest Harewood (MG)   10:41.8, 69.90 mph
Fastest lap: Peter Gammon (MG TC) - 1:51.6, 77.42 mph

Event 6 - 5-lap Handicap (C)
1   Tony Brooks (Frazer Nash LMR)   10:02.6, 78.66 mph
Fastest lap: Lawrence Mitchell (Frazer Nash HS) - 1:46.0, 81.51 mph

Event 7 - 5-lap Handicap (D)
1   Michael Head (Jaguar XK120)   9:32.2, 75.92 mph
Fastest lap: Graham Whitehead (Jaguar C-type) - 1:47.8, 80.15 mph

Event 8 - 5-lap Handicap (E)
1   A.H. Greig (MG TC)   11:29.0, 62.70 mph
Fastest lap: A.H. Greig - 2:05.2, 69.01 mph

Event 9 - 5-lap Handicap (F)
1   Claude Hamilton (Invicta)   10:56.0, 65.26 mph
Fastest lap: David Lewis (Alfa Romeo 8C) - 1:54.4, 75.52 mph

25 JULY 1953 - 13th MEMBERS' MEETING

Event 1 - 5-lap Handicap for Closed Cars
1   Len Potter (Dyna Panhard)   12:24.0, 58.15 mph
Fastest lap: Tony Everard (Aston Martin DB2) - 1:54.2, 75.76 mph

Event 2 - 5-lap Scratch Race (A) up to 1100cc non s/c
1   Colin Chapman (Lotus-Ford MkVI)   10:19.86, 69.73 mph
Fastest lap: Colin Chapman - 2:00.4, 71.76 mph

Event 3 - 5-lap Scratch Race (B) 1100-1500cc non s/c
1   Peter Gammon (MG TC)   9:30.4, 75.79 mph
Fastest lap: Cliff Davis (Cooper-MG T14) - 1:51.4, 77.56 mph

Event 4 - 5-lap Scratch Race (C) 1500-3000cc non s/c
1   Lawrence Mitchell (Frazer Nash HS)   9:01.4, 79.85 mph
Fastest lap: Cliff Davis (Tojeiro-Bristol) - 1:46.0, 81.51 mph

Event 5 - 5-lap Scratch Race (D) over 3000cc non s/c
1   Oscar Moore (HWM-Jaguar)   9:23.0, 76.73 mph
Fastest lap: Oscar Moore - 1:49.2, 79.12 mph

Event 6 - 5-lap Handicap (B)
1   Roy Watling-Greenwood (RWG)   11:20.8, 69.90 mph
Fastest lap: Roy Watling-Greenwood - 1:59.6, 72.24 mph

Event 7 - 5-lap Handicap (C)
1   Archie Lusty (MG TD)   10:49.6, 66.51 mph
Fastest lap: Don Beauman (Riley TT Sprite) - 1:52.6, 76.73 mph

Event 8 - 5-lap Handicap (D)
1   A.H. Greig (MG TC)   10:48.2, 68.25 mph
Fastest lap: Lawrence Mitchell (Frazer Nash HS) - 1:46.2, 81.36 mph

Event 9 - 5-lap Handicap (E)
1   Ronnie Symondson (Bugatti T57S)   10:38.4, 74.68 mph
Fastest lap: Michael Head (Jaguar XK120)/Ronnie Symondson - 1:52.8, 76.60 mph

Event 10 - 5-lap Handicap (F)
1   P.J. Morgan (Bentley)   11:45.0, 61.27 mph
Fastest lap: A.H. Greig (MG TC) - 2:04.0, 69.68 mph

22 AUGUST 1953 -

SECOND NINE-HOUR INTERNATIONAL SPORTS CAR RACE

1   Reg Parnell/Eric Thompson (Aston Martin DB3S)   297 laps, 78.94 mph
2   Peter Collins/Pat Griffith (Aston Martin DB3S)   295 laps
3   Peter Whitehead/Ian Stewart (Jaguar C-type)   295 laps
4   Jimmy Stewart/Bob Dickson (Jaguar C-type)   282 laps
5   Jock Lawrence/Frank Curtis (Jaguar C-type)   281 laps
6   Bob Gerard/David Clarke (Frazer Nash LMR)   280 laps

12 SEPTEMBER 1953 - 14th MEMBERS' MEETING

Event 1 - 5-lap Handicap (A) for Closed Cars
1   Len Potter (Dyna Panhard)   12:32.6, 59.86 mph
Fastest lap: Tony Everard (Aston Martin DB2) - 1:54.2, 75.66 mph

Event 2 - 5-lap Scratch Race (A) up to 1100 cc non s/c
1   Colin Chapman (Lotus-Ford MkVI)   10:26.0, 69.01 mph
Fastest lap: Ellis Cuff Miller (Riley Brooklands 9) - 2:02.6, 70.47 mph

Event 3 - 5 lap Scratch Race (B) 1100-1500cc non s/c
1   Peter Gammon (MG TC)   9:37.4, 74.80 mph
Fastest lap: Peter Gammon - 1:51.6, 77.42 mph

Events 4 & 5 - 5 lap Scratch Races (C) 1500-3000cc non s/c &
(D) over 3000cc non s/c, run concurrently

1500-3000cc non s/c
1   Tony Brooks (Frazer Nash LMR)   9:20.2, 77.14 mph
Fastest lap: Tony Brooks - 1:48.4, 79.70 mph

Over 3000cc non s/c
1   Tony Page (Allard J2)   9:20.0, 77.14 mph
Fastest lap: Tony Page 1:47.8, 80.15 mph

Event 6 - 5-lap Bentley Handicap
1   Bill Mason (Bentley)   11:31.0, 64.86 mph
Fastest lap: Hamish Orr-Ewing (Bentley) - 1:58.6, 72.85 mph

Event 7 - 5-lap Handicap Race (B)
1   Tom Dargue (MG Special)   11:30.2, 73.85 mph
Fastest lap: Tom Dargue - 1:54.8, 75.26 mph

Event 8 - 5-lap Handicap Race (C)
1   Tony Everard (Aston Martin DB2)   10:02.0, 74.61 mph
Fastest lap: Tony Page (Allard J2) - 1:47.2, 80.60 mph

Event 9 - 5-lap Handicap Race (D)
1   Tom Haig (MG TC)   10:50.6, 67.34 mph
Fastest lap: Peter Gammon (MG TC) - 1:50.2, 78.40 mph

Event 10 - 5-lap Handicap Race (E)
1   Hamish Orr-Ewing (Bentley)   11:27.6, 70.88 mph
Fastest lap: Tony Brooks (Healey Silverstone) - 1:51.6, 77.42 mph

26 SEPTEMBER 1953 - SEPTEMBER MEETING

Event 1 - Madgwick Cup for Formula 2 Cars - 7 laps
1   Roy Salvadori (Connaught A)   11:15.0, 89.63 mph
2   Stirling Moss (Cooper-Alta T24)   11:18.4
3   Tony Rolt (Connaught A)   11:18.8
Fastest lap: Roy Salvadori - 1:35.0, 90.95 mph

Event 2 - Sports Car Race over 1500cc non s/c - 5 laps
1   George Abecassis (HWM-Jaguar)   8:40.6, 83.00 mph
2   Ken Wharton (Frazer Nash LMR)   8:48.0
3   Tony Brooks (Frazer Nash LMR)   8:53.8
Fastest lap: George Abecassis - 1:42.4, 84.37 mph

Event 3 - Woodcote Cup for *Formule Libre* Cars - 5 laps
1   Mike Hawthorn (Ferrari 'Thin Wall Special')   7:49.2, 92.11 mph
2   Juan Fangio (BRM Type 15)   8:05.4
3   Ken Wharton (BRM Type 15)   8:17.6
Fastest lap (RECORD): Mike Hawthorn - 1:32.0, 93.91 mph

Event 4 - 500cc Race- 5 laps
1   Don Parker (Kieft-Norton)   8:51.0, 81.36 mph
2   Stuart Lewis Evans (Cooper-Norton)   8:51.4
3   Reg Bicknell (Erskine Staride-Norton)   8:51.6
Fastest lap: Stuart Lewis-Evans - 1:43.8, 83.24 mph

Event 5 - Goodwood Trophy for *Formule Libre* Cars - 15 laps
1   Mike Hawthorn (Ferrari 'Thin Wall Special')   23:17.8, 92.70 mph
2   Ken Wharton (BRM Type 15)   23:40.8
3   Bob Gerard (Cooper Bristol T23)   14 laps
Fastest lap (RECORD): Mike Hawthorn - 1:31.4, 94.53 mph

Event 6 - First September Handicap for Sports Cars - 5 laps
1   Peter Woozley (Allard J2X)   9:37.0, 75.52 mph
2   John Hogg (Allard J2)   9:38.0
3   Tony Page (Allard J2)   9:42.4
Fastest lap: Duncan Hamilton (Jaguar C-type) -1:45.6, 81.82 mph

Event 7 - Second September Handicap for Racing Cars - 5 laps
1   Graham Whitehead (ERA C Type)   9:14.8, 85.42 mph
2   Leslie Marr (Connaught A)   9:16.4
3   Keith Hall (Cooper-Bristol T20)   9:22.0
Fastest lap: Graham Whitehead - 1:39.0, 87.27 mph

1954

27 MARCH 1954 - 15th MEMBERS' MEETING

Event 1 - 5-lap Handicap Race (A) for Closed Cars
1   K.W. Moore (Renault 750)   12:46.0, 56.40 mph
Fastest lap: Alan Brown (Aston Martin DB2) - 1:59.6, 72.24 mph

Event 2 - 5-lap Scratch Race (A)
1   Roy Watling-Greenwood (RWG)   10:32.0, 68.35 mph
Fastest lap: Roy Watling-Greenwood - 2:03.2, 70.13 mph

Event 3 - 5-lap Scratch Race (B)
1   Michael Head (Jaguar XK120C)   9:21.8, 76.87 mph
Fastest lap: Bob Berry (Jaguar XK120) - 1:50.2, 78.40 mph

Event 4 - 5-lap Scratch Race (C)
1   John Coombs (Connaught ALSR)   9:29.0, 75.92 mph
Fastest lap: John Coombs - 1:49.6, 78.83 mph

Shades of 1940 - though at ground level - as this 'vic' of Britain's finest drift round the West Sussex perimeter track with aggressive intent; a pride of Jaguar C-types on the prowl - Goodwood, 1954.

Event 5 - 10-lap Scratch Race (D)
1   Tony Brooks (Frazer Nash LMR)   18:03.6, 79.70 mph
Fastest lap: Alan Brown (Cooper-Bristol T20) -1:44.0, 83.08 mph

Event 6 - 5-lap Handicap Race (B)
1   Peter Gammon (Lotus MG MkVI)   10:57.8, 78.12 mph
Fastest lap: John Coombs (Connaught ALSR) - 1:48.2, 79.85 mph

Event 7 - 5-lap Handicap Race (C)
1   Roy Watling-Greenwood (RWG)   11:07.0, 71.40 mph
Fastest lap: Michael Burn (Frazer Nash LMR) - 1:55.2, 75.00 mph

Event 8 - 5-lap Handicap Race (D)
1   Basil de Mattos (Morgan +4)   11:13.4, 71.58 mph
Fastest lap: Nigel Mann (Alfa Romeo 8C) - 1:55.4, 74.87 mph

Event 9 - 5 lap-Handicap Race (E)
1   Dick Shattock (RGS-Atalanta)   9:28.6, 78.76 mph
Fastest lap: Tony Brooks (Frazer Nash LMR) - 1:46.2, 81.36 mph

Event 10 - 5-lap Handicap Race (F)
1   Peter Scott-Russell (Cooper-Bristol)   10:28.0, 77.42 mph
Fastest lap: Peter Scott-Russell - 1:48.6, 79.56 mph

19 APRIL 1954 – EASTER MEETING

Event 1 - Lavant Cup for Formula 1 Cars - 7 laps
1   Reg Parnell (Ferrari 500/625)   11:21.4, 88.77 mph
2   Roy Salvadori (Maserati 250F)   11:22.0
3   Ken McAlpine (Connaught A)   11:51.4
Fastest lap: Reg Parnell/Roy Salvadori - 1:36.2, 89.81 mph

Event 2 - First Easter Handicap for Sports Cars
1   Jimmy Stewart (Jaguar C-type)   9:26.2, 82.11 mph
2   Tony Rolt (Jaguar C-type)   9:29.0
3   Ellis Cuff Miller (Allard)   9:29.0
Fastest lap: Jimmy Stewart/George Abecassis (HWM-Jaguar) - 1:43.0, 83.88 mph

Event 3 - Chichester Cup for *Formule Libre* Cars - 5 laps
1   Ken Wharton (BRM P30 MkII)   8:07.2, 88.70 mph
2   Roy Salvadori (Maserati 250F)   8:07.6
3   Reg Parnell (Ferrari 500/625)   8:08.4
Fastest lap: Ken Wharton/Ron Flockhart (BRM Type 15)/Roy Salvadori - 1:35.6, 90.38 mph

Event 4 - Second Easter Handicap for Sports Cars - 5 laps
1   Tony Crook (Cooper-Bristol T24)   9:44.2, 81.50 mph
2   Dick Steed (JAG-MG)   9:48.8
3   Cliff Davis (Tojeiro-Bristol)   9:58.2
Fastest lap: Tony Crook - 1:42.4, 84.37 mph

Event 5 - Third Easter Handicap for Racing Cars - 5 laps
1   Tony Rolt (Connaught A)   9:18.8, 87.28 mph
2   Claude Hamilton (ERA B Type)   9:19.4
3   Reg Parnell (Ferrari 500/625)   9:20.2
Fastest lap: Reg Parnell - 1:35.6, 90.38 mph

Event 6 - Earl of March Trophy for 500cc Racing Cars - 5 laps
1   Les Leston (Cooper-Norton)   8:48.2, 82.19 mph
2   Reg Bicknell (Revis-Norton)   8:49.4
3   Don Parker (Kieft-Norton)   8:49.8
Fastest lap: Les Leston - 1:43.6, 83.40 mph

Event 7 - Fourth Easter Handicap for Racing Cars - 5 laps
1   Claude Hamilton (ERA B Type)   9:13.2, 78.46 mph
2   Jock Somervail (ERA B Type)   9:14.4
3   J. Goodhew (Maserati 4CL)   9:27.4
Fastest lap: J. Goodhew - 1:46.0, 81.51 mph

Event 8 - Richmond *Formule Libre* Race for the Glover Trophy - 21 laps
1   Ken Wharton (BRM Type 15)   35:00.0, 86.40 mph
2   Kenneth McAlpine (Connaught A)   35:40.0
3   Leslie Marr (Connaught A)   36:00.4
4   Ron Flockhart (BRM P30 MkII)   36:08.0
5   Peter Whitehead (Cooper Alta T24)   37:29.4
6   Charles Boulton (Connaught A)   N/A
Fastest lap: Ken Wharton/Roy Salvadori (Maserati 250F) - 1:37.8, 88.34 mph

1 MAY 1954 – 16th MEMBERS' MEETING

Event 1 - 5-lap Handicap Race (A) for Closed Cars
1   Ian Forbes (Jowett Jupiter)   12:25.6, 63.02 mph
Fastest lap: Alan Brown (Jaguar XK120 Coupé) - 1:50.6, 78.12 mph

Event 2 - 5-lap Scratch Race (A) over 3000cc non s/c
1   Jimmy Stewart (Jaguar C-type)   8:38.6, 83.36 mph
Fastest lap: Jimmy Stewart - 1:42.2, 84.54 mph

Event 3 - 5-lap Scratch Race (B) up to 1500cc non s/c
1   John Coombs (Connaught AL/SR)   9:33.4, 75.33 mph
Fastest lap: John Coombs - 1:52.4, 76.87 mph

Event 4 - 10-lap Scratch Race (C) 1500cc-3500cc non s/c
1   Jimmy Stewart (Jaguar C-type)   17:02.0, 84.54 mph
Fastest lap: Jimmy Stewart - 1:41.0, 85.54 mph

Event 5 - 5-lap Handicap Race (B)
1   A.D. Stevens (Lea Francis)   11:05.6, 68.84 mph
Fastest lap: Roy Watling-Greenwood (RWG) - 1:58.0, 73.22 mph

Event 6 - 5-lap Handicap Race (C)
1   John Deeley (Austin-Healey 100)   10:18.0, 72.60 mph
Fastest lap: Mike Keen (Cooper-Bristol T20) - 1:46.0, 81.51 mph

Event 7 - 5-lap Handicap Race (D)
1   John Deeley (Austin-Healey 100)   10:17.0, 72.73 mph
Fastest lap: Alan Brown (Cooper-Bristol T20) - 1:43.6, 83.40 mph

Event 8 - 5-lap Handicap Race (E)
1   A.D. Stevens (Lea-Francis)   11:17.2, 69.45 mph
Fastest lap: Bert Rogers (Cooper-Bristol) - 1:50.6, 78.12 mph

7 JUNE 1954 – WHITSUN MEETING

Event 1 - Goodwood National 500 - 15 laps
1   Reg Bicknell (Revis-Norton)   26:27.2, 81.66 mph
2   Keith Hall (Cooper-JAP)   26:50.8
3   Ken Tyrrell (Cooper-Norton)   26:56.4
Fastest lap: Reg Bicknell - 1:44.2, 82.92 mph

Event 2 - Formula 1 Race
1   Reg Parnell (Ferrari 500/625)   8:13.2, 87.63 mph
2   Roy Salvadori (Maserati 250F)   8:13.8
3   Jock Somervail (Cooper-Bristol T20)   8:38.8
Fastest lap: Roy Salvadori - 1:35.0, 90.95 mph

Event 3 - Johnson's Sports Car Challenge Trophy - lap 21
1   Jimmy Stewart (Jaguar C-type)   36:38.4, 82.52 mph
2   Ninian Sanderson (Jaguar C-type)   36:59.0
3   Gerry Dunham (Jaguar C-type)   37:02.2
Fastest lap: Roy Salvadori (Maserati A6GCS) - 1:39.0, 87.27 mph

Event 4 - Goodwood Whitsun Trophy for *Formule Libre* Cars - 15 laps
1   Peter Collins (Ferrari '*Thin Wall Special*')   23:35.4, 91.53 mph
2   Ron Flockhart (BRM P30 MkII)   23:50.4
3   Roy Salvadori (Maserati 250F)   23:58.0
Fastest lap: Peter Collins - 1:32.6, 93.30 mph

Event 5 - First Whitsun Handicap non s/c Sports Cars - 5 laps
1   Sir Jeremy Boles (Aston Martin DB3)   9:40.4, 76.06 mph
2   Dick Protheroe (Jaguar XK120)   9:41.2
3   Michael Head (Jaguar C-type)   9:42.0
Fastest lap: Jimmy Stewart (Jaguar C-type) - 1:43.4, 83.56 mph

Event 6 - Second Whitsun Handicap non s/c Sports Cars - 5 laps
1   Desmond Titterington (Triumph TR2)   11:21.8, 70.99 mph
2   Basil de Mattos (AC Ace)   11:30.4
3   P.H. Scarf (Triumph TR2)   11:33.0
Fastest lap: Bert Rogers (Cooper-Bristol) - 1:49.6, 78.83 mph

21 AUGUST 1954 – 17th MEMBERS' MEETING

Event 1 - 5-lap Handicap Race (A) for Closed Cars
1   J. Corps (Citroen)   12:45.6, 59.80 mph
Fastest lap: Dick Jacobs (MG Coupé) - 2:07.4, 67.82 mph

Event 2 - 5-lap Scratch Race (A) up to 1250cc non s/c
1   Roy Watling-Greenwood (RWG)   11:15.0, 64.00 mph
Fastest lap: Jack Richards (Lotus-Climax MkVI) - 2:10.2, 66.36 mph

Event 3 - 5-lap Scratch Race (B) over 3000cc non s/c
1   Michael Head (Jaguar C-type)   10:01.2, 71.88 mph
Fastest lap: Michael Head - 1:56.8, 73.97 mph

Event 4 - 5-lap Scratch Race (C) up to 1500cc non s/c
1   John Coombs (Lotus-Connaught MkVIII)   10:06.4, 71.23 mph
Fastest lap: John Coombs/Cyril Wick (Lester MG) - 1:59.4, 72.36 mph

Event 5 - 10-lap Scratch Race (D) 1500cc-3500cc non s/c
1   Michael Head (Jaguar C-type)   19:04.4, 75.52 mph
Fastest lap: Tony Brooks (Frazer Nash LMR) - 1:48.6, 79.56 mph

Event 6 - 5-lap Handicap Race (B)
1   R.B. Watson (MG Special)   10:58.2, 67.71 mph
Fastest lap: Roy Watling-Greenwood (RWG) - 1:58.8, 72.73 mph

Event 7 - 5 lap-Handicap Race (C)
1   Chris Threlfall (Turner-Lea-Francis)   10:42.8, 70.47 mph
Fastest lap: John Coombs (Lotus-Connaught MkVIII) - 1:47.4, 80.45 mph

Event 8 - 5-lap Handicap Race (D)
1   Dick Fitzwilliam (Talbot-Lago T26)   9:47.4, 75.13 mph
Fastest lap: Tony Brooks (Frazer Nash LMR) - 1:46.8, 80.90 mph

Event 9 - 5-lap Handicap Race (E)
1   Bill Constable (MG TD)   11:21.4, 66.92 mph
Fastest lap: P. Johnson (Triumph TR2) - 2:02.0, 70.82 mph

25 SEPTEMBER 1954 – SEPTEMBER MEETING

Event 1 - Madgwick Cup for Formula 2 Cars - 7 laps
1   Bob Gerard (Cooper-Bristol T23)   11:36.0, 86.89 mph
2   Don Beauman (Connaught A)   11:39.4
3   Mike Keen (Cooper-Alta T23)   11:51.6
Fastest lap: Bob Gerard/Don Beauman - 1:37.8, 88.34 mph

Event 2 - 500cc Race (A) - 5 laps
1   Don Parker (Kieft-Norton)   8:50.8, 81.39 mph
2   Stirling Moss (Cooper-Norton)   8:51.0
3   Reg Bicknell (Revis-Norton)   8:51.8
Fastest lap: Stirling Moss - 1:43.0, 83.88 mph

Event 3 - Sports Car Race (A) up to 2000cc non s/c - 5 laps
1   Roy Salvadori (Maserati A6GCS)   8:46.0, 82.13 mph
2   Stirling Moss (Lister-Bristol)   8:46.6
3   Alan Brown (Cooper-Bristol)   8:51.2
Fastest lap: Stirling Moss - 1:43.2, 83.72 mph

Event 4 - Goodwood Trophy for Formula 1 Cars - 21 laps
1   Stirling Moss (Maserati 250F)   33:03.2, 91.49 mph
2   Peter Collins (Vanwall Special)   33:23.6
3   Roy Salvadori (Maserati 250F)   34:20.6
4   Bob Gerard (Cooper-Bristol T23)   34:24.8
5   Don Beauman (Connaught A)   34:28.4
6   Mike Keen (Cooper-Alta T23)   N/A
Fastest lap: Stirling Moss - 1:33.0, 92.90 mph

Event 5 - Sports Car Race (B) unlimited cc - 5 laps
1   Roy Salvadori (Jaguar C-type)   8:35.0, 83.88 mph
2   Masten Gregory (Ferrari 375MM Spider)   8:35.2
3   George Abecassis (HWM-Jaguar)   8:40.6
Fastest lap: Mike Hawthorn (Ferrari 750 *Monza*) - 1:40.0, 86.40 mph

Event 6 - Woodcote Cup for *Formule Libre* Cars - 10 laps
1   Peter Collins (Ferrari '*Thin Wall Special*')   15:38.4, 92.07 mph
2   Ken Wharton (BRM P30 Mk2)   15:44.4
3   Stirling Moss (Maserati 250F)   15:48.0
Fastest lap: Peter Collins - 1:32.2, 93.71 mph

Event 7 - 500cc Race (B) - 5 laps
1   Noel Berrow Johnson (Martin Special-Norton) 9:10.2, 78.52 mph
2   Alan Cowley   9:11.6
3   John Denley (Cooper-Norton)   9:18.4
Fastest lap: Alan Cowley - 1:46.4, 81.20 mph

One of the formative photographs which shaped the Goodwood Motor Circuit Revival's 'set-dressing' in 1998: vintage baler, long-stem corn-stalk sheaves and stooks, the tricky plunging sweep out of St Mary's - oh, and a motor race too... the 1955 Nine-Hours.

1955

26 MARCH 1955 - 18th MEMBERS' MEETING

Event 1 - First Novices 5-lap Handicap Race
1   M.P. Froggatt (Triumph TR2)   10:36.0, 67.92 mph
Fastest lap: Dennis Barthel (Aston Martin DB3) - 1:56.2, 74.35 mph

Event 2 - Ladies 5-lap Handicap Race
1   Pat Moss (MG TF)   13:15.0, 63.53 mph
Fastest lap: Hazel Dunham (AC Ace) - 2:09.0, 66.98 mph

Event 3 - Second Novices 5-lap Handicap Race
1   J.K. Bell (Morris Minor)   12:59.8, 55.80 mph
Fastest lap: B.P. Odoni (Morgan +4) - 2:04.2, 69.56 mph

Event 4 - 5-lap Scratch Race (A) up to 1250cc non s/c
1   Mark Lund (RWG)   10:19.8, 69.68 mph
Fastest lap: Mark Lund - 2:00.0, 72.00 mph

Event 5 - 5-lap Scratch Race over 3000cc non s/c
1   Michael Head (Jaguar C-type)   9:20.0, 77.14 mph
Fastest lap: Michael Head - 1:49.4, 78.98 mph

Event 6 - 5-lap Handicap Race (A)
1   Bill Constable (MG TD)   11:30.4, 66.50 mph
Fastest lap: Basil de Mattos (Morgan +4) - 1:59.2, 72.48 mph

Event 7 - 5-lap Scratch Race up to 1500cc non s/c
1   John Coombs (Lotus-Connaught)   9:29.8, 75.86 mph
Fastest lap: John Coombs - 1:51.8, 77.28 mph

Event 8 - 10-lap Scratch Race 1500cc-3500cc non s/c
1   Michael Head (Jaguar C-type)   18:38.8, 77.21 mph
Fastest lap: Mike Keen (Cooper-Bristol T20) - 1:48.6, 79.56 mph

Event 9 - 5-lap Handicap Race (B) for Closed Cars
1   Michael Head (Ford Zephyr)   12:28.4, 62.29 mph
Fastest lap: G.M. Walters (Aston Martin DB2/4) - 2:04.4, 69.45 mph

Event 10 - 5-lap Handicap Race (C)
1   Anthony Dennis (Austin-Healey 100)   10:20.4, 72.00 mph
Fastest lap: Tony Brooks (Frazer Nash LMR) - 1:49.6, 78.83 mph

11 APRIL 1955 - EASTER MEETING

Event 1 - Lavant Cup for Formula 2 Cars - 7 laps
1   Roy Salvadori (Connaught A)   11:36.8, 86.57 mph
2   Bob Gerard (Cooper-Bristol T23)   11:39.4
3   Don Beauman (Connaught A)   11:42.8
Fastest lap: Roy Salvadori - 1:38.0, 88.16 mph

Event 2 - Sports Car Race (A) up to 1500cc non s/c - 5 laps
1   Les Leston (Connaught AL/SR)   8:49.0, 81.66 mph
2   Ken McAlpine (Connaught AL/SR)   8:50.4
3   Ivor Bueb (Cooper-Climax T39)   9:00.8
Fastest lap: Les Leston - 1:43.8, 83.24 mph

Event 3 - Chichester Cup for *Formule Libre* Cars - 7 laps
1   Peter Collins (BRM P30 MkII)   11:09.8, 90.29 mph
2   Roy Salvadori (Maserati 250F)   11:15.2
3   Stirling Moss (Maserati 250F)   11:20.0
Fastest lap: Peter Collins - 1:34.4, 91.52 mph

Event 4 - Earl of March Trophy for 500cc Racing Cars - 7 laps
1   Iver Bueb (Cooper-Norton)   12:16.6, 82.13 mph
2   Don Parker (Kieft-Norton)   12:24.2
3   Colin Davis (Cooper-Norton)   12:24.6
Fastest lap: Les Leston (Cooper Norton) - 1:43.0, 83.88 mph

Event 5 - Sports Car Race (B) over 2000cc non s/c - 5 laps
1   Roy Salvadori (Aston Martin DB3S)   8:37.8, 83.40 mph
2   Mike Sparken (Ferrari 750 *Monza*)   8:25.6
3   Duncan Hamilton (Jaguar D-type)   8:29.6
Fastest lap: Mike Sparken - 1:59.2, 86.22 mph

Event 6 - Sports Car Race (C) up to 2000 cc non s/c - 5 laps
1   Archie Scott Brown (Lister-Bristol)   8:40.6, 83.06 mph
2   Tony Brooks (Frazer Nash LMR)   8:40.8
3   Mike Anthony (Lotus-Bristol MkX)   8:49.8
Fastest lap: Archie Scott Brown - 1:41.6, 85.10 mph

Event 7 - Richmond Trophy for Formula 1 Cars - 21 laps
1   Roy Salvadori (Maserati 250F)   33:53.0, 89.26 mph
2   Bob Gerard (Cooper-Bristol T23)   34:20.4
3   Don Beauman (Connaught A)   34:26.0
4   Mike Keen (Cooper-Alta T23)   35:19.0
5   Bill Holt (Connaught A)   35:34.0
6   John Young (Connaught A)   20 laps
Fastest lap: Roy Salvadori - 1:33.8, 92.11 mph

Event 8 - Easter Handicap - 5 laps
1   Bob Gerard (Cooper-Bristol T23)   9:09.8, 88.25 mph
2   Roy Salvadori (Maserati 250F)   9:16.0
3   John Young (Connaught A)   9:16.2
Fastest lap: Peter Collins (BRM P30 MkII) - 1:33.0, 92.90 mph

30 MAY 1955 - WHITSUN MEETING

Event 1 - Sports Car Race (A) up to 1500cc non s/c - 10 laps
1   Colin Chapman (Lotus-MG MkIX)   17:39.2, 81.75 mph
2   Reg Parnell (Cooper-Connaught T39)   17:40.8
3   Ken McAlpine (Connaught AL/SR)   17:45.0
Fastest lap: Colin Chapman - 1:42.2, 84.54 mph

Event 2 - Sports Car Race (B) up to 2000cc non s/c - 10 laps
1   Mike Anthony (Lotus-Bristol MkX)   17:20.0, 82.83 mph
2   Tony Brooks (Frazer Nash LMR)   17:28.6
3   Peter Scott Russell (Lotus-Bristol MkX)   18:10.0
Fastest lap: Mike Anthony/Tony Brooks - 1:42.4, 84.37 mph

Event 3 - Sports Car Race (C) over 2000cc non s/c
1   Duncan Hamilton (Jaguar D-type)   17:12.0, 83.72 mph
2   Bob Berry (Jaguar D-type)   17:30.0
3   Dick Protheroe (Jaguar C-type)   18:10.0
Fastest lap: Duncan Hamilton - 1:41.8, 84.87 mph

Event 4 - Vintage Car Handicap - 5 laps
1   John Tozer (Amilcar C6)   11:09.8, 72.26 mph
2   Jack Sears (Sunbeam)   11:13.6
3   Gordon McDonald (Bentley)   11:25.6
Fastest lap: John Tozer - 1:56.0, 74.48 mph

Event 5 - Ladies Handicap - 5 laps
1   Nancy Mitchell (Daimler Conquest)   12:24.0, 64.57 mph
2   Hazel Dunham (AC Ace)   12:24.2
3   Jean Bloxam (Aston Martin DB2)   12:32.0
Fastest lap: Hazel Dunham - 2:01.2, 71.29 mph

Event 6 - Celebrities Handicap - 3 laps
1   Richard Murdoch (Rolls-Royce 20/25)   2:51.6, 49.27 mph
2   Chris Brasher (Jowett Javelin)   4:34.6
3   John Gregson (Hillman Minx)   4:40.2
Fastest lap: Brian Reece (Sunbeam Alpine) - 2:19.2, 62.07 mph

Event 7 - Johnsons Challenge Trophy for Sports Cars - 21 laps
1   Duncan Hamilton (Jaguar D-type)   35:49.4, 84.41 mph
2   Bob Berry (Jaguar D-type)   36:04.6
3   Mike Anthony (Lotus-Bristol MkX)   36:17.0
Fastest lap: Duncan Hamilton - 1:40.2, 86.22 mph

18 JUNE 1955 - 19th MEMBERS' MEETING

Event 1 - 5-lap Scratch Race (A) up to 1250cc non s/c
1   Tommy Sopwith (Cooper-Climax T39)   9:10.0, 78.54 mph
Fastest lap: Tommy Sopwith - 1:47.8, 80.15 mph

Event 2 - Ladies' 5-lap Handicap Race
1   Lorna Snow (Jaguar XK120 Coupé)   11:48.4, 67.66 mph
Fastest lap: Hazel Dunham (AC Ace) - 1:57.2, 73.72 mph

Event 3 - 5-lap Scratch Race (B) up to 1500cc non s/c
1   Tommy Sopwith (Cooper-Climax T39)   9:15.6, 77.75 mph
Fastest lap: Tommy Sopwith - 1:47.2, 80.60 mph

Event 4 - 5-lap Handicap Race (A)
1   Innes Ireland (Riley Brooklands 9)   10:50.8, 66.41 mph
Fastest lap: Michael MacDowel (Lotus-Ford MkIX) - 1:49.6, 78.83 mph

Event 5 - 10-lap Scratch Race (C) 1500cc-3500cc non s/c
1   George Abecassis (HWM-Jaguar)   17:22.0, 82.92 mph
Fastest lap: George Abecassis - 1:42.8, 84.05 mph

Event 6 - 5-lap Handicap Race (B) for Closed Cars
1   Tommy Sopwith (Armstrong-Siddeley Sapphire)   12:03.6, 69.28 mph
Fastest lap: G.M. Walters (Aston Martin DB2/4) - 2:01.4, 71.17 mph

Event 7 - 5-lap Handicap Race (C)
1   W.E. Parkin (Triumph TR2)   10:12.0, 70.59 mph
Fastest lap: George Abecassis (HWM-Jaguar) - 1:42.2, 84.54 mph

Event 8 - 5-lap Handicap Race (D)
1   George Abecassis (HWM-Jaguar)   10:37.2, 83.51 mph
Fastest lap: George Abecassis - 1:41.4, 85.21 mph

20 AUGUST 1955 -
THIRD NINE-HOUR INTERNATIONAL SPORTS CAR RACE

1   Peter Walker/Dennis Poore (Aston Martin DB3S)   82.24 mph, 309 laps
2   Desmond Titterington/Ninian Sanderson (Jaguar D-type) 308 laps
3   Peter Collins/Tony Brooks (Aston Martin DB3S)   305 laps
4   Lance Macklin/Bill Smith (HWM-Jaguar)   301 laps
5   Bob Berry/Norman Dewis (Jaguar D-type)   301 laps
6   Les Leston/Archie Scott Brown (Connaught AL/SR)   288 laps
Fastest lap - Mike Hawthorn (Ferrari 750 Monza) - 1:34.8, 91.14 mph

24 SEPTEMBER 1955 - 20th MEMBERS' MEETING

Event 1 - 5-lap Scratch Race (A) up to 1250 cc non s/c
1   Colin Chapman (Lotus-Climax MkIX)   8:57.8, 80.30 mph
Fastest lap: Colin Chapman - 1:43.8, 83.24 mph

Event 2 - Ladies 5-lap Handicap Race
1   Mary Morton (Austin-Healey 100)   10:40.2, 71.84 mph
Fastest lap: Mrs A.D.N. Vickers (Jaguar C-type) - 1:57.5, 73.47 mph

Event 3 - 5-lap Scratch Race (B) up to 1500cc non s/c
1   Colin Chapman (Lotus-Climax MkIX)   8:43.4, 82.53 mph
Fastest lap: Colin Chapman - 1:42.2, 84.54 mph

Event 4 - 5-lap Handicap Race (A)
1   David Piper (Lotus-MG MkVI)   10:20.0, 72.00 mph
Fastest lap: D. Laver (Lotus-Connaught MkIX) - 1:52.6, 76.37 mph

Event 5 - 10-lap Scratch Race (C) for Sports Cars 1500-3500cc
1   George Abecassis (HWM-Jaguar)   17:24.6, 82.71 mph
Fastest lap: Michael Head (Jaguar D-type)/Peter Sargent (Jaguar XK120) - 1:43.2, 83.72 mph

Event 6 - 5-lap Handicap Race for Closed Cars
1   I.M. Gillett (Jaguar MkVII)   11:35.0, 65.45 mph
Fastest lap: Tony Everard (Aston Martin DB2/4) - 1:56.6, 74.10 mph

Event 7 - 5-lap Handicap Race (C)
1   Dick Protheroe (Jaguar C-type)   9:23.8, 81.66 mph
Fastest lap: Michael Head (Jaguar D-type) - 1:42.0, 84.71 mph

Event 8 - 5-lap Handicap Race (D)
1   H. Giles (Triumph TR2)   10:20.2, 71.40 mph
Fastest lap: Hon. Patrick Lindsay (HWM-Alta) - 1:52.8, 76.60 mph

1956

17 MARCH 1956 - 21st MEMBERS' MEETING

Event 1 - 5 lap Scratch Race (A) up to 1250cc non s/c
1   Dick Steed (Lotus-Climax MkVI)   8:58.0, 80.30 mph
Fastest lap: Dick Steed/Peter Ashdown (Lotus-Climax MkIX) - 1:45.6, 81.82 mph

Event 2 - Ladies 5 lap Handicap Race
1   Bluebelle Gibbs (HRG Lightweight)   11:59.8, 67.52 mph
Fastest lap: Jean Bloxam (Lotus MG MkVIII) - 1:56.4, 74.23 mph

Event 3 - 5-lap Scratch Race (B) up to 1500cc non s/c
1   Peter Lumsden (Lotus-Climax MkIX)   9:04.6, 79.30 mph
Fastest lap: Dick Steed (Lotus-Climax MkIX) - 1:44.4, 82.76 mph

Event 4 - First 5-lap Novices Handicap Race
1   Keith Greene (Cooper-Climax T39)   10:07.8, 75.42 mph
Fastest lap: Keith Greene - 1:51.6, 77.42 mph

Event 5 - 10-lap Scratch Race (C) 1500cc-3500cc non s/c
1   George Abecassis (HWM-Jaguar)   17:05.4, 84.26 mph
Fastest lap: George Abecassis - 1:39.6, 86.75 mph

Event 6 - Second Novices 5-lap Handicap Race
1   R. Dore (Morris Minor Jowett)   12:33.2, 65.15 mph
Fastest lap: A.G. Cochrane (Morgan +4) - 2:01.0, 71.40 mph

Event 7 - 5-lap Handicap Race (A)
1   Berwyn Baxter (Aston Martin DB3S)   10:38.2, 81.02 mph
Fastest lap: George Abecassis (HWM-Jaguar) - 1:38.8, 87.45 mph

Event 8 - 5-lap Handicap Race (B) for Closed Cars
1   Jeff Sparrowe (MG Special)   11:55.8, 69.03 mph
Fastest lap: Tony Everard (Mercedes-Benz 300SL) - 1:53.4, 76.19 mph

2 APRIL 1956 - EASTER MEETING

Event 1 - Lavant Cup for Racing and Sports Cars up to 2000cc non s/c - 7 laps
1   Roy Salvadori (Cooper-Climax T39)   11:33.6, 87.17 mph
2   Bob Gerard (Cooper-Bristol T23)   11:34.6
3   John Young (Connaught A)   11:51.6
Fastest lap: Bob Gerard - 1:37.2, 88.89 mph

Event 2 - Earl of March Trophy 500cc Racing Cars - 7 laps
1   Ivor Bueb (Cooper-Norton)   12:06.6, 83.24 mph
2   Colin Davis (Cooper-Norton)   12:10.4
3   Cliff Allison (Cooper-Norton)   12:22.4
Fastest lap: Ivor Bueb - 1:42.4, 84.37 mph

Event 3 - Sports Car Race (A) over 1500cc non s/c - 15 laps
1   Stirling Moss (Aston Martin DB3S)   24:13.2, 89.18 mph
2   George Abecassis (HWM-Jaguar)   24:36.2
3   Bob Berry (Jaguar D-type)   24:39.8
Fastest lap: Stirling Moss - 1:35.0, 90.95 mph

Event 4 - Sports Car Race (B) up to 1500cc non s/c - 7 laps
1   Roy Salvadori (Cooper-Climax T39)   11:40.8, 86.30 mph
2   Jim Russell (Cooper-Climax T39)   11:41.2
3   Les Leston (Cooper-Climax T39)   11:56.6
Fastest lap: Jim Russell/Roy Salvadori - 1:38.8, 87.45 mph

Event 5 - Richmond Formula 1 Race for the Glover Trophy - 32 laps
1   Stirling Moss (Maserati 250F)   48:50.4, 94.35 mph
2   Roy Salvadori (Maserati 250F)   49:53.6
3   Les Leston (Connaught B)   50:25.8
4   Bob Gerard (Connaught B)   31 laps
5   Reg Parnell (Connaught B)   31 laps
6   Robert Manzon (Gordini T32)   30 laps
Fastest lap (RECORD): Stirling Moss - 1:30.2, 95.79 mph

Event 6 - Production Car Race - 13 laps
1   Ken Rudd (AC-Bristol)   23:44.6, 78.84 mph
2   Dick Utley (Frazer Nash LMR)   24:42.4
3   John Dalton (Austin-Healey 100S)   24:49.6
Fastest lap: Ken Rudd - 1:47.8, 80.15 mph

Event 7 - Easter Handicap - 7 laps
1   Ron Flockhart (Jaguar D-type)   12:41.0, 86.77 mph
2   Alan Brown (Jaguar D-type)   12:49.0
3   Reg Parnell (Connaught B)   12:49.2
Fastest lap: Reg Parnell - 1:34.0, 91.91 mph

14 APRIL 1956 - 22nd MEMBERS' MEETING

Event 1 - 5-lap Scratch Race (A) & (B) up to 1250 cc non s/c
1   Roy Bloxam (Lotus-MG MkVIII)   9:11.2, 78.37 mph
Fastest lap: Peter Lumsden (Lotus-Climax MkIX) - 1:48.4, 79.70 mph

Event 2 - Ladies 5-lap Handicap Race
1   Jean Bloxam (Lotus-MG MkVIII)   10:47.6, 71.69 mph
Fastest lap: Jean Bloxam/Patsy Burt (Aston Martin DB2/4) - 1:57.0, 73.85 mph

Event 3 - 10-lap Scratch Race 1500cc-3500cc non s/c
1   Michael Head (Cooper-Jaguar T38)   17:44.0, 81.20 mph
Fastest lap: Michael Head - 1:44.0, 83.08 mph

Event 4 - 5-lap Handicap Race (A) for Closed Cars
1   J.K. Bell (Morris Minor)   12:22.2, 60.66 mph
Fastest lap: D.F. Cornell (Aston Martin DB2) - 1:59.6, 72.24 mph

Event 5 - 5-lap Handicap Race (B)
1   Mike Sleep (Healey Silverstone)   11:20.2, 68.55 mph
Fastest lap: Stuart Young (*Weldangrind* [Par-Son] MG) - 1:56.0, 74.48 mph

Event 6 - 5-lap Handicap Race (C)
1   M.J. Clay (Lotus-Climax MkVI)   11:23.2, 73.44 mph
Fastest lap: Peter Lumsden (Lotus-Climax MkIX) - 1:48.4, 79.70 mph

Event 7 - 5-lap Handicap Race (D)
1   Tom Kyffin (Aston Martin DB3S)   9:23.6, 80.96 mph
Fastest lap: Michael Head (Cooper-Jaguar T38) - 1:43.0, 83.88 mph

Event 8 - 5-lap Handicap Race (E)
1   Innes Ireland (Riley Brooklands 9)   10:57.4, 70.52 mph
Fastest lap: John Fredman (Jaguar XK120) - 1:56.6, 74.10 mph

21 MAY 1956 - WHITSUN MEETING

Event 1 - Sports Car Race (A) up to 1500cc non s/c - 26 laps
1   Colin Chapman (Lotus-Climax 11)   43:35.2, 85.88 mph
2   Mike Hawthorn (Lotus-Climax 11)   43:53.2
3   Jack Brabham (Cooper-Climax T39)   44:35.2
Fastest lap: Mike Hawthorn/Colin Chapman - 1:37.4, 88.71 mph

Event 2 - 500cc race - 12 laps
1   Jim Russell (Cooper-Norton)   21:02.2, 82.14 mph
2   Eric Fenning (Staride-Norton)   21:36.6
3   Reg Bicknell (Revis-Norton)   22:04.2
Fastest lap: Jim Russell - 1:42.6, 84.21 mph

Event 3 - Sports Car Race (B) over 1500cc non s/c - 26 laps
1   Bob Berry (Jaguar D-type)   42:37.0, 87.85 mph
2   Ron Flockhart (Jaguar D-type)   42:57.0
3   Desmond Titterington (Jaguar D-type)   43:49.2
Fastest lap: Ron Flockhart - 1:36.8, 89.26 mph

Event 4 - Whitsun Trophy for *Formule Libre* Cars - 26 laps
1   Desmond Titterington (Jaguar D-type)   42:43.0, 87.65 mph
2   Mike Hawthorn (Lotus-Climax 11)   42:44.8
3   Ron Flockhart (Jaguar D-type)   42:48.0
Fastest lap (RECORD): Desmond Titterington - 1:36.6, 89.44 mph

Event 5 - Vintage Car Handicap - 5 laps
1   Barry Eastick (Bentley)   11:22.8, 67.21 mph
2   Sir Francis Samuelson (Sunbeam)   11:25.6
3   John Tozer (Amilcar)   11:41.0
Fastest lap: John Tozer - 1:52.8, 76.60 mph

7 JULY 1956 - 23rd MEMBERS' MEETING

Event 1 - 5-lap Scratch Race (A) up to 1250cc non s/c
1   Peter Ashdown (Lotus-Climax MkIX)   8:47.8, 81.97 mph
Fastest lap: Peter Ashdown/Bill Frost (Lotus-Climax 11) - 1:43.4, 83.56 mph

Event 2 - Ladies 5-lap Handicap Race
1   Gillian Spooner (Triumph TR2)   11:12.6, 66.21 mph
Fastest lap: Jean Bloxam (Aston Martin DB2) - 2:00.6, 71.64 mph

'Gorgeous George' at 'Glorious Goodwood' - hard-driving Aston Martin distributor and sometime works team driver George Abecassis built his own HWM cars in partnership with John Heath (who tragically lost his life in one of their HWM-Jaguar sports cars in the 1956 Mille Miglia). George pressed on briefly, and here finished second to Moss's DB3S - Easter Monday 1956.

Event 3 - 5-lap Scratch Race (B) up to 1500cc non s/c
1   Bill Frost (Lotus-Climax 11)   8:50.8, 81.38 mph
Fastest lap: Peter Ashdown (Lotus-Climax MkIX) - 1:43.6, 83.40 mph

Event 4 - 5-lap Handicap Race (A)
1   C.J. Freeman (Aston Martin)   10:45.0, 71.40 mph
Fastest lap: John Fredman (Jaguar XK120) - 1:56.8, 73.97 mph

Event 5 - 10-lap Scratch Race (C) 1500cc-3500cc non s/c
1   Michael Head (Cooper-Jaguar T38)   17:28.6, 82.36 mph
Fastest lap: Michael Head - 1:42.2, 84.54 mph

Event 6 - 5-lap Handicap Race (B) for Closed Cars
1   Ellis Cuff Miller (Ford)   12:25.0, 64.00 mph
Fastest lap: G. Livanos (Aston Martin DB2/4) - 1:55.0, 75.13 mph

Event 7 - 5-lap Handicap Race (C)
1   Peter Farquharson (Allard)   10:07.2, 75.52 mph
Fastest lap: Michael Head (Cooper-Jaguar T33) - 1:43.6, 83.4 mph

Event 8 - 5-lap Handicap Race (D)
1   Robin Benson (Morgan +4)   10:55.4, 73.16 mph
Fastest lap: Colin Davis (Lotus-Climax 11) - 1:51.0, 77.84 mph

8 SEPTEMBER 1956 – SEPTEMBER MEETING

Event 1 - Madgwick Cup for Sports Cars up to 1100cc non s/c - 5 laps
1   Keith Hall (Lotus-Climax 11)   8:30.6, 84.62 mph
2   Michael MacDowel (Cooper-Climax T39)   8:31.6
3   Cliff Allison (Lotus-Climax 11)   8:35.4
Fastest lap: Keith Hall - 1:39.6, 86,75 mph

Event 2 - 500cc Race - 5 laps
1   Jim Russell (Cooper-Norton)   8:38.4, 83.33 mph
2   Don Parker (Cooper-Norton)   8:40.6
3   Colin Davis (Beart Cooper-Norton)   8:41.0
Fastest lap (RECORD): Jim Russell - 1:41.8, 84.87 mph

Event 3 - Woodcote Cup for Sports or Racing Cars up to 2000cc - 10 laps
1   Roy Salvadori (Cooper-Climax T39)   16:18.0, 88.34 mph
2   Colin Chapman (Lotus-Climax 11)   16:33.2
3   Les Leston (Cooper-Climax T39)   16:33.6
Fastest lap: Roy Salvadori - 1:36.2, 89.81 mph

Event 4 - First September Handicap - 5 laps
1   Alan Stacey (Lotus-Climax 11)   9:22.0, 82.76 mph
2   Mark Zervudachi (Lotus-Climax 11)   9:25.2
3   Robbie MacKenzie-Low (Cooper-Climax T39)   9:25.4
Fastest lap: Colin Chapman (Lotus-Climax 11) - 1:37.4, 88.71 mph

Event 5 - Sussex Trophy for Sports and Racing Cars up to 1500cc - 10 laps
1   Roy Salvadori (Cooper-Climax T41)   16:10.0, 89.07 mph
2   Colin Chapman (Lotus-Climax 11)   16:22.2
3   Les Leston (Cooper-Climax T39)   16:35.6
Fastest lap: Roy Salvadori - 1:35.4, 90.57 mph

Event 6 - Goodwood Trophy for Sports Cars over 1500cc - 21 laps
1   Tony Brooks (Aston Martin DB3S)   34:17.4, 88.19 mph
2   Roy Salvadori (Aston Martin DB3S)   34:34.6
3   Ron Flockhart (Jaguar D-type)   34:35.6
Fastest lap: Ninian Sanderson (Jaguar D-type) - 1:37.0, 89.07 mph

Event 7 - Second September Handicap - 5 laps
1   Jock Lawrence (Jaguar D-type)   8:54.6, 84.44 mph
2   Noel Cunningham Reid (HWM-Jaguar)   8:57.2
3   Paul Emery (Emeryson)   8:59.6
Fastest lap: Ron Flockhart (Jaguar D-type)/Tony Brooks (Aston Martin DB3S) - 1:37.2, 88.89 mph

22 SEPTEMBER 1956 – 24th MEMBERS' MEETING

Event 1 - 5-lap Scratch Race (A) up to 1250cc non s/c
1   Alan Stacey (Lotus-Climax 11)   8:40.0, 83.08 mph
Fastest lap: Alan Stacey - 1:42.4, 84.37 mph

Event 2 - 5-lap Ladies Handicap Race
1   Hazel Dunham (MG A)   11:09.2, 68.66 mph
Fastest lap: Gillian Spooner (Triumph TR2) - 2:02.0, 70.82 mph

Event 3 - 5-lap Scratch Race (B) up to 1500cc non s/c
1   Alan Stacey (Lotus-Climax 11)   8:36.0, 83.72 mph
Fastest lap: Alan Stacey - 1:41.2, 85.37 mph

Event 4 - 5-lap Handicap Race (A)
1   N.N. Bentley (Triumph TR2)   10:49.2, 72.10 mph
Fastest lap: John Hickman (Elva-Climax Mk1) - 1:52.4, 76.87 mph

Event 5 - 10-lap Scratch Race (C) 1500cc-3500cc non s/c
1   Graham Whitehead (Aston Martin DB3S)   17:06.2, 84.19 mph
Fastest lap: Graham Whitehead 1:41.2, 85.37 mph

Event 6 - 5-lap Handicap Race for Closed Cars
1   D.E. Howard (Aston Martin DB3)   13:42.8, 72.26 mph
Fastest lap: D.E. Howard - 1:55.4, 74.87 mph

Event 7 - 5-lap Handicap Race (C)
1   Len Gibbs (Lotus-Climax 11)   9:22.8, 78.15 mph
Fastest lap: Graham Whitehead (Aston Martin DB3S) - 1:40.0, 86.40 mph

Event 8 - 5-lap Handicap Race (D)
1   R C B Ashby (Leco-MG)   10:52.0, 66.25 mph
Fastest lap: Chris Bristow (Leonard-MG) - 1:53.6, 76.06 mph

1957

22 APRIL 1957 – EASTER MEETING

Event 1 - 'Autosport' Series for Production Sports Cars - 13 laps
1   Ken Rudd (AC Bristol)   23:30.0, 79.66 mph
2   Dickie Stoop (Frazer Nash Sebring)   23:46.6
3   John Dalton (Austin-Healey 100S)   24:41.0
Fastest lap: Ken Rudd - 1:44.4, 82.76 mph

Event 2 - Lavant Cup for Formula 2 Cars - 12 laps
1   Tony Brooks (Cooper-Climax T41)   19:22.0, 88.84 mph
2   Jack Brabham (Cooper-Climax T43)   19:40.2
3   Ron Flockhart (Lotus-Climax 11)   20:03.6
Fastest lap: Roy Salvadori (Cooper-Climax T43) - 1:34.4, 91.52 mph

Event 3 - Chichester Cup for Sports Cars up to 1500cc non s/c - 10 laps
1   Colin Chapman (Lotus-Climax 11)   16:29.4, 87.32 mph
2   Ron Flockhart (Lotus-Climax 11)   16:30.0
3   Keith Hall (Lotus-Climax 11)   16:41.4
Fastest lap: Roy Salvadori (Cooper-Climax T39) - 1:37.0, 89.07 mph

Event 4 - Richmond Formula 1 Race for the Glover Trophy - 32 laps
1   Stuart Lewis-Evans (Connaught B)   50:49.8, 90.66 mph
2   Jack Fairman (Connaught B)   51:13.2
3   Ron Flockhart (BRM Type 25)   51:33.0
4   Jack Brabham (Cooper-Climax T43)   31 laps
5   Jim Russell (Maserati 250F)   30 laps
6   Tony Brooks (Vanwall)   27 laps
Fastest lap (RECORD): Tony Brooks - 1:29.6, 96.43 mph

Event 5 - Sussex Trophy for Sports Cars over 1500cc non s/c - 21 laps
1   Archie Scott Brown (Lister-Jaguar)   33:49.0, 89.42 mph
2   Roy Salvadori (Aston Martin DBR1)   34:10.2
3   Tony Brooks (Aston Martin DB3S)   34:38.6
Fastest lap (RECORD): Archie Scott Brown - 1:34.6, 91.33 mph

Event 6 - Earl of March Trophy 500cc Racing Cars - 10 laps
1   Stuart Lewis Evans (Beart Cooper-Norton)   17:19.2, 83.14 mph
2   Eugene Hall (Cooper-Norton)   17:49.4
3   Derek Strange (Cooper-Norton)   17:49.6
Fastest lap: Stuart Lewis-Evans - 1:42.2, 84.54 mph

11 MAY 1957 – 25th MEMBERS' MEETING

Event 1 - 5-lap Scratch Race (A) up to 1250cc non s/c
1   Innes Ireland (Lotus-Climax 11)   8:52.0, 81.20 mph
Fastest lap: Innes Ireland/Chris Bristow (Cooper-Climax T39) - 1:44.4, 82.76 mph

Event 2 - 5-lap Novices Handicap Race
1   J. Baker Courtney (MG T Type)   10:35.0, 68.03 mph
Fastest lap: Hon. Mark Fitzalan-Howard (Lotus-Climax 11) - 1:53.2, 76.32 mph

Event 3 - 5-lap Scratch Race (B) up to 1500 cc non s/c
1   Innes Ireland (Lotus-Climax 11)   8:36.6, 83.63 mph
Fastest lap: Tommy Sopwith (Cooper-Climax T39) - 1:40.6, 85.88 mph

Event 4 - 5-lap Handicap Race (A)
1   Alan Foster (MG A)   12:30.4, 72.53 mph
Fastest lap: C.J. Freeman (Aston Martin SM) - 1:55.0, 75.13 mph

Event 5 - 5-lap Handicap Race (B)
1   Maurice Charles (Jaguar D-type)   8:52.2, 83.52 mph
Fastest lap: Tommy Sopwith (Cooper-Climax T39) - 1:41.6, 85.04 mph

Event 6 - 5-lap Handicap Race for Closed Cars
1   Jean Bloxam (Aston Martin DB2)   12:27.4, 72.31 mph
Fastest lap: Jean Bloxam - 1:55.0, 75.13 mph

Event 7 - 5-lap Handicap Race (C)
1   Ian Baillie (Jaguar D-type)   10:32.2, 78.95 mph
Fastest lap: Maurice Charles (Jaguar D-type) - 1:42.2, 84.54 mph

Event 8 - 5-lap Handicap Race (D)
1   Tony Page (Lotus-Climax MkIX)   10:40.8, 75.03 mph
Fastest lap: Tony Page - 1:50.6, 78.12 mph

The inimitable crowd favourite Archie Scott Brown in untypically peaceful poise with the Cambridge works team's original 1957 Lister-Jaguar.

10 JUNE 1957 – WHITSUN MEETING

Event 1 - Closed Car Handicap - 7 laps
1   John Sprinzel (Austin A35)   14:57.4, 62.65 mph
2   J.K. Bell (Morris Minor)   14:58.0
3   W.G. Wright (Morris 1000)   15:07.8
Fastest lap: Jean Bloxam (Aston Martin DB2) - 1:52.8, 76.60 mph

Event 2 - Sports Car Race (A) up to 1100cc non s/c - 26 laps
1   Alan Stacey (Lotus-Climax 11)   45:00.8, 83.18 mph
2   Keith Greene (Cooper-Climax T39)   45:25.0
3   Bryan Hewitt (Lotus-Climax MkIX)   45:46.2
Fastest lap: Innes Ireland (Lotus-Climax 11) - 1:41.8, 84.87 mph

Event 3 - Bentley '21st' Handicap - 7 laps
1   Donald Day (Bentley)   14:46.2, 65.11 mph
2   M.J. Bradley (Bentley)   15:08.8
3   A.P.K. Chaffey (Bentley)   15:12.8
Fastest lap: George Burton (Bentley) - 1:52.2, 77.00 mph

Event 4 - Sports Car Race (B) unlimited non s/c - 26 laps
1   Michael Head (Cooper-Jaguar T38)   43:44.8, 85.88 mph
2   Peter Blond (Aston Martin DB3S)   43:50.6
3   Maurice Charles (Jaguar D-type)   43:53.2
Fastest lap: Michael Head - 1:38.6, 87.63 mph

Event 5 - Ladies Handicap - 5 laps
1   Avril Scott-Moncrieff (Lotus-MG MkVI)   10:53.8, 68.27 mph
2   Rosemary Seers (Cooper-Zephyr T14)   11:04.8
3   Jean Bloxam (Aston Martin DB2)   11:16.4
Fastest lap: Jean Bloxam - 1:52.0, 77.14 mph

Event 6 - Marque Scratch Race - 7 laps
1   Paul Fletcher (AC Ace)   13:19.8, 75.62 mph
2   John Looker (Morgan +4)   13:23.4
3   Robin Carnegie (MG A Le Mans)   13:24.4
Fastest lap: Paul Fletcher - 1:53.0, 76.46 mph

22 JUNE 1957 - 26th MEMBERS' MEETING

Event 1 - 5-lap Scratch Race (A) up to 1250cc non s/c
1   Innes Ireland (Lotus-Climax 11)   8:34.6, 83.95 mph
Fastest lap: Innes Ireland - 1:41.0, 85.54 mph

Event 2 - 5-lap Handicap Race (A)
1   N.D. Sheffield (Triumph TR2)   11:02.0, 72.36 mph
Fastest lap: Peter Sargent (Jaguar XK120) - 1:50.8, 77.98 mph

Event 3 - 5-lap Scratch Race (B) up to 1500cc non s/c
1   Innes Ireland (Lotus-Climax 11)   8:38.2, 83.37 mph
Fastest lap: Keith Greene (Cooper-Climax T39) - 1:41.8, 84.87 mph

Event 4 - 5-lap Handicap Race (B)
1   Ellis Cuff-Miller (Lago Talbot-Lago T26)   11:13.2, 67.80 mph
Fastest lap: Maurice Charles (Jaguar D-type) - 1:55.0, 75.13 mph

Event 5 - 5-lap Marque Scratch Race
1   Alan Foster (MG A)   9:44.4, 73.92 mph
Fastest lap: N.N. Bentley (Triumph TR2) - 1:53.2, 76.32 mph

Event 6 - 5-lap Handicap Race for Closed Cars
1   R. Dore (Morris Minor-Javelin)   11:15.2, 65.93 mph
Fastest lap: Jean Bloxam (Aston Martin DB2) - 1:55.6, 74.74 mph

Event 7 - 5-lap Handicap Race (C)
1   Tony Page (Lotus-Climax MkIX)   9:13.8, 79.88 mph
Fastest lap: Innes Ireland (Lotus-Climax 11) - 1:41.6, 85.04 mph

Event 8 - 5-lap Handicap Race (D)
1   Jon Goddard-Watts (Berkeley)   11:17.2, 58.86 mph
Fastest lap: Chris Lawrence (Rotacks MG) - 2:09.2, 66.87 mph

31 AUGUST 1957 - 27th MEMBERS' MEETING

Event 1 - 10-lap Scratch Race (A) up to 1250cc non s/c
1   Chris Bristow (Cooper-Climax T39)   17:32.6, 82.05 mph
Fastest lap: Innes Ireland (Lotus-Climax 11) - 1:42.4, 84.37 mph

Event 2 - 5-lap Handicap Race (A)
1   Dick Fitzwilliam (Talbot-Lago T26C)   10:55.0, 77.00 mph
Fastest lap: Dick Fitzwilliam - 1:49.2, 79.12 mph

Event 3 - 5-lap Scratch Race (B) up to 350cc non s/c
1   Jon Goddard-Watts (Berkeley)   11:25.4, 63.02 mph
Fastest lap: Jon Goddard-Watts - 2:14.2, 64.38 mph

Event 4 - 5-lap Handicap Race for Closed Cars
1   Bob Shaw (Fiat-Abarth 750)   11:42.8, 62.79 mph
Fastest lap: Jean Bloxam (Aston Martin DB2) - 1:53.2, 76.32 mph

Event 5 - 5-lap Scratch Race (C) up to 1500cc
1   Innes Ireland (Lotus-Climax 11)   8:32.6, 84.29 mph
Fastest lap: Chris Bristow (Cooper-Climax T39) - 1:40.0, 86.40 mph

Event 6 - 10-lap Marque Scratch Race
1   I.W. McCulloch (Triumph TR2)   19:14.8, 75.26 mph
Fastest lap: John Looker (Morgan +4) - 1:51.8, 77.28 mph

Event 7 - 5-lap Handicap Race (B)
1   Ellis Cuff-Miller (Talbot-Lago T26)   10:17.0, 76.87 mph
Fastest lap: Maurice Charles (Jaguar D-type) - 1:45.6, 81.82 mph

Event 8 - 5-lap Handicap Race (C)
1   Keith Greene (Cooper-Climax T39)   10:24.0, 82.76 mph
Fastest lap: Keith Greene - 1:41.0, 85.54 mph

14 SEPTEMBER 1957 - VSCC MEETING

Event 1 - Vintage Sports Car Race - 10 laps
1   George Burton (Bentley)   74.80 mph
Fastest lap: George Burton - 1:51.4, 77.56 mph

Event 2 - Vintage and Historic Racing Cars Race - 10 laps
1   Bill Moss (ERA B Type)   74.17 mph
Fastest lap: 'Nobby' Spero (ERA B Type) - 1:52.4, 76.87 mph

28 SEPTEMBER 1957 - SEPTEMBER MEETING

Event 1 - 500cc Race - 10 laps
1   Stuart Lewis-Evans (Beart Cooper-Norton)   16:48.2, 85.70 mph
2   Jim Russell (Cooper-Norton)   17:04.4
3   Don Parker (Cooper-Norton)   17:26.8
Fastest lap (RECORD): Stuart Lewis-Evans - 1:39.4, 86.92 mph

Event 2 - Madgwick Cup for Sports Cars up to 1100cc - 10 laps
1   Alan Stacey (Lotus-Climax 11)   16:32.8, 87.01 mph
2   Keith Hall (Lotus-Climax 11)   16:38.6
3   Peter Ashdown (Lotus-Climax 11)   16:46.6
Fastest lap (RECORD): Innes Ireland (Lotus-Climax 11)/Alan Stacey - 1:37.4, 88.71 mph

Event 3 - Woodcote Cup for Formula 2 Cars - 10 laps
1   Roy Salvadori (Cooper-Climax T43)   15:15.0, 94.42 mph
2   Jack Brabham (Cooper-Climax T43)   15:15.6
3   Cliff Allison (Lotus-Climax 12)   15:43.4
Fastest lap (RECORD): Jack Brabham - 1:30.0, 96.00 mph

Event 4 - Goodwood Trophy for Unlimited Sports Cars - 21 laps
1   Archie Scott Brown (Lister-Jaguar)   34:03.0, 88.84 mph
2   Jack Brabham (Tojeiro-Jaguar)   34:37.0
3   Henry Taylor (Jaguar D-type)   34:46.2
Fastest lap (RECORD): Archie Scott Brown - 1:35.6, 90.38 mph

Event 5 - Marque Sports Car Race - 10 laps
1   John Dalton (Austin-Healey 100/6)   18:46.0, 76.72 mph
2   Robin Carnegie (MG A Le Mans)   18:47.2
3   Alan Foster (MG A)   18:56.0
Fastest lap: John Dalton - 1:51.2, 77.70 mph

Event 6 - September Sports Car Handicap - 5 laps
1   Patsy Burt (Cooper-Climax T39)   9:19.6, 79.33 mph
2   Robbie MacKenzie-Low (Elva-Climax MkIII)   9:20.0
3   Keith Greene (Cooper-Climax T39)   9:24.4
Fastest lap: Henry Taylor (Jaguar D-type)/Michael Head (Cooper-Jaguar T38) - 1:39.4, 86.92 mph

1958

7 APRIL 1958 - EASTER MEETING

Event 1 - Earl of March Trophy for 500cc cars - 10 laps
1   Stuart Lewis Evans (Beart Cooper-Norton)   17:13.2, 83.62 mph
2   Trevor Taylor (Beart Cooper-Norton)   17:30.0
3   John Pitcher (Cooper-Norton)   18:00.2
Fastest lap: Stuart Lewis-Evans - 1:41.6, 85.04 mph

Event 2 - Lavant Cup for Formula 2 Cars - 15 laps
1   Jack Brabham (Cooper-Climax T43)   23:02.2, 93.76 mph
2   Graham Hill (Lotus-Climax 12)   23:02.6
3   Cliff Allison (Lotus-Climax 12)   23:14.2
Fastest lap: Graham Hill - 1:30.2, 95.79 mph

Event 3 - Sussex Trophy for Sports Cars over 1100cc - 21 laps
1   Stirling Moss (Aston Martin DBR2)   33:37.4, 89.94 mph
2   Peter Collins (Ferrari Dino 206S)   34:25.0
3   Duncan Hamilton (Jaguar D-type)   34:30.6
Fastest lap (RECORD): Stirling Moss - 1:33.4, 92.50 mph

Event 4 - Goodwood International '100' for the Glover Trophy - 42 laps
1   Mike Hawthorn (Ferrari Dino 246)   63:14.4, 94.96 mph
2   Jack Brabham (Cooper-Climax T45)   64:20.4
3   Roy Salvadori (Cooper-Climax T45)   41 laps
4   Cliff Allison (Lotus-Climax 12)   41 laps
5   Stuart Lewis-Evans (Connaught B)   40 laps
6   Archie Scott Brown (Connaught B)   40 laps
Fastest lap (RECORD): Mike Hawthorn/Stirling Moss (Cooper-Climax T43) - 1:28.8, 97.30 mph

Event 5 - Chichester Cup for Sports Cars up to 1100cc - 10 laps
1   John Campbell-Jones (Lotus-Climax 11)   16:32.2, 87.08 mph
2   Tom Dickson (Lotus-Climax 11)   16:32.4
3   Roy Salvadori (Lotus-Climax 11)   16:44.0
Fastest lap (RECORD): John Campbell-Jones - 1:37.2, 88.89 mph

26 APRIL 1958 - 28th MEMBERS' MEETING

Event 1 - 10-lap Scratch Race (A) up to 1250 cc non s/c
1   Keith Greene (Lotus-Climax 11)   17:11.2, 83.79 mph
Fastest lap: John Campbell-Jones (Lotus-Climax 11) - 1:39.6, 86.75 mph

Event 2 - 5-lap Handicap Race (A) for Closed Cars
1   G. M. Hopkinson (Austin A35)   13:30.0, 61.28 mph
Fastest lap: Mike Barker (Ford Anglia) - 2:11.6, 65.68 mph

Event 3 - 10-lap Marque Scratch Race
1   Paul Fletcher (AC Ace)   20:24.0, 70.59 mph
Fastest lap: Paul Fletcher - 1:58.6, 72.85 mph

Event 4 - 5-lap Scratch Race (B) up to 1500cc non s/c
1   Keith Greene (Lotus-Climax 11)   9:29.4, 75.85 mph
Fastest lap: Chris Bristow (Hume Lotus-Climax 11) - 1:46.0, 81.53 mph

Event 5 - 5-lap Handicap Race (B) for Closed Cars
1   Edgar Wadsworth (Healey)   11:06.8, 66.79 mph
Fastest lap: Jean Bloxam (Aston Martin DB3S Coupé) - 1:55.8, 74.61 mph

Ferrari's only works team victory at Goodwood lies within sight for Mike Hawthorn - International '100' for the Glover Trophy, Easter Monday 1958. By year's end 'The Farnham Flyer' would have become the first ever British World Champion. In a year's time he would be dead.

Event 6 - 5-lap Handicap Race (C)
1   John Dashwood (Frazer Nash LMR)   10:58.4, 71.00 mph
Fastest lap: Dennis Barthel (Aston Martin DB3S) - 1:54.6, 75.30 mph

Event 7 - 5-lap Handicap Race (D)
1   Philip Arnold (Triumph TR2)   11:36.4, 68.97 mph
Fastest lap: Philip Arnold - 2:01.4, 71.17 mph

Event 8 - 5-lap Handicap Race (E)
1   R. Rye (Lotus-MG MkVI)   11:00.0, 69.12 mph
Fastest lap: Dennis Barthel (Aston Martin DB3S) - 1:54.8, 75.26 mph

26 MAY 1958 – WHITSUN MEETING

Event 1 - 'Autosport' Series for Production Sports Car Race - 12 laps
1   Ted Whiteaway (AC-Bristol)   22:02.3, 78.36 mph
2   Bill Wilks (Frazer Nash LMR)   22:08.4
3   Mike Anthony (AC-Bristol)   22:22.6
Fastest lap: Ted Whiteaway - 1:47.8, 80.15 mph

Event 2 - Historic Racing Cars - 10 laps
1   Bill Moss (ERA B Type)   17:31.8, 82.14 mph
2   Douglas Hull (ERA B Type)   17:52.4
3   J. Goodhew (ERA-Delage 15S8)   18:19.4
Fastest lap: Bill Moss - 1:41.0, 85.54 mph

Event 3 - Whitsun Trophy - 21 laps
1   Graham Whitehead (Lister-Jaguar)   35:49.6, 84.41 mph
2   Duncan Hamilton (Jaguar D-type)   35:56.6
3   Chris Bristow (Hume Lotus-Climax 11)   36:14.0
Fastest lap: Graham Whitehead - 1:37.6, 88.52 mph

Event 4 - Marque Sports Car Race - 10 laps
1   Jack Sears (Austin-Healey 100/6)   18:46.4, 76.70 mph
2   Paul Fletcher (AC Ace)   19:10.2
3   Roy North (Triumph TR2)   19:16.8
Fastest lap: Jack Sears - 1:50.0, 78.54 mph

Event 5 - Production Saloon Car Race - 10 laps
1   Duncan Hamilton (Jaguar 3.4)   18:14.4, 78.95 mph
2   Tommy Sopwith (Jaguar 3.4)   18:36.6
3   Sir Gawaine Baillie (Jaguar 3.4)   19:04.6
Fastest lap: Duncan Hamilton - 1:48.2, 79.85 mph

Event 6 - Whitsun Handicap - 10 laps
1   Bruce Halford (Lister-Jaguar)   17:09.4, 87.33 mph
2   Bob Hicks (Lotus-Climax 11)   17:15.4
3   Duncan Hamilton (Jaguar D-type)   17:24.4
Fastest lap: Graham Whitehead (Lister-Jaguar)/Bruce Halford - 1:37.0, 89.07 mph

14 JUNE 1958 – 29th MEMBERS' MEETING

Event 1 - 10-lap Scratch Race (A) up to 1250 cc non s/c
1   Michael Taylor (Lotus-Climax 11)   16:33.4, 86.97 mph
Fastest lap: Michael Taylor - 1:38.0, 88.16 mph

Event 2 - 5-lap Handicap Race for Closed Cars
1   D.E. Hicks (Standard 8)   12:27.2, 60.64 mph
Fastest lap: Mike Barker (Ford Anglia)/Fred Marriott (Morris 1000) - 2:07.6, 67.71 mph

Event 3 - 10-lap Marque Scratch Race
1   Sid Hurrell (Triumph TR3)   19:11.0, 75.06 mph
Fastest lap: Sid Hurrell - 1:51.8, 77.28 mph

Event 4 - 5-lap Handicap Race (B) for Closed Cars
1   Ron Brightman (AC Aceca-Bristol)   11:05.4, 73.17 mph
Fastest lap: Ron Brightman - 1:54.2, 75.66 mph

Event 5 - 5-lap Handicap Race (C)
1   Julian Sutton (Austin-Healey 100)   9:58.4, 75.34 mph
Fastest lap: Ian Baillie (Jaguar D-type) - 1:44.6, 82.60 mph

Event 6 - 5-lap Scratch Race (B) up to 1500cc non s/c
1   Michael Taylor (Lotus-Climax 11)   8:16.0, 87.10 mph
Fastest lap: Keith Greene (Lotus-Climax 11) - 1:37.4, 88.71 mph

Event 7 - 5-lap Handicap Race (D)
1   Ron Brightman (AC Aceca-Bristol)   9:38.4, 75.34 mph
Fastest lap: Ian Baillie (Jaguar D-type) - 1:43.4, 83.56 mph

Event 8 - 5-lap Handicap Race (E)
1   R.C.G. Ashby (Berkeley B65)   10:20.0, 53.08 mph
Fastest lap: Mick Sleep (AC Ace) - 1:53.0, 76.46 mph

12 JULY 1958 – 30th MEMBERS' MEETING

Event 1 - 10-lap Scratch Race (A) up to 1250cc non s/c
1   Michael Taylor (Lotus-Climax 11)   16:25.2, 87.70 mph
Fastest lap: Keith Greene (Lotus-Climax 11)/Michael Taylor - 1:37.2, 88.89 mph

Event 2 - 5-lap Handicap Race (A) for Closed Cars
1   George Lawrence (Austin A35)   12:09.0, 64.10 mph
Fastest lap: Fred Marriott (Morris 1000) - 2:09.0, 66.98 mph

Event 3 - 10-lap Marque Scratch Race
1   David Shale (Austin-Healey 100/6)   19:08.0, 75.26 mph
Fastest lap: David Shale - 1:51.0, 77.84 mph

Event 4 - 5-lap Handicap Race (B) for Closed Cars
1   W.P. Sheppard (Jaguar XK120)   10:51.0, 70.70 mph
Fastest lap: Ron Brightman (AC Aceca-Bristol) - 1:53.2, 76.32 mph

Event 5 - 5-lap Scratch Race up to 1500cc non s/c
1   Michael Taylor (Lotus-Climax 11)   8:13.6, 87.52 mph
Fastest lap: Michael Taylor - 1:37.2, 88.89 mph

Event 6 - 5-lap Handicap Race (C)
1   John Fredman (Lotus-Climax 11)   10:30.0, 76.87 mph
Fastest lap: F.B. Birch (Cooper-Jaguar T38) - 1:48.2, 79.85 mph

Event 7 - 5-lap Handicap Race (D)
1   David Shale (Lotus-Climax 11)   9:44.2, 83.21 mph
Fastest lap: David Shale - 1:41.0, 85.54 mph

Event 8 - 5-lap Handicap Race (E)
1   Chris Steele (Cooper-Zephyr T14)   11:41.6, 71.81 mph
Fastest lap: John Quick (Triumph TR2) - 1:54.0, 75.79 mph

23 AUGUST 1958 – 31st MEMBERS' MEETING

Event 1 - 10-lap Scratch Race (A) up to 1100cc non s/c
1   Michael Taylor (Lotus-Climax 11)   16:43.2, 86.12 mph
Fastest lap: Eric Broadley (Lola-Climax Mk1) - 1:37.4, 88.71 mph

Event 2 - 5-lap Handicap Race (A) for Closed Cars
1   Rosemary Massey (Jaguar XK150)   10:46.0, 69.57 mph
Fastest lap: Jean Bloxam (Aston Martin DB3S Coupé) - 1:49.6, 78.83 mph

Event 3 - 10-lap Marque Scratch Race
1   David Shale (Austin-Healey 100/6)   19:00.6, 75.75 mph
Fastest lap: David Shale - 1:52.0, 77.14 mph

Event 4 - 5-lap Handicap Race (B) for Closed Cars
1   J. Wheeler (Austin A35)   12:01.2, 63.89 mph
Fastest lap: 'Paddy' Gaston (Austin A35) - 2:09.0, 66.98 mph

Event 5 - 5-lap Scratch Race (B) up to 1500cc non s/c
1   Michael Taylor (Lotus-Climax 11)   8:23.8, 84.08 mph
Fastest lap: Michael Taylor/John Campbell-Jones (Lotus-Climax 11) - 1:39.4, 86.92 mph

Event 6 - 5-lap Handicap Race (C)
1   John Bekaert (HWM-Jaguar)   10:19.6, 80.80 mph
Fastest lap: John Bekaert - 1:44.2, 82.92 mph

Event 7 - 5-lap Handicap Race (D)
1   Chris Threlfall (Tojeiro-Climax)   10:00.0, 80.75 mph
Fastest lap: John Bekaert (HWM -aguar) - 1:43.0, 83.88 mph

Event 8 - 5-lap Handicap Race (E)
1   Geoff Breakell (Triumph TR3)   10:17.4, 73.67 mph
Fastest lap: John Quick (Triumph TR2) - 1:51.2, 77.70 mph

13 SEPTEMBER 1958 – 23rd RAC TOURIST TROPHY

1   Stirling Moss/Tony Brooks (Aston Martin DBR1)   4h 00:51.2, 148 laps, 88.83 mph
2   Roy Salvadori/Jack Brabham (Aston Martin DBR1)   4h 01:17.4, 148 laps
3   Carroll Shelby/Stuart Lewis Evans (Aston Martin DBR1) 4h 01:18.7, 148 laps
4   Jean Behra/Edgar Barth (Porsche RSK)   4h 01:18.0, 144 laps
5   Masten Gregory/Innes Ireland (Jaguar D-type)   4h 00:44.0, 143 laps
6   Duncan Hamilton/Peter Blond (Jaguar D-type)   4h 00:51.2, 142 laps
Fastest lap (RECORD): Stirling Moss - 1:32.6, 93.30 mph
Team Award - Aston Martin

27 SEPTEMBER – 32nd MEMBERS' MEETING

Event 1 - 10-lap Scratch Race (A) for 500cc Racing Cars
1   Tommy Bridger (Cooper-Norton)   17:02.4, 84.51 mph
Fastest lap: Trevor Taylor (Beart Cooper-Norton) - 1:40.4, 86.06 mph

Event 2 - 10-lap Scratch Race for Sports Cars up to 1100 cc non s/c
1   Keith Greene (Lotus-Climax 11)   16:47.4, 85.77 mph
Fastest lap: John Campbell-Jones (Lotus-Climax 11) - 1:38.8, 87.45 mph

Event 3 - 5-lap Handicap Race (A) for Closed Cars
1   Dennis Barthel (Mercedes-Benz 300SL)   10:51.6, 75.58 mph
Fastest lap: John Lawry (Lotus Elite) - 1:47.2, 80.60 mph

Event 4 - 10-lap Marque Scratch Race
1   David Shale (Austin-Healey 100/6)   18:46.4, 76.70 mph
Fastest lap: Chris Lawrence (Morgan +4) - 1:50.6, 78.12 mph

Event 5 - 5-lap Handicap Race (B) for Closed Cars
1   D.E. Osborne (Morris Minor)   11:35.0, 62.15 mph
Fastest lap: 'Paddy' Gaston (Austin A35) - 2:03.8, 69.79 mph

Event 6 - 5-lap Handicap Race (C) incorporating Ladies Handicap Race
1   J. Hayles (MG A)   10:36.4, 73.67 mph
Fastest lap: Richard Green (AC Aceca-Bristol) - 1:51.0, 77.84 mph

Event 7 - 5-lap Handicap Race (D)
1   Stuart Young (Par-Son-Maserati)   9:48.6, 82.51 mph
Fastest lap: David Piper (Lotus-Climax 11) - 1:40.4, 86.06 mph

Event 8 - 5-lap Handicap Race (E)
1   Ken MacKenzie (MG A)   10:14.0, 73.97 mph
Fastest lap: Sid Hurrell (Triumph TR3) - 1:51.6, 77.42 mph

1959

14 MARCH 1959 – 33rd MEMBERS' MEETING

Event 1 - 10-lap Scratch Race for Sports Cars up to 1100cc
1   Dick Prior (Lotus-Climax 11)   16:59.0, 84.79 mph
Fastest lap: Dick Prior - 1:39.6, 86.75 mph

Event 2 - 5-lap Handicap Race (A) for Closed Cars
1   Albert Gay (Peerless)   10:40.6, 69.61 mph
Fastest lap: Jonathan Williams (Lotus Elite)/Richard Shepherd Barron (Alfa Romeo GSV) - 1:55.2, 75.00 mph

Event 3 - 10-lap Marque Scratch Race
1   Chris Lawrence (Morgan +4)   18:30.2, 77.82 mph
Fastest lap: Bill de Selincourt (Triumph TR3) - 1:48.6, 79.56 mph

Event 4 - 5-lap Handicap Race (B)
1   Derek Howard (Lotus-Climax 11)   9:28.2, 80.72 mph
Fastest lap: Derek Howard - 1:45.2, 82.13 mph

Event 5 - 5-lap Handicap Race (C)
1   Peter Riley (Lotus-Climax 11)   10:03.8, 82.47 mph
Fastest lap: Peter Riley - 1:42.8, 84.05 mph

Event 6 - 5-lap Handicap Race (D) for Closed Cars
1   John Turner (LMB Ford Popular)   11:40.0, 68.03 mph
Fastest lap: John Turner - 2:02.2, 70.70 mph

Event 7 - 5-lap Handicap Race (E)
1   Chris Lawrence (Morgan +4)   10:20.8, 77.08 mph
Fastest lap: Chris Lawrence - 1:48.4, 79.70 mph

30 MARCH 1959 - EASTER MEETING

Event 1 - Chichester Cup for Sports Cars up to 1100 cc - 10 laps
1   Peter Ashdown (Lola-Climax Mk1)   16:23.0, 87.89 mph
2   Peter Gammon (Lola-Climax Mk1)   16:28.0
3   Michael Taylor (Lola-Climax Mk1)   16:39.0
Fastest lap: Peter Ashdown - 1:35.6, 90.38 mph

Event 2 - Lavant Cup for Formula 2 Cars - 15 laps
1	Jack Brabham (Cooper-Climax T45)	23:08.4, 93.34 mph
2	Roy Salvadori (Cooper-Climax T43)	23:08.8
3	Jim Russell (Cooper-Climax T45)	23:20.8

Fastest lap: Roy Salvadori - 1:30.2, 95.79 mph

Event 3 - Sussex Trophy for Sports Cars over 1100cc - 21 laps
1	Ivor Bueb (Lister-Jaguar)	38:27.2, 78.64 mph
2	Peter Blond (Lister-Jaguar)	38:34.0
3	Graham Whitehead (Aston Martin DBR1)	38:34.6

Fastest lap: Peter Blond - 1:44.2, 82.92 mph

Event 4 - Goodwood International 100 for the Glover Trophy - 42 laps
1	Stirling Moss (Cooper-Climax T51)	66:58.0, 90.31 mph
2	Jack Brabham (Cooper-Climax T51)	67:14.6
3	Harry Schell (BRM Type 25)	67:15.6
4	Joakim Bonnier (BRM Type 25)	67:16.2
5	Masten Gregory (Cooper-Climax T51)	41 laps
6	Bruce McLaren (Cooper-Climax T45)	39 laps

Fastest lap: Stirling Moss - 1:31.8, 94.12 mph

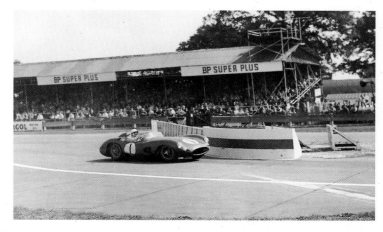

Goodwood's greatest day - 5th September 1959 - saw the first ever British victory in the FIA Sports Car World Championship. Moss's first Aston Martin DBR1/300 would burn out in the pits - his second would win!

Event 5 - Fordwater Trophy for Saloon Cars - 10 laps
1	Ivor Bueb (Jaguar 3.4)	18:22.0, 78.40 mph
2	Roy Salvadori (Jaguar 3.4)	18:28.6
3	Sir Gawaine Baillie (Jaguar 3.4)	19:07.6

Fastest lap: Ivor Bueb - 1:48.6, 79.56 mph

25 APRIL 1959 - 34th MEMBERS' MEETING

Event 1 - 10-lap Scratch Race (A) for Sports Cars up to 1100cc non s/c
1	Tony Maggs (Lotus-Climax 11)	19:59.2, 72.05 mph

Fastest lap: Tony Maggs/Tony Hegbourne (Tojeiro-Climax) - 1:57.8, 73.34 mph

Event 2 - 5-lap Handicap Race (A) for Closed Cars
1	Peter Lumsden (Lotus Elite)	11:11.0, 70.70 mph

Fastest lap: Peter Lumsden - 2:00.2, 71.88 mph

Event 3 - 10-lap Marque Scratch Race
1	Bill de Selincourt (Triumph TR3)	19:33.2, 73.64 mph

Fastest lap: Chris Lawrence (Morgan +4) - 1:55.0, 75.13 mph

Event 4 - 5-lap Handicap Race (B) for Closed Cars
1	B.M.S. Levy (Austin A35)	12:47.0, 62.43 mph

Fastest lap: 'Paddy' Gaston (Austin A35) - 2:13.4, 64.77 mph

Event 5 - 5-lap Scratch Race (B) up to 1500cc non s/c
1	Alan Rees (Lotus-Climax 11)	9:45.6, 73.77 mph

Fastest lap: Tony Maggs (Lotus-Climax 11) - 1:54.2, 75.66 mph

Event 6 - 5-lap Handicap Race (C)
1	Ken MacKenzie (Austin-Healey Sprite)	11:41.2, 66.28 mph

Fastest lap: V.D. Clark (MG TC) - 2:02.6, 70.47 mph

Event 7 - 5-lap Handicap Race (D)
1	J.M. Mann (AC-Bristol)	11:09.6, 69.92 mph

Fastest lap: Derek Howard (Lotus-Climax 11) - 1:59.8, 72.12 mph

Event 8 - 5-lap Handicap Race (E)
1	Ken MacKenzie (Austin-Healey Sprite)	10:53.8, 67.10 mph

Fastest lap: J.M. Mann (AC-Bristol) - 1:59.4, 72.36 mph

18 MAY 1959 - WHITSUN MEETING

Event 1 - Touring and Grand Touring Cars - 10 laps
1	Peter Lumsden (Lotus Elite)	18:07.0, 79.48 mph
2	Sir Gawaine Baillie (Jaguar 3.4)	18:07.6
3	John Lawry (Lotus Elite)	18:20.8

Fastest lap: Sir Gawaine Baillie - 1:46.6, 81.05 mph

Event 2 - Pre-War Racing Cars - 10 laps
1	Douglas Hull (ERA B Type)	18:04.2, 79.69 mph
2	Gordon Chapman (ERA A Type)	18:06.0
3	J. Goodhew (ERA-Delage 15S8)	18:41.0

Fastest lap: Douglas Hull - 1:45.4, 81.97 mph

Event 3 - Whitsun Trophy for Sports Cars - 21 laps
1	Ron Flockhart (Tojeiro-Jaguar)	34:10.0, 88.51 mph
2	John Bekaert (Lister-Jaguar)	34:20.6
3	Peter Blond (Lister-Jaguar)	34:29.4

Fastest lap: John Bekaert - 1:35.8, 90.19 mph

Event 4 - Marque Sports Cars - 10 laps
1	Syd Hurrell (Triumph TR3)	18:09.4, 79.31 mph
2	Chris Lawrence (Morgan +4)	18:11.4
3	Bill de Selincourt (Triumph TR3)	18:23.2

Fastest lap: Syd Hurrell - 1:45.8, 81.66 mph

Event 5 - First Whitsun Handicap - 10 laps
1	Richard Utley (Lotus-Climax 11)	17:22.2, 82.90 mph
2	John Coundley (Jaguar D-type)	17:30.8
3	Peter Blond (Lister-Jaguar)	17:46.2

Fastest lap: Ron Flockhart (Tojeiro-Jaguar) John Bekaert (Lister-Jaguar) - 1:35.2, 90.76 mph

Event 6 - Second Whitsun Handicap - 10 laps
1	Paul Fletcher (MG A t/c)	19:21.0, 77.42 mph
2	Bill de Selincourt (Triumph TR3)	19:26.2
3	Chris Lawrence (Morgan +4)	19:27.6

Fastest lap: Bill de Selincourt/Chris Lawrence - 1:47.8, 80.15 mph

6 JUNE 1959 - 35th MEMBERS' MEETING

Event 1 - 10-lap Scratch Race (A) up to 1100cc non s/c
1	Bill de Selincourt (Lotus-Climax 11)	17:15.4, 83.44 mph

Fastest lap: Bill de Selincourt - 1:41.4, 85.21 mph

Event 2 - 5-lap Handicap Race (A) for Closed Cars
1	'Paddy' Gaston (Austin-Healey Sprite)	11:10.2, 72.58 mph

Fastest lap: 'Paddy' Gaston - 1:56.6, 74.10 mph

Event 3 - 10-lap Marque Scratch Race
1	Chris Lawrence (Morgan +4)	18:17.6, 79.08 mph

Fastest lap: Chris Lawrence - 1:46.2, 81.36 mph

Event 4 - 5-lap Scratch Race up to 1000cc ohv & 1200cc sv
1	'Paddy' Gaston (Austin-Healey Sprite)	9:50.8, 73.12 mph

Fastest lap: 'Paddy' Gaston - 1:55.8, 74.61 mph

Event 5 - 5-lap Scratch Race (C) up to 1500 cc non s/c
1	Count Stephen Ouvaroff (Willment Climax)	8:32.6, 84.28 mph

Fastest lap: Count Stephen Ouvaroff - 1:40.2, 86.22 mph

Event 6 - 5-lap Handicap Race (B)
1	Donald Wagner (GSM Dart)	10:27.4, 69.97 mph

Fastest lap: Derek Howard (Lotus-Climax 11) - 1:45.4, 81.97 mph

Event 7 - 5-lap Handicap Race (C) for Closed Cars
1	Simon Hill (Peerless)	10:40.2, 72.55 mph

Fastest lap: Jonathan Williams (Lotus Elite) - 1:52.4, 76.87 mph

Event 8 - 5 lap Handicap Race (D)
1	S. Chitty (Triumph TR3)	11:20.8, 71.90 mph

Fastest lap: Kathleen Howard (Lotus-Climax 11) - 1:52.6, 76.73 mph

27 JUNE 1959 - 36th MEMBERS' MEETING

Event 1 - 10-lap Scratch Race (A) up to 1100cc non s/c
1	Jack Westcott (Lotus-Climax 11)	17:04.4, 84.34 mph

Fastest lap: Jack Westcott - 1:40.6, 85.88 mph

Event 2 - 5-lap Handicap Race (A) for Closed Cars
1	Robin Bryant (Austin A35)	11:27.2, 66.75 mph

Fastest lap: Rosemary Massey (Jaguar XK150) - 1:58.4, 72.97 mph

Event 3 - 10-lap Marque Scratch Race
1	Chris Lawrence (Morgan +4)	18:28.8, 77.92 mph

Fastest lap: Syd Hurrell (Triumph TR3) - 1:46.8, 80.90 mph

Event 4 - 5-lap Scratch Race up to 1000cc ohv or 1200cc sv non s/c
1	Jon Derisley (Lotus-Ford 7)	10:02.8, 71.67 mph

Fastest lap: John Derisley - 1:58.2, 73.10 mph

Event 5 - 5-lap Scratch Race up to 1500cc non s/c
1	Stuart Young (Par-Son-Maserati)	8:36.8, 83.59 mph

Fastest lap: Stuart Young - 1:40.6, 85.88 mph

Event 6 - 5-lap Handicap Race (B)
1	R. Levett (Scorpion)	10:18.4, 71.01 mph

Fastest lap - J. Menzies - 1:56.4, 74.23 mph

Event 7 - 5-lap Handicap Race (C)
1	B.P.W. Playford (Playford-MG)	9:49.4, 73.30 mph

Fastest lap: Stuart Young (Par-Son Maserati) - 1:40.0, 86.40 mph

Event 8 - 5-lap Handicap Race (D)
1	John Quick (Triumph TR2)	10:36.2, 74.97 mph

Fastest lap - Jonathan Williams (Lotus Elite) - 1:49.0, 79.27 mph

11 JULY 1959 - 37th MEMBERS' MEETING

Event 1 - 10-lap Scratch Race (A) up to 1100cc non s/c
1	Jack Westcott (Lotus-Climax 11)	17:00.8, 84.64 mph

Fastest lap: Jack Westcott - 1:40.0, 86.40 mph

Event 2 - 5-lap Handicap Race (A) for Closed Cars
1	Alan Foster (MG Magnette)	10:58.4, 65.61 mph

Fastest lap: Jonathan Williams (Lotus Elite) - 1:52.4, 76.87 mph

Event 3 - 10-lap Marque Scratch Race
1	Chris Lawrence (Morgan +4)	18:06.4, 79.53 mph

Fastest lap: Chris Lawrence - 1:46.2, 81.36 mph

Event 4 - 5-lap Scratch Race (B) up to 1000cc ohv or 1200cc sv non s/c
1	'Paddy' Gaston (Austin Healey Sprite)	9:58.6, 72.12 mph

Fastest lap: 'Paddy' Gaston - 1:56.4, 74.23 mph

Event 5 - 5-lap Scratch Race (C) up to 1500cc non s/c
1	Peter Arundell (Lotus-Climax 11)	8:40.0, 83.08 mph

Fastest lap: Peter Arundell - 1:41.6, 85.04 mph

Event 6 - 5-lap Handicap Race (B)
1 Paul Fletcher (MG A t/c)   10:32.2, 76.84 mph
Fastest lap: Paul Fletcher - 1:49.4, 78.89 mph

Event 7 - 5-lap Handicap Race (C)
1 Mike Bowling (Austin-Healey 100S)   9:56.0, 75.00 mph
Fastest lap: Derek Howard (Lotus-Climax 11) - 1:44.2, 82.92 mph

Event 8 - 5 -ap Handicap Race (D)
1 Geoff Coles (MG)   10:18.0, 69.90 mph
Fastest lap: Kathleen Howard (Lotus-Climax 11) - 1:50.6, 78.12 mph

5 SEPTEMBER 1959 – 24TH R.A.C. TOURIST TROPHY

1	Carroll Shelby/Jack Fairman/Stirling Moss (Aston Martin DBR1)	6h 00:46.8, 224 laps
2	Wolfgang von Trips/Joakim Bonnier (Porsche RS60 718)	6h 00:14.4, 223 laps
3	Olivier Gendebien/Giulio Cabianca/Tony Brooks/ Phil Hill (Ferrari 250TR59)	6h 00:16.4, 223 laps
4	Maurice Trintignant/Paul Frère (Aston Martin DBR1)	6h 00:39.2, 221 laps
5	Tony Brooks/Dan Gurney (Ferrari 250TR59)	6h 00:55.2, 220 laps
6	Peter Ashdown/Alan Ross (Lola-Climax Mk1)	6h 00:38.4, 210 laps

Fastest lap (RECORD): Tony Brooks - 1:31.8, 94.12 mph
Team Award - Lola Cars Ltd

26 SEPTEMBER 1959 – 38th MEMBERS' MEETING

Event 1 - 10-lap Scratch Race up to 1100cc non s/c
1 Bill de Selincourt (Lola-Climax Mk1)   16:37.8, 86.59 mph
Fastest lap: Bill de Selincourt - 1:37.6, 88.52 mph

Event 2 - 5-lap Handicap Race for Closed Cars
1 Jeff Uren (Ford Zephyr)   10:28.4, 74.69 mph
Fastest lap: Jeff Uren - 1:53.2, 76.32 mph

Event 3 - 10-lap Marque Scratch Rce
1 Chris Lawrence (Morgan +4)   18:15.0, 78.90 mph
Fastest lap: Paul Fletcher (MG A t/c) - 1:46.8, 80.90 mph

Event 4 - 5 lap Scratch Race (B) up to 1000cc ohv or 1200cc non s/c
1 John Venner-Pack (Austin-Healey Sprite)   9:32.2, 75.50 mph
Fastest lap: John Venner-Pack - 1:51.6, 77.42 mph

Event 5 - 5-lap Scratch Race (C) up to 1500cc non s/c
1 Alan Rees (Lotus-Climax 11)   8:31.0, 84.54 mph
Fastest lap: Stuart Young (Par-Son-Maserati)/Alan Rees - 1:39.2, 87.10 mph

Event 6 - 5-lap Handicap Race (B)
1 Mary Wheeler (Triumph TR2)   9:49.8, 65.85 mph
Fastest lap: Tony Maggs (Tojeiro Jaguar) - 1:42.2, 84.54 mph

Event 7 - 5-lap Handicap Race (C)
1 John Venner-Pack (Austin Healey Sprite)   10:31.6, 75.98 mph
Fastest lap: John Venner-Pack - 1:50.2, 78.40 mph

Event 8 - 5-lap Handicap Rce (D)
1 Peter Leuch (Triumph TR2)   10:13.6, 74.66 mph
Fastest lap: Tony Maggs (Tojeiro Jaguar) - 1:42.4, 84.37 mph

1960

19 MARCH 1960 – 39th MEMBERS' MEETING

Event 1 - 10-lap Scratch Race (A) for Sports Cars to 1100cc
1 James van Sickle (Lotus-Climax 11)   17:17.4, 83.29 mph
Fastest lap: James van Sickle - 1:41.4, 85.21 mph

Event 2 - 5-lap Handicap Race (A) for Closed Cars
1 C.J. Parkinson (Austin A40)   10:39.6, 69.72 mph
Fastest lap: V.H. Parness (Jaguar XK120) - 1:53.0, 76.46 mph

Event 3 - 10-lap Scratch Race (B) for Formula Junior
1 Jim Clark (Lotus-Ford 18)   16:16.2, 88.51 mph
Fastest lap: Jim Clark - 1:35.6, 90.38 mph

Event 4 - 10-lap Marque Scratch Race
1 Paul Fletcher (AC-Bristol)   18:15.0, 78.90 mph
Fastest lap: Paul Fletcher - 1:46.6, 81.05 mph

Event 5 - 5-lap Scratch Race (C) Unlimited Sports Cars
1 Mike Salmon (Jaguar D-type)   8:27.0, 85.21 mph
Fastest lap: Mike Salmon - 1:39.2, 87.10 mph

Event 6 - 5-lap Scratch Race (D) 1000cc ohv or 1200cc sv
1 John Venner-Pack (Austin-Healey Sprite)   9:28.2, 76.00 mph
Fastest lap: John Venner-Pack - 1:52.0, 77.14 mph

Event 7 - 5-lap Handicap Race (B)
1 R.D. Paine (Frazer Nash MM)   9:44.8, 77.17 mph
Fastest lap: Mike Salmon - 1:39.6, 86.75 mph

18 APRIL 1960 – EASTER MEETING

Event 1 - Chichester Cup for Formula Junior Cars - 10 laps
1 Jim Clark (Lotus-Ford 18)   15:55.0, 90.47 mph
2 Trevor Taylor (Lotus-Ford 18)   15:57.4
3 Mike McKee (Lotus-Ford 18)   16:19.0
Fastest lap (RECORD): Jim Clark - 1:33.6, 92.31 mph

Event 2 - Lavant Cup for Formula 2 Cars - 15 laps
1 Innes Ireland (Lotus-Climax 18)   22:24.2, 96.41 mph
2 Stirling Moss (Porsche 718)   22:30.6
3 Roy Salvadori (Cooper-Climax T51)   22:47.4
Fastest lap (RECORD): Innes Ireland - 1:28.8, 97.30 mph

Event 3 - Sussex Trophy for Sports Cars - 21 laps
1 Roy Salvadori (Cooper Monaco T49)   33:36.8, 89.96 mph
2 Jimmy Blumer (Cooper Monaco T49)   33:53.8
3 Tom Dickson (Lotus-Climax 15)   34.03.2
Fastest lap (RECORD): Roy Salvadori - 1:29.6, 96.43 mph

Event 4 - Goodwood International '100' for the Glover Trophy - 42 laps
1 Innes Ireland (Lotus-Climax 18)   60:14.8, 100.39 mph
2 Stirling Moss (Cooper-Climax T51)   60:17.6
3 Chris Bristow (Cooper-Climax T51)   61:19.8
4 Bruce McLaren (Cooper-Climax T45)   61:32.4
5 Graham Hill (BRM P48)   41 laps
6 Joakim Bonnier (BRM Type 25)   41 laps
Fastest lap: Innes Ireland - 1:24.6, 102.13 mph

Event 5 - Fordwater Trophy for Closed Cars - 10 laps
1 Stirling Moss (Aston Martin DB4GT)   17:20.6, 83.03 mph
2 Roy Salvadori (Jaguar 3.8)   17:42.2
3 Jack Sears (Jaguar 3.8)   17:49.2
Fastest lap: Stirling Moss - 1:42.8, 84.05 mph

Trend-setter - Innes Ireland enjoyed several truly great days at Goodwood, this being one of the best: Easter Monday 1960, when his new works lightweight rear-engined Lotus 18s twice beat Moss to win both the Formula 1 and Formula 2 events.

7 MAY 1960 – 40th MEMBERS' MEETING

Event 1 - 10-lap Scratch Race (A) for Sports Cars to 1100cc
1 Ken Lyon (Lotus-Climax 11)   17:19.0, 83.16 mph
Fastest lap: Ken Lyon - 1:41.6, 85.04 mph

Event 2 - 5-lap Scratch Race (B) for Closed Cars
1 Bill Blydenstein (Borgward Isabella)   9:55.6, ????
Fastest lap: Bill Blydenstein - 1:57.2, 73.72 mph

Event 3 - 10-lap Marque Scratch Race
1 Chris Lawrence (Morgan +4)   18:06.2, 79.54 mph
Fastest lap: Chris Lawrence - 1:45.6, 81.82 mph

Event 4 - 5-lap Scratch Race (C) 1000cc ohv 1200cc sv non s/c
1 C.J. Parkinson (Yimkin)   9:37.6, 74.79 mph
Fastest lap: C.J. Parkinson - 1:50.6, 78.12 mph

Event 5 - 5-lap Scratch Race (D) for Formula Junior
1 Colin Boden (Elva-DKW 100)   18:01.0, 79.93 mph
Fastest lap: Colin Boden - 1:45.4, 81.97 mph

Event 6 - 5-lap Scratch Race (E) for Unlimited Sports Cars
1 Derek Howard (Lotus-Climax 11)   8:32.2, 84.34 mph
Fastest lap: Derek Howard - 1:40.8, 85.71 mph

Event 7 - 5-lap Handicap Race (A)
1 Fred Marriott (Austin-Healey Sprite)   10:07.8, 72.87 mph
Fastest lap: Kathleen Howard - 1:50.2, 78.40 mph

Event 8 - 5-lap Handicap Race (B)
1 Derek Howard (Lotus-Climax 11)   9:31.6, 82.82 mph
Fastest lap: Derek Howard - 1:40.4, 86.05 mph

6 JUNE 1960 – WHITSUN MEETING

Event 1 - Cibié Cup for Closed Cars - 10 laps
1 'Paddy' Gaston (Austin A40)   19:45.0, 72.91 mph
2 George Lawrence (Austin A40)   19:46.0
3 Bill Blydenstein (Borgward Isabella)   19:47.0
Fastest lap: George Lawrence - 1:56.4, 74.10 mph

Event 2 - Autosport Series for Production Sports Cars - 10 laps
1 Julian Sutton (Austin-Healey)   18:21.0, 78.47 mph
2 Peter Sargent (Jaguar 3.4)   18:23.0
3 Sid Hurrell (Lotus Elite)   18:34.0
Fastest lap: Julian Sutton/Peter Sargent - 1:48.4, 79.70 mph

Event 3 - Whitsun Trophy for Sports Cars - 21 laps
1 Tom Dickson (Cooper Monaco T49)   34:11.2, 88.46 mph
2 Doug Graham (Lotus-Climax 15)   34:36.0
3 Chris Martyn (Lotus-Climax 15)   35:09.4
Fastest lap: Tom Dickson - 1:34.2, 91.72 mph

Event 4 - Pre-War Racing Cars - 10 laps
1 J. Goodhew (ERA-Delage 15S8)   18:19.0, 78.62 mph
2 Gordon Chapman (ERA A Type)   18:22.2
3 Keith Schellenberg (Bentley Barnato-Hassan)   18:24.8
Fastest lap: J. Goodhew - 1:47.6, 80.30 mph

Event 5 - Marque Sports Cars - 10 laps
1 Colin Hextall (Triumph TR2)   18:14.6, 78.94 mph
2 Bill McCowen (AC-Bristol)   18:25.4
3 Jack Turner (Austin-Healey 3000)   18:26.6
Fastest lap: Julian Sutton (Austin-Healey 100) - 1:46.6, 81.05 mph

Event 6 - Whitsun Handicap - 10 laps
1   Chris Kerrison (Lotus-Climax 11)   17:54.6, 84.33 mph
2   Tom Dickson (Cooper-Climax T49)   18:03.0
3   Ken Yeates (Lister-Bristol)   18:04.0
Fastest lap: Tom Dickson - 1:32.8, 93.10 mph

25 JUNE 1960 - 41st MEMBERS' MEETING

Event 1 - 10-lap Scratch Race (A) for Sports Cars up to 1100 cc non s/c
1   Peter Boshier-Jones (Lotus-Climax 11)   17:12.0, 83.72 mph
Fastest lap: Peter Boshier-Jones - 1:40.8, 85.74 mph

Event 2 - 5-lap Handicap Race (A)
1   Ian Wylie (Austin-Healey 3000)   9:26.6, 76.24 mph
Fastest lap: Peter Sargent (Jaguar D-type) - 1:39.8, 86.57 mph

Event 3 - 10-lap Scratch Race (B) for Formula Junior
1   Chris Andrews (Lotus-Ford 18)   16:34.4, 86.89 mph
Fastest lap: Chris Andrews - 1:38.2, 87.98 mph

Event 4 - 10-lap Marque Scratch Race
1   Colin Hextall (Triumph TR2)   18:42.0, 77.00 mph
Fastest lap: Colin Hextall - 1:48.8, 79.41 mph

Event 5 - 5-lap Scratch Race for Unlimited Sports Cars
1   Peter Sargent (Jaguar D-type)   8:24.8, 85.88 mph
Fastest lap: 'Dizzy' Addicott (Lotus-Ford 11) - 1:38.2, 87.98 mph

Event 6 - 5-lap Scratch Race (D) for Sports Cars to 1000cc ohv & 1200cc sv non s/c
1   Jack Murrell (DRW-Ford)   9:19.6, 77.20 mph
Fastest lap: Jack Murrell - 1:49.4, 78.89 mph

Event 7 - 5-lap Handicap Race (B) for Closed Cars
1   Bill Aston (Jaguar 3.4)   10:17.0, 73.59 mph
Fastest lap: Peter Sargent (Jaguar 3.4) - 1:51.2, 77.70 mph

Event 8 - 5-lap Handicap Race (C)
1   A.J.S. Bullen (Lotus 7)   9:43.2, 76.70 mph
Fastest lap: A.J.S. Bullen - 1:49.8, 78.69 mph

9 JULY 1960 - 42nd MEMBERS' MEETING

Event 1 - 10-lap Scratch Race (A) for Sports Cars to 1100cc non s/c
1   Bill de Selincourt (Lola-Climax Mk1)   24:53.0, 57.87 mph
Fastest lap: Bill de Selincourt - 2:17.8, 62.70 mph

Event 2 - 5-lap Handicap Race (A)
1   John Binns (Triumph TR3A)   12:05.8, 65.65 mph
Fastest lap: Eric Martin (Tornado Thunderbolt) - 2:01.0, 71.40 mph

Event 3 - 10-lap Scratch Race (B) for Formula Junior
1   Chris Andrews (Lotus-Ford 18)   18:40.0, 78.99 mph
Fastest lap: Chris Andrews - 1:46.4, 81.20 mph

Event 4 - 10-lap Marque Scratch Race
1   Bill McCowen (AC-Bristol)   18:25.4, 78.16 mph
Fastest lap: Bill McCowen - 1:47.6, 80.30 mph

Event 5 - 5-lap Scratch Race (C) for Unlimited Sports Cars
1   Mike Salmon (Jaguar D-type)   8:30.0, 84.70 mph
Fastest lap: Mike Salmon - 1:40.0, 86.40 mph

Event 6 - 5-lap Scratch Race (D) for Sports Cars to 1100 cc ohv or 1200cc sv
1   Jack Murrell (DRW-Ford)   9:18.2, 77.40 mph
Fastest lap: Jack Murrell - 1:48.2, 79.85 mph

Event 7 - 5-lap Handicap Race (B) for Closed Cars
1   E.J. Roach (Austin A35)   11:24.8, 66.99 mph
Fastest lap: Bill Aston - 1:53.6, 76.06 mph

Event 8 - 5-lap Handicap Race (C)
1   Hugh Dibley (AC Aceca)   10:12.2, 77.53 mph
Fastest lap: Mike Salmon (Jaguar D-type) - 1:39.8, 86.57 mph

20 AUGUST 1960 - TOURIST TROPHY MEETING

Event 1 - BARC Formula Junior Championship Heat 1 - 7 laps
1   Trevor Taylor (Lotus-Ford 18)   11:10.0, 90.27 mph
2   Dick Prior (Lola-Ford Mk2)   11:19.8
3   Cliff Johnson (Lotus-Ford 18)   11:27.6
Fastest lap: Tony Maggs (Gemini-Ford Mk3)/Trevor Taylor - 1:34.2, 91.72 mph

Event 2 - BARC Formula Junior Championship Heat 2 - 7 laps
1   Jim Clark (Lotus-Ford 18)   11:15.2, 89.57 mph
2   Mike McKee (Lotus-Ford 18)   11:16.2
3   Peter Ashdown (Lola-Ford Mk2)   11:20.4
Fastest lap: Jim Clark/Mike McKee - 1:34.2, 91.72 mph

Event 3 - BARC Formula Junior Championship Final - 21 laps
1   Trevor Taylor (Lotus-Ford 18)   33:20.8, 90.68 mph
2   Jim Clark (Lotus-Ford 18)   33:23.0
3   Mike McKee (Lotus-Ford 18)   33:39.4
Fastest lap (RECORD): Trevor Taylor/Jim Clark - 1:33.4, 92.50 mph

Event 4 - 25th RAC Tourist Trophy
1   Stirling Moss (Ferrari 250GT SWB)   108 laps, 85.58 mph
2   Roy Salvadori (Aston Martin DB4GT)   106 laps
3   Innes Ireland/John Whitmore (Aston Martin DB4GT)   106 laps
4   Graham Hill (Porsche 1600GS)   104 laps
5   Graham Whitehead/Jack Fairman (Ferrari 250GT SWB)   103 laps
6   Colin Davis (Ferrari 250GT LWB)   103 laps
Fastest lap (RECORD): Stirling Moss - 1:36.6, 89.44 mph

10 SEPTEMBER 1960 - 43rd MEMBERS' MEETING

Event 1 - 10-lap Scratch Race (A) for Formula Junior
1   Chris Andrews (Lotus-Ford 18)   16:40.0, 86.40 mph
Fastest lap: Chris Andrews/John Fenning (Lotus-BMC 18) - 1:38.2, 87.98 mph

Event 2 - 10-lap Scratch Race (B) for Sports Cars to 1100cc non s/c run concurrently
with Event 1
1   Bill de Selincourt (Lola-Climax Mk1)   16:49.4, 83.94 mph
Fastest lap: Bill de Selincourt - 1:38.6, 87.63 mph

Event 3 - 5-lap Cibié Cup Race for 4-Seat Closed Cars
1   Alan Hutcheson (Riley 1.5)   9:37.2, 74.85 mph
Fastest lap: Alan Hutcheson - 1:51.8, 77.28 mph

Event 4 - 10-lap Marque Scratch Race
1   Chris Lawrence (Morgan +4)   17:52.8, 80.54 mph
Fastest lap: Bill McCowen (AC-Bristol) - 1:44.6, 82.60 mph

Event 5 - 5-lap Scratch Race (C) for Unlimited Sports Cars
1   Mike Salmon (Jaguar D-type)   8:16.8, 86.96 mph
Fastest lap: Jim Tiller (Allard J2) - 1:38.2, 87.98 mph

Event 6 - 5-lap Scratch Race (D) for Sports Cars to 1000cc ohv or 1200cc sv
1   Jack Murrell (DRW-Ford)   9:03.0, 79.56 mph
Fastest lap: Jack Murrell/Bob van Niekirk (GSM Delta) - 1:46.2, 81.36 mph

Event 7 - 5-lap Handicap Race (A) for Closed Cars
1   David Hobbs (Jaguar XK140)   10:13.6, 75.97 mph
Fastest lap: Jack Hobbs - 1:50.2, 78.40 mph

Event 8 - 5 -lap Handicap Race (B)
1   George Naylor (Austin-Healey Sprite)   9:30.8, 75.68 mph
Fastest lap: Mike Salmon (Jaguar D-type) - 1:37.0, 89.07 mph

Event 9 - 5-lap Invitation Scratch Race
1   Ronald Barker (Morris Mini)   11:59.6, 60.03 mph
Fastest lap: Roger Bell (Morris Mini) - 2:17.6, 62.79 mph

1961

11 MARCH 1961 - 44th MEMBERS' MEETING

Event 1 - 5-lap Scratch Race (A) Sports Cars to 1100 cc non s/c
1   Peter Boshier-Jones (Lola-Climax Mk1)   8:30.6, 84.60 mph
Fastest lap: Laurie Keens (Lola-Climax Mk1) - 1:38.8, 87.45 mph

Event 2 - 5-lap Handicap Race (A) for Closed Cars
1   Maurice Baring (Fiat-Abarth)   10:04.6, 72.66 mph
Fastest lap: D. Howard (Aston Martin DB2/4) - 1:54.8, 75.26 mph

Event 3 - 10-lap Scratch Race (B) for Formula Junior
1   Trevor Taylor (Lotus-Ford 20)   15:50.6, 90.89 mph
Fastest lap: Trevor Taylor/Peter Arundell (Lotus-Ford 20) - 1:33.4, 92.50 mph

Event 4 - 10-lap Marque Scratch Race
1   Bob Staples (AC-Bristol)   18:20.0, 78.54 mph
Fastest lap: Bob Staples - 1:45.4, 81.97 mph

Event 5 - 10-lap Scratch Race (C) for Unlimited Sports Cars
1   Henry Taylor (Lola-Climax Mk1)   16:30.6, 87.24 mph
Fastest lap: Henry Taylor - 1:35.8, 90.19 mph

Event 6 - 5 lap Scratch Race (D) for Sports Cars to 1200cc (ex ohv)
1   Jon Derisley (Lotus-Ford 7)   9:12.2, 78.23 mph
Fastest lap: John Derisley - 1:46.2, 81.36 mph

Event 7 - 5 lap Handicap Race (B)
1   Ray Dilley (Frazer Nash TF)   9:55.0, 81.51 mph
Fastest lap: Mike Salmon (Jaguar D-type) - 1:35.0, 90.95 mph

3 APRIL 1961 - EASTER MEETING

Event 1 - St Mary's Trophy for Saloon Cars - 10 laps
1   Mike Parkes (Jaguar 3.8)   18:52.2, 76.30 mph
2   Graham Hill (Jaguar 3.8)   18:58.0
3   Dennis Taylor (Jaguar 3.8)   19:01.0
Fastest lap: Mike Parkes - 1:50.8, 77.98 mph

Event 2 - Lavant Cup for InterContinental Formula Cars - 21 laps
1   Stirling Moss (Cooper-Climax T53)   33:25.6, 90.47 mph
2   Bruce McLaren (Cooper-Climax T53)   33:26.0
3   Graham Hill (BRM P48)   33:45.0
Fastest lap: Bruce McLaren - 1:30.4, 95.57 mph

Event 3 - Chichester Cup for Formula Junior Cars - 10 laps
1= Peter Arundell (Lotus-Ford 20)   16:55.4, 85.08 mph
1= Tony Maggs (Cooper-BMC T56)   16:55.4
3   Peter Ashdown (Lola-Ford Mk3)   17:09.0
Fastest lap: Peter Arundell - 1:34.4, 91.52 mph

Event 4 - Goodwood International '100' for the Glover Trophy - 42 laps
1   John Surtees (Cooper-Climax T53)   1h 03:10.0, 95.76 mph
2   Graham Hill (BRM P57-Climax)   1h 03:36.6
3   Roy Salvadori (Cooper-Climax T53)   1h 04:19.4
4   Stirling Moss (Lotus-Climax 18)   1h 04:43.6
5   Innes Ireland (Lotus-Climax 18)   41 laps
6   Henry Taylor (Lotus-Climax 18)   41 laps
Fastest lap (RECORD): John Surtees - 1:28.0, 98.18 mph

Event 5 - Sussex Trophy for Sports Cars - 15 laps
1   Stirling Moss (Lotus-Climax 19)   26:29.0, 81.57 mph
2   Henry Taylor (Lotus-Climax 19)   26:31.2
3   Tom Dickson (Cooper Monaco T49)   27:10.8
Fastest lap: Henry Taylor - 1:43.4, 83.56 mph

Event 6 - Fordwater Trophy for GT Cars - 10 laps
1   Mike Parkes (Ferrari 250GT SWB)   17:18.2, 83.22 mph
2   Innes Ireland (Aston Martin DB4GT)   17:25.0
3   Stirling Moss (Aston Martin DB4GTZ)   17:26.6
Fastest lap: Mike Parkes - 1:41.2, 85.37 mph

6 MAY 1961 - 45th MEMBERS' MEETING

Event 1 - 5-lap Scratch Race (A) for Sports Cars to 1100cc non s/c
1   Peter Boshier-Jones (Lola-Climax Mk1)   8:34.6, 83.96 mph
Fastest lap: Peter Boshier-Jones - 1:40.2, 86.22 mph

Event 2 - 5-lap Scratch Race (B) for Sports Cars to 1200cc ex ohc
1   Jon Derisley (Lotus-Ford 7)   8:56.2, 80.56 mph
Fastest lap: Harry Epps (Lotus-Ford 7) - 1:42.4, 84.37 mph

Event 3 - 10-lap Scratch Race (C) for Formula Junior
1   Terry Wilson (Lotus Ford 18)   17:15.0, 83.48 mph
Fastest lap: Terry Wilson - 1:38.8, 87.45 mph

Event 4 - 10-lap Scratch Race (D) for Unlimited Sports Cars
1   Dizzy Addicott (Lotus-Climax 11)   19:09.2, 75.18 mph
Fastest lap: Bill de Selincourt (Lister-Jaguar) - 1:48.7, 78.76 mph

Event 5 - 10-lap Marque Scratch Race
1   Bill Shaw (AC-Bristol)   19:55.2, 72.30 mph
Fastest lap: Bob Staples (AC-Bristol) - 1:55.4, 74.87 mph

Event 6 - 5-lap Handicap Race (A) for Closed Cars
1   G.C. Burrows (Austin Se7en)   10:46.0, 67.92 mph
Fastest lap: Mick Cave (Austin A40) - 2:02.6, 70.36 mph

Event 7 - 5-lap Handicap Race (B)
1   Bill de Selincourt (Lister-Jaguar)   10:30.6, 77.07 mph
Fastest lap: Bill de Selincourt - 1:49.6, 78.83 mph

Event 8 - 5-lap Handicap Race (C)
1   John Sparrow (Triumph TR3)   10:54.6, 67.55 mph
Fastest lap: John Sparrow - 2:00.8, 71.10 mph

22 MAY 1961 – WHITSUN MEETING

Event 1 - Cibié Cup Race for Saloon Cars - 10 laps
1   Bob Jankel (Ford Anglia)   19:02.0, 75.66 mph
2   George Lawrence (Austin A40)   19:02.4
3   Robin Bryant (Sunbeam Rapier)   19:13.6
Fastest lap: Bob Jankel - 1:52.2, 77.00 mph

Event 2 - Formula Junior Race - 10 laps
1   Angus Hyslop (Lotus-Ford 20)   16:12.4, 88.85 mph
2   Brian Hart (Terrier-Ford Mk4)   16:35.4
3   Bob Hicks (Caravelle-Ford Mk3)   16:36.0
Fastest lap: Chris Meek (Elva-Ford 300) - 1:35.8, 90.19 mph

Event 3 - Whitsun Trophy for Sports Cars - 21 laps
1   Bruce Halford (Cooper Monaco T49)   33:34.8, 90.05 mph
2   Bill de Selincourt (Lister-Jaguar)   33:40.8
3   Mike Salmon (Jaguar D-type)   34:24.0
Fastest lap: Bruce Halford - 1:32.0, 93.91 mph

Event 4 - Marque Sports Car Race - 10 laps
1   Bob Staples (AC-Bristol)   18:02.4, 79.82 mph
2   Bill Shaw (AC-Bristol)   18:14.6
3   Neil Dangerfield (Triumph TR3)   18:21.4
Fastest lap: Bob Staples - 1:45.6, 81.82 mph

Event 5 - Pre-War Racing Car Handicap - 10 laps
1   Hon. Patrick Lindsay (ERA B Type)   20:06.2, 79.54 mph
2   Richard Bergel (Bugatti T35)   20:16.0
3   Peter Waller (ERA B Type)   20:27.6
Fastest lap: Hon. Patrick Lindsay - 1:46.2, 81.36 mph

Event 6 - GT Race - 10 laps
1   Gordon Jones (Marcos-Climax)   17:52.8, 80.54 mph
2   Robin Benson (Porsche 356 Carrera)   17:53.0
3   David Howard (Jaguar XK120)   18:02.4
Fastest lap: David Howard - 1:45.0, 82.29 mph

Event 7 - Whitsun Handicap - 10 laps
1   'Dizzy' Addicott (Lotus-Climax 11)   17:14.4, 81.67 mph
2   Jack Wober (Jaguar D-type)   17:28.0
3   Mike Salmon (Jaguar D-type)   17:29.4
Fastest lap: Bill de Selincourt (Lister-Jaguar) - 1:34.0, 91.91 mph

10 JUNE 1961 – 46th MEMBERS' MEETING

Event 1 - 5-lap Scratch Race (A) for Sports Cars to 1100cc non s/c
1   Peter Dodd (Lotus-Climax 11)   8:51.2, 81.33 mph
Fastest lap: Laurie Keens (Lola-Climax Mk1) - 1:40.6, 85.88 mph

Event 2 - 5-lap Scratch Race (B) for Sports Cars to 1200cc ex ohc
1   Jon Derisley (Lotus-Ford 7)   9:05.4, 79.21 mph
Fastest lap: Jon Derisley - 1:46.0, 81.51 mph

Event 3 - 10-lap Scratch Race (C) for Formula Junior
1   Ken Lyon (Lotus-Ford 20)   16:14.0, 88.72 mph
Fastest lap: Bill McCowen (Lola-Ford Mk3) - 1:35.8, 90.19 mph

Event 4 - 10-lap Scratch Race (D) for Unlimited Sports Cars
1   Peter Dickinson (Lotus-Climax 11)   17:27.6, 82.47 mph
Fastest lap: Peter Dodd (Lotus-Climax 11) - 1:42.0, 84.71 mph

Event 5 - 10-lap Marque Scratch Race
1   Neil Dangerfield (Triumph TR3)   19:00.6, 75.75 mph
Fastest lap: Kostas Pateras (AC Bristol) - 1:49.4, 78.89 mph

Event 6 - 5-lap Handicap Race (A) for Closed Cars
1   Chris Williams (Austin-Healey Sprite)   10:02.6, 74.15 mph
Fastest lap: Chris Barber (Lotus Elite) - 1:49.4, 78.89 mph

Event 7 - 5-lap Handicap Race (B)
1   Mike Sumner (Lotus-BMC)   9:24.4, 76.54 mph
Fastest lap: Mike Beckwith (Lotus-Climax 11) - 1:42.6, 84.21 mph

Event 8 - 5-lap Handicap Race (C)
1   Geoff Oliver (DRW-Ford)   10:22.0, 75.52 mph
Fastest lap: Dick Crossfield (MG A t/c) - 1:51.0, 77.8 mph

1 JULY 1961 – 47th MEMBERS' MEETING

Event 1 - 5-lap Scratch Race (A) for Sports Cars to 1100cc non s/c
1   Laurie Keens (Lola-Climax Mk1)   8:37.4, 83.48 mph
Fastest lap: Laurie Keens - 1:40.6, 85.88 mph

Performers of true pedigree - Jaguar 3.8 Mk II saloons pack the front row for the St Mary's Trophy race - Easter Monday, Goodwood, 1961 - drivers Michael Parkes, Roy Salvadori, Graham Hill and Bruce McLaren; class indeed.

Event 2 - 5-lap Scratch Race (B) for Sports Cars to 1200cc non s/c ex ohc
1   Geoff Oliver (DRW-Ford)   8:46.6, 82.07 mph
Fastest lap: Geoff Oliver - 1:42.2, 84.54 mph

Event 3 - 10-lap Scratch Race (C) Formula Junior
1   'Dizz'y Addicott (Lola Ford Mk3)   16:43.0, 86.18 mph
Fastest lap: 'Dizzy' Addicott - 1:37.4, 88.71 mph

Event 4 - 10-lap Scratch Race (D) for Unlimited Sports Cars
1   Laurie Keens (Lola-Climax Mk1)   17:18.2, 83.21 mph
Fastest lap: 'Dizzy' Addicott (Lotus-Climax 11) - 1:38.0, 88.16 mph

Event 5 - Cibie Cup Race for 4-seater Closed Cars - 5 laps
1   Doc Merfield (Ford Anglia)   9:32.2, 75.49 mph
Fastest lap: Alan Hutcheson (Riley 1.5) - 1:52.4, 76.87 mph

Event 6 - 10-lap Marque Scratch Race
1   Bob Staples (AC-Bristol)   18:11.4, 79.17 mph
Fastest lap: Bob Staples - 1:45.2, 82.13 mph

Event 7 - 5-lap Handicap Race (A) for Closed Cars
1   David Howard (Jaguar XK120)   9:44.8, 80.78 mph
Fastest lap: David Howard - 1:44.8, 82.44 mph

Event 8 - 5-lap Handicap Race (B)
1   Kostas Pateras (AC-Bristol)   9:32.4, 78.21 mph
Fastest lap: Peter Heath (Lotus-Climax 15) - 1:43.4, 83.56 mph

19 AUGUST 1961 - TOURIST TROPHY MEETING

Event 1 - BARC Formula Junior Championship Heat 1 - 7 laps
1   Frank Gardner (Lotus-Ford 20)   11:08.2, 90.51 mph
2   John Rhodes (Cooper-BMC T56)   11:08.6
3   Bill Moss (Gemini-Ford Mk3a)   11.09.0
Fastest lap: Bill Moss - 1:33.6, 92.31 mph

Event 2 - BARC Formula Junior Championship Heat 2 - 7 laps
1   Alan Rees (Lotus-Ford 20)   11:05.4, 90.89 mph
2   Dick Prior (Lola-Ford Mk3)   11:06.2
3   Dennis Taylor (Lola-Ford Mk3)   11:08.6
Fastest lap: Alan Rees - 1:33.4, 92.50 mph

Event 3 - BARC Formula Junior Championship Final - 15 laps
1   Alan Rees (Lotus-Ford 20)   23:41.0, 91.20 mph
2   Gavin Youl (MRD-Ford)   23:57.6
3   Dennis Taylor (Lola-Ford Mk3)   24:00.4
Fastest lap: Alan Rees - 1:33.6, 92.31 mph

Event 4 - 26th RAC Tourist Trophy - 3 hours
1   Stirling Moss (Ferrari 250GT SWB)   109 laps, 86.62 mph
2   Mike Parkes (Ferrari 250GT SWB)   108 laps
3   Roy Salvadori (Aston Martin DB4GTZ) 108 laps
4   Jim Clark (Aston Martin DB4GTZ)   107 laps
5   Innes Ireland (Aston Martin DB4GT)   107 laps
6   Graham Hill (Porsche 695GS)   104 laps
Fastest lap: Mike Parkes - 1:35.4, 90.57 mph

16 SEPTEMBER 1961 - 48th MEMBERS' MEETING

Event 1 - 5-lap Scratch Race (A) for Sports Cars to 1100cc non s/c
1   Laurie Keens (Lola-Climax Mk1)   8:26.4, 85.31 mph
Fastest lap: Ian Harrison-Hansley (Lola-Climax Mk1) - 1:38.0, 88.16 mph

Event 2 - 5-lap Scratch Race (B) for Sports Cars to 1200cc non s/c ex ohc
1   Geoff Oliver (DRW-Ford)   8:42.6, 82.66 mph
Fastest lap: Jon Derisley (Lotus-Ford 7) - 1:41.8, 84.87 mph

Event 3 - 10 lap Scratch Race (C) for Formula Junior
1   Dickie Attwood (Cooper-Ford T56)   16:19.2, 88.24 mph
Fastest lap: Dickie Attwood - 1:35.2, 90.76 mph

Event 4 - 10-lap Scratch Race (D) for Unlimited Sports Cars
1   Mike Salmon (Jaguar D-type)   16:29.0, 87.36 mph
Fastest lap: Mike Salmon - 1:36.4, 89.63 mph

Event 5 - Cibié Cup Race for 4-Seat Closed Cars - 5 laps
1   'Doc' Merfield (Ford Anglia)   9:30.4, 75.74 mph
Fastest lap: 'Doc' Merfield/Bob Jankel (Ford Anglia) - 1:50.0, 78.54 mph

Event 6 - 10-lap Marque Scratch Race
1   Bob Olthoff (MG A t/c)   17:46.4, 81.02 mph
Fastest lap: Bob Olthoff - 1:44.4, 82.76 mph

Event 7 - 5-lap Handicap Race (A) for Closed Cars
1   Jeff Uren (GSM Delta)   10:14.6, 77.20 mph
Fastest lap: Peter Woodroffe (Jaguar 3.4) - 1:49.2, 79.12 mph

Event 8 - 5-lap Handicap Race (B)
1   Jon Derisley (Lotus-Ford 7)   9:41.6, 82.82 mph
Fastest lap: Peter Lumsden (Jaguar E-type) - 1:40.0 86.40 mph

1962

24TH MARCH 1962 - 49th MEMBERS' MEETING

Event 1 - 5-lap Scratch Race Sports Cars to 1100cc non s/c
1   Tony Hegbourne (Lola-Climax Mk1)   8:25.4, 85.48 mph
Fastest lap: Tony Hegbourne - 1:39.0, 87.27 mph

Event 2 - 7-lap Veedol Marque Scratch Race
1   Bob Burnard (AC-Bristol)   12:58.6, 77.68 mph
Fastest lap: David Eva (MG A) - 1:45.0, 82.29 mph

Event 3 - 7-lap Veedol Scratch Race
1   David Soley (DRW-Ford)   12:06.8, 83.21 mph
Fastest lap: Lionel Brooke (Lotus-Ford 7)/David Soley - 1:42.0, 84.71 mph

Event 4 - 10-lap Scratch Race for Formula Junior
1   Dick Prior (Lola-Ford Mk5)   15:04.8, 95.49 mph
Fastest lap (RECORD): Dick Prior - 1:29.0, 97.08 mph

Event 5 - 10-lap Scratch Race for Unlimited Sports and GT Cars
1   Bill de Selincourt (Lister-Jaguar)   16:09.6, 89.11 mph
Fastest lap: Bill de Selincourt - 1:33.0, 92.90 mph

Event 6 - 5-lap Scratch Race for Sports Cars to 1200cc ex ohc
1   James Manfield (DRW-Ford)   8:51.0, 81.36 mph
Fastest lap: James Manfield - 1:43.4, 83.56 mph

Event 7 - 10-lap Marque Scratch Race
1   David Eva (MG A)   17:53.2, 80.51 mph
Fastest lap: David Eva - 1:44.0, 83.08 mph

Event 8 - 5-lap Handicap Race
1   Ray Meredith (Morgan +4)   9:05.8, 77.98 mph
Fastest lap: Bill de Selincourt (Lister-Jaguar) - 1:33.8, 92.11 mph

New car, novice winner, but a glittering future - Graham Hill notched his first outright Formula I win in BRM P578 chassis '5781' - Easter Monday 1962. By the end of the year the Londoner would have become only the second British World Champion Driver, and '5781' his legendary 'Old Faithful' car.

23 APRIL 1962 - EASTER MEETING

Event 1 - St Mary's Trophy for Saloon Cars - 10 laps
1   Graham Hill (Jaguar 3.8)   16:37.8, 86.59 mph
2   Roy Salvadori (Jaguar 3.8)   16:41.4
3   Jack Sears (Jaguar 3.8)   16:45.8
Fastest lap: Roy Salvadori/Graham Hill - 1:37.8, 88.34 mph

Event 2 - Lavant Cup for 4-Cylinder Formula 1 Cars - 21 laps
1   Bruce McLaren (Cooper-Climax T55)   30:31.8, 99.05 mph
2   Roy Salvadori (Lola-Climax 4)   31:17.6
3   Tony Shelly (Lotus-Climax 18/21)   31:28.0
Fastest lap: Bruce McLaren - 1:25.4, 101.17 mph

Event 3 - Chichester Cup for Formula Junior Cars - 10 laps
1   Peter Arundell (Lotus-Ford 22)   14:59.6, 96.04 mph
2   Dennis Taylor (Lola-Ford Mk5)   15:00.2
3   Mike Spence (Lotus-Ford 22)   15:00.6
Fastest lap: Tony Maggs (Cooper-BMC T59) -1:27.8, 98.40 mph

Event 4 - Goodwood International 100 for the Glover Trophy - 42 laps
1   Graham Hill (BRM P578)   58:55.2, 102.65 mph
2   Bruce McLaren (Cooper-Climax T55)   59:38.6
3   Innes Ireland (Lotus-Climax 18/21)   59:13.6
4   Roy Salvadori (Lola-Climax 4)   41 laps
5   Masten Gregory (Lotus-Climax 18/21)   41 laps
6   Tony Shelly (Lotus-Climax 18/21)   40 laps
Fastest lap (RECORD): John Surtees (Lola-Climax 4)/Stirling Moss (Lotus-18/21 V8) - 1:22.0, 105.37 mph

Event 5 - Sussex Trophy for GT and Sports Cars - 15 laps
1   Innes Ireland (Lotus-Climax 19)   22:36.4, 95.5 mph
2   Mike Parkes (Ferrari 250GTO)   23:35.0
3   Bill de Selincourt (Lister-Jaguar)   23:48.2
Fastest lap: Innes Ireland - 1:27.4, 98.85 mph

26 MAY 1962 - 50th MEMBERS' MEETING

Event 1 - 10-lap Scratch Race for Formula Junior
1   Hugh Dibley (Lola-Ford Mk5)   15:22.4, 90.72 mph
Fastest lap: Hugh Dibley - 1:32.4, 93.51 mph

Event 2 - 7-lap Veedol Marque Scratch Race
1   David Eva (MG A t/c)   12:28.0, 80.86 mph
Fastest lap: David Eva - 1:44.0, 83.08 mph

Event 3 - 5-lap Handicap Race for Closed Cars
1   'Doc' Merfield (Ford Anglia)   10:20.0, 80.00 mph
Fastest lap: 'Doc' Merfield - 1:44.6, 82.60 mph

Event 4 - 10-lap Scratch Race Sports & GT Cars
1   'Dizzy' Addicott (Lotus-Buick 15)   15:45.0, 91.43 mph
Fastest lap: 'Dizzy' Addicott - 1:31.2, 94.74 mph

Event 5 - 10-lap Marque Scratch Race
1   David Eva (MG A t/c)   18:00.0, 79.78 mph
Fastest lap: Tommy Entwistle (TVR Grantura) - 1:44.4, 82.76 mph

Event 6 - 5-lap Handicap Race (A)
1   Tommy Entwistle (TVR Grantura)   9:25.0, 80.75 mph
Fastest lap: Tommy Entwistle/Philip Arnold (Lotus-Ford) - 1:44.0, 83.08 mph

Event 7 - 5-lap Handicap Race (B)
1   Charles Hodgson (Lotus-Climax 11)   9:11.6, 85.78 mph
Fastest lap: Charles Hodgson - 1:36.8, 89.26 mph

Event 8 - 7-lap Veedol Scratch Race
1   David Cole (Lotus-Ford 7)   12:01.4, 83.84 mph
Fastest lap: David Cole/David Soley (DRW-Ford) - 1:41.6, 85.04 mph

11 JUNE 1962 - WHITSUN MEETING

Event 1 - Saloon Car Race - 10 laps
1   Peter Woodroffe (Jaguar 3.8)   17:35.6, 81.85 mph
2   John Sparrow (Jaguar 3.8)   18:12.0
3   Nicky Byrne (Mercedes-Benz 220SE)   18:35.2
Fastest lap: Peter Woodroffe - 1:41.8, 84.87 mph

Event 2 - Formula Junior Scratch Race - 10 laps
1   Keith Francis (Lotus-Ford 20)   15:36.2, 92.29 mph
2   Bob Hicks (Caravelle-Ford Mk3)   15:39.0
3   Geoff Breakell (Lotus-Ford 20)   16:12.0
Fastest lap: Hugh Dibley (Lola Ford Mk5) - 1:30.8, 95.15 mph

Event 3 - Whitsun Trophy for GT and Sports Cars - 21 laps
1   Jimmy Blumer (Cooper-Monaco T49)   33:14.4, 90.98 mph
2   Laurie Keens (Lotus-Ford 23)   33:35.2
3   Chris Spender (Lotus-Climax 11)   33:47.4
Fastest lap: Jimmy Blumer - 1:30.2, 95.79 mph

Event 4 - Marque Sports Car Race - 10 laps
1   Bill Jones (Morgan +4)   17:54.4, 80.44 mph
2   Bob Burnard (AC Bristol)   17:54.8
3   Neil Dangerfield (Triumph TR4)   18:20.2
Fastest lap: Chris Lawrence (Morgan +4) - 1:42.8, 84.05 mph

Event 5 - Pre-War Racing Cars - 10 laps
1   Gordon Chapman (ERA A Type)   17:22.8, 82.86 mph
2   Hon. Patrick Lindsay (ERA B Type)   17:45.0
3   Basil Bowman (Talbot-Lago T26SS)   17:59.8
Fastest lap: Donald Day (ERA B Type) - 1:41.6, 85.04 mph

Event 6 - Sports Car Race up to 1200cc exc ohc - 10 laps
1   George Naylor (Elva-BMC Mk6)   16:57.8, 84.94 mph
2   Mike Adlington (Lotus-Ford 7)   17:01.2
3   David Porter (Lotus-Ford 7)   17:10.0
Fastest lap: Laurie Keens (Lotus-Ford 23) - 1:34.2, 91.72 mph

Event 7 - Whitsun Handicap - 10 laps
1   Lord Clydesdale (Lola-Climax Mk1)   17:01.4, 85.43 mph
2   Jon Derisley (Lotus Elite)   17:07.0
3   John Nicholson (Lola-Climax Mk1)   17:08.0
Fastest lap: Jimmy Blumer (Cooper-Monaco T49) - 1:31.6, 94.32 mph

23 JUNE 1962 - 51st MEMBERS' MEETING

Event 1 - 5-lap Scratch Race for Sports Cars to 1100cc
1   Mike Beckwith (Lotus-Ford 23)   7:55.0, 90.94 mph
Fastest lap: Laurie Keens (Lotus-Ford 23) - 1:33.2, 92.70 mph

Event 2 - 10-lap Marque Scratch Race
1   'Pip' Arnold (Morgan +4)   17:47.8, 80.91 mph
Fastest lap: 'Pip' Arnold - 1:43.4, 83.56 mph

Event 3 - 5-lap Scratch Race for Sports Cars to 1200cc ex ohc
1   George Naylor (Elva-BMC Mk6)   8:26.0, 85.38 mph
Fastest lap: George Naylor 1:40.0, 86.40 mph

Event 4 - 10-lap Scratch Race for Formula Junior
1   Hugh Dibley (Lola-Ford 5)   15:21.4, 93.77 mph
Fastest lap: Hugh Dibley - 1:30.4, 95.57 mph

Event 5 - 10-lap Scratch Race for Unlimited Sports & GT Cars
1   'Dizzy' Addicott (Lotus-Buick 15)   15:26.6, 93.24 mph
Fastest lap: 'Dizzy' Addicott - 1:31.4, 94.53 mph

Event 6 - 7-lap Veedol Marque Scratch Race
1   Tommy Entwistle (TVR Grantura)   12:19.8, 81.75 mph
Fastest lap: Bob Burnard (AC-Bristol)/Bill Jones (Morgan +4)/David Eva (MG A t/c) -
1:43.8, 83.24 mph

Event 7 - 5-lap Handicap for Closed Cars
1   John Sparrow (Jaguar 3.8)   9:57.8, 78.86 mph
Fastest lap: 'Doc' Merfield (Ford Anglia) - 1:44.2, 82.92 mph

Event 8 - 5-lap Handicap Race
1   Bill Belcher (Terrier-Ford)   9:50.0, 81.51 mph
Fastest lap: Peter Skidmore (Jaguar D-type) - 1:42.6, 84.21 mph

7 JULY 1962 - 52nd MEMBERS' MEETING

Event 1 - 10-lap Scratch Race for Formula Junior & non-s/c Sports Cars to 1100cc
1   Brian Berrow-Johnson (Lotus-Ford 20)   15:36.0, 92.31 mph
Fastest lap: Brian Berrow-Johnson - 1:32.0, 93.91 mph

Event 2 - 7-lap Veedol Scratch Race
1   David Cole (Lotus-Ford 7)   11:55.6, 84.50 mph
Fastest lap: David Cole/David Soley (DRW-Ford) - 1:39.6, 86.75 mph

Event 3 - 10-lap Scratch Race for Unlimited Sports & GT Cars
1   Mike Beckwith (Lotus-Ford 23)   15:41.6, 91.87 mph
Fastest lap: Mike Beckwith - 1:32.8, 93.10 mph

Event 4 - 10-lap Marque Scratch Race
1   Tommy Entwistle (TVR Grantura)   17:45.2, 81.12 mph
Fastest lap: Tommy Entwistle - 1:42.8, 84.05 mph

Event 5 - 5-lap Handicap Race (A)
1   D.M. Green (Triumph TR3A)   10:24.0, 75.26 mph
Fastest lap: D. Bedford (Lotus-Ford) - 1:42.4, 84.37

Event 6 - 5-lap Scratch Race for Sports Cars to 1200cc non s/c ex ohc
1   Mike Adlington (Lotus-Ford 7)   8:24.0, 85.71 mph
Fastest lap: Clive Lacey (Lotus-Ford 7) - 1:36.0, 90.00 mph

Event 7 - 5 lap Handicap Race (B)
1   Joe Hicks (Lotus-Climax 11)   8:44.6, 84.78 mph
Fastest lap: Peter Skidmore (Jaguar D-type) - 1:39.0, 87.27 mph

18 AUGUST 1962 - TOURIST TROPHY MEETING

Event 1 - Veedol Championship Race - 15 laps
1   David Cole (Lotus Ford 7)   25:23.4, 85.07 mph
2   David Soley (DRW Ford)   25:24.6
3   Bob Deverell (Lotus Ford 7)   26:20.0
Fastest lap: David Soley - 1:39.2, 87.10 mph

Event 2 - BARC Formula Junior Championship - 21 laps
1   Peter Arundell (Lotus-Ford 22)   30:51.4, 98.00 mph
2   Dickie Attwood (Cooper-Ford T59)   31:24.2
3   Bob Anderson (Lotus-Ford 22)   31:30.4
Fastest lap (RECORD): Peter Arundell - 1:27.2, 99.08 mph

Event 3 - 27th RAC Tourist Trophy - 100 laps
1   Innes Ireland (Ferrari 250GTO)   2h 33:06.8, 94.05 mph
2   Graham Hill (Ferrari 250GTO)   2h 33:01.0
3   Mike Parkes (Ferrari 250GTO)   2h 34:01.0
4   Roy Salvadori (Jaguar E-type)   99 laps
5   David Piper (Ferrari 250GTO)   98 laps
6   Dick Protheroe (Jaguar E-type)   93 laps
Fastest lap: John Surtees (Ferrari 250GTO) - 1:28.6, 97.52 mph

1 SEPTEMBER 1962 - 53rd MEMBERS' MEETING

Event 1 - 10-lap Scratch Race for Formula Junior & 1100cc Sports Cars
1   Tony Hegbourne (Lola-Climax Mk1)   15:38.2, 92.09 mph
Fastest lap: Tony Hegbourne - 1:32.4, 93.51 mph

Event 2 - 5-lap Scratch Race for Sports Cars to 1200cc non s/c ex ohc
1   David Porter (Lotus-Ford 7)   8:22.0, 86.06 mph
Fastest lap: David Porter - 1:37.8, 88.34 mph

Event 3 - 10-lap Marque Scratch Race
1   David Eva (MG A t/c)   17:47.4, 80.94 mph
Fastest lap: David Eva - 1:44.0, 83.08 mph

Event 4 - 10-lap Scratch Race for Sports & GT Cars
1   Tony Hegbourne (Lola-Climax Mk1)   15:54.6, 90.51 mph
Fastest lap: Tony Hegbourne - 1:33.4, 92.50 mph

Event 5 - 5-lap Handicap Race (A) for Closed Cars
1   Mick Cave (Austin A40)   9:38.4, 76.54 mph
Fastest lap: Peter Woodroffe (Jaguar 3.8) - 1:43.6, 83.40 mph

Event 6 - 5-lap Handicap Race (E)
1   D.S. Jones (Triumph TR3)   9:16.6, 78.32 mph
Fastest lap: David Eva (MG A t/c) - 1:42.6, 84.21 mph

Event 7 - 5-lap Handicap Race (C)
1   Rob Beck (Jaguar XK120)   9:06.0, 81.36 mph
Fastest lap: Mike Renny (Lotus-Climax 11) - 1:41.2, 85.37 mph

22 SEPTEMBER 1962 - 54th MEMBERS' MEETING

Event 1 - 10-lap Scratch Race for Formula Junior
1   John Fenning (Lola-Ford 5)   15:05.6, 95.41 mph
Fastest lap: John Fenning - 1:28.4, 97.74 mph

Event 2 - 5-lap Scratch Race for Sports Cars to 1100cc non s/c
1   Mike Beckwith (Lotus-Climax 23)   7:47.4, 92.43 mph
Fastest lap: Tony Hegbourne (Lola-Climax Mk1) - 1:31.6, 94.32 mph

Event 3 - 5-lap Scratch Race for Sports Cars to 1200cc ex ohc
1   James Manfield (DRW-Ford)   8:33.8, 84.08 mph
Fastest lap: Clive Lacey (Lotus Ford 7) - 1:38.4, 87.80 mph

Event 4 - 10-lap Marque Scratch Race
1   David Eva (MG A t/c)   17:24.6, 82.71 mph
Fastest lap: David Eva - 1:43.0, 83.88 mph

Event 5 - 10-lap Scratch Race for Unlimited Sports & GT Cars
1   Mike Beckwith (Lotus-Ford 23)   15:26.6, 93.24 mph
Fastest lap (RECORD): 'Dizzy' Addicott (Lotus-Buick 15) - 1:30.0, 96.00 mph

Event 6 - 5-lap Handicap Race (A) for Closed Cars
1   'Doc' Merfield (Ford Anglia)   9:41.0, 82.13 mph
Fastest lap: 'Doc' Merfield - 1:43.2, 83.72 mph

Event 7 - 5-lap Handicap Race (B)
1   Roger Nathan (Lotus Elite)   9:21.6, 79.76 mph
Fastest lap: David Eva (MG A t/c) - 1:41.2, 85.37 mph

Event 8 - 5-lap Handicap Race (C)
1   Charles Hodgson (Lotus-Climax 11)   8:39.2, 89.22 mph
Fastest lap: Charles Hodgson - 1:34.2, 91.72 mph

6 OCTOBER 1962 - 55th MEMBERS' MEETING

Event 1 - 10-lap-Scratch Race for Formula Junior
1   Rod Banting (Lotus-Ford 20)   15:36.0, 92.32 mph
Fastest lap: Brian Berrow-Johnson (Lotus-Ford 20)/Rod Banting/John Dunn (Lotus
Ford 18) - 1:32.0, 93.91 mph

Event 2 - 10-lap Scratch Race for Unlimited Sports Cars up to 1150 cc
1   Charles Hodgson (Lotus-Climax 11)   16:23.0, 87.90 mph
Fastest lap: Charles Hodgson - 1:36.0, 90.00 mph

Event 3 - 10-lap Scratch Race GT & Sports Cars to 1000cc GT Cars
1   David Porter (Lotus-Ford 7)   16:40.2, 85.86 mph
Fastest lap: David Porter - 1:38.0, 88.16 mph

Event 4 - 5-lap Handicap Race for Closed Cars
1   Mark Konig (Lotus Elite)   9:59.6, 77.75 mph
Fastest lap: 'Doc' Merfield (Ford Anglia) - 1:41.8, 84.87 mph

Event 5 - 10-lap Scratch Race for GT Cars
1   Mike Johnson (Lotus Elite)   17:07.0, 84.12 mph
Fastest lap: Mike Johnson - 1:40.4, 86.06 mph

Event 6 - 10-lap Scratch Race for *Formule Libre* Cars
1   Brian Berrow-Johnson (Lotus-Ford 20) 15:40.6, 91.90 mph
Fastest lap: Alan Rollinson (Cooper-Ford T59) - 1:32.6, 93.30 mph

Event 7 - 5-lap Handicap Race for Sports & GT Cars
1   Hugh Braithwaite (Morgan +4)   9:48.8, 83.26 mph
Fastest lap: Bill Belcher (Terrier Ford) - 1:39.6, 86.75 mph

Event 8 - 5-lap Cibié Cup Handicap Race
1   A.G. Payne (Austin A40)   9:56.2, 76.30 mph
Fastest lap: 'Doc' Merfield (Ford Anglia) - 1:42.0, 84.71 mph

1963

23 MARCH 1963 – 56th MEMBERS' MEETING

Event 1 - 10-lap Scratch Race for Formula Junior & '64 F2 Cars
1   Eddie Fletcher (Lotus-Ford 20)   15:33.8, 92.53 mph
Fastest lap: Roy James (Brabham-Ford BT6)/David Cole (Cooper-BMC T59) - 1:30.8, 95.15 mph

Event 2 - 10-lap Scratch Race for GT Cars over 1600cc
1   Brian Hetreed (Aston Martin DB4GTZ)   17:00.2, 84.69 mph
Fastest lap: Brian Hetreed - 1:39.8, 86.57 mph

Event 3 - 10-lap Scratch Race for Sports Cars
1   Rodney Bloor (Lotus-Ford 23B)   15:30.8, 92.82 mph
Fastest lap: Rodney Bloor - 1:31.6, 94.32 mph

Event 4 - 5-lap Scratch Race for Saloons to 1200cc non s/c over 1200cc and any s/c cars
1   'Doc' Merfield (Ford Anglia)   8:47.6, 81.88 mph
Fastest lap: 'Doc' Merfield - 1:43.6, 83.40 mph

Event 5 - 10-lap Scratch Race for Sports Cars to 1000cc non s/c ex ohc and GT Cars to 1150cc and 1151cc-1600cc
1   Mike Johnson (Lotus Elite)   16:52.6, 85.32 mph
Fastest lap: Mike Johnson - 1:38.6, 87.63 mph

Event 6 - 10-lap *Formule Libre* Scratch Race
1   Rodney Bloor (Lotus-Ford 23B)   15:08.6, 95.90 mph
Fastest lap: Rodney Bloor - 1:28.8, 97.30 mph

Event 7 - 5-lap Handicap Race (A)
1   E. Hardwicke (Morgan +4)   10:29.2, 73.95 mph
Fastest lap: Richard Seth-Smith - 1:46.2, 81:36 mph

Event 8 - 5-lap Handicap Race (B)
1   Alan Deacon (Lister-Jaguar)   9:15.6, 89.89 mph
Fastest lap: Chris Williams (Lotus-Ford 23) - 1:34.0, 91.91 mph

Timeless beauty - Dick Protheroe's peerless Malcolm Sayer-styled E-type Jaguar *'Low-Drag Coupé'* in the 1963 Tourist Trophy. 'CUT 7' ran again in the 1998 TT Celebration race.

15 APRIL 1963 – EASTER MEETING

Event 1 - Chichester Cup for Formula Junior Cars - 10 laps
1   Frank Gardner (Brabham-Ford BT6)   16:04.8, 89.68 mph
2   Denny Hulme (Brabham-Ford BT6)   16:04.8
3   Dickie Attwood (Lola-Ford Mk5A)   16:05.6
Fastest lap: Frank Gardner - 1:32.4, 93.51 mph

Event 2 - St Mary's Trophy for Touring Saloons - 10 laps
1   Graham Hill (Jaguar 3.8)   16:50.2, 85.02 mph
2   Roy Salvadori (Jaguar 3.8)   16:57.6
3   Mike Salmon (Jaguar 3.8)   17:08.2
Fastest lap: Graham Hill - 1:39.0, 87.27 mph

Event 3 - Goodwood International '100' for the Glover Trophy - 42 laps
1   Innes Ireland (Lotus-BRM 24)   59:02.4, 102.44 mph
2   Bruce McLaren (Cooper-Climax T66)   59:07.4
3   Tony Maggs (Lotus-Climax 24)   41 laps
4   Jim Hall (Lotus-BRM 24)   41 laps
5   Chris Amon (Lola-Climax 4A)   40 laps
6   Jack Brabham (Brabham-Climax BT3)   40 laps
Fastest lap: Graham Hill (BRM P578) - 1:22.4, 104.85 mph

Event 4 - Sussex Trophy for GT Cars - 15 laps
1   Graham Hill (Jaguar E-type)   22:21.4, 96.62 mph
2   Mike Parkes (Ferrari 250GTO)   22:22.8
3   Roy Salvadori (Jaguar E-type)   22:26.8
Fastest lap: Graham Hill - 1:28.4, 97.74 mph

Event 5 - Lavant Cup for Sports Cars - 21 laps
1   Roy Salvadori (Cooper Monaco T61M)   35:49.4, 84.14 mph
2   Alan Rees (Lotus-Ford 23B)   36:04.8
3   Keith Greene (Lotus-Ford 23B)   36:45.2
Fastest lap: Innes Ireland (Lotus-Climax 19) - 1:38.0, 88.16 mph

18 MAY 1963 – 57th MEMBERS' MEETING

Event 1 - 10-lap Scratch Race for Sports Cars
1   Chris Williams (Lotus-Ford 23)   15:55.6, 90.42 mph
Fastest lap: Chris Williams - 1:33.4, 92.50 mph

Event 2 - 10-lap Scratch Race for GT Cars up to 1150cc
1   Kevin Keegan (Lotus Elan)   16:53.2, 85.27 mph
Fastest lap: Bob Duggan (Lotus Elite) - 1:39.6, 86.75 mph

Event 3 - 5-lap Scratch Race for Saloon Cars up to 1200cc
1   Mike Pendleton (Jaguar 3.8)   9:00.0, 80.00 mph
Fastest lap: Mike Pendleton - 1:46.0, 81.51 mph

Event 4 - 10-lap Scratch Race for *Formule Libre* and Formula Junior
1   Bill de Selincourt (Lotus-Climax 19)   15:36.6, 92.25 mph
Fastest lap: David Prophet (Brabham Ford BT6) - 1:31.4, 94.53 mph

Event 5 - 5-lap Marque Scratch Race
1   Jonathan Harris (Austin-Healey 3000)   8:44.2, 82.41 mph
Fastest lap: Neil Dangerfield (Triumph TR4) - 1:43.0, 83.88 mph

Event 6 - 5-lap Saloon Car Handicap Race
1   Alan Allard (Ford Allardette)   10:20.6, 77.75 mph
Fastest lap: Mike Pendleton (Jaguar 3.8) - 1:44.6, 82.60 mph

Event 7 - 5-lap Handicap Race (A)
1   Bobby Buchanan-Michaelson (Fiat Abarth)   9:35.8, 77.72 mph
Fastest lap: Mike Beard (Lotus-Climax 17) - 1:38.0, 88.16 mph

Event 8 - 5-lap Handicap race (B)
1   Mark Fielden (Triumph TR4)   9:46.0, 73.72 mph
Fastest lap: Tom Fletcher (Lister Jaguar) - 1:39.6, 86.75 mph

3 JUNE 1963 – WHITSUN MEETING

Event 1 - Spring Grove Saloon Car Race - 10 laps
1   Mike Salmon (Jaguar 3.8)   16:47.4, 85.77 mph
2   Doc Merfield (Lotus-Cortina)   18:13.0
3   John Lewis (Morris Cooper S)   18:13.6
Fastest lap: Mike Salmon - 1:39.2, 87.10 mph

Event 2 - Historic Racing Cars Race - 10 laps
1   Peter Waller (ERA Type B)   18:48.0, 76.62 mph
2   Hon. Patrick Lindsay (ERA Type B)   18:49.4
3   John Freeman (Aston Martin SM)   20:14.2
Fastest lap: Hon. Patrick Linday - 1:50.0, 78.54 mph

Event 3 - Whitsun Trophy for GT Cars - 21 laps
1   Mike Parkes (Ferrari 250GTO)   .34:50.0, 86.81 mph
2   Michael MacDowel (Ferrari 250GTO)   35:06.4
3   Chris Kerrison (Ferrari 250GT 'Speciale')   35:18.0
Fastest lap: Mike Parkes - 1:35.6, 90.38 mph

Event 4 - Sports Car Race - 15 laps
1   Bill de Selincourt (Lotus-Climax 19)   24:14.6, 89.10 mph
2   Syd Fox (Lola-Climax Mk1)   24:26.0
3   Chris Williams (Lotus-Ford 23)   24:31.0
Fastest lap: Bill de Selincourt - 1:33.2, 92.70 mph

Event 5 - Marque Sports Car Race
1   John Dangerfield (Morgan +4)   17:09.8, 80.90 mph
2   Adrian Dence (Morgan +4)   17:10.6
3   Neil Dangerfield (Triumph TR4)   17:18.0
Fastest lap: John Dangerfield - 1:40.8, 85.71 mph

Event 6 - Whitsun Handicap - 10 laps
1   Peter Sutcliffe (Aston Martin DB3S Coupé)   16:43.8, 86.07 mph
2   Chris Harding (Lotus-Climax 1)   17:03.2
3   Kostas Pateras (AC-Bristol)   17:04.6
Fastest lap: Bill de Selincourt (Lotus-Climax 19) - 1:30.4, 95.57 mph

22 JUNE 1963 – 58th MEMBERS' MEETING

Event 1 - 10-lap Scratch Race for Sports Cars
1   Chris Williams (Lotus-Ford 23)   15:44.6, 91.47 mph
Fastest lap: Chris Williams/Robin Benson (Elva-Climax Mk7) - 1:33.2, 92.70 mph

Event 2 - 10-lap Scratch Race for GT Cars over 1600cc
1   Brian Hetreed (Aston Martin DB4GTZ)   16:30.0, 87.27 mph
Fastest lap: Brian Hetreed - 1:37.0, 89.07 mph

Event 3 - 10-lap Scratch Race for GT Cars
1   Bob Duggan (Lotus Elite)   17:07.4, 84.10 mph
Fastest lap: Bob Duggan - 1:40.4, 86.06 mph

Event 4 - 5-lap Scratch Race for Saloon Cars
1   'Doc' Merfield (Lotus-Cortina)   8:47.8, 81.85 mph
Fastest lap: Brian Muir (Ford Cortina GT) - 1:43.0, 83.88 mph

Event 5 - 10 lap Scratch Race Formula Junior & *Formule Libre*
1   Roy James (Brabham-Ford BT6)   15:26.4, 93.27 mph
Fastest lap: Rod Banting (Brabham-Ford BT6)/Roy James - 1:31.2, 94.74 mph

Event 6 - 5-lap Marque Scratch Race
1   Adrian Dence (Morgan +4)   8:38.6, 83.30 mph
Fastest lap: Adrian Dence - 1:41.8, 84.87 mph

Event 7 - 5-lap Handicap Race
1   Raymond Jackson (Elva-Alfa Romeo Mk6)   9:45.0, 83.88 mph
Fastest lap: Raymond Jackson - 1:40.0, 86.40 mph

Event 8 - 5-lap Handicap Race for Closed Cars
1   John Adams (Vauxhall VX/490)   10:15.4, 75.74 mph
Fastest lap: 'Doc' Merfield (Lotus-Cortina) - 1:43.6, 83.40 mph

24 AUGUST 1963 – TOURIST TROPHY MEETING

Event 1 - BARC Formula Junior Championship - 21 laps
1 Peter Arundell (Lotus-Ford 27)   30:29.4, 99.18 mph
2 Dickie Attwood (Lola-Ford Mk5A)   30:32.2
3 Denny Hulme (Brabham-Ford BT6)   30:34.4
Fastest lap: Peter Arundell - 1:25.6, 100.93 mph

Event 2 - 28th RAC Tourist Trophy - 130 laps
1 Graham Hill (Ferrari 250GTO)   3.15:45.6, 95.14 mph
2 Mike Parkes (Ferrari 250GTO)   3.16:46.0
3 Roy Salvadori (Jaguar E-type)   129 laps
4 Jack Sears (Jaguar E-type)   129 laps
5 David Piper (Ferrari 250GTO)   128 laps
6 Dick Protheroe (Jaguar E-type)   128 laps
Fastest lap: Graham Hill - 1:27.4, 98.95 mph

21 SEPTEMBER 1963 – 59th MEMBERS' MEETING

Event 1 - 10-lap Combined Race for *Formule Libre* and Formula Junior
1 Jackie Stewart (Cooper Monaco Climax T49)   14:51.8, 96.88 mph
Fastest lap: Jackie Stewart - 1:27.4, 98.85 mph

Event 2 - 5-lap 'Spring Grove' Scratch Race
1 'Doc' Merfield (Lotus-Cortina)   8:38.0, 83.40 mph
Fastest lap: 'Doc' Merfield/Mick Cave (Austin A40) - 1:42.0, 84.71 mph

Event 3 - 5-lap Marque Scratch Race
1 Adrian Dence (Morgan +4)   8:41.0, 82.92 mph
Fastest lap: Adrian Dence/B. Kendall (Morgan +4)/Gordon Spice (Morgan +4) - 1:42.2,
84.54 mph

Event 4 - 10-lap Scratch Race for Sports Cars
1 Mike Warner (Lotus-Ford 23B)   15:27.0, 93.20 mph
Fastest lap: Mike Warner - 1:31.0, 94.94 mph

Event 5 - 10-lap Scratch Race for Sports and GT Cars
1 James Manfield (Lotus-Ford 23)   16:24.6, 87.75 mph
Fastest lap: David Porter (Lotus-Ford 7) - 1:37.0, 89.07 mph

Event 6 - 10-lap Scratch Race for GT Cars
1 Jackie Stewart (Tojeiro-Buick EE)   15:18.6, 94.06 mph
Fastest lap: Jackie Stewart - 1:30.0, 96.00 mph

Event 7 - 5-lap Handicap Race
1 Harry Digby (Austin A40)   10:17.4, 81.91 mph
Fastest lap: 'Doc' Merfield (Lotus-Cortina) - 1:43.2, 83.72 mph

Event 8 - 5-lap Handicap Race
1 T.N. Crisp (Daimler SP250)   9:29.4, 80.84 mph
Fastest lap: Brian Hetreed (Aston Martin DB4GTZ) - 1:35.0, 90.95 mph

1964

14 MARCH 1964 – 60th MEMBERS' MEETING

Event 1 - 10-lap Formula 3 and *Formule Libre*
1 Bill Bradley (Cooper-Ford)   19:39.0, 73.28 mph
Fastest lap: Bill Bradley - 1:56.2, 74.35 mph

Event 2 - 7-lap Spring Grove Saloons
1 Boley Pittard (Ford Anglia)   13:24.8, 75.15 mph
Fastest lap: Boley Pittard - 1:49.8, 78.69 mph

Event 3 - 5-lap Marque Sports
1 John Sharp (MG B)   9:30.0, 75.79 mph
Fastest lap: John Sharp - 1:50.8, 77.98 mph

Event 4 - 10-lap Sports Cars
1 Peter Gethin (Lotus-Ford 23)   17:43.4, 80.49 mph
Fastest lap: John Hine (Lotus-Ford 23) - 1:45.2, 82.13 mph

Event 5 - 10-lap Grand Touring Cars
1 John E. Miles (Turner-Ford)   18:39.4, 77.18 mph
Fastest lap: Chris McLaren (Marcos GT) - 1:49.0, 79.27 mph

Event 6 - 5-lap Handicap Saloons
1 Boley Pittard (Ford Anglia)   11:06.8, 73.00 mph
Fastest lap: John Nicholson (Lotus Cortina) - 1:53.8, 75.92 mph

Event 7 - 5-lap Handicap for Grand Touring Cars
1 Tony Flory (GSM Delta)   10:55.0, 66.46 mph
Fastest lap: John Glyde Walker (Turner-Ford) - 1:58.6, 72.85 mph

Event 8 - 5 lap Handicap Sports
1 Derek Bell (Lotus-Ford 7)   11:09.8, 66.48 mph
Fastest lap: F. Crombie (Lotus-Ford 7) - 2:06.6, 68.25 mph

30 MARCH 1964 – EASTER MEETING

Event 1 - Chichester Cup for Formula 3 Cars - 10 laps
1 Jackie Stewart (Cooper-Austin T72)   15:34.4, 92.47 mph
2 John Fenning (Lotus-BMC 22)   15:47.8
3 Warwick Banks (Cooper-Morris T72)   15:48.8
Fastest lap: Jackie Stewart - 1:32.2, 93.71 mph

Event 2 - St Mary's Trophy for Touring Saloons - 10 laps
1 Jack Sears (Ford Galaxie)   16:08.0, 89.26 mph
2 Jim Clark (Lotus-Cortina)   16:14.4
3 Peter Arundell (Lotus-Cortina)   16:27.4
Fastest lap: Jack Sears - 1:35.2, 90.76 mph

Event 3 - '*News of the World*' International Trophy for Formula 1 Cars
1 Jim Clark (Lotus-Climax 25)   57:39.0, 104.91 mph
2 Peter Arundell (Lotus-Climax 25)   59:00.6
3 Trevor Taylor (Lotus-BRM 24)   41 laps
4 Dickie Attwood (BRM P57)   41 laps
5 Mike Hailwood (Lotus-BRM 25)   40 laps
6 Graham Hill (BRM P261)   39 laps
Fastest lap (RECORD): Graham Hill - 1:21.0, 106.67 mph

Event 4 - Sussex Trophy for GT Cars - 15 laps
1 Graham Hill (Ferrari 250GTO/64)   22:19.4, 96.76 mph
2 Jack Sears (AC Cobra)   22:20.2
3 David Piper (Ferrari 250GTO)   22:25.6
Fastest lap: Graham Hill - 1:28.0, 98.18 mph

Event 5 - Lavant Cup for Sports Cars
1 John Coundley (Lotus-Climax 19)   31:05.6, 97.26 mph
2 Jackie Stewart (Cooper Monaco T49)   31:11.4
3 Jack Brabham (Brabham-BRM BT8)   31:16.6
Fastest lap: John Coundley/Jackie Stewart - 1:27.0, 99.31 mph

A new generation of 'schoolroom class' single-seaters charge away towards Madgwick Corner:
the Reg Parnell Trophy race for 1-litre Formula 3 cars - Whit Monday 1964.

25 APRIL 1964 – 61st MEMBERS' MEETING

Event 1 - 10-lap Formula 3 & *Formule Libre*
1 Chris Williams (Lotus-Ford 23)   17:09.4, 83.93 mph
Fastest lap: John Coundley (Lotus-Climax 19) - 1:40.2, 86.22 mph

Event 2 - 5-lap Marque Sports
1 John Haynes (Elva Courier)   9:03.4, 79.50 mph
Fastest lap: John Haynes - 1:43.8, 83.24 mph

Event 3 - 7-lap Saloon Cars
1 Boley Pittard (Ford Anglia)   12:2.2, 83.74 mph
Fastest lap: Boley Pittard - 1:41.5, 85.21 mph

Event 4 - 10-lap Sports Cars over 1200cc
1 Chris Williams (Lotus-Ford 23)   15:06.0, 95.36 mph
Fastest lap: John Coundley (Lotus-Climax 19) - 1:27.6, 98.63 mph

Event 5 - 10-lap Grand Touring Cars
1 John Miles (Turner-Ford)   16:29.4, 87.33 mph
Fastest lap: Kostas Pateras (Lotus Elan) - 1:36.6, 89.44 mph

Event 6 - 5-lap Sports and Grand Touring Handicap
1 Valerie Pirie (Lotus Elan)   8:43.8, 82.47 mph
Fastest lap: Mike Beard (Lotus-Climax 17) - 1:35.2, 90.67 mph

Event 7 - 5-lap Handicap for Saloons
1 David Dunnell (Austin Cooper S)   9:42.4, 79.65 mph
Fastest lap: Roger Swanton (Lotus-Cortina) - 1:39.2, 87.10 mph

Event 8 - 5-lap Handicap for Grand Touring Cars
1 B. Kendall (Morgan +4)   10:00.0, 77.84 mph
Fastest lap: John Haynes (Elva Courier) - 1:43.2, 83.72 mph

18 MAY 1964 – WHITSUN MEETING

Event 1 - Reg Parnell Trophy Race for Formula 3 Cars - 10 laps
1 Roger Mac (Brabham-Ford BT6)   15:45.6, 91.37 mph
2 Bruce Eglington (Lotus-Ford)   16:00.2
3 Robert Burton (Lotus-Ford)   16:42.6
Fastest lap: Roger Mac/Rod Banting (Lotus-BMC 31) - 1:32.4, 93.51 mph

Event 2 - Vintage Sports Car Race - 10 laps
1 Jonty Williamson (Bentley)   19:16.2, 74.43 mph
2 Tony Charnock (Alvis Speed 20 Spl)   19:22.0
3 John Freeman (Aston Martin SM)   19:23.4
Fastest lap: George Bishop (Aston Martin SM) - 1:51.6, 77.42 mph

Event 3 - Whitsun Trophy Race for Sports & GT Cars - 21 laps
1 Roy Salvadori (CooperMaserati T61P)   31:27.0, 96.15 mph
2 Hugh Dibley (Brabham-Climax BT8)   31:36.0
3 Bob Olthoff (AC Cobra)   31:37.6
Fastest lap: Roy Salvadori - 1:27.0, 99.31 mph

Event 4 - Saloon Car Race - 15 laps
1 Bob Olthoff (Ford Cortina GT)   25:06.4, 86.03 mph
2 Roger Swanton (Lotus-Cortina)   25:35.6
3 John Nicholson (Lotus-Cortina)   25:46.4
Fastest lap: 'Doc' Merfield (Ford Cortina V8) - 1:38.6, 87.63 mph

Event 5 - Historic Racing Car Race
1 Bill Wilks (Cooper-Bristol T20)   17:27.2, 82.51 mph
2 Peter Waller (ERA B Type)   17:27.4
3 Bill Morris (ERA B Type)   18:15.0
Fastest lap: Peter Waller - 1:42.0, 84.71 mph

Event 6 - Saloon Car Handicap - 5 laps
1   Mike Cox (Austin A40)   9:13.4, 78.06 mph
2   Rupert Jones (Morris Cooper S)   9:17.0
3   A.B. Stracey (Volvo B18)   9:19.6
Fastest lap: Bob Olthoff (Ford Cortina GT) - 1:39.0, 87.27 mph

30 MAY 1964 - 62nd MEMBERS' MEETING

Event 1 - 10-lap Formula 3
1   Rodney Banting (Lotus-BMC 22)   15:49.4, 91.00 mph
Fastest lap: Rodney Banting - 1:33.8, 92.11 mph

Event 2 - 10-lap Grand Touring up to 1150cc
1   Clive Lacey (Merlyn-Ford GT Mk4)   16:55.4, 85.09 mph
Fastest lap: Bob Deverell (Lotus 7GT) - 1:38.6, 87.63 mph

Event 3 - 10-lap *Formule Libre*
1   Hugh Dibley (Brabham-Climax BT8)   14:55.4, 96.49 mph
Fastest lap: Hugh Dibley - 1:27.2, 99.08 mph

Event 4 - 5-lap Marque Sports
1   John Sharp (MG B)   8:36.2, 83.69 mph
Fastest lap: John Sharp - 1:41.2, 85.37 mph

Event 5 - 10-lap Sports Cars
1   Hugh Dibley (Brabham-Climax BT8)   14:56.6, 96.36 mph
Fastest lap: Hugh Dibley - 1:26.2, 100.23 mph

Event 6 - 7-lap Saloon Cars
1   Boley Pittard (Ford Anglia)   11:41.2, 86.25 mph
Fastest lap: Boley Pittard - 1:37.8, 88.34 mph

Event 7 - 10-lap Grand Touring over 1151cc
1   John Miles (Turner-Ford)   16:11.2, 88.96 mph
Fastest lap: Adrian Chambers (Lotus Elan) - 1:33.6, 92.31 mph

Event 8 - 5-lap Handicap Saloons
1   Roger Swanton (Lotus-Cortina)   9:35.0, 84.71 mph
Fastest lap: Boley Pittard (Ford Anglia) - 1:39.2, 87.10 mph

Event 9 - 5-lap Handicap - Sports and Grand Touring
1   Mike Hawkesworth (Falcon 515)   9:21.2, 81.33 mph
Fastest lap: James Manfield (Lotus-Ford 23) - 1:35.8, 90.19 mph

29 AUGUST 1964 - TOURIST TROPHY MEETING

Event 1 - Race for GT Cars - 21 laps
1   Mike Spence (Lotus Elan)   32:36.0, 92.76 mph
2   Dickie Stoop (Porsche 904GTS)   32:49.2
3   Mike de'Udy (Porsche 904GTS)   33:17.0
Fastest lap: Mike Spence - 1:31.6, 94.32 mph

Event 2 - 29th RAC Tourist Trophy - 130 laps
1   Graham Hill (Ferrari 330P)   3h 12:43.6, 97.13 mph
2   David Piper (Ferrari 250LM)   129 laps
3   Dan Gurney (AC Cobra Daytona)   129 laps
4   Jack Sears (AC Cobra)   127 laps
5   Bob Olthoff (AC Cobra)   126 laps
6   Innes Ireland (Ferrari 250GTO/64)   125 laps
Fastest lap: Bruce McLaren (Cooper-Oldsmobile) - 1:23.8, 103.10 mph

12 SEPTEMBER 1964 - 63rd MEMBERS' MEETING

Event 1 - 10-lap Formula 3 & *Formule Libre*
1   Chris Irwin (Merlyn-Ford 7)   15:18.4, 94.08 mph
Fastest lap: Chris Irwin/Denis O'Sullivan (Brabham-Ford BT6) - 1:31.0, 94.94 mph

Event 2 - 7-lap Spring Grove Saloons
1   Boley Pittard (Ford Anglia)   11:38.0, 88.65 mph
Fastest lap: Boley Pittard - 1:38.2, 87.98 mph

Event 3 - 5-lap Marque Sports
1   Tommy Entwistle (TVR Grantura)   8:03.0, 84.21 mph
Fastest lap: Tommy Entwistle - 1:40.6, 85.88 mph

Event 4 - 7-lap Spring Grove Saloons 1001 to 1300cc
1   Harry Digby (Austin A40)   12:10.2, 82.83 mph
Fastest lap: George Lawrence (Austin Cooper S) - 1:42.4, 84.37 mph

Event 5 - 10-lap Sports Cars
1   Tony Lanfranchi (Elva-BMW Mk7)   14:45.4, 97.58 mph
Fastest lap: Tony Lanfranchi - 1:26.8, 99.54 mph

Event 6 - 10-lap Grand Touring Cars
1   Clive Lacey (Merlyn GT-Ford Mk4)   16:14.6, 88.65 mph
Fastest lap: Jim Moore (Diva Ford) - 1:35.4, 90.57 mph

Event 7 - 5-lap Handicap (A)
1   J.S. Woodfield (Morris Cooper S)   9:38.0, 74.74 mph
Fastest lap: Mick Cave (Austin A40)/Tom Fletcher (Lotus Cortina) - 1:42.0, 84.71 mph

Event 8 - 5-lap Handicap (B)
1   Don Jones (Lola-Climax Mk1)   9:02.2, 88.67 mph
Fastest lap: Jim Moore (Diva Ford) - 1:35.0, 90.95 mph

1965

13 MARCH 1965 - 64th MEMBERS' MEETING

Event 1 - 10-lap Grand Touring Cars
1   John Miles (Diva GT)   16:54.4, 85.17 mph
Fastest lap: John Miles - 1:40.0, 86.40 mph

Event 2 - 10-lap *Formule Libre*
1   Chris Williams (Lotus-Brabham-BMW)   15:10.0, 94.95 mph
Fastest lap: John Dean (Lotus Ford 30) - 1:27.0, 99.31 mph

Event 3 - 7-lap Saloon Cars
1   Peter Dodd (Jaguar 3.8)   11:52.4, 84.90 mph
Fastest lap: 'Doc' Merfield (Ford Cortina V8) - 1:39.2, 87.10 mph

Event 4 - 10-lap Sports Cars and Clubmans Sports
1   Tommy Hitchcock (Brabham-Climax BT8)   17:10.0, 83.88 mph
Fastest lap: Tommy Hitchcock - 1:40.0, 86.40 mph

Event 5 - 10-lap Formula 3
1   Charles Crichton-Stuart (Brabham-Ford BT10)   17:47.6, 80.93 mph
Fastest lap: Charles Crichton-Stuart - 1:44.2, 82.92 mph

Event 6 - 10-lap Grand Touring Cars
1   Keith Burnand (Lotus Elan)   20:05.6, 71.67 mph
Fastest lap: Keith Burnand - 1:55.0, 75.13 mph

Event 7 - 5-lap Handicap
1   David Negus (Morris Cooper S)   10:58.4, 71.01 mph
Fastest lap: Harry Digby (Austin A40) - 1:52.6, 76.73 mph

3 APRIL 1965 - 65th MEMBERS' MEETING

Event 1 - 5-lap Marque
1   Mike Campbell (Elva Sebring MG)   8:28.6, 84.94 mph
Fastest lap: John Wingfield (TVR Grantura) - 1:39.4, 86.92 mph

Event 2 - 7-lap Spring Grove Saloons up to 1000cc
1   Terry Kirby (Austin Cooper S)   12:53.4, 78.20 mph
Fastest lap: Terry Kirby - 1:47.6, 80.30 mph

Event 3 - 10-lap Sports & Clubman's
1   Sid Taylor (Brabham-Climax BT8)   15:26.4, 93.26 mph
Fastest lap: Sid Taylor - 1:30.4, 95.57 mph

Event 4 - 10-lap Grand Touring Cars
1   Peter Lumsden (Jaguar E-type)   15:24.0, 93.51 mph
Fastest lap: Peter Lumsden - 1:30.4, 95.57 mph

Event 5 - 7-lap 'Spring Grove' Saloons over 1000cc
1   'Doc' Merfield (Ford Cortina V8)   11:47.0, 85.54 mph
Fastest lap: 'Doc' Merfield - 1:38.6, 87.63 mph

Event 6 - 5-lap Handicap
1   B.W. Boardman (MG B)   9:07.6, 80.36 mph
Fastest lap: Charles Sawyer-Hoare (Lotus Ford 23) - 1:36.0, 90.00 mph

Event 7 - 5-lap Handicap
1   Peter Whitaker (Morris Cooper S)   9:38.0, 79.56 mph
Fastest lap: Harry Digby - 1:40.2, 86.22 mph

19 APRIL 1965 - EASTER MEETING

Event 1 - Chichester Cup for Formula 3 Cars - 10 laps
1   Roy Pike (Brabham-Ford BT16)   16:17.2, 88.42 mph
2   Piers Courage (Brabham-Ford BT10)   16:17.8
3   Jonathan Williams (Brabham-Ford BT10)   16:26.4
Fastest lap: Piers Courage - 1:33.0, 92.90 mph

Team-mates: gentlemanly double World Champion Jim Clark and 'Gentleman Jack' Sears glissade out of the Club Corner chicane in their twin works Lotus-Cortina saloons, en route to yet another tin-topped triumph - Easter Monday 1965.

Event 2 - St Mary's Trophy for Touring Saloons - 10 laps
1   Jim Clark (Lotus-Cortina)   9:01.0, 79.85 mph
2   Jack Sears (Lotus-Cortina)   9:12.0
3   Mike Salmon (Ford Mustang)   9:23.6
Fastest lap: Jim Clark - 1:46.0, 81.51 mph

Event 3 - 'Sunday Mirror' International Trophy Race for Formula 1 Cars - 42 laps
1   Jim Clark (Lotus-Climax 25)   57:33.8, 105.07 mph
2   Graham Hill (BRM P261)   57:58.0
3   Jack Brabham (Brabham-Climax BT11)   58:24.6
4   Bruce McLaren (Cooper-Climax T77)   41 laps
5   Joakim Bonnier (Brabham-Climax BT7)   41 laps
6   Dickie Attwood (Lotus-BRM 25)   41 laps
Fastest lap (RECORD): Jackie Stewart (BRM P261)/Jim Clark - 1:20.4, 107.46 mph

Event 4 - Sussex Trophy Race for GT Cars - 15 laps
1   Roger Mac (AC Cobra)   22:34.2, 95.70 mph
2   Jack Sears (AC Cobra Coupé)   22:40.0
3   Peter Sutcliffe (Ferrari 250GTO)   23:04.8
Fastest lap: Peter Lumsden - 1:28.2, 97.96 mph

Event 5 - Lavant Cup Race for Sports Cars - 21 laps
1	Jim Clark (Lotus Ford 30)	29:14.0, 103.44 mph
2	Bruce McLaren (McLaren-Elva-Oldsmobile M1A)	29:34.0
3	David Hobbs (Lola Ford T70)	30:38.0

Fastest lap (RECORD): Jim Clark - 1:20.8, 106.93 mph

22 MAY 1965 - 66th MEMBERS' MEETING
Event 1 - 10-lap Grand Touring Cars
1 Bob Burnard (Simca-Abarth 2000)   17:03.6, 84.41 mph
Fastest lap: Bob Burnard - 1:38.4, 87.80 mph

Event 2 - 10-lap Saloons up to 1000cc
1 Ralph Wilding (Austin Cooper S)   18:10.4, 79.24 mph
Fastest lap: Ralph Wilding - 1:43.6, 83.40 mph

Event 3 - 10-lap Formula 3 Race
1 Derek Bell (Lotus-Ford 31)   15:30.8, 92.82 mph
Fastest lap: Derek Bell - 1:31.0, 94.94 mph

Event 4 - 10-lap Grand Touring Cars
1 Keith Burnard (Lotus Elan)   16:07.8, 89.28 mph
Fastest lap: Keith Burnard - 1:35.2, 90.67 mph

Event 5 - 10-lap Saloon Cars over 1000cc
1 Mick Cave (Austin A40)   16:44.4, 86.02 mph
Fastest lap: Mick Cave - 1:38.6, 87.63 mph

Event 6 - 10-lap Sports and Clubman's
1 Clive Lacey (Merlyn-Ford Mk4)   16:08.4, 89.22 mph
Fastest lap: Clive Lacey - 1:34.8, 91.14 mph

Event 7 - 5-lap Handicap
1 Richard Miles (Austin A40)   10:02.0, 80.45 mph
Fastest lap: Peter Dodd - 1:42.2, 83.54 mph

Event 8 - 5-lap Handicap
1 Charles Sawyer-Hoare (Lotus Ford 23)   9:23.8, 87.49 mph
Fastest lap: Charles Sawyer-Hoare - 1:36.8, 89.26 mph

7 JUNE 1965 - WHITSUN MEETING
Event 1 - Reg Parnell Trophy Race for Formula 3 Cars - 10 laps
1	Piers Courage (Brabham-Ford BT10)	15:01.2, 95.87 mph
2	Charles Crichton-Stuart (Brabham-Ford BT10)	15:09.6
3	Mike Knight (Cooper-Ford T76)	15:14.4

Fastest lap (RECORD): Piers Courage - 1:29.0, 97.08 mph

Event 2 - Historic Racing and Vintage Sports Cars race - 10 laps
1	Bob Salvage (Connaught A Type)	17:34.4, 81.94 mph
2	Colin Crabbe (Maserati 250F)	17:35.4
3	Hon. Patrick Lindsay (ERA B Type)	17:35.4

Fastest lap: Brian Allart (Connaught A Type) - 1:40.4, 86.06 mph

Event 3 - Whitsun Trophy for Sports and GT Cars - 21 laps
1	John Coundley (McLaren-Elva-Oldsmobile M1A)	30:38.8, 98.67 mph
2	Roy Salvadori (Ford GT40)	31:33.4
3	Roger Mac (AC Cobra)	31:52.2

Fastest lap: Roger Nathan (Brabham BT8 Oldsmobile) - 1:24.8, 101.89 mph

Event 4 - Spring Grove Saloon Car Race - 15 laps
1	Mike Salmon (Ford Mustang)	24:32.8, 88.00 mph
2	Terry Drury (Ford Anglia)	24:59.0
3	Alan Peer (Ford Anglia)	24:59.0

Fastest lap: Mike Salmon - 1:36.8, 89.26 mph

Event 5 - *Formule Libre* Race - 10 laps
1	John Sparrow (AC Cobra)	15:34.0, 92.51 mph
2	Bob King (Lotus-Climax 24)	15:44.2
3	A.D. Bennett (Brabham-Ford BT14)	15:45.2

Fastest lap: John Dean (Lotus-Ford 30) - 1:28.2, 97.96 mph

3 JULY 1965 - 67th MEMBERS' MEETING
Event 1 - 10-lap Saloons up to 1000cc
1 Ray Calcutt (Hillman Imp)   17:57.2, 80.21 mph
Fastest lap: Ralph Wilding (Austin Cooper S) - 1:44.8, 82.44 mph

Event 2 - 10-lap Formula 3
1 David Cole (Brabham-Ford BT15)   15:11.2, 94.82 mph
Fastest lap: David Cole - 1:29.6, 96.43 mph

Event 3 - 10-lap Marque Sports
1 Richard Skilbeck (Elva Courier)   17:03.2, 84.44 mph
Fastest lap: Mike Campbell - 1:38.4, 87.80 mph

Event 4 - 10-lap 'Autosport' Championship Sports Cars
1 Simon de Lautour (Lotus Ford 30)   15:40.0, 91.91 mph
Fastest lap (RECORD): Robin Widdows (Lotus BRM 23) - 1:30.2, 95.79 mph

Event 5 - 10-lap 'Autosport' Championship Grand Touring Cars
1 Peter Harper (Sunbeam Tiger)   15:57.0, 90.28 mph
Fastest lap: Peter Harper - 1:33.0, 92.90 mph

Event 6 - 10-lap Saloons over 1000cc
1 Mick Cave (Austin A40)   16:43.0, 86.14 mph
Fastest lap: Peter Dodd (Jaguar 3.8) - 1:38.4, 87.80 mph

Event 7 - 5-lap Handicap
1 Peter Dodd (Jaguar 3.8)   9:09.6, 84.77 mph
Fastest lap: Mick Cave (Austin A40) - 1:38.6, 87.63 mph

1966

19 MARCH 1966 - 68th MEMBERS' MEETING
Event 1 - 10-lap 'Spring Grove' Saloon Cars up to 1000cc
1 Nick Brittan (Hillman Imp)   17:04.6, 84.33 mph
Fastest lap: Roger Nathan (Hillman Imp) - 1:40.8, 85.71 mph

Event 2 - 10-lap Grand Touring Cars
1 John Miles (Lotus Elan)   15:29.2, 92.98 mph
Fastest lap: John Hine (Lotus Elan) - 1:30.6, 95.36 mph

Event 3 - 10-lap Formula 3
1 Chris Williams (Brabham-Ford)   14:48.0, 97.30 mph
Fastest lap (RECORD): Chris Williams/Chris Lambert (Brabham-Ford BT18) -
1:27.0, 99.31 mph

Event 4 - 10-lap 'Spring Grove' Saloon Cars over 1000cc
1 'Doc' Merfield (Ford Cortina V8)   15:50.8, 90.95 mph
Fastest lap: 'Doc' Merfield - 1:33.4, 92.50 mph

Event 5 - 10-lap *Formule Libre*
1 Tommy Weber (Lotus-BRM 23)   15:10.6, 94.88 mph
Fastest lap: Mac Daghorn (Felday 4-BRM) - 1:27.2, 99.08 mph

Goodwood's greatest graduate? Jackie Stewart lining up his Ken Tyrrell-entered Formula 2
Matra-Cosworth on the grid for the Sussex circuit's final front-line International - Easter
Monday 1966.

Event 6 - 10-lap Clubmans and Sports Cars
1 John Bromilow (DRW-Ford)   16:51.2, 85.37 mph
Fastest lap (RECORD): John Bromilow/Tony Youlten (Lotus-Ford 7) - 1:39.8, 86.57 mph

Event 7 - 10-lap Marque Sports
1 Chris Lawrence (Morgan SLR)   16:31.8, 87.11 mph
Fastest lap (RECORD): Chris Lawrence - 1:37.8, 88.34 mph

Event 8 - 5-lap Handicap
1 Tony Flory (Elva Courier)   8:58.8, 85.75 mph
Fastest lap: Tommy Weber (Lotus-BRM 23) - 1:34.8, 91.15 mph

11 APRIL 1966 - EASTER MEETING
Event 1 - Chichester Cup for Formula 3 Cars - 10 laps
1	Chris Irwin (Brabham-Ford BT18)	14:42.2, 97.94 mph
2	John Fenning (Brabham-Ford BT18)	14:51.6
3	Peter Gethin (Brabham-Ford BT18)	14:52.4

Fastest lap (RECORD): Chris Irwin - 1:26.6, 99.77 mph

Event 2 - St Mary's Trophy for Saloon Cars - 10 laps
1	Brian Muir (Ford Galaxie)	15:46.8, 91.25 mph
2	Jack Brabham (Ford Mustang)	15:47.2
3	Mike Salmon (Ford Mustang)	15:48.0

Fastest lap (RECORD): Brian Muir - 1:32.2, 93.71 mph

Event 3 - Sunday Mirror Trophy for Formula 2 Cars - 42 laps
1	Jack Brabham (Brabham-Honda BT18)	58:50.2, 102.79 mph
2	Denny Hulme (Brabham-Honda BT18)	58:50.6
3	Jochen Rindt (Brabham-Cosworth BT18)	59:29.2

Fastest lap: Denny Hulme - 1:22.2, 105.10 mph

Event 4 - Sussex Trophy for GT Cars - 15 laps
1	John Miles (Lotus Elan)	23:26.6, 92.14 mph
2	Peter Pollard (Lotus Elan)	24:01.6
3	Peter Creasey (Lotus Elan)	24:03.2

Fastest lap: John Hine (Lotus Elan) - 1:31.4, 94.53 mph

Event 5 - Lavant Cup for Sports Racing Cars - 21 laps
1	Mike Spence (Parnell-BRM)	30:55.6, 97.78 mph
2	Tony Dean (Brabham-Climax BT8)	31:00.6
3	Mac Daghorn (Felday 4-BRM)	31:05.4

Fastest lap: Mike Spence - 1:24.4, 102.37 mph

30 APRIL 1966 - 69th MEMBERS' MEETING
Event 1 - 10-lap Grand Touring Cars
1 Eric Oliver (Lotus Elan)   16:22.6, 87.93 mph
Fastest lap: Chris St Quentin (Lotus Elan) - 1:36.4, 89.63 mph

Event 2 - 10-lap Saloon Car Race (A)
1 David George (Austin Cooper S)   17:48.6, 80.85 mph
Fastest lap: David George/Don Jones (Ford Anglia) - 1;45.0, 82.29 mph

Event 3 - 10-lap Marque Race
1   Bill Bradley (Triumph Spitfire)   16:46.8, 85.82 mph
Fastest lap: Bill Bradley - 1:39.0, 87.27 mph

Event 4 - 10-lap Formula 3 Race
1   Chris Lambert (Brabham-Ford BT15)   14:55.4, 96.49 mph
Fastest lap: Chris Lambert - 1:28.4, 97.74 mph

Event 5 - 10-lap Saloon Car Race (B)
1   Chris Montague (Austin Cooper S)   16:42.0, 86.23 mph
Fastest lap: Harry Digby (Austin A40) - 1:38.4, 87.80 mph

Event 6 - 10-lap Sports and Clubman's Race
1   Clive Lacey (Brabham-Climax BT8)   15:40.2, 91.90 mph
Fastest lap: Clive Lacey - 1:31.0, 94.94 mph

Event 7 - 5-lap Handicap
1   Dickie Metcalfe (Lola-Climax Mk1)   9:36.4, 82.82 mph
Fastest lap: Mick Cave ((Austin A40) - 1:37.8, 88.34 mph

30 MAY 1966 – WHITSUN MEETING

Event 1 - Marque Race - 15 laps
1   Chris Lawrence (Morgan SLR)   24:35.6, 87.83 mph
2   Tommy Entwistle (TVR Grantura)   24:57.8
3   Roger Connel (Daimler SP250)   25:02.6
Fastest lap: Chris Lawrence - 1:36.6, 89.44 mph

Event 2 - Saloon Car Race - 15 laps
1   Alan Peer (Ford Anglia 1798 cc)   24:36.8, 87.76 mph
2   Tony Dean (Lotus Cortina)   24:40.6
3   Ian Mitchell (Austin Cooper S)   25:06.0
Fastest lap: Alan Peer - 1:36.6, 89.44 mph

Event 3 - Reg Parnell Trophy for Formula 3 Cars - 20 laps
1   David Cole (Brabham-Ford BT18)   29:54.6, 96.29 mph
2   Derek Bell (Lotus-Ford 41)   30:06.4
3   Mo Nunn (Lotus-Ford 41)   30:07.8
Fastest lap: Derek Bell - 1:27.0, 99.31 mph

Event 4 - Sports and GT Car Race - 15 laps
1   Tony Dean (Brabham-Climax BT8)   22:25.8, 94.20 mph
2   John Miles (Lotus Elan)   23:15.0
3   Sid Fox (Elva-BMW 7)   23:32.4
Fastest lap: Tony Dean - 1:29.0, 97.08 mph

Event 5 - Historic Racing and Vintage Sports Car Race - 10 laps
1   Peter Brewer (Aston Martin DBR4)   17:02.0, 84.54 mph
2   Bob Salvage (Connaught A Type)   17:04.2
3   Peter Waller (ERA B Type)   17:12.2
Fastest lap: Bob Salvage/Peter Brewer - 1:40.2, 86.22 mph

11 JUNE 1966 – 70th MEMBERS' MEETING

Event 1 - 10-lap Grand Touring Cars
1   Mike Crabtree (Lotus Elan)   15:41.8, 91.74 mph
Fastest lap: Mike Crabtree - 1:32.8, 93.10 mph

Event 2 - 10-lap Saloon Car Race (A)
1   Roger Nathan (Hillman Imp)   17:42.4, 81.33 mph
Fastest lap: Roger Nathan - 1:44.2, 82.92 mph

Event 3 - 10-lap Clubman's Sports Car Race
1   Harry McLaughlin (Mallock U2-Ford)   16:20.4, 88.13 mph
Fastest lap: Harry McLaughlin - 1:35.0, 90.95 mph

Event 4 - 10-lap Marque Race
1   Jim Donnelly (Morgan SLR)   16:53.0, 85.29 mph
Fastest lap: Jim Donnelly - 1:39.0, 87.27 mph

Event 5 - 10-lap Saloon Car Race (B)
1   Chris Montague (Austin Cooper S)   16:54.6, 85.16 mph
Fastest lap: George Lawrence (Austin Cooper S) - 1:39.6, 86.75 mph

Event 6 - 10-lap Formula 3
1   Derek Bell (Lotus-Ford 41)   14:50.0, 97.08 mph
Fastest lap: David Cole - 1:27.4, 98.85 mph

Event 7 - 5-lap Handicap
1   R.N. Griffith (Austin Cooper S)   9:37.4, 78.92 mph
Fastest lap: Peter Lawrence (Austin Cooper S) - 1:42.8, 84.05 mph

2 JULY 1966 – 71st MEMBERS' MEETING

Event 1 - 10 lap Special GT Race
1   Peter Pollard (Lotus Elan)   16:29.0, 87.36 mph
Fastest lap: Stuart Hands (Austin-Healey 3000) - 1:35.6, 90.38 mph

Event 2 - 10-lap Saloon Car Race (A)
1   Andrew Mylius (Fiat-Abarth 1000)   17:43.6, 81.23 mph
Fastest lap: Andrew Mylius - 1:45.0, 82.29 mph

Event 3 - 10-lap Sports Car Race
1   Clive Lacey (Brabham-Climax BT8)   15:17.2, 94.20 mph
Fastest lap: Clive Lacey - 1:29.2, 96.86 mph

Event 4 - 10-lap Marque Race
1   Stuart Hands (Austin-Healey 3000)   16:32.2, 87.08 mph
Fastest lap: Jim Donnelly (Morgan SLR) - 1:36.0, 90.00 mph

Event 5 - 10-lap Saloon Car Race B
1   Richard Cluley (Austin Cooper S)   16:39.6, 86.44 mph
Fastest lap: Richard Cluley - 1:38.0, 88.16 mph

Event 6 - 10-lap Clubman's Sports
1   Brian Classick (Chevron-Ford)   15:58.4, 90.15 mph
Fastest lap: Brian Classick - 1:34.6, 91.33 mph

Event 7 - 5-lap Handicap
1   Dickie Metcalfe (Lola-Climax Mk1)   9:32.4, 84.31 mph
Fastest lap: Neil Dangerfield (Triumph SLR) - 1:38.8, 87.45 mph

1998

18-20 SEPTEMBER 1998 – THE GOODWOOD MOTOR CIRCUIT REVIVAL MEETING

Event 1 - Woodcote Cup for Formula 1,2 and *Libre* Cars 1948-53 - 15 laps
1   Ludovic Lindsay (ERA B Type)   23:30.2, 91.90 mph
Fastest lap: Gregor Fisken (Cooper-Bristol Mk2) - 1:32.245, 93.66 mph

Event 2 - Earl of March Trophy for 500cc/F3 Cars 1948-58 - 10 laps
1   Julian Majzub (Cooper-Norton Mk8)   18:09.177, 79.32 mph
Fastest lap: Julian Majzub - 1:44.875, 82.38 mph

Event 3 - Lennox Cup for 350cc/500cc Group 1 Motor-cycles 1948-66 - 8 laps
1   Mick Hemmings (McIntyre-Matchless 500)   13:15.444, 86.89 mph
Fastest lap: Mick Hemmings - 1:34.389, 91.54 mph

Event 4 - Sussex Trophy for Production Sports-Racing Cars 1955-60 - 15 laps
1   Robert Brooks (Lotus-Climax 15)   22:39.653, 95.31 mph
Fastest lap: John Harper (Cooper-Climax Monaco) - 1:28.487, 97.64 mph

Event 5 - Freddie March Memorial Trophy for Goodwood Nine-Hour Cars 1953-55 - 11 laps
1   Gary Pearson (Jaguar C-type)   18:03.025, 87.75 mph
Fastest lap: Andrew Garner (Cooper-Jaguar T38) - 1:35.789, 90.20 mph

Event 6 - St Mary's Trophy for Group 2 Saloon Cars 1948-53 - 15 laps
1   Richard Dodkins (Austin Cooper S)   25:12.593, 85.68 mph
Fastest lap: Richard Dodkins - 1:38.279, 87.91 mph

Event 7 - Lennox Cup for 350cc/500cc Group 1 Motor-cycles 1948-66 - 8 laps
1   Mick Hemmings (McIntyre-Matchless 500)   12:59.682, 88.65 mph
Fastest lap: Malcolm Clark (Matchless G50 500) - 1:33.380, 92.53 mph

Event 8 - RAC TT Celebration for GT Cars 1960-64 - 1 hour, 38 laps
1   Nigel Corner/Barrie Williams (Jaguar E-type 'Lightweight')1h 00:04.802, 91.07 mph
Fastest lap: Nigel Corner - 1:30.958, 94.99 mph

Event 9 - Richmond Trophy for 2½ litre Formula 1 Cars 1956-60 - 15 laps
1   Rod Jolley (Cooper-Climax T51)   22:53.298, 94.37 mph
Fastest lap: Rod Jolley - 1:26.885, 99.44 mph

Event 10 - Glover Trophy for 1½-litre Formula 1 Cars 1961-65 - 21 laps
1   Danny Sullivan (Lola-Climax Mk4)   31:55.775, 94.70 mph
Fastest lap: Alan Baillie (Lotus-BRM 24) - 1:28.676, 97.43 mph

Event 11 - Lavant Cup for World Championship Sports Cars 1957-60 - 21 laps
1   Peter Hardman (Ferrari Dino 246S)   32:02.282, 94.38 mph
Fastest lap: Peter Hardman - 1:31.126, 95.87 mph

Event 12 - Chichester Cup for Formula Junior Cars 1958-63 - 12 laps
1   Jean-Michel Farine (Lotus-Ford 20)   19:41.214, 87.77 mph
Fastest lap: Joos Tollanaar (Lola-Ford Mk3) - 1:35.559, 90.42 mph

Event 13 - 'Ebby' Ebblewhite Handicap for Saloon, Sports and GT Cars - 10 laps
1   Peter Hardman (Ferrari Dino 246S)   16:27.858, 87.46 mph
Fastest lap: Robert Brooks (Lotus-Climax 15) - 1:29.400, 96.64 mph

Event 14 - Scott Gaze Handicap for Single-Seater Cars - 10 laps
1   Rod Jolley (Cooper-Climax T51)   14:44.405, 97.69 mph
Fastest lap: Rod Jolley - 1:26.799, 99.54 mph

ACKNOWLEDGMENTS

Mike Lawrence would like to give special thanks to: Robert Barker, for sharing his exhaustive research on racing at Goodwood; John Brierley, for his recollections as photographer and local publican; Ted Croucher, Chief Marshal at the Goodwood Circuit; Eric Marsden, for reminiscences of RAF Westhampnett in 1940; and the staff at Goodwood House.

Simon Taylor would like to thank everyone who gave him so much of their time, on the phone and face to face, in the course of conducting the interviews: Sir John Whitmore, Damon Hill, Jackie Stewart, Jack Sears, Robin McKay, Lady Watson (Miss Christabel Carlisle), John Surtees, Murray Walker, Sir Jack Brabham, the Earl of March & Kinrara, Dan Gurney, Bill Boddy, Raymond Baxter, Tony Rudd, John Cooper, Roy Salvadori, Brian Lister, Nick Mason, Stirling Moss, Graham Macbeth, Derek Bell, Tony Gaze, David Piper, Frank Gardner, Ronald 'Steady' Barker, Tim Parnell, Phil Hill.

Doug Nye would like to give thanks to: Ted Croucher, veteran Chief Marshal at Goodwood and his staff; to Tony Houghton, airfield/circuit manager; and above all to the thousands of enthusiasts and casual fans alike who have supported Goodwood's historic events, rain and dry, since 1993 and whose warmth, understanding and knowledge is now acknowledged internationally as 'The World's Best Motor Racing Crowd'.

Virgin Publishing and Slatter-Anderson would like to thank: Di Skinner; Stirling and Susie Moss; Robert Barker; Enid Smith at the BARC; and Marion Calver Smith, Janet Bradley, Rob Widdows, Ellen Westbrook and Dee Heap at Goodwood House.

Chapter opener illustrations: Peter Hearsey • Rostrum photography: Johnny Ring at RSA • Front cover re-colouring: Robin Anderson

Picture credits: Jesse Alexander: pages 2/3, 11 top, 159, 162, 167 top, 170, 171 top, 175, 181, 281 • Archivio Ruote Classiche: page 246 middle left and bottom centre • 'Autocar': page 285 • BARC archive: pages 8, 17, 23 bottom, 46, 49, 52 top, 53, 55, 56 top and bottom, 57, 58, 59, 60/61, 62, 63, 64, 66, 67 all photos, 68/69, 72, 73 top and bottom, 75, 77, 78/79, 87, 94, 98, 100, 104, 106 top, 107 all photos, 115, 126, 143 bottom, 146, 148 top, 149 bottom, 151 bottom, 156, 157 bottom, 158 top, 214, 216, 217, 264, 269, 276, 284 • Chris Bayley: page 9, 105 bottom, 109, 123 bottom, 135, 144/145, 152, 189, 258 - Jackie Stewart, 259 - Sir Jack Brabham • Russell Brockbank/Temple Press: 110 bottom, 288 • Christopher Brooks: page 228 • Peter Burn: page 45, 76 bottom, 116, 160, 206/207, 241 top, 248 bottom, 249 top and bottom, 252 top, 255 • Diana Burnett: page 247 top right, 258 - Ken Tyrrell and John Cooper • Clicksport: pages 241 bottom, 245 bottom, 248 top, 259 - Damon Hill • Michael Cooper: pages 183, 197, 224 top, 225 bottom, 244 top • Tony Gaze: page 48 middle and bottom • the GP Collection: pages 10, 76 top, 80, 84 top and bottom, 89, 93, 99 middle, 111, 118, 119 bottom, 120, 121, 123 top, 124/125, 131, 132/133, 136, 137, 180 bottom, 147, 192 top, 194/195, 198, 200, 203, 218/219, 220, 221, 224 bottom, 265 top, 272, 273, 275, 279, 283, 286 • Evi Gurney: page 39 • S.J. Havelock: pages 223, 234, 235, 259 - Rowan Atkinson • Barry Hathaway: pages 65, 140, 141, 154/155, 242, 245 top, 246 all black and whites, 247 all black and whites, 256/257 • Stephen Hayward: pages 1, 32, 90/91, 210, 222/223, 262/263 • Malcolm Jeal: page 215 • Dafydd Jones: pages 40, 41, 247 bottom 2nd from right, 258 - John Surtees, 259 - Dan Gurney, 260 all photos • Mark Kehoe: pages 138/139 the Klementaski Collection: pages 112/113 • LAT archive: pages 37, 71, 97, 99 top and bottom, 101, 102/103, 106 bottom, 114, 117, 122, 128, 129, 134, 137 top, 142, 143 top, 150, 153 bottom, 157 top, 161 bottom, 164, 165 bottom, 166, 173, 174 bottom, 179, 182, 184, 185 top and bottom, 190, 191 top and bottom, 196, 199, 201 top and bottom, 202, 208, 243, 253 bottom, 265 bottom, 266, 268, 270, 274, front cover, back cover middle • A. Loader: page 237 • James Mann: pages 32, 42/43, 70, 105 top, 186/187, 188, 226, 238/239, 246 top centre and bottom left, 247 bottom left, 250/251, 253 top, 258 - Phil Hill, back cover knockback • Bill Mason: 149 top • Mortons Motorcycle Media: page 213 • National Motor Museum: pages 148/149 knockback, 211 • Xavier de Nombel: pages 54, 240 • Paul Parker/Ludvigsen Library: pages 110 top, 176/177, 252 bottom • Terry Pickering: page 232 • Graham Piggott: 212, 236 all photos, 246 middle right lower, 247 bottom 2nd from left, 258 - Derek Bell, back cover top and bottom • Royal Air Force Museum: pages 34, 35 top and bottom, 38 top • Benedict Redgrove: page 225, 244 bottom, 246 middle right upper and knockback, 247 top left and bottom right, 259 - Roy Salvadori • RSA: pages 38 bottom • Sallon (of 'The Daily Mirror'): pages 11 bottom, 85 top, 119 top • Nigel Snowdon: pages 178, 205 • 'The Tatler': page 85 bottom • Steve Walsh Racing Photographs: page 108 • Graham White Photographic Library/John Brierley: pages 163 bottom, 168/169, 280 • Graham White Photographic Library/Max Le Grand: page 204 • Glynn Williams: page 230.

BARC memorabilia on pages 82 and 83 supplied courtesy of Lawrence Edscer • Loona Doone Snow memorabilia on page 158 supplied courtesy of George Wheatley • All other photographs and illustrations courtesy of the Goodwood Archive.

Quotes by Freddie, Duke of Richmond on pages 47 and 212 from 'Goodwood: The Sussex Motor Racing Circuit'
(Dalton Watson/National Motor Museum Trust)
Quote by Laura Doone Snow on page 158 courtesy of George Wheatley

Every effort has been made to source and contact copyright holders. If any omissions do occur, the publisher will be happy to give full credit in subsequent reprints and editions.

"All I'm getting is a high-pitched screech rising in pitch"